ESTATE VALUATION HANDBOOK

ESTATE VALUATION HANDBOOK

LAWRENCE H. AVERILL, Jr.
Dean and Professor
University of Arkansas at Little Rock
School of Law

Wiley Law Publications
JOHN WILEY & SONS
New York • Chichester • Brisbane • Toronto • Singapore

Library of Congress Cataloging in Publication Data

Averill, Lawrence H.
Estate valuation handbook.

(Wiley law publications)
Includes bibliographical references and index.
1. Estate planning—United States. 2. Valuation—Law and legislation—United States. I. Title. II. Series.

KF750.A83 1983 346.7305'2 82-17574
ISBN 0-471-89859-7 347.30652

Printed in the United States of America

10 9 8 7 6 5 4 3 2 1

Dedicated to those who have taught and who continue to teach me that love is truly the most valuable asset of life:

Suzanne, my wife
Larry, my son
Liz, my daughter
and
My Mother,
Margaret W. Averill

PREFACE

Please take a few minutes to read this Preface. Several technical matters concerning the organization, style and content of this Handbook deserve mention. A thorough understanding of these matters will greatly aid the reader's enjoyment and enrichment when reading the remainder of this Handbook.

First, a little explanation of the organization is helpful. This Handbook is separated into three parts. The first part has two chapters (1–2). Chapter 1 explains the importance and application of valuation determinations. In effect it establishes the setting for what follows.

The second chapter is very important. It provides definitions and explanations of the pervasive terms and concepts used for valuation determination purposes. Significantly, the matters in Chapter 2 are frequently referred to in the other chapters. Although the scope of its content should be examined before reading Part II, the particular section need not be read until reference to it is made in Part II.

Chapters 3–11 are in Part II and concern the substantive portion of the Handbook. They are divided into related groups of assets that have common characteristics from a valuation standpoint. Consult the Detailed Contents for a breakdown of these asset groupings.

Part III contains Chapter 12 which is designed to give you an overview of valuation philosophy and strategies for estate planning purposes. It summarizes the general approach you should take in making valuation decisions.

The style used for the text is designed for easy readability and understanding. Numerous sections are used so that you are aware of the subject matter of the discussion. In addition, illustrations, tables and charts are frequently provided in order to facilitate understanding. Also, to improve readability quotations are kept to a minimum.

For the purpose of readability, citations are not included in the text but are footnoted for reference purposes. Within the realm of a handbook's purposes, the cited authorities constitute a useful reference and research tool. Although the citations are selective and not exhaustive, they still include reference to the most significant primary and secondary authority on valuation.

At the end of the Handbook, a complete and composite set of reference tables is included. These tables are divided into relatively convenient and obvious categories:

1. Internal Revenue Code Citations;
2. Internal Revenue Code Regulations Citations;

3. Revenue Rulings, Revenue Procedures and Letter Rulings Citations;
4. Case Citations (alphabetized by case name):
    a. United States Supreme Court Decisions,
    b. Federal Circuit Court Decisions,
    c. Federal District Court Decisions,
    d. Federal Court of Claims Decisions,
    e. Tax Court and Board of Tax Appeal Decisions,
    f. Tax Court Memorandum Decisions;
5. Major Text and Treatise Citations (alphabetized by author's name);
6. Law Review and Periodical Citations (alphabetized by author's name);
7. Miscellaneous Citations:
    a. Statutory References;
    b. Other References.

These tables not only provide the reader with the full citation but also indicate where the reference is cited in the Handbook.

The Handbook also contains a substantial number of cross references to other parts of its text. These are made by a reference to a section sign, the relevant section number and the section heading. For example, a reference "**§5.17** The Cost Approach to Real Property Valuation" refers to section **5.17** which is found in Chapter 5 and which discusses the cost approach to valuing real property. For easy access to the cross references, the top center of odd number pages indicate a section discussed on the page.

LAWRENCE H. AVERILL, JR.

Little Rock, Arkansas
July 1982

ACKNOWLEDGMENTS

It goes without saying, this book required a great deal of effort from other persons in addition to my own. Written in part both at the University of Wyoming and at the University of Illinois, there are certain people who were or are at each of these Universities and who deserve recognition and an expression of my appreciation.

First, I want to express my sincere and deep gratitude to Steven Jay Landau, C.P.A., while he was a second year student at the University of Illinois, College of Law, for his tireless dedication and efforts to both the Handbook's substantive and technical quality. My sincere gratitude Steve. Another student deserving an expression of my gratitude is Anne Buchenroth Tallmadge, a second year student at the University of Wyoming, College of Law. She was a terrific help in finalizing and authenticating the citations and the reference tables. Thank you Ann.

Second, a whole list of secretaries deserve an expression of my appreciation, too. At the University of Illinois, Cynthia Utley deserves special recognition. In addition to typing more than one-half of the early drafts, she also typed eighty percent or more of the final draft. Thank you Cynthia for an excellent job.

At the University of Wyoming, there are a covey of secretaries who deserve recognition for their typing and retyping of the manuscript as it slowly matured to completion. Realizing that I may omit someone who did work on the Handbook, I am naming only those who were primarily responsible for my work. These include in alphabetical order, Lory A. Godfrey, Jan L. Halter, Cecilia M. Kirkwood, Marilyn R. Mathis and Tresa Lee Smith. Thank you Lory, Jan, Cecilia, Marilyn and Tresa for your outstanding cooperation, patience and assistance.

Finally, I desire to express my deepest appreciation to my family for their cooperation and encouragement to finish the task. They are the ones who have really had to sacrifice in this endeavor. All my love, appreciation and respect to Sue, Larry and Liz.

L.H.A.

SHORT REFERENCE LIST

Shortened forms of reference are used throughout this text for authorities and sources that are frequently cited. The shortened forms are as follows:

Short Reference	Full Reference
I.R.C.	Internal Revenue Code, Title 26 United States Code
I.R.M. Audit	Internal Revenue Manual—Audit (CCH 1977)
I.R.S.	Internal Revenue Service
I.R.S. App. Off.	Internal Revenue Service, Appeals Officer Valuation Training Program (1980)
I.R.S. Tax Law Course	Internal Revenue Service, Estate, Gift and Generation Skipping Tax Law Course for Attorneys (1979)
Letter Ruling or Letter Rul.	Internal Revenue Service Letter Ruling
Regulation or Reg.	Treasury Department Regulation
Revenue Procedure or Rev. Proc.	Internal Revenue Service Procedure
Revenue Ruling or Rev. Rul.	Internal Revenue Service Ruling

SUMMARY CONTENTS

DETAILED CONTENTS

PART I

TECHNIQUES AND PROCEDURES FOR ESTATE VALUATION

CHAPTER 1

THE WHY AND WHEN OF VALUATION

§1.1 Introduction

In certain social circles, it is not uncommon to hear bards of a sort jape that every rancher or farmer has three different valuations for his real property. The first, and highest is used to get loans from lending institutions. The second, more moderate amount, is the value he puts on land for sale. The third, rock bottom price, is the land's value for tax purposes including real property tax assessment and gift and estate tax valuations. Although the actual value in the above three situations obviously would not be substantially different, the point of the tale is more fact than fiction. For practical purposes the value of an asset will neither remain the same for all purposes nor at all times. Even the tax law specifically gives limited recognition to this concept; a decedent's estate may elect under prescribed circumstances, a special use value for farm and small business real estate.[1]

Because value is determined by human judgment from an indefinite number of subjective variables, the process of valuation is one of art and not science. In practice, an asset's stated value is an opinion determined or agreed upon at a particular time and place. However, these judgments are not whimsical, and the valuator's discretion is not unlimited. When proper procedures and techniques are employed using substantial and accurate information, the estimated value of the property should be relatively accurate and credible.

Normally each determination of the value of an asset is a unique effort calling for an individual approach and analysis. Appraisals do not even have siblings—much less twins. At best, some have distant cousins that may be useful for comparison purposes but cannot be copied. Therefore, the techniques and methods in this book are guidelines for the attorney and not dogma.

The attorney's job is difficult because there are often several different techniques which are proper for valuing an asset depending on the type, time, and place of valuation. Even for the same asset, at the same time, and in the same place, there may be several applicable and appropriate methods for determining its value.

To begin with, valuation concerns things (assets) that have monetary value. In order for assets to have value from an economic and legal standpoint, they must have to some degree all of the following four elements: utility, scarcity, demand and transferability.[2] Their actual value according to the relevant monetary standard depends upon the degree to which each of these elements is lacking or present. Procedurally, valuation determination issues may be separated into two parts: substantive value and evidentiary value.[3]

Substantive value refers to the valuation method or to the particular or specific type of value being determined. The most common types include fair market value and its derivations, and value to the owner and its derivations. Although these valuation techniques may yield identical results, frequently their results will differ significantly.

Evidentiary value refers to the type of evidence necessary to prove the substantive value. The type of evidence used affects the value. Evidence includes actual or original cost, sale price, current asset value, capitalized income valuation and projection of earning capacity. All of these evidentiary matters may be relevant in a particular case. The particular facts used to justify them, however, may vary significantly from case to case. For example, the facts necessary to show a firm's capitalized income may differ greatly depending upon whether the firm's income derives from an operating mine, rental property or some other form of business or enterprise.

---

[1] I.R.C. §2032a. *See* **§5.20** Special Use Valuation Generally.

[2] A. Ring, The Valuation of Real Estate 8 (2d ed. 1970).

[3] *See* 1 J. Bonbright, Valuation of Property 10-38 (1937).

However, for the practicing lawyer, valuation techniques and valuation evidentiary factors are concomitant issues and cannot be separated from each other.[4]

Generally, fair market value refers to the price at which a seller sells an asset and a buyer buys it.[5] "The worth of a thing is the price it will bring." Although the technique has its variations and often implies recourse to a hypothetical price, it is the starting point for most valuations, including those required for estate planning. The rest of this Handbook deals with the meaning of this technique, its variations and proof of valuation.

The issue of the "ascertainability" of the value of an asset or interest has two aspects.[6] The first concerns the factual question of when an asset or interest is valueless or can be said to have no value.

The second aspect of the situation deals with an asset that has "no ascertainable value." This issue is a mixed question of fact and law. It assumes that an asset or interest has value but that the evidence is inadequate to set a fixed value for the property. Most of these situations arise in an income tax context—more specifically, in the context of capital gain or loss.

The I.R.S. takes a firm position that "only in rare and in extraordinary cases will property be considered to have no fair market value."[7] Consequently, when a determination of the value of an asset is made for tax purposes, all relevant evidence and factors must be considered. "Approximate valuations" and "a rough estimate" are sufficient to overcome an objection raised due to the "difficulties of evaluation."[8] Even where it has been determined that an asset has no ascertainable value at a particular time, the I.R.S. position is that this is only temporary; the asset must be given a value at the earliest possible date.

Most of the litigated cases on this issue deal with income tax, where the value must be ascertained to close a transaction. Otherwise, the transaction remains open, and the possibility of tax avoidance increases significantly.[9] Usually the taxpayer contends the value is greater than the I.R.S. contends.

In the estate and gift tax area, however, this has not been a serious problem. The value under these taxes must be determined as of a particular date and the parties are resigned to that task. This does not mean, however, that all assets or interests for estate and gift tax purposes will have a value. If it can be substantiated that an asset has a zero or a negative value, a zero value will be assigned to that asset.[10]

An issue that frequently arises is the relevance of events after the appropriate valuation date. Generally, these events will not be considered in determining fair

---

[4] *Id.* at 12.

[5] *See* §**2.9** Fair Market Value.

[6] *See* Research Institute of America, Estate Planning & Taxation Coordinator ¶¶82,075-79, at p. 82,058-61 (1979).

[7] Reg. §1.1001-1(a).

[8] Rev. Rul. 58-402, 1958-2 C.B. 15.

[9] Webster, *Ascertainable Value,* 19 N.Y.U. Inst. Fed. Tax'n 509 (1961).

[10] *See e.g.,* May v. McGowan, 194 F.2d 396 (2d Cir. 1952).

market value except to the extent that they were reasonably foreseeable at the valuation date.[11]

VALUATION PRACTICALITIES

§1.2 When and Where Valuation Determinations Are Made

Almost all aspects of our society give rise to questions of valuation. Clearly, valuations are necessary for determining income, gift, estate taxes, and all other forms of taxation related to assets and their transfer. Because these questions are so important to the estate planner, this book emphasizes valuation for tax purposes.

Valuation for most purposes is only relevant with regard to a particular date. The date on which valuation must be made, however, varies depending on the purpose for which the valuation is being made. The following lists the most important valuation dates for estate planning purposes:

Chart I-1

Purpose of Valuation	Date of Valuation
1. Sale or exchange of asset	Date of sale or exchange [Reg. §1.1001-1(a)]
2. Gift of asset	Date of gift [I.R.C. §2512]
3. Asset in a decedent's gross estate	**(a)** Date of death [I.R.C. §2031] or **(b)** The earlier of **(i)** Date of sale of asset after date of death or **(ii)** Date six months after date of death [I.R.C. §2037]
4. Generation Skipping	Date of **(a)** "Taxable Distribution" [I.R.C. §2613(a)] or **(b)** "Taxable Termination" [I.R.C. §2613(b)]
5. Various income tax transactions	Date on which the transaction finalizes.

[11] Estate of Tully v. United States, 78-1 U.S.T.C. (CCH) ¶13,228 (Ct. Cl. 1978); Estate of Ridgely v. United States, 180 Ct. Cl. 1220 (1967).

The following is an outline of the basic steps in the process of valuing assets of all types:

1. Identify asset (obtain complete data concerning its physical and legal descriptions, its location and any other important attributes)
2. Collect extrinsic data that may affect value of asset (this includes all relevant economic, historical, legal and other value concerned matters)
3. Determine the valuation technique or techniques applicable to the valuation of the particular asset
4. Calculate the estimated valuations using the appropriate techniques
5. Calculate and deduct applicable discounts
6. Calculate and add applicable premiums
7. Prepare substantiating appraisal, if necessary.

Obviously, some assets will require a great deal more research and effort than will other assets. Even additional steps may be necessary.[12]

In addition, when an asset is composed of several separate and identifiable assets, such as a business interest, valuation processes may require valuation both of the individual assets and of the composite asset. You are often required to identify the asset, that, in a sense, equals the least common denominator. Then, in turn, you must determine the synergistic effect, if any, of the whole entity. The sum of the parts may be less or greater than the value of the whole. When greater, the relevance of liquidation value is significantly increased. When less, then techniques such as the market or income approaches to valuation may be more relevant.

§1.3 The Varying Degrees of Importance of an Accurate Value Determination

Even the importance of a valuation varies depending upon the circumstances surrounding, and the purposes behind, the value determination. Sometimes the law requires a value determination but the interested parties do not really care. For example, consider the solvent decedent's estate that passes entirely to a sole heir or devisee. Unless tax issues are involved, this successor cares very little about the accuracy of any valuation made. On the other hand, sometimes the parties are greatly concerned with valuation and the law is apathetic. Obviously, the buyer and seller in any significant private sales transaction are especially concerned, though the law seldom attempts to influence or set market value.

The necessary degree of accuracy also depends on the effect that the value has on the principal issue or transaction. Some value determinations have a dollar-for-dollar effect. The sales transaction is the most obvious example. Tax consequences aside, the buyer pays a full dollar more for each additional dollar of value. The seller correspond-

12 *See* **§4.2** Checklists for Business Interest Valuation.

ingly receives an additional dollar. Of course, the opposite occurs if value decreases. Other value determinations have less than a dollar-for-dollar effect. For example, the party who accepts collateral for a loan is not interested in the collateral's precise value so long as its value adequately covers the debt in case of default.

In a sense, the treatment of valuation for tax matters is anomalous. Tax values have an effect only with respect to the marginal rate of the tax. Therefore, a difference in value will not have a dollar-for-dollar effect. Nonetheless, tax enforcers have typically taken a very strict approach to value. Sometimes the rules are arguably too picayune, *e.g.,* the *ex-dividend* rules with respect to traded stocks and bonds.[13]

§1.4 How the Courts Look at Valuation

Although the courts, often with the approval of legislation, have had a tendency to refer to the concept of "market value" as "fair market value," ordinarily these two have been treated as synonymous.[14] And, although other definitions exist, the most prevalent definition of market value or fair market value is the one adopted for tax purposes.[15] Because valuation issues for tax purposes are so pervasive, the tax definition is the one that will most frequently be dealt with by the courts for estate planning and estate valuation purposes.

Many court decisions have to a large degree been disappointing from a developmental standpoint.[16] For reasons not discernable from the reports, most court decisions concerning valuation lack the clarity of standard and justification for result that is desired and expected in other areas of the law.

The courts' problems exhibit themselves in many ways. First, because valuation disputes are questions of fact rather than of law, the courts have tended to operate on a case-by-case approach. Decisions, then, range from automatic affirmance of decisions by administrative agencies or other triers of fact, to what appear to be an arbitrary alteration or reversal of such decisions without adequate explanation of the bases or underlying theories.

Second, courts have often looked for the easiest way out of their dilemma. This probably accounts for the preference many have shown for market price as the primary determinant of market value. It could also possibly explain the phenomena that decisions frequently split the difference between the contesting parties' valuations. The classic case is the district court opinion that states, "By giving consideration to all relevant facts which may be considered" the value equals X dollars. The facts of the case, however, specifically reveal that the court merely split the difference between the IRS' and the taxpayer's value contentions.[17]

Commendably, the Tax Court recently expressed its concern about this tendency to

---

13 *See* **§3.3** Valuation of Stocks.

14 1 J. Bonbright, Valuation of Property 56-74 (1937).

15 *See* **§1.28** How the I.R.S. Looks at Valuation.

16 Banks, *Measuring the Value of Corporate Stock,* 11 Cal. W.L. Rev. 1, 59 (1974).

17 Schnorbach v. Kavanagh, 102 F. Supp. 828 (W.D. Mich. 1951).

split the difference.[18] It warned value antagonists that as a rule, this court would not make valuation decisions in this manner but would make them on the evidence before them. The court expressed the opinion that valuation compromises should be obtained before litigation. In later proceedings in the same case and in a fit of judicial pique, Chief Judge of the Tax Court, Tannenwold, expressed the court's frustration at having to reach a valuation between the contesting parties and their refusal to settle the matter privately.[19]

A later decision clearly indicates that the Tax Court is going to analyze the antagonists' position carefully and will derive its own conclusions as to value from the record.[20]

Despite these problems, court decisions still constitute a key source of valuation criteria and will be discussed and cited throughout this Handbook.

§1.5 How the I.R.S. Looks at Valuation

Although the income tax provisions use the term "fair market value" and the estate and gift tax provisions use the term "value," they are defined similarly.[21] The I.R.S.' definition is: "The fair market value is the price at which the property would change hands between a willing buyer and a willing seller, neither being under any compulsion to buy or to sell and both having reasonable knowledge of relevant facts."[22]

As interpreted, this definition has several points deserving mention:

1. The word "fair" adds nothing to the phrase "market value"[23]
2. Forced sale price and other related abnormal price situations such as compulsory sale price, price as affected by unusual market conditions, and manipulated market price, are eliminated from consideration[24]
3. Generally, the relevant price equals the retail price and not the wholesale or dealer price[25]
4. The value is not reduced by expected sales costs such as sales commissions[26]
5. Fair market value is the price obtainable in cash and not by the extension of credit or installment payments by the seller[27]
6. Fair market value is ordinarily an objective standard and not a subjective evaluation dependent upon peculiar fitness, usefulness or adaptability of the

[18] Buffalo Tool & Die Mfg. Co., 74 T.C. 441 (1980).

[19] Buffalo Tool & Die Mfg. Co., 50 T.C.M. (P-H) ¶81,456 (1981).

[20] *See* Estate of A. Little, 51 T.C.M. (P-H) ¶82,026 (1982).

[21] I.R.S. App. Off., 1-2.

[22] Reg. §20.2031-1(b).

[23] United States v. Miller, 317 U.S. 369 (1943).

[24] Regs. §§20.2031-1(b), 25.2512-1.

[25] Regs. §§20.2031-1(b), 25.2512-1; Goldman v. Commissioner, 388 F.2d 476 (6th Cir. 1967).

[26] Estate of D. Smith, 57 T.C. 650 (1972), *aff'd on other grounds,* 510 F.2d 479 (2d Cir. 1975), *cert. denied,* 423 U.S. 827 (1975), *acq.* 1974-2 C.B. 4.

[27] H. Epstein, 53 T.C. 459 (1969), *acq.* 1970-2 C.B. xix.

property to special uses by the owner or prospective purchasers[28]

7. Fair market value must be determined even though there are neither standard markets to sell the asset nor known buyers to purchase it.[29]

The I.R.S. recognizes that the determination of fair market value is basically a question of fact.[30] The I.R.S. requires that all relevant circumstances and factors as of the value date are to be considered in determining value. Further, it is admitted that no mathematical answer is absolutely correct and that there is a range of right answers under the circumstances.[31] Because of the variability and fluctuation of market value, the I.R.S. recognizes the importance of opinion evidence provided by expert witnesses. It also recognizes the merit and persuasive force of appraisals made by qualified persons using appropriate and accurate data.

The risk of nonpersuasion (burden of proof) of the value of an asset is on the taxpayer.[32] I.R.S. valuations are considered prima facie correct. Once the taxpayer has produced evidence to rebut the presumption, however, the burden of going forward with the evidence shifts to the Service.

Because of the diversity of valuation issues that arise for tax purposes, it is not unusual to discover that the I.R.S. may at different times be on both sides of a valuation issue. It is helpful, then, to understand what the typical I.R.S. position will be under common situations. The following indicates the tax value issue and whether the I.R.S. in litigation will usually seek a higher or lower value.

Chart I-2

Income Tax Cases	Value Issue	Value Desired by I.R.S.
Compensation in Kind	Gross Income	Higher
Deduction in Kind	Deduction	Lower
Sale of Property	Capital Gain	
	Basis	Lower
	Sale Price	Higher
Estate and Gift Tax Cases	**Value Issue**	**Value Desired by I.R.S.**
Gift Value	Gift Tax	Higher
Gross Estate Value	Estate Tax	Higher
Adjusted Gross Estate	Deduction	Lower

The I.R.S. has released to the public two separate manuals that deal with the valuation of assets: the Appeals Officer Valuation Training Program (1980), and the Estate, Gift

28 Colonial Fabrics v. Commissioner, 202 F.2d 105 (2d Cir. 1953), *cert. denied,* 346 U.S. 814 (1953).

29 I.R.S. Tax Law Course, 20-1.

30 I.R.S. App. Off., 1-2; I.R.S. Tax Law Course, 20-1 to -3.

31 *See* Rev. Rul. 59-60 §3, 1959-1 C.B. 237; reproduced in Appendix A of this text.

32 Welch v. Helvering, 290 U.S. 111 (1933).

and Generation Skipping Tax Law Course for Attorneys (1979). Both manuals are designed for training I.R.S. employees. They are clearly slanted toward the collection of the maximum tax and thus must be read with caution.

For the practitioner, these manuals have the useful feature that they do provide some guidance as to how various I.R.S. personnel will react. When this aspect is important, the appropriate manual should be consulted. This Handbook cites these manuals when the I.R.S. position on a matter is relevant or determinative.

§1.6 How to Determine Basis for Estate Valuation Purposes

For estate planning purposes, there are two distinct basis determination methods. Choice of method depends on whether the assets are transferred to a taxpayer from an estate or as an inter vivos gift. If property is received from an estate, all assets included in the taxable gross estate receive a new income tax basis for income tax purposes. The basis equals the asset's value used on the federal estate tax return for federal estate tax purposes. If there is no estate tax return, the basis equals the asset's fair market value on the date of the decedent's death.[33] The basis rule with regard to gifts is that gifts of capital assets carry over the donor's basis, subject to adjustment for transfer expenses and gift taxes incurred, and subject to the limitation that basis cannot exceed fair market value as adjusted at the date of the gift.[34]

§1.7 Estate Planning Strategy

Pre-death estate planning calls for judgments about the value of the client's property. The following sections will discuss some of the most important valuation considerations that are relevant to such a client.

The rules governing the taxation of estates make it very important for a prospective donor to know the basis of the property to be transferred. First, the donor should avoid *inter vivos* gifts of property that have a basis higher than market value at the time of the gift. Instead, the donor should sell that property, take the appropriate capital loss deduction, and give the proceeds. Second, when the donor's basis is substantially less than market value, he or she should consider the potential adverse income tax consequences to the donee if the donee has to sell the property. The problem becomes particularly acute if sale of the property by the donee is anticipated. For very low basis-very high market value property, it is often desirable for the donor to retain such property in his or her estate in order to obtain the new, higher stepped-up basis.

The Economic Recovery Tax Act of 1981 adds a new section to the Internal Revenue Code that makes it even more important to make accurate valuations of assets for income tax purposes. Applicable to any return filed after December 31, 1981, this new

---

33 I.R.C. §1014.

34 I.R.C. §1015.

section imposes a special surcharge against the underpayment of income taxes due to a valuation overstatement.[35] The surcharges are as follows:

Surcharge Against Tax Underpayment	Percent of Overstatement
10%	150% to 200%
20%	Above 200% to 250%
30%	Above 250%

The appropriate surcharge is applicable only if all of the following conditions are met:

1. The stated value exceeds the determined correct value or adjusted basis by 150 percent
2. The overstated value is made on a return filed after December 31, 1981
3. The return is filed by an individual (including a partner of a partnership), closely held corporation or personal service corporation
4. The resultant underpayment of the income tax equals $1,000 or more
5. The property valued was held by the taxpayer for five years or less.

The Secretary is also given discretion to waive the surcharge in whole or in part if the taxpayer, in good faith, had a reasonable basis for the valuation or adjusted basis.

It is important to understand some of the areas of taxation to which the new section applies. For estate planning purposes the section applies to the following determination of value:

1. Adjusted basis of gifted property for capital gain or loss purposes upon sale by the donees
2. Adjusted basis of property passing as part of a decedent's estate for capital gain and loss purposes upon sale by the estate or the distributees
3. The value of stock contributed to an ESOP for deduction purposes by a close corporation
4. The value of property contributed to charity for charitable deduction purposes on the taxpayer's return.

The stated legislative purpose of the surcharge is to discourage taxpayer from grossly overstating values in order to obtain valuation compromises that have tended to "split the difference," and to take advantage of the tax interest rate that is below prevailing interest rates.[36]

---

35 I.R.C. §6659.

36 Joint Comm. on Tax, 97th Cong., 1st Sess., General Explanation of the Economic Recovery Tax Act of 1981, 332 (1981).

Two important limitations on the applications of the surcharge deserve mention. First, it only applies to overstatements of value and thus not to understatements. Second and consistent with the first, it does not apply to valuations for gift and estate taxes. Normally when gift and estate taxes are involved, the taxpayer does not want to overvalue an asset.

There are situations, however, where it could be advantageous to overvalue assets in a decedent's estate. Because the estate tax value and the income tax basis of assets that are part of a decedent's estate are the same, it may be desirable to value estate assets as high as possible particularly when there is, in effect, little or no estate tax due because of the unified credit or deductions or both. In this situation the surcharge may be applicable to capital gains taxes when the assets are sold by the estate or successors.

Illustration I-1

Assumptions

1. H, the Decedent, dies in 1987 survived by his wife, W;
2. Decedent's only assets at death are:
   (a) $20,000 cash held in joint account with W;
   (b) $30,000 life insurance payable to W as beneficiary;
   (c) Residence held in joint tenancy, with right of survivorship;
   (d) Closely Held Business;
3. W, the executor, estimates the value of the residence to equal $50,000 and the Business to equal $500,000;
4. W does not file an estate tax return because the total estate is less than the $600,000 filing threshhold (I.R.C. § 6018);
5. W sells Business in 1988 for $500,000 and declares no capital gain;
6. W is in the 50% income tax bracket;
7. I.R.S. audits W's return and determines that the fair market value and basis of the Business at the date of decedent's death equals $250,000.

Calculations

1.	Overstated Value	$500,000
2.	Divide 1. by Market Value or Adjusted Basis	÷250,000
3.	Overstated Percentage	2.00 = 200%
4.	Excess Value—Subtract 2. from 1.	250,000
5.	Tax on Excess Value (Capital Gain = Maximum Tax = 20%)	.20
6.	Tax Underpayment	$ 50,000
7.	Surcharge Percentage (10% for 200% Overvalue or less)	.10
8.	Surcharge Amount	5,000
9.	Total Tax Due (Without Interest) add 6. and 8.	$ 55,000

If the decedent's estate must file an estate tax return or returns for state inheritance or transmission tax, the value listed on those returns establishes a prima facie basis value for the asset.[37] Although no recent authority can be found, the values appearing on these filings are not conclusive.[38] Because of the new surcharge rule and because few estates are subject to estate taxes, the I.R.S. may scrutinize the values attributed to assets of a decedent when the sales of these assets are tested for capital gain or loss purposes.

Obviously, valuation determination and income taxation have significant importance to estate planning in general. Although some of the circumstances discussed above are not subject to planning (e.g., losses and thefts), others can be determined and controlled by the estate planner. If the planner's goal is the overall reduction of taxation, valuation determinations clearly are important factors.

TAX CONSIDERATIONS

§1.8 Estate Tax Considerations

Many of the pre- and post-mortem estate tax valuation considerations are interrelated and in some regards inseparable. When feasible, post-mortem considerations should be integrated into pre-mortem estate planning.

Lifetime techniques for after-death tax savings are needed because some of the considerations are substantive in nature, related to the taxation scheme in general. For example, *inter vivos* gifts can be used to reduce a client's estate and reduce the unified tax. This strategy takes advantage of the annual exclusion available during the client's lifetime but not available after his or her death.[39]

When estate taxes are payable, the valuation problems are greatly magnified. First, there is an immediate need to make more careful and precise valuation decisions. The tax collector is much more concerned with value than is the typical probate court, creditor or successor who receives some windfall assets. Second, two different valuation dates become potentially relevant. Not only is the market value at the date of death important[40] but the market value at the alternate valuation date, six months after the date of death, is also important.[41]

With estates, as with gifts, there are some benchmarks of which the practitioner must be aware. Initially, there is the federal estate tax threshold called the equivalent exemp-

---

37 Reg. §1.1014-3(a).

38 A. Evans, Trustee, 29 B.T.A. 710 (1934); Rev. Rul. 54-97, 1954-1 C.B. 113.

39 *See* §**1.12** Gift Tax Considerations.

40 I.R.C. §2031.

41 I.R.C. §2032.

tion.[42] This threshold amount determines whether the estate has to file an estate tax return. Congress has provided a new sliding scale for this amount depending on the date of death.[43] This scale is as follows:

Chart I-3

Year	Amount
1982	$225,000
1983	275,000
1984	325,000
1985	400,000
1986	500,000
1987	600,000

Unless Congress changes the exemption again, it will continue at $600,000 in 1987 and thereafter. Under these guides, an estate tax return is necessary only if the estate is valued at or above the appropriate prescribed amount less the amount of adjusted taxable gifts. The taxable estate is also reduced by the amount of the pre-1977 $30,000 specific gift tax lifetime exemption taken by the decedent for gifts he or she made between September 8, 1976 and December 31, 1976.

Because you must file a return does not mean that a tax will be paid. For example, 100 percent of qualified transfers to the decedent's spouse is deductible.[44] If these and other relevant deductions reduce the estate tax below the applicable unified credit, then no federal estate tax would be due.

§1.9 Considerations for the Estate Practitioner

A special value election with respect to the decedent's agricultural real estate and closely-held business real estate may be taken after the taxpayer's death.[45] The availability of the use of this election may require pre-mortem planning so that the percentage figure requirements of the election may be satisfied in the decedent's estate. Basically, the qualifying real estate comprise at least 25 percent of the adjusted value of the decedent's estate. The qualifying real estate and other property in the qualifying closely-held business must comprise at least 50 percent of the adjusted value of the decedent's gross estate. Although the qualifying percentages are absolute and are not subject to adjustment after the death of the client, during a client's lifetime it might be possible to structure assets so that the client's real property will qualify for the election.

The Internal Revenue Code contains several other relief provisions for post-mortem

42 I.R.C. §6018.

43 Economic Recovery Tax Act of 1981, §401; I.R.C. §6018.

44 I.R.C. §2056.

45 I.R.C. §2032A. *See* **§5.20** Special Use Valuation Generally.

elections for estates containing closely-held businesses. Typically these businesses' assets are non-liquid; cash to pay taxes is seldom available.

I.R.C. §303 deals with corporate redemption of a decedent's close corporation stock. Similar to the special valuation election method above, this section requires that over 35 percent of the adjusted gross estate be held in the close corporation. There are special rules concerning the inclusion of two or more close corporations and the inclusion of the interests of the surviving spouse.[46] Under special circumstances, to meet the 35 percent test, the decedent's estate may supplement its qualified holdings with the value of interests held by the decedent in two or more businesses and with the value of interests held by the decedent's surviving spouse. If the percentage and other requirements are met, and if the person who receives the stock upon the death of the testator is obligated to pay the appropriate taxes and expenses, the corporation is permitted to redeem the testator's stock to pay the portion of the testator's death taxes, funeral and administration expenses attributable to the value of the stock.[47]

The advantages of an I.R.C. §303 redemption are: it offers a means to obtain liquid assets in exchange for the non-liquid close corporation stock, and the transfer of the stock is considered a capital exchange rather than a distribution of dividends.

The Internal Revenue Code contains several other sections that can help with liquidity problems. For example, estates may pay estate tax in installments, postpone payment, or both. I.R.C. §§6166 and 6166A apply to the estates of persons dying before January 1, 1982. Revised I.R.C. §6166 applies to the estates of those dying later.[48] These sections, like I.R.C. §303, deal with closely held business interests (proprietorships, partnerships, and corporations). They also have their own important percentage qualification requirements.

Former I.R.C. §6166 allowed deferred payments of estate tax if a closely held business constituted more than 65 percent of the value (subject to supplementation due to family ownership)[49] of the adjusted gross estate of those dying before January 1, 1982. If the percentage and other requirements were met, the personal representative could elect to pay the relevant portion of the estate in the following manner: interest only on the tax due for the first five years, then ten years of equal installments to pay tax and interest due. In addition, the interest rate on the tax due on the first $1,000,000 of the closely held business was only 4 percent.

Former I.R.C. §6166A permitted installment payments of estate tax where a closely held business represented more than 35 percent of the value of the gross estate or 50 percent of the value of the taxable estate. As with I.R.C. §6166, 35 percent and 50 percent requirements could be supplemented under special circumstances by the interest of two or more businesses and by the value of interests held by certain relatives of the decedent. If the estate qualified for this section, the personal representative could

[46] Economic Recovery Tax Act of 1981, §442(b)(1); I.R.C. §303(b)(2).

[47] *See* **§1.16** Worksheet for Section 303 Redemption of Stock.

[48] Economic Recovery Tax Act of 1981, §442.

[49] Subject to supplementation refers to the provision in I.R.C. §6166(b)(2)(d): "All stock and all partnership interests held by the decedent or by any member of his family (within the meaning of section 267(c)(4)) shall be treated as owned by the decedent."

elect to pay the taxes attributable to the closely-held business in two to ten equal annual installments. There is no 4 percent interest rule; therefore, the interest on the taxes due must be paid at the ordinary tax interest rate.

The new I.R.C. §6166, relating to the estates of those who die after December 31, 1981, is a composite of the prior two sections and incorporates the advantageous features of each.[50] First, the value of the decedent's closely held business need only exceed 35 percent of the value of the adjusted gross estate. Second, for purposes of the 35 percent requirement, the decedent's estate may supplement its qualified holding under special circumstances with the value of interests held by the decedent in two or more businesses and with the value of interest held by decedent's surviving spouse and other certain relatives. Third, if the percentage and other requirements are met, the personal representative may elect to pay only interest on the tax due during the first five years and thereafter pay the tax and interest in equal installments for up to the next ten years. Fourth, the interest rate on the tax due on the first $1,000,000 of the closely-held business is only four percent.[51] Installment payments of estate tax can help an estate's liquidity problems. Even if cash is available, these provisions, in effect, offer loans from the government. A qualified estate does not have to give a reason for making the election. If the rate of interest is favorable (and a four percent rate is *extremely* favorable) the estate planner should consider using the election. Two points are important here: pre-death planning is often required to qualify an estate; and other factors may make the election undesirable.

§1.10 Estate Distribution Considerations

The distribution of assets among successors and beneficiaries seldom raises valuation questions. This is particularly true where the distribution provision is a cash bequest to be funded in cash or where it is a residuary-type clause that merely distributes a fractional share among named or identifiable beneficiaries. Valuation problems in such distributions may, however, become important when the particular fiduciary involved (whether a personal representative or trustee) has the power or responsibility to distribute assets in kind and/or in nonfractional share proportions, in equal shares to named or otherwise identifiable beneficiaries. Such distributions ordinarily require that the fiduciary make valuation determinations. The fiduciary must be careful that the valuation made does not prejudice or favor one beneficiary over the other.

Another related problem of valuation concerns in-kind distributions in satisfaction of pecuniary bequests or of income distributions. Again, the fiduciary must be careful that the valuation of the assets distributed is not insufficient or do not exceed the amount to be distributed.[52]

---

[50] Economic Recovery Tax Act of 1981, §442; I.R.C. §6166.

[51] I.R.C. §6601(j). *See* **§1.17** Worksheets for Section 6166 Deferrals of Estate Tax.

[52] To satisfy partial distributions in kind, the in kind distributions may exceed in value the relevant value of the testamentary gift. For example, a $1,000 legacy could be funded by distributing in kind assets that have a value greater or lesser than $1,000.

Valuation techniques for these distribution problems are usually the same as for other matters requiring the valuation of assets, although a will or trust can specify particular valuation techniques.

§1.11 State Gift and Death Transfer Tax Considerations

Most states do not tax gifts and have inheritance rather than estate tax provisions.[53] Despite the fact that some of the existing state gift, estate or inheritance laws are less effective than federal tax provisions in coverage and rate, when applicable they all ordinarily require valuations to be made of covered assets for estate planning purposes. Generally, the states follow the "market value" rule with regard to the valuation of assets. In addition, the valuation dates are usually the same or are compatible with the federal dates.

Valuation problems with state death taxes are less numerous, and when relevant are most often similar to federal estate tax problems. One significant difference is the exemption or exclusions available to the successors. Because most state death taxes are inheritance taxes, these exemptions and exclusions depend on the successor's relationship to the decedent.[54] Closer relatives such as the surviving spouse and descendants are provided higher exemptions and exclusions than successors who are more distant relatives or nonrelatives. The estate planner must take advantage of these tax-saving exemptions and exclusions. Because they are phrased in dollar terms, they necessarily relate directly to the question of valuation of the estate.

Federal estate taxes and state death taxes are integrated by the "pick-up" or "sponge" tax that most states have adopted in order to take full advantage of the federal estate tax's state tax credit.[55] In many estates this will be the only state tax due.

Often (but not always) state tax administrators will accept the final valuations used for federal estate and gift tax purposes; a separate valuation will not be required. The states, however, are particularly sensitive when different (usually lower) values are submitted for state tax purposes than for federal tax purposes. Practitioners should be careful to be consistent in this regard. Also, state officials generally demand that they be alerted to alterations in the values made by the federal authorities.

§1.12 Gift Tax Considerations

The making of gifts is a natural and beneficial activity in our society. Parents frequently make gifts to their children and grandparents are well known for their generosity. Gifts of small items and small amounts of cash raise few or no valuation issues. They constitute merely private transactions between the individuals involved. Congress recently reaffirmed the idea that small gifts are private in nature and should not have estate or gift tax consequences when it raised the annual gift tax exclusion from gifts

[53] Institute for Business Planning, Lawyer's Desk Book 546-74 (6th ed. 1980).

[54] W. Behrenfeld, Estate Planning Desk Book 230-36 (4th ed. 1978).

[55] *See* I.R.C. §2011.

valued up to $3,000 to gifts valued up to $10,000.[56] The new exclusion applies to transfers made after December 31, 1981. Not entirely in jest, it has often been said that the exclusion is necessary so that the I.R.S. agent will not be found hiding under the Christmas tree.

For larger gifts, a gift tax valuation is often essential.[57] Even the exclusion raises significant valuation problems.[58] This exclusion is a benchmark. Qualified gifts below the permitted figure are immune from both gift and estate tax consequences. Consequently, a non-cash gift must be evaluated in order to stay within the exclusion. Even accidental errors in valuation may cause adverse tax consequences. The $10,000 maximum applies to annual gifts to a single donee; the donor can give up to $10,000 per person per year to any number of donees.

"Qualified gifts" must conform to a basic requirement and a specific limitation on the exclusion. First, in order to qualify, gifts must be of a present interest in property.[59] Second, although within the exclusion amount at the date of the gift, gifts of life insurance policies may trigger estate tax if the donor dies within three years of making the gift and the face value of the policy is above the exclusion threshold.[60]

The I.R.S. has made it more important than ever to make accurate valuation determinations for gift tax purposes. In a recent letter ruling the I.R.S. provided its interpretation of two important related matters.[61] First, no gift tax is due or payable until a taxpayer has exhausted the taxpayer's unified credit. This means that a voluntary payment of a gift tax, when a sufficient amount of the unified credit still exists to cover the gift is not permitted. It constitutes overpayment, not payment.[62] Second, use of the unified credit on a gift tax return is not equivalent to a tax assessment or payment. In other words, a gift tax is assessed or paid only after the gift taxes due exceed the available unified credit. Therefore, valuations listed on prior tax returns may be adjusted on subsequent gift tax returns to calculate the aggregate value of prior taxable gifts unless: (a) a tax was actually assessed or paid as interpreted by this ruling and (b) the statutory gift tax assessment period has expired.[63] If this gift tax assessment period has expired, the unpaid gift tax on the previous gift is uncollectible even if no tax was assessed or paid. Illustration I-2 clarifies these points.

This example shows an increased tax of $5,000 due to the revaluation of the 1981 gift. Although the additional value assigned to the 1981 gift is added to aggregate gift value, the taxpayer will not have to pay the additional $40,800 of taxes that would have been due on that return because the limitations on collecting taxes on that return assumably have expired. It does, however, increase taxpayer's taxes on the 1985 return and for taxable gifts in subsequent years due to the increase in total values of all gifts.

---

[56] Economic Recovery Tax Act of 1981, §441; I.R.C. §2503(b).
[57] I.R.C. §2503.
[58] I.R.C. §2503(b).
[59] *See* Reg. §25.2503-3.
[60] I.R.C. §§2035(b), (d)(2).
[61] Letter Rul. 8132011.
[62] I.R.C. §2505.
[63] I.R.C. §2504(c).

Illustration I-2

Assumptions	
Taxpayer makes taxable gift in 1981 and 1985, only.	
Taxpayer's Gift Tax Form for 1981	
Value of current and total taxable gifts	$150,000
Tax on taxable gifts	38,800
Less unified credit taken	−38,799
Gift tax paid	1
Unused Unified Credit [= Maximum credit ($47,000) minus Unified Credit taken ($38,799)]	[$ 8,201]
Taxpayer's Gift Tax Form for 1985	
Value of current taxable gifts	$300,000
Prior taxable gifts	150,000
Total taxable gifts	450,000
Tax on taxable gifts	138,800
Less tax on prior gifts	−38,800
Tax balance due	100,000
Less unused credit [Maximum 1985 credit ($121,800) less Unified Credit taken ($38,799)]	−83,001
Tax due	$ 16,999
I.R.S. Contentions	
1985 Taxable gift	$300,000
Revalued prior 1981 taxable gift	300,000
Total taxable gifts	600,000
Tax on taxable gifts	192,800
Less tax on prior gifts as revalued	−87,800
Tax balance due	105,000
Less unused credit [Maximum 1985 credit ($121,800) less Unified Credit taken ($38,799)]	−83,001
Tax due	$ 21,999

It may be assumed that the I.R.S. will make the same contention in estates when calculating the values of adjusted taxable gifts on the estate tax return.

§1.13 Income Tax Considerations

The federal income tax law demands that assets be valued under many and diverse circumstances.[64] These issues cannot be discussed exhaustively here; this is a short review of the income tax considerations to give the reader an overall perspective.

64 *See* Alfred, *General Considerations,* 14 W. Reserve L. Rev. 173-74 (1963); Alfred, *Current Problem Areas in Income Taxation,* 14 W. Reserve L. Rev. 217-32 (1963).

The most common situations in which valuation decisions must be made include:

1. Receipt of property as income including, for example
   (a) Employee's discount price for goods[65]
   (b) Compensation paid in goods or in kind[66]
   (c) Distribution by a corporation that constitutes a dividend[67]
2. Capital gain or loss, including
   (a) Transfer of property for consideration[68]
   (b) Incorporation of a business[69]
   (c) Liquidation of a business[70]
   (d) Distribution of taxable stock rights[71]
3. Deductions taken including
   (a) Casualty and theft losses[72]
   (b) In-kind contributions (including the stock of the employer corporation) to an exempt employee's profit-sharing trust[73]
   (c) In-kind charitable contributions[74]
   (d) Basis of property upon which to calculate depreciation[75]
   (e) Bad debts[76]
4. The value of the property in order to classify the property for other tax consequences including, for example
   (a) Existence of a collapsible corporation[77]
   (b) Existence of a personal holding company[78]
   (c) Character of a transaction as a reorganization[79]
   (d) Existence of a regulated investment company.[80]

The importance of basis determination is that many of these valuation situations require the determination of the property's "basis" or "adjusted basis." These concepts are

---

[65] Reg. §1.61-2(d)(2)(i).
[66] Reg. §1.61-2(d)(1).
[67] I.R.C. §301(b)(1).
[68] I.R.C. §61(a)(3).
[69] I.R.C. §§356(a)(1), 356(b), 361(b).
[70] I.R.C. §331(a).
[71] I.R.C. §307(a).
[72] I.R.C. §§165(c)(3), 165(e).
[73] I.R.C. §404(a)(3).
[74] Reg. §1.170-1(c).
[75] I.R.C. §§167(a), 1011; also used for calculating cost recovery, *see* I.R.C. §168.
[76] I.R.C. §166(b).
[77] I.R.C. §§341(c)(1)(A), (e)(1)(C), (e)(8).
[78] I.R.C. §§542(a)(2), 543(a)(6)(A).
[79] I.R.C. §368(a)(2)(B)(iii).
[80] I.R.C. §§851(b)(4), 851(c)(1).

relevant here only when one or more of the valuation techniques is employed in order to determine basis. Necessarily, when basis or its other terms employ a valuation technique, the discussion of this technique is applicable.

Valuation to determine capital gain and loss is discussed in §1.5. Also remember that many wills and trusts permit the relevant fiduciary to fund a beneficiary's income rights in kind or in other assets. This approach requires a valuation of the assets used to satisfy these rights. Ordinarily, it is desirable to use assets that are valued as close as possible to the valuation of the income payments to be made.

PROPERTY TRANSFER CONSIDERATIONS

§1.14 Credit Considerations

A prudent lender must have information about the borrower's financial condition. This sometimes requires that the lender (particularly the secured lender) obtain information concerning the value of the borrower's assets.

The precision with which asset values must be determined depends significantly upon both the repayment protection necessary and the amount of the loan. A substantial loan, which greatly exceeds the borrower's ordinary earning capacity, may require an extensive inspection and valuation of the borrower's assets. Special appraisals may be necessary in order for the borrower to obtain the loan. Most frequently, however, a much more casual and simpler approach will be taken. After all, a lender is often aware of the general value of property in his or her community and does not require an extensive valuation process to be undertaken.

Ordinary valuation procedures are used before credit is extended. The most significant difference is that the lender is thinking in terms of loan or credit security and is ordinarily not dealing with a protective margin of only 100 per cent value. For example, mortgages typically cover only 60 percent to 90 per cent of the estimated value of the asset. Other protective security reductions will even be more severe. Pledge values of securities may run as low as 30 percent of the current value of the asset.

§1.15 Exchange of Property and Its Considerations

Sound estate planning often requires the purchase, sale, or exchange of assets, and valuation of these assets is necessary. As with other matters in this area, the degree to which the seller and buyer will proceed in order to determine the value depends upon a variety of factors. Some of these factors include:

1. The time within which the transfer must be made (forced sale)
2. The type of asset involved (incidental personal property items versus extensive commercial properties)
3. The anticipated value of the property (incidental inexpensive personal property versus expensive commercial properties)
4. The degree of certainty necessary (a purchase for consumption versus a purchase as an investment by a fiduciary for a trust).

In practical terms, the actual definition of value may significantly differ in these situations. Not only will market value be considered but the intrinsic value to the owner or purchaser is also relevant.[81] This means that utility, usefulness or productivity may be irrelevant to the purchaser and that the most important consideration is a pure desire to have the asset. Consequently, the sales price may be higher than what ordinarily would be considered market value. On the other hand, sometimes sales will be at values below market value because of an urgent desire on the part of the seller to dispose of the goods.

§1.16 Worksheet for Section 303 Redemption of Stock

SECTION 303
REDEMPTION OF STOCK
HELD IN DECEDENT'S GROSS ESTATE
[CONSIDERED SALE OR EXCHANGE
RATHER THAN DIVIDEND]
(FOR DECEDENTS WHO DIE AFTER 12-31-81, ONLY)

Qualification checklist

Check numbered right hand boxes if requirement is satisfied:

1. The decedent has corporate stock included in his or her gross estate. **1.** ☐
2. Corporate distributions in redemption of part or all of stock are feasible. **2.** ☐
3. The recipient of the stock is liable for payment of taxes and funeral and administration expenses. **3.** ☐
4. The recipient of stock did not obtain the stock by purchase or in satisfaction of a pecuniary bequest. **4.** ☐

If all right hand column boxes above are checked, make the following calculations:

[81] 1 J. Bonbright, Valuation of Property 15-16 (1937).

SECTION 303 (*Continued*)

Qualification checklist (*Continued*)

5. **A.** The total gross estate (Form 706, page 1, line 1) ________

B. Less allowable deductions under §§ 2053 and 2054 (Form 706, page 3, item 14) ________

C. Result equals the adjusted gross estate. **5.** ________

6. The Federal Estate Tax return (Form 706) value of the qualified stock(s) included in the gross estate. (Use Section 303 Appendix A for calculation) **6.** ________

7. **A.** The adjusted gross estate [Item (5)] ________

B. Multiply by 35% × .35

C. Result equals test amount **7.** ________

8. Subtract result of item 7. from item 6. **8.** ________

If item 8. results in a positive number above zero, the stock qualifies for a §303 redemption and it is necessary to make the following calculations.

9. Calculation of the actual reduction of the stock recipient's interest due to the payment of the following:

	Total Deduction	Recipient's Proportion	Actual Reduction
A. Federal Estate Taxes	________	× .______	________
B. State Death Taxes	________	× .______	________
C. Interest on A. and B.	________	× .______	________
D. Allowable Funeral and Administration Expenses under § 2053	________	× .______	________

E. Add A.-D. under Actual Reduction Column **9.** ________

10. Maximum allowable §303 redemption: Lesser of Item 6. or Item 9. **10.** ________

SECTION 303 APPENDIX A

Columns		# 1	# 2	# 3	# 4
Items (If the stock of only one corporation is held, complete items A-1. and A-9., only.)		Name	Name	Name	Name
A-1. The Federal Estate Tax value of qualified corporation in gross estate	A-1				
A-2. Add value of corporation stock owned be decedent's surviving spouse as community property, joint tenants, tenants by the entirety or tenants in common	A-2				
A-3. Total value of both spouses' corporation stock	A-3				
A-4. Total value of all of the outstanding stock	A-4				
A-5. Multiply by 20%	A-5	× .20	× .20	× .20	× .20
A-6. Result equals multiple corporation stock qualification amount	A-6				

A-7. Add the item A-1. amounts of all of decedent's corporations in which each of their item A-3. values are equal to or greater than their item A-6. values

A-7. #1 ______
#2 ______
#3 ______
#4 ______

A-8. Result equals the value of qualified interests of multiple corporations

A-9. Enter highest Federal Estate Tax value of interest of single corporation held in gross estate

A-8. ______
A-9. ______

Insert at item 6. of the Qualification Checklist for §303 the higher amount indicated in item A-8. or A-9.

§1.17 Worksheets for Section 6166 Deferrals of Estate Tax

SECTION 6166
UP TO 15 YEARS OF DEFERRAL
5-YEAR DEFERRAL—10-YEAR INSTALLMENT PAYMENT
(FOR DECEDENTS WHO DIE AFTER 12-31-81, ONLY)

Qualification checklist

Check numbered right hand boxes if requirement is satisfied:

1. Decedent is an U.S. citizen or resident at death. **1.** ☐

2. The gross estate includes one or more or combination of the following interests in a closely held business:
- **A.** A proprietor of a trade or business
  OR
- **B.** A partner in a trade or business
  OR
- **C.** A shareholder in a corporation **2.** ☐

3. The decedent either:
- **A.** Is the sole proprietor
  OR
- **B.** Owns 20%[a] or more of the capital interest in the relevant partnership
  OR
- **C.** Is one of 15 or fewer partners[b] in the relevant partnership
  OR
- **D.** Owns 20%[a] or more in value of the voting stock of the relevant corporation included in the estate
  OR
- **E.** Is one of 15 or fewer shareholders[b] in the relevant corporation **3.** ☐

If all right hand column boxes are checked, make the following calculations:

---

[a] For purposes of satisfying the 20% requirement, the value of the surviving spouse's community property, joint tenant, tenant by the entirety or tenant in common interest in the closely held business is combined with the value of the decedent's interest in the closely held business.

[b] The following interests may be combined together and counted as only one partner or one shareholder: (1) the surviving spouse's and decedent's interest in the closely held business which is held as community property, joint tenants, tenants by the entirety or tenants in common; and (2) the interests in the closely held business held by the decedent and the decedent's spouse or descendants of the decedent's grandparents or both.

SECTION 6166 *(Continued)*

Qualilfication checklist *(Continued)*

4. A. The total gross estate (Form 706, page 1, line 1) __________

B. Less allowable deductions under Sections 2053 and 2054 (Form 706, page 3, item 14) – __________

C. Result equals the adjusted gross estate **4.** __________

5. The Federal Estate Tax return (Form 706) value of the qualified closely held business(es) included in the gross estate (Use Section 6166 Appendix A for calculation) **5.** __________

6. A. The adjusted gross estate (Item 4.) __________

B. Multiply by 35% × .35

C. Result equals test amount **6.** __________

7. Subtract result of item 6. from item 5. **7.** __________

If item 7. results in a positive number above zero, the estate qualifies for a Section 6166 installment payout and it is necessary to make the following calculations:

8. A. Net Estate Tax (Form 706, page 1, line 19) __________

B. Multiply by item 5. × __________

C. Result __________

D. Divide by the value of the adjusted gross estate (Item 4.) ÷ __________

E. Result equals tax deferrable **8.** __________

9. A. Net Estate Tax (Form 706, page 1, line 19) __________

B. Less Tax deferrable (Item 8.) – __________

C. Result equals tax not deferrable (due at time for paying estate tax) __________ **9.** __________

SECTION 6166 (*Continued*)

Qualification checklist (*Continued*)

10.	**A.**	Tax on $1,000,000	$345,800		
	B.	Less Allowable unified credit (Form 706, page 1, line 11)	– ______		
	C.	Result equals first alternative test amount	______		
	D.	Tax deferrable (Item 8.)	______		
	E.	Lesser of C. or D. above equals the four percent portion		**10.**	______
11.	**A.**	Tax deferrable (Item 8.)	______		
	B.	Less four percent portion (Item 10.)	– ______		
	C.	A positive number above zero equals the non-four percent portion		**11.**	______
12.	**A.**	Four percent portion (Item 10.)	______		
	B.	Divided by number of annual install-ments in which tax is to be paid (No less than 2 nor more than 10)	÷ ______		
	C.	Result equals the annual installment payment on the four percent portion		**12.**	______
13.	**A.**	Non-four percent portion (Item 11.)	______		
	B.	Divided by number of annual installments in which tax is to be paid (Same as Item 12.B.)	÷ ______		
	C.	Result equals the annual installment payment on the non-four percent portion		**13.**	______

SECTION 6166 APPENDIX A

Columns		# 1	# 2	# 3	# 4
Items (If the interest of only one closely held business is held, complete items A-1. and A-9., only.)		Name	Name	Name	Name
A-1. The Federal Estate Tax value of qualified closely held business in gross estate	**A-1.**				
A-2. Add value of closely held business owned by decedent's surviving spouse as community property, joint tenants, tenants by the entirety or tenants in common	**A-2.**				
A-3. Total value of both spouses' closely held business interests	**A-3.**				
A-4. Total value of closely held business	**A-4.**				
A-5. Multiply by 20%	**A-5.**	× .20	× .20	× .20	× .20
A-6. Result equals multiple closely held business qualification amount	**A-6.**				

A-7. Add the item (A-1) amounts of all closely held businesses in which each of their item (A-3) values are equal to or greater than their item (A-6) values

A-7. #1 ______
#2 ______
#3 ______
#4 ______

A-8. Result equals the value of qualified interests of multiple closely held businesses **A-8.** ______

A-9. Enter highest Federal Estate Tax value of interest of single closely held business held in gross estate **A-9.** ______

Insert at item 5. of the Qualification Checklist for §6166 the higher amount indicated in item A-8. or A-9.

PAYMENT SCHEDULE–6166

(YEARS 6–15)

[USE TWO OF THESE SCHEDULES]

	Payment is due on ____________, ________ of each year:				
Installment No.	6/11	7/12	8/13	9/14	10/15
Year of Payment	(19)	(19)	(19)	(19)	(19)
A. Balance due on four percent portion[a]	$________ (Item 10.)	$________	$________	$________	$________
B. Multiply by 4%	× .04	× .04	× .04	× .04	× .04
C. Interest due on four percent portion	$________	$________	$________	$________	$________
D. Balance due on non-four percent portion[b]	$________ (Item 11.)	$________	$________	$________	$________
E. Multiply by current interest rate	× .	× .	× .	× .	× .
F. Interest due on non-four percent portion	$________	$________	$________	$________	$________

G. Installment amount due on four percent portion (Item 12. or other proportionate greater amount)	$______	$______	$______	$______	$______
H. Installment amount due on non-four percent portion (Item 13. or other proportionate greater amount)	$______	$______	$______	$______	$______
I. Total installment payment due (Add C, F, G and H)	$______	$______	$______	$______	$______

[a] Balance due for each installment in each year is calculated by subtracting the previous year's installment payment without interest from the previous year's balance due, *e.g.*, balance due, item A., year 7, equals balance due, item A., year 6 less installment amount, item G., year 6.

[b] Same procedure as Note a, above, *e.g.*, balance due, item D., year 7, equals balance due, item D., year 6 less installment amount, item H., year 6.

SECTION 6166
(ATTRIBUTION ELECTION)
UP TO 10 YEARS DEFERRAL
(FOR DECEDENTS WHO DIE AFTER 12-31-81, ONLY)

Qualification checklist

Check numbered right hand boxes if requirement is satisfied:

1. Decedent is an U.S. citizen or resident at death. **1.** ☐

2. The gross estate includes one or more or combination of the following interests in a closely held business:
- **A.** A partner in a trade or business
  OR
- **B.** A shareholder in a corporation **2.** ☐

3. The decedent either:
- **A.** Owns 20%[a] or more of the capital interest in the relevant partnership
  OR
- **B.** Owns 20%[a] or more in the value of the voting stock of the relevant corporation included in the gross estate **3.** ☐

If all right hand column boxes are checked, make the following calculations:

4. **A.** The total gross estate (Form 706, page 1, line 1) ____________
- **B.** Less allowable deductions under Sections 2053 and 2054 (Form 706, page 3, item 14) ____________
- **C.** Result equals the adjusted gross estate **4.** ____________

5. The federal Estate Tax return (Form 706) value of the qualified closely held business(es) included in the gross estate [Use Section 6166 (Attribution Election) Appendix A for calculations] **5.** ____________

[a]For purposes of the 20% requirement, the value of all stock or partnership interests which are not readily tradable (owned by the decedent, the decedent's spouse and the descendants of decedent's grandparents can be combined.

SECTION 6166 (*Continued*)

Qualification checklist

6.	**A.**	The adjusted gross estate (Item 4.)	______	
	B.	Multiply by 35%	× .35	
	C.	Result equals test amount		**6.** ______
7.		Subtract result of item 6. from item 5.		**7.** ______

If item 7. results in a positive number above zero, the estate qualifies for a Section 6166 (Attribution Election) installment payout and it is necessary to make the following calculations:

8.	**A.**	Net Estate Tax (Form 706, page 1, line 19)	______	
	B.	Multiply by item 5.	______	
	C.	Result	______	
	D.	Divide by the value of the adjusted gross estate (Item 4.)	______	
	E.	Result equals tax deferrable		**8.** ______
9.	**A.**	Tax deferrable (Item 8.)	______	
	B.	Divide by number of annual installments in which tax is to be paid (No less than 2 nor more than 10)	÷ ______	
	C.	Result equals annual installment payments		**10.** ______
10.	**A.**	Net Estate Tax (Form 706, page 1, line 19)	______	
	B.	Less tax deferrable (Item 8.)	− ______	
	C.	Result equals tax not deferrable	______	
	D.	Add first annual installment (Item 9.)	______	
	E.	Result equals Estate Tax due at time for paying estate tax		**10.** ______

SECTION 6166 (ATTRIBUTION ELECTION) APPENDIX A

Columns		Stock # 1	Stock # 2	Stock # 3	Stock # 4
Items (If the interest of only one appropriate closely held business is held, complete items A-1. and A-9., only.)		______ Name	______ Name	______ Name	______ Name
A-1. The Federal Estate Tax value of qualified closely held business in gross estate	**A-1.**	______	______	______	______
A-2. Add value of closely held business owned by decedent's surviving spouse and descendants of decedent's grandparents	**A-2.**	______	______	______	______
A-3. Total value of spouses' and relatives' closely held business	**A-3.**	______	______	______	______
A-4. Total value of closely held business	**A-4.**	______	______	______	______
A-5. Multiply by 20%	**A-5.**	× .20	× .20	× .20	× .20
A-6. Result equals multiple closely held business qualification amount	**A-6.**	______	______	______	______

A-7. Add the item A-1. amounts of all closely held businesses in which each of their item A-3. values are equal to or greater than their item A-6. values

A-7. #1 ______
#2 ______
#3 ______
#4 ______

A-8. Result equals the value of qualified interests of multiple closely held businesses **A-8.** ______

A-9. Enter highest Federal Estate Tax value of interest of single closely held business held in gross estate **A-9.** ______

Insert at item 5. of the Qualification Checklist for § 6166 the higher amount indicated in item (A-8) or (A-9).

SECTION 6166 PAYMENT SCHEDULE (ATTRIBUTION ELECTION)

	Installment No./ Annual Payment	1. (19_)	Payment is due on ______, ______ of each year: 2. (19_)	3. (19_)	4. (19_)	5. (19_)
A.	Balance due[a]	$______ (Item 8.)	$______	$______	$______	$______
B.	Multiply by current interest rate	NA	×.___	×.___	×.___	×.___
C.	Interest due	(None)	______	______	______	______
D.	Add Installment amount due (Item 9. or other greater amount)	$______	$______	$______	$______	$______
E.	Total installment payment due	$ (Same)	$______	$______	$______	$______

	Installment No./ Annual Payment	6. (19_)	7. (19_)	8. (19_)	9. (19_)	10. (19_)
A.	Balance due[a]	$______	$______	$______	$______	$______
B.	Multiply by current interest rate	×.___	×.___	×.___	×.___	×.___
C.	Interest due	$______	$______	$______	$______	$______
D.	Add Installment amount due (Item 9. or other greater amount)	$______	$______	$______	$______	$______
E.	Total installment payment due	$______	$______	$______	$______	$______

[a] Balance Due for each installment in each year is calculated by subtracting the previous year's installment payment without interest (Item D.) from the previous year's balance due, e.g., item A., year 7, equals balance due, item A., year 6, less installment amount, item D., year 6.

CHAPTER 2

THE BASIC GROUND RULES FOR VALUATION

§2.1 Introduction to Valuation of Assets

Although there are many special rules with respect to particular types of assets, many generalizations can be made, and several terms and concepts recur throughout discussions of valuation.

There are two ways to use this Handbook. Either read this chapter to gain general knowledge of asset valuation—fourteen concepts are discussed in this chapter—or refer to these topics as you need them:

1. Actuarial Calculations
2. Appraisals and Expert Analysis
3. Book Value (Asset Value)
4. Capitalization of Income
5. Cost (Purchase Price)
6. Discounts and Premiums
7. Fair Market Value
8. Market
9. Proof of Value
10. Replacement or Reproduction Costs
11. Special Use Value
12. Statistical and Regression Analyses
13. Valuation Mathematics
14. Weighting of Valuation Factors.

APPRAISALS

§2.2 Valuation Determination Strategies - "How Much Effort Should I Take to Make a Particular Valuation?"

The effort necessary to make valuations may range from "eyeballing" or "horseback" estimates to elaborate and comprehensive written or printed appraisals. Unfortunately, as with so many issues concerned with valuation, there is no set formula to follow. The answer basically lies solely in your judgment as the valuator. A few points of reference can help:

1. You need only satisfy ordinary standards for valuation of that type. For example, is the valuation merely a general reference point (e.g., in a credit investigation) or is it highly determinative (e.g., in tax situations)? For the former, appraisals are not necessary, and the valuation determinations ordinarily can be made short form or rule of thumb valuation guides. For example, a bank deciding how much money to loan to a purchaser of an apartment house might accept the gross rental multiplier technique (multiplying the gross rent of the apartment house by a known locally developed factor) as an adequate valuation technique.[1]

2. Numerous assets of low value (e.g., personal effects in a decedent's estate) ordinarily can be valued in a very casual way. It is common for the evaluator to select an arbitrary amount as the value of the entire class of assets. Unless specifically required by law, detailed appraisals of these assets would generally be counterproductive and too expensive.

3. Determinative valuations of high valued assets ordinarily call for careful and complete appraisals by persons qualified to make them.[2] Frequently, money and time can be saved by making these appraisals immediately, not waiting until a valuation disagreement arises. Still, some discretion must be employed in these situations: there is no need to pay $1,500 for an appraisal when a $200 appraisal would do.

4. The amount you should spend on an appraisal or appraisals depends upon many things. Certainly, the importance of the valuation is the most significant factor. A sort of cost-benefit analysis is necessary. You must decide how much the appraisals will cost versus how much financial benefit will be derived in making the valuation in this manner. For example, the effect of a high or low valuation of an asset for estate and gift tax purposes depends on the rate of the tax applicable: it is never a dollar-for-dollar trade-off.

5. The best advice: use reasonable judgment under the circumstances.

The process of value determination is not a science; it often depends on opinion evidence from expert appraisers.[3] Appraisals are required by the law of many states to set the value of a decedent's estate. Unless the assets have an identifiable market price or have little value, these appraisals may lack accuracy and foundation. In most situations, they remain unquestioned and unreviewed. Frequently, these appraisals can be used only for the satisfaction of the inventory and appraisement requirement of probate statutes. Their lack of more general applicability is due to the fact that they

---

[1] *See* **§5.4** Short Form Valuation Techniques for Real Property.

[2] *See* **§§2.3–2.7** on APPRAISALS.

[3] *See* **§2.8** Proof of Value.

are commonly made by inexpert appraisers as a friendship gesture, solely to satisfy the statutory requirement. Sometimes, any resemblance between these appraisals and fair market value is purely coincidental.

§2.3 Significance of Appraisals and Expert Testimony

Under proper conditions, qualified appraisals may have significant usefulness in the determination of value. The I.R.S. not only obtains and uses them,[4] it even sometimes requires them.[5] In addition, appraisals have been used in many ways by the courts. When the expert's opinion has been formed by proper, thorough and comprehensive methods and factors, the testimony of the expert witness may have great weight on the final valuation determination.[6] For example, appraisals may permit the court to weigh the merits of a particular valuation technique or between various valuation techniques.[7] This is particularly true when several appraisals have been introduced and accepted into evidence. Under other proper circumstances, the courts have used appraisals to rebut other evidence that might ordinarily be conclusive. For example, fair market value of a par-value stock might be significantly different than the stated par value.[8] Finally, because appellate courts use the substantial evidence rule to review valuation decisions made by the trier of fact, the existence of bona fide and qualified appraisals can help satisfy this test.[9]

When a bona fide expert appraiser testifies in court, the weight to be given to a *bona fide* expert appraiser's testimony depends on circumstances similar to those affecting the weight to be given to any other expert witness' testimony.[10] Many factors are considered to determine the degree of a particular witness' expertise. In selecting an appraiser you should consider the following:

1. The length of experience
2. The amount and quality of any special study or training in appraising
3. The relationship between the person's experience and training to the particular type and location of property involved
4. The degree to which the appraiser is performing and committed to the art of appraising.

None of these criteria provides a satisfactory test for distinguishing an expert from a nonexpert with an opinion. Although the latter's opinion may be admissible, it is typically given less weight than opinion testimony provided by experts. Even expert

---

4 *See* I.R.S. Tax Law Course, 2-17; I.R.S. App. Off., 16-1 to -7.

5 *See, e.g.,* Reg. §20.2031-6(b). *See* **§2.29** Documentation for Federal Tax Returns.

6 Loesch & Green Const. Co. v. Commissioner, 211 F.2d 210 (6th Cir. 1954).

7 *See, e.g.,* Estate of J. Salsbury, 44 T.C.M. (P-H) ¶75,333 (1975).

8 *See* H. Testard, 6 B.T.A.M. (P-H) ¶37,272 (1937).

9 *See* Elmhurst Cemetery Co. v. Commissioner, 300 U.S. 37 (1937).

10 *See* 2 Am. Jur. Proof of Facts, *Appraisals* §1 (1959).

testimony is weighted according to the expert's individual qualifications.[11]

§2.4 When to Get an Appraisal

Appraisals should be obtained when:

1. The I.R.S. requires it[12]
2. Other interested parties require it (e.g., financial institutions, buyers, insurers)
3. Litigation has or may arise over valuation.

There are two primary situations when appraisals are not necessary for estate planning purposes:

1. When only rough estimates of valuation are required (e.g., some credit situations)
2. When market price data is readily available (e.g., traded securities).

The following assets may require appraisal under the standards mentioned above:

1. Large blocks of or restricted traded securities (Chapter 3)
2. Untraded business interests (Chapter 4)
3. Real estate (Chapter 5)
4. Some agricultural personalty (Chapter 6)
5. Mineral interests (Chapter 7)
6. Some contractual properties (Chapter 8)
7. Intellectual and other unique property (Chapter 9)
8. Some significant personal effects (Chapter 10)
9. Any asset that does not have an identifiable market price (Chapter 11).

§2.5 Types of Appraisals

The most common type of value estimate received from appraisers is the point estimate. This estimate is a statement of an estimated single value for the property and is ordinarily required for tax valuation purposes.

Another type of estimate occasionally given is the interval estimate. Rather than a single figure, this estimate expresses the value in a range of values. For example, the appraisal would conclude that the property is to be valued from X to Y dollars. Although generally insufficient for tax valuation purposes, an interval estimate may be a sufficient indication of value for many planning purposes. When interval estimates

[11] Estate of T. Folks, 51 T.C.M. (P-H) ¶82,043 (1982).

[12] *See* **§2.29** Documentation for Federal Tax Returns.

are made, it is common to state the approximate reliability of the prediction by percentages. In other words, the appraiser states that he or she is 100 percent, 90 percent, 50 percent or whatever percent confident that market value lies within the range of the appraisal. A 50 percent confidence factor might be satisfactory in some cases; a 95 percent or more confidence factor might be required in other situations. Statistical techniques are commonly employed to predict the confidence factor by calculating the standard error in the estimate.[13]

§2.6 Appraisal Standards

Clearly, appraisals will have a greater significance if they satisfy certain minimum standards. The following paragraphs outline the basic substantive standards that your appraisals should satisfy.

1. Appraisals should be made as close to the date of valuation as possible. The longer the time between the date of valuation and the appraisal, the more speculative the basic data necessary to determine the market condition at the date of valuation, and the less weight the appraisal may be accorded.

On this point you have the advantage over the I.R.S. because of tax return filing dates. Get the appraisal, then, as soon as you decide you need it.

2. Appraisals should be as factually complete as possible. The omission of an important factor has been a significant reason for discounting the validity of an appraisal. You should consider all relevant factors related to valuation including the asset's physical properties (size, condition, shape, composition, type, design, and function), its geography or location (proximity, social and economic status, and restrictions) and usability (highest and best use, operating costs, alterability, repairability, and suitability).

3. Appraisals should make use of all techniques relevant to the appraisal of the particular asset. You might include, for example, book value, comparable sales of similar assets, cost, replacement and reproduction costs, and earning capacity analysis.

4. Appraisals should set out clearly the basis upon which the appraised value is determined. Substantiation of the determined value is a very important factor in determining the weight to be given to an appraisal.

5. Appraisals should indicate their purpose clearly. Naturally, this purpose should be appropriate to the context in which they are introduced. For example, your appraisals for credit purposes may have little weight in proceedings to determine estate tax

---

13 *See* Brown, Encyclopedia of Real Estate Appraising 166-71 (Friedman 3d ed. 1978). *See also* §2.25 Statistical and Regression Analysis.

value; credit appraisals typically are too conservative to be accepted by the I.R.S. or for most tax purposes.

The I.R.S. has set out a list of the minimal information it requires for appraisals of charitable gifts for income tax deduction purposes.[14] Because this list is just as applicable to all tax appraisals, all of your appraisals must state:

1. A summary of the appraiser's qualifications
2. The value of the asset and the appraiser's definition of value
3. The bases upon which the appraisal was made including asset use limitations
4. The valuation dates
5. The appraiser's signature and date of the appraisal.

§2.7 Limitations on Appraisals and Expert Testimony

You could say that if you have five expert appraisers you'll get five different values; six or more if the property is income-producing. This joke is not rooted in the venality of the appraising profession, but in the need for judgment on the appraiser's part. Although disagreement between qualified experts on the same side of a case may be detrimental to that party's position, uniform or formula determined valuations are not necessary. In fact, they can be detrimental. The courts appear to be willing to consider the cumulative effect of all appraisals and to accommodate their differences.[15]

Several qualifications about appraisals deserve mention. First, appraising is not a science. It is clear that appraisals constitute opinion evidence subject to being ignored, rejected or given only slight weight. Second, appraisals by experts are not necessary for all assets or in all situations. Appraisals cost money and should be employed only where they will serve a legitimate purpose.[16]

VALUATION TERMINOLOGY

§2.8 Proof of Value

Discussion of "proof of value" assumes that litigation has occurred concerning the valuation of an asset. The determination of the value of an asset is basically a question of fact,[17] and must be proved by all of the admissible and competent evidence.

In tax cases the burden of proof (or risk of non persuasion) of an asset's value is on the taxpayer, because the commissioner's determination of value is prima facie cor-

---

[14] Rev. Proc. 66-49, 1966-2 C.B. 1257.

[15] *See* Cullers v. Commissioner, 237 F.2d 611 (8th Cir. 1956).

[16] *See* **§2.2** Valuation Determination Strategies.

[17] Tracy v. Commissioner, 53 F.2d 575 (6th Cir. 1931), *cert. denied,* 287 U.S. 632 (1932).

rect.[18] Under a few circumstances, the courts have held that the burden is on the I.R.S.; for example, when the I.R.S.' valuation lacks reasonable basis under the facts available, is based on some error of law or where the I.R.S. attempts to change its original valuation determination.[19]

The rules of evidence concerning valuation are the same used to prove any fact. Proof of valuation will quite frequently involve the testimony of an expert witness.[20]

The determination of value by the trier of fact is given substantial weight on appeal. Appellate courts will not overrule the decision of the trier of fact provided there is "substantial evidence" to support the decision.[21] This substantial-evidence rule will prevent a reversal even where the trier of fact has failed to give a detailed analysis of the reasons behind the valuation determination.

§2.9 Fair Market Value

The determination of fair market value is the most important factor for estate valuation purposes. Although the various definitions vary slightly, basically the definition has remained constant for estate valuation purposes. The oft-quoted IRS definition is: "The fair market value is the price at which the property would change hands between a willing buyer and a willing seller, neither being under any compulsion to buy or to sell and both having reasonable knowledge of relevant facts."[22]

One of the most lucid explanations of fair market value appears in an instruction to the jury made by District Judge Ewing T. Kerr in *Lewis* v. *United States*.[23] The following paraphrases this instruction to make it a more pervasive statement.

The term "fair market value" means that price, in money or its equivalent, that the property would have brought on or about the valuation date considered at its highest and best use when the buyer is not compelled to buy and the seller is not compelled to sell. When the expression "highest and best use" of property is used, it means that use that would give the property its highest fair market value as of the valuation date. This may be the actual use of the property on that date, or a use to which it was then adaptable, even though on the date in question the property was not being put to such use.

It must be assumed that the purchaser in such a transaction wanted to buy the property, but was not forced to buy, and that the seller wanted to sell the property, but was not forced to sell. It must also be assumed that both the buyer and the seller were fully informed on that date as to all favorable circumstances and factors about the property; as to all uses to which the property was then being put, and as to the

---

18 Welch v. Helvering, 290 U.S. 111 (1933).

19 *See, e.g.,* Andrews v. Commissioner, 135 F.2d 314 (2d Cir. 1943), *cert. denied,* 320 U.S. 748 (1943).

20 *See* §§**2.3–2.7** on APPRAISALS.

21 Elmhurst Cemetery Co. v. Commissioner, 300 U.S. 37 (1937).

22 Reg. §20.2031-1(b); *see also* Reg. §25.2512-1; *see* §**1.5** How the I.R.S. Looks at Valuation.

23 Lewis v. United States, 27 A.F.T.R.2d 71-1650 (D. Wyo. 1970).

highest and best use, of all other uses, for which the property was at that time actually and potentially suitable and adaptable.

In determining fair market value of the asset, it is necessary to consider what amount could have been realized by a reasonably efficient disposal of the asset on the valuation date or within a reasonable time thereafter.

In this regard, the best evidence of value would be a sale of the asset itself, during the period of time relevant to valuation. However, if the asset has not been sold the sale of similar property in the immediate vicinity may be considered in arriving at a value.

When considering whether other property sold is similar to the asset in question, "similar" means "having a resemblance," not "identical." Obviously, no two assets will be identical: there will be differences in the size, shape, location, and immediate surroundings of the two assets. To the extent that they are similar, the price for which one sold on the open market is the best indication of the fair market value of the other.

As a general rule, because of his or her ownership, an assets owner is allowed to testify as to its value. This testimony is to be weighed and considered in the same manner as that of any other witness expressing an opinion as to fair market value.

For gift and estate tax purposes, the I.R.S. takes the position that an item's fair market value is the price at which that item or comparable items would sell at retail.[24] For estate tax purposes, however, the I.R.S. recognizes price for tangible personal property other than retail price, under two limited circumstances.

First, the service permits you to value tangible personal property in an estate at the price for which it sells; if the property is sold at public auction, or if the property is sold through newspaper classified ads, and property of this nature is ordinarily sold in this manner.[25] Such sales must be made within a reasonable time after the applicable valuation date. Furthermore, this method may not be used if there have been substantial changes in market conditions or other circumstances affecting the value of the item between the date of valuation and the date of sale.

Second, when an asset is sold to a dealer, the difference between the retail market price on the applicable valuation date and the actual price received from the dealer may be treated as a cost for the estate and taken as an administration expense.[26] However, the sale must be necessary in order to pay debts, expenses of administration, taxes, to preserve the estate or to effect distribution. In effect, this dealer-sale exception permits an estate, under these circumstances, to value these types of assets at wholesale rather than retail prices.

§2.10 Market

The terms "market value" and "fair market value" imply that value is related to a particular market. However, this is not necessarily the case.

---

[24] Regs. §§20.2031-1(b), 25.2512-1. *See* **§2.10** Market.

[25] Rev. Proc. 65-19, 1965-2 C.B. 1002.

[26] Reg. §20.2053-3(d)(2).

For our purposes, the word "market" can be defined as "the area of economic activity in which buyers and sellers come together and forces of supply and demand affect prices."[27] Clearly when homogeneous property is traded in such a market, the value of such property is readily obtainable and identifiable. An obvious example: readily-marketable securities that are traded frequently on the recognized securities exchange.

Unfortunately from efficiency and predictability standpoints, many types of assets do not have such markets available to determine value. Nonetheless, the law requires that these assets be given a "market value" or "fair market value." Consequently, the word "market" is used in a hypothetical sense. In determining the value of such assets, therefore, you must consider all relevant data to make the valuation decision (e.g., compare actual sales of similar properties). For some types of assets, this is the principal valuation technique.[28] Naturally, selecting the properties to compare and determining what sales or transactions are comparable are matters of opinion and judgment. The "market" in such situations is clearly a fiction.

Even when markets exist, you may have more than one from which to choose and must select carefully. For example, there may be both retail and wholesale markets. The I.R.S. position (which has specific limited exceptions) is that, for estate and gift tax purposes, the assets are to be valued at their retail market value.[29] One federal Circuit Court has taken the same position on the income tax value of a charitable contribution.[30] The exception recognized in the Regulations permits a price other than retail price to prevail for estate tax purposes under specified circumstances when dealing with tangible personal property.[31]

You may find that there are different retail markets depending, for example, on the volume of assets ordinarily traded by the owner. Generally, in these situations, you should refer to the market that usually serves the asset owner involved.

§2.11 Sales of the Asset

The price at which an asset has sold may be very relevant if not determinative of market value. Obviously, there is no better evidence of market value than the value of the asset received in the market place.[32] Even when assets are not traded on a recognized market, the sale price received for an asset or parts of it are, subject to qualifications, relevant to market value. The four general requirements for relevance are:[33]

1. The sale must be made from arm's length dealing

---

27 Webster's New Collegiate Dictionary (1977).

28 *See* **§4.17** Traded Securities Comparative Analysis, **§5.11** The Market Approach to Real Property Valuation.

29 Regs. §§20.2031-1(b), 25-2512-1.

30 Goldman v. Commissioner, 388 F.2d 476 (6th Cir. 1967).

31 *See* **§2.9** Fair Market Value.

32 *See* Duncan Industries, Inc., 75 T.C. 266 (1979).

33 *See* I.R.S. App. Off., 6-4 to -8.

2. The sale must be for a reasonable consideration
3. The sale must not have been forced or made under distress conditions and,
4. The sale must have been made at a time reasonably close to the valuation date.

If you have sales that meet these requirements, then the sale price for the asset may be the best criterion to determine market value.[34] This technique is applicable to all types of assets.[35]

The arm's-length requirement is designed to prevent market value from being set by parties who do not have a desire to press for the best deal. Obviously, sales between close business associates and family members are most suspect if not irrelevant.[36] Notwithstanding, such sales could qualify if the basic philosophy of fair market value has been satisfied.

The reasonable-consideration and non-forced sale requirements merely carry out the definition of fair market value.[37]

The timing requirement is designed to guarantee that the market price reflects economic considerations at the valuation date. The longer the time between the dates, the greater the chances are that economic conditions have changed. Even when economic changes have occurred, however, sales prices may still be relevant if appropriate economic adjustments can be made. A reasonable period of time may vary, depending on the type of asset involved and the volatility of the market for that asset.

When sales are a valid valuation factor, several other factors are relevant in determining the degree of weight you should give to the sale prices. Greater or lesser weight will be given to sales prices depending upon where on the various scales the particular sales transactions fall:

Chart II-1

Greater Weight	Lesser Weight
1. Large number of sales	Few or sporadic sales
2. Sales date close in time from valuation date	Sales date distant in time from valuation date
3. Quantity of sales to be valued similar	Quantity of sales to be valued dissimilar
4. Sales of same kind or quality of interest as interest to be valued	Sales not of same kind or quality of interest to be valued

It will be very relevant if other valuation techniques arrive at values that are similar to the sales prices received.

---

34 Duncan Industries, Inc., 75 T.C. 266 (1979).

35 *See, e.g.*, **§5.11** The Market Approach to Real Property Valuation, **§10.2** Household Effects Valuation.

36 *See, e.g.*, Estate of Kinney v. Commissioner, 80 F.2d 568 (9th Cir. 1935); M. Hooper, 41 B.T.A. 114 (1940).

37 *See* **§2.9** Fair Market Value.

§2.12 Book Value (Asset Value)

The term "book value" is primarily an accountancy term with several applications.[38] It refers to an amount entered on the accountant's books to record the cost of an asset or group of assets, less reductions such as depreciation and amortization. The "book value" of an entire firm or business or corporation, refers to the difference between total assets and total liabilities. Although not in itself a benchmark for fair market value, book value is still a relevant factor in making accurate decisions concerning values of assets and firms.

When book value is recast in a more appropriate form, "adjusted book value," which rejects the mere historical value and accepts the actual market value on the date in question, book value and fair market value may be synonymous. In valuing a firm, for example, adjusted book value is particularly useful when the firm is a holding company or financial institution or when the corporation, as a going concern, is operating at a deficit.[39] In addition, because adjusted book value sometimes equals the lowest value for the asset or firm, adjusted book value is indicative of liquidation value. This would not, however, set or establish your asset's highest and best use value.

A thorough explanation of this term is included in §4.4 Adjusted Book Value of the Business Interest.

§2.13 Cost (Purchase Price)

Actual cost is another accountancy term commonly used with regard to valuation. Typically, it refers to an asset's acquisition or historical cost.[40] Its usefulness for estate valuation purposes is limited. Its most common use is to set the basis of an asset that has been sold or retired from use for capital gain or loss determination for income tax purposes.

Occasionally the term "actual cost" will in fact be used to mean replacement and reproduction costs.[41] These different terms will be separately discussed.[42]

Unless your purchase price is contemporary, actual cost does not necessarily equal fair market value. When very contemporaneous purchases are involved, your cost may be very relevant to the determination of fair market value. Actual cost ordinarily will be one relevant factor among many for making all fair market value determinations. There are a few situations when it is the predominant factor.[43]

---

38 S. Davidson, C. Stickney, & R. Weil, Accounting: The Language of Business 11 (4th ed. 1979).
39 I.R.S. Tax Law Course, 24-7 to -9.
40 S. Davidson, C. Stickney, & R. Weil, Accounting: The Language of Business 17 (4th ed. 1979).
41 1 J. Bonbright, Valuation of Property 19 (1937).
42 *See* **§2.15** Replacement and Reproduction Costs.
43 *See* **§5.17** The Cost Approach to Real Property Valuation.

§2.14 Discounts and Premiums

Potential discounts from or premiums to normal value are often considered (e.g., valuation of nontraded business interests).[44] Issues of valuation discounts and premiums arise in other contexts, although clearly the most controversial and litigated examples involve nontraded business interests. Nearly every kind of asset's value could involve a discount or premium, if the asset has some attribute that either restricts its marketability (discount) or increases its desirability (premium). For example, a parcel of real estate may be saleable only at a discount because of an existing disadvantageous long-term lease on the property.[45] A collection might sell at a premium over its value as individual pieces.

It is important to note that, no matter what type of asset being valued, a discount or premium is relevant only if the technique employed to derive the asset's "normal" value does not include the discount or premium in its valuation calculations. For example, the real estate price discussed above would not be discounted if the valuation technique considered the effect of the lease in its calculation. Presumably an income analysis technique would include consideration of the unfavorable lease.

The following lists the most commonly raised discount factors for valuation matters and where such factor is discussed in this Handbook:

Factor	Section and Title	
Blockage	**§3.5**	Blockage Discount for Traded Securities
	§5.6	Fractional Interest and Other Discounts for Real Property Valuation
Lack of Marketability	**§4.26**	Lack of Marketability Discount
	§5.6	Fractional Interest and Other Discounts for Real Property Valuation
Loss of Key Person	**§4.27**	Loss of Key Manager/Owner Discount
Minority Interest	**§4.23**	Minority Interest Discount
Restriction on Sale	**§3.8**	Restricted and Control Securities Discount
	§4.29	Private Restrictive Agreements
	§5.6	Fractional Interest and Other Discounts for Real Property Valuation Discount

[44] The relevance of discounts and premiums as it relates to such assets is explained in detail in **§4.20** Discounts and Premiums in General.

[45] *See* Saunders v. United States, 48 A.F.T.R.2d ¶148,481 (M.D. Ga. 1981).

§2.15 Replacement and Reproduction Costs

Although the term "replacement cost" and "reproduction cost" are often used interchangeably, they are properly given different meanings.[46] For one thing, reproduction costs are more exacting. They equal the cost that would be necessary to reproduce the asset in a manner as similar as possible in all important aspects. Replacement cost, on the other hand, merely refers to the cost necessary to produce or purchase an asset of similar utility, not necessarily using the same or equal quality raw materials. Under both concepts, value is subject to depreciation.

Although replacement and reproduction cost methods are seldom the determining factor for fair market value, they are useful as a reference point because they often equal an asset's highest relevant value.[47] These methods have also received greater recognition as a valuation determinator in several special situations, e.g.:

1. Tax accounting techniques for inventory[48]
2. Valuing life insurance[49]
3. Valuing unique and special purpose assets such as churches, schools, libraries and museums.[50]

§2.16 Special Use Value

"Special Use Value" is the antithesis of the usual meaning of fair market value.[51] Ordinarily, fair market value refers to an asset's highest and best use value. Special use value refers to the asset's particular value in its present use. It is sort of a "value to the owner" concept. As a general rule, special use value is not determinative of an asset's fair market value.

The Tax Reform Act of 1976, however, specifically recognized a special use value situation.[52] Congress was persuaded that one effect of the federal estate and gift tax law was to cause small businesses, farms, and ranches to go on the selling block to pay these taxes. It was contended and accepted that the highest and best value of much of this real estate far exceeded the value of the real property's current beneficial use. For example, farm land near metropolitan areas might have a highest and best use value for subdivision purposes exceeding that for farm purposes. Farm and ranch land near recreational areas might have a highest and best use value for homestead and recreational development exceeding that for ranches or farms. Consequently, under formulas and limitations to be discussed subsequently, Congress enacted I.R.C. §2032A which permits a decedent's estate to value qualified real property (for estate tax purposes only)

---

46 I.R.S. Tax Law Course, 21-5.

47 I.R.S. Tax Law Course, 21-14 to -15; *see* 2 Am. Jur. Proof of Facts, *Appraisals* §1 (1959).

48 *See* **§10.6** Inventory Valuation.

49 *See* **§8.5** Life Insurance Valuation.

50 *See* **§5.17** The Cost Approach to Real Property Valuation.

51 *See* **§2.9** Fair Market Value.

52 I.R.C. §2032A.

at its current or "special" use value even if its highest and best use value would be significantly higher.[53] However, for tax valuation purposes, I.R.C. §2032A is the only specific statutory recognition of special use value for an asset. Highest and best use value is still the standard test for determining fair market value.

COMPUTATION

§2.17 Valuation Mathematics

The process of making valuation determinations requires that you understand a little bit about monetary or money mathematics. The following is intended to give you this little bit of knowledge—nothing more. The amateur valuator should be sure to consult an expert when the valuation problems exceed his or her capabilities or competence.

There are six basic calculations you should understand and be able to use and apply if you expect to make or review value determinations frequently.[54] Two of the calculations concern the value of a single fund or dollar amount. The other four calculations concern four separate valuation issues involving a series of consecutive and equal dollar amounts. Generally, any series of periodic payments is called an annuity.

Although mathematical formulas are available for all six calculations, ordinarily you will use readily available precalculated valuation tables or certain calculators that can make the needed computations quickly. The factors in these valuation tables are calculated for one dollar. You take the appropriate factor and multiply it by the known amount. Be sure you use the right table: selecting the wrong table guarantees that errors will be made.

Also be sure that the table employs the desired rate of interest and also calculates the factor on the appropriate compounding timetable. Most tables are calculated on the basis of compounding interest annually; different tables must be used or the tables used adjusted, if interest is compounded on a more frequent basis (e.g., quarterly, monthly).

Given relatively inexpensive sophisticated preprogrammed or programmable calculators, to a great extent the use of tables has become obsolete. Calculators enable you, as a valuator, to make the necessary mathematical calculations quickly and simply, usually merely by entering the appropriate figures.

For example, the typical calculator that is programmed or programmable for financial matters can calculate compound interest, sinking fund arrangements, various annuity factors, various types of depreciation, and many other statistical problems. Anyone who plans to deal with valuation matters frequently should consider obtaining such a calculator. The mini-computers that are currently becoming more readily available can also be programmed for these calculations.

Another mathematical concept you should understand is the "reciprocal." It is

---

[53] *See* **§5.20** Special Use Valuation Generally.

[54] *See generally* Cox, *Income Approach to Value,* Encyclopedia of Real Estate Appraising 52-55 (E. Friedman 3d ed. 1978).

frequently said in value determinations that one calculation or factor is the reciprocal of another calculation or factor. This simply means that one calculation or factor equals 1 divided by the other calculation or factor and vice versa. For example:

Illustration II-1

The reciprocal of 5 = .20

Proof:

$$5 = 1 \div .20$$

$$.20 = 1 \div 5.$$

An understanding of this principle is very helpful when one is valuing assets according to a capitalization or multiplier technique.[55] For example, if income is to be capitalized, the answer is the same whether you multiply the income by 5 or divide the income by .20.

Compounded interest is another concept you will frequently have to consider. Basically, compound interest is the process by which interest is earned on accumulated interest as well as on the principal. In other words, each time interest is determined, it is added to the principal plus all prior interest additions.

§2.18 The Six Principal Calculations

1. Future value of a set amount (one dollar) that will earn compounded interest at a specific rate for a determinable period of time. See column 1 of Table II-1.

Illustration II-2

What would $10,000 be worth at the end of ten years if it were invested at a 12 percent rate of interest compounded annually?

The factor in column 1 on line 10 is 3.105848. To determine the future value, multiply this factor by the principal:

$$3.105848 \times \$10{,}000 = \$31{,}058.48$$

This calculation can be used for determining the present value of a prior investment, assuming an annually-compounded interest rate. In other words, if you had invested $10,000 ten years earlier, how much should you receive today if the investment had

55 *See* **§2.19** Capitalization of Income.

been earning 12 percent interest compounded annually? The answer is the same as the above example.

2. Present value of a set amount (one dollar) receivable at a certain future date and discounted at a specific rate of compounded interest for a determinable period of time. See column 4 in Table II-1.

Illustration II-3

What is today's value of $10,000 that will be paid ten years from now discounted at a 12 percent rate of interest compounded annually?

The proper factor in column A on line 10 is .321973. To determine the present value, multiply the factor by the future fund:

$$.321973 \times \$10{,}000 = \$3{,}219.73$$

This technique is used to value, or discount, sums of money or assets with fixed values to be received in the future.

The 1. and 2. calculations used above are reciprocals.

3. Future value of a set amount (one dollar) deposited serially for a determinable period of time that will earn a specific compounded interest rate for the same determinable period of time. See column 2 in Table II-1.

Illustration II-4

What would the value of an account be ten years from now if the depositor deposited $1,000 per year for ten years and if the account earned a rate of interest of 12 percent compounded annually?

The proper factor in column 2 on line 10 is 17.548735. To determine the future value, multiply the factor by the amount of the annual deposit:

$$17.548735 \times \$1{,}000 = \$17{,}548.74$$

This calculation proves very useful when an estate plan calls for accumulation of a sinking fund. This factor permits you to calculate exactly how much will be in the fund at the expiration of a period of time if a set amount is to be put in the fund periodically and the fund is to earn a specified rate of compound interest.

4. Value of a set amount deposited serially for a determinable period of time that, assuming a compounded interest rate will accumulate to a future determined sum. See column 3 in Table II-1.

Illustration II-5

How much do you have to put aside each year if you want to have a fund of $10,000 available at the end of ten years, assuming the deposits will receive a rate of interest of 12 percent compounded annually?

The proper factor in column 3, line 10, is .056984. The calculation to determine the annual deposit is to multiply the factor by the desired fund:

$$.056984 \times \$10{,}000 = \$569.84$$

This means that you would have to deposit $569.84 each year for ten years in order to have a fund of $10,000.

This calculation is very useful to determine the amount necessary to satisfy amortization of assets. Amoritzation anticipation may be very useful from an estate planning standpoint particularly where assets have a limited life.[56]

The results of calculations 3. and 4. are reciprocals.

5. Present value of a set amount (one dollar) deposited serially in an account at a specific compounded interest rate for a determinable period of time. See column 5, line 10, in Table II-1.

Illustration II-6

What would be the present value of ten annual payments of $1,000 if each were discounted at 12 percent interest compounded annually?

The proper factor in column 5, line 10 is 5.650223. To determine the present value of the annual deposits, multiply the factor by the annual deposits:

$$5.650223 \times \$1{,}000 = \$5{,}650.22$$

This calculation is useful to determine the value of any asset to be paid in the future on a regular basis at a regular rate of interest—e.g., leases for a term of years.[57]

6. Amount of each installment to be paid to recover a set amount including a specific rate of interest, within a determinable period of time. See column 6, line 10, in Table II-1.

Illustration II-7

What would the installment payment have to be for a $10,000 loan that must be paid back within ten years at an annual rate of return of 12 percent?

The proper factor in column 6, line 10 is .176984. To determine the necessary installment is to multiply the factor by the amount of the loan:

$$.176984 \times \$10{,}000 = \$1{,}769.84$$

56 *See* **§7.4** The Income Method of Mineral Interest Valuation.

57 *See* **§8.3** Lease and Leasehold Valuation.

Table II-1[a]

12% ANNUAL COMPOUND INTEREST TABLE 12%
EFFECTIVE RATE = 12% BASE = 1.1200

YEARS	1 Amount Of 1 At Compound Interest $S^n = (1+i)^n$	2 Accumulation Of 1 Per Period $S_{\overline{n}\vert} = \frac{S^n - 1}{i}$	3 Sinking Fund Factor $1/S_{\overline{n}\vert} = \frac{i}{S_n - 1}$	4 Pres. Value Reversion Of 1 $V^n = \frac{1}{S^n}$	5 Present Value Ord. Annuity 1 Per Period $a_{\overline{n}\vert} = \frac{1 - V^n}{i}$	6 Instalment To Amortize 1 $1/a_{\overline{n}\vert} = \frac{i}{1 - V^n}$	n YEARS
1	1.120000	1.000000	1.000000	.892857	.892857	1.120000	1
2	1.254400	2.120000	.471698	.797194	1.690051	.591698	2
3	1.404928	3.374400	.296349	.711780	2.401831	.416349	3
4	1.573519	4.779328	.209234	.635518	3.037349	.329234	4
5	1.762342	6.352847	.157410	.567427	3.604776	.277410	5
6	1.973823	8.115189	.123226	.506631	4.111407	.243226	6
7	2.210681	10.089012	.099118	.452349	4.563757	.219118	7
8	2.475963	12.299693	.081303	.403883	4.967640	.201303	8
9	2.773079	14.775656	.067679	.360610	5.328250	.187679	9
10	3.105848	17.548735	.056984	.321973	5.650223	.176984	10
11	3.478550	20.654583	.048415	.287476	5.937699	.168415	11
12	3.895976	24.133133	.041437	.256675	6.194374	.161437	12
13	4.363493	28.029109	.035677	.229174	6.423548	.155677	13
14	4.887112	32.392602	.030871	.204620	6.628168	.150871	14
15	5.473566	37.279715	.026824	.182696	6.810864	.146824	15
16	6.130394	42.753280	.023390	.163122	6.973986	.143390	16
17	6.866041	48.883674	.020457	.145644	7.119630	.140457	17
18	7.689966	55.749715	.017937	.130040	7.249670	.137937	18
19	8.612762	63.439681	.015763	.116107	7.365777	.135763	19
20	9.646293	72.052442	.013879	.103667	7.469444	.133879	20

Table II-1 (*Continued*)

YEARS	1 Amount Of 1 At Compound Interest $S^n = (1 + i)^n$	2 Accumulation Of 1 Per Period $S_{\overline{n}\vert} = \frac{S^n - 1}{i}$	3 Sinking Fund Factor $1/S_{\overline{n}\vert} = \frac{i}{S_n - 1}$	4 Pres. Value Reversion Of 1 $V^n = \frac{1}{S^n}$	5 Present Value Ord. Annuity 1 Per Period $a_{\overline{n}\vert} = \frac{1 - V^n}{i}$	6 Instalment To Amortize 1 $1/a_{\overline{n}\vert} = \frac{i}{1 - V^n}$	n YEARS
21	10.803848	81.698736	.012240	.092560	7.562003	.132240	21
22	12.100310	92.502584	.010811	.082643	7.644646	.130811	22
23	13.552347	104.602894	.009560	.073788	7.718434	.129560	23
24	15.178629	118.155241	.008463	.065882	7.784316	.128463	24
25	17.000064	133.333870	.007500	.058823	7.843139	.127500	25
26	19.040072	150.333934	.006652	.052521	7.895660	.126652	26
27	21.324881	169.374007	.005904	.046894	7.942554	.125904	27
28	23.883866	190.698887	.005244	.041869	7.984423	.125244	28
29	26.749930	214.582754	.004660	.037383	8.021806	.124660	29
30	29.959922	241.332684	.004144	.033378	8.055184	.124144	30
31	33.555113	271.292606	.003686	.029802	8.084986	.123686	31
32	37.581726	304.847719	.003280	.026609	8.111594	.123280	32
33	42.091533	342.429445	.002920	.023758	8.135352	.122920	33
34	47.142517	384.520979	.002601	.021212	8.156564	.122601	34
35	52.799620	431.663496	.002317	.018940	8.175504	.122317	35
36	59.135574	484.463116	.002064	.016910	8.192414	.122064	36
37	66.231843	543.598690	.001840	.015098	8.207513	.121840	37
38	74.179664	609.830532	.001640	.013481	8.220993	.121640	38
39	83.081224	684.010196	.001462	.012036	8.233030	.121462	39
40	93.050970	767.091420	.001304	.010747	8.243777	.121304	40

41	104.217087	860.142390	.001163	.009595	8.253372	.121163	41
42	116.723137	964.359477	.001037	.008567	8.261939	.121037	42
43	130.729914	1081.082614	.000925	.007649	8.269589	.120925	43
44	146.417503	1211.812527	.000825	.006830	8.276418	.120825	44
45	163.987604	1358.230031	.000736	.006098	8.282516	.120736	45
46	183.666116	1522.217634	.000657	.005445	8.287961	.120657	46
47	205.706050	1705.883750	.000586	.004861	8.292822	.120586	47
48	230.390776	1911.589800	.000523	.004340	8.297163	.120523	48
49	258.037669	2141.980576	.000467	.003875	8.301038	.120467	49
50	289.002189	2400.018245	.000417	.003460	8.304498	.120417	50
51	323.682452	2689.020434	.000372	.003089	8.307588	.120372	51
52	362.524346	3012.702886	.000332	.002758	8.310346	.120332	52
53	406.027268	3375.227233	.000296	.002463	8.312809	.120296	53
54	454.750540	3781.254500	.000264	.002199	8.315008	.120264	54
55	509.320605	4236.005040	.000236	.001963	8.316972	.120236	55
56	570.439077	4745.325645	.000211	.001753	8.318725	.120211	56
57	638.891767	5315.764723	.000188	.001565	8.320290	.120188	57
58	715.558779	5954.656489	.000168	.001398	8.321687	.120168	58
59	801.425832	6670.215267	.000150	.001248	8.322935	.120150	59
60	897.596932	7471.641099	.000134	.001114	8.324049	.120134	60

[a] Reproduced from Ellwood Tables for Real Estate Appraising and Financing, 4th edition, copyright 1977 by the American Institute of Real Estate Appraisers of the National Association of Realtors.

This factor has many estate planning valuation uses. For example, you could use it to determine the necessary annual payments for mortgage loan financing. You might also use it to determine annual payments for private annuities.[58]

The results of calculations 5. and 6. are reciprocals.

Calculation 1. assumes the amount is deposited at the beginning of the year; calculations 2.–6. assume that the amount involved is deposited or paid at the end of the year.

§2.19 Capitalization of Income

Fair market value is often determined by converting an asset's known or projected income flow to its present value.[59] For many assets, particularly ones that earn income, this well-recognized method, commonly called "income capitalization," produces an accurate estimate of fair market value. Given appropriate data, the calculation is simple. The data you need is: (1) what constitutes the proper income; and (2) what is the capitalization rate.[60]

The standard definition for income capitalization is that estimated present value (V) equals adjusted earnings (E) divided by the capitalization rate (C), or:

$$V = \frac{E}{C}$$

Illustration II-8

Assume that the adjusted earnings of an asset equal $10,000 and that the appropriate rate of return is 10%. Using the above formula the calculation is:

$$V = \frac{\$10{,}000}{.10} = \$100{,}000$$

The estimated present value equals $100,000.

Another method of making the same calculation is to use the following formula:

$$V = \frac{1}{C} \times E$$

Illustration II-9

Using the facts in Illustration II-8, the calculation is:

$$V = 1/.10 \times 10{,}000 = 10 \times 10{,}000 = 100{,}000$$

Again, estimated present value equals $100,000.

---

58 *See* **§8.8** Annuity Valuation.

59 *See* **§2.17** Valuation Mathematics.

60 *See* I.R.S. Tax Law Course, 21-10 to -14.

For some assets, particularly stocks, a slightly different calculation is made, using the price/earnings (P/E) ratio technique. Mathematically, the price/earnings ratio is the reciprocal of the capitalization rate. (See §2.17 Valuation Mathematics.) However, the price/earnings ratio calculation is usable only when there are comparable figures from other, similar business interests with an established market price. Using the valuation of traded stocks and a business interest for illustration, the formula for this calculation is as follows:

Traded Security(ies)	Subject Business Interest
$\dfrac{\text{Per Share Market Price}}{\text{Earnings Per Share}}$	$\dfrac{\text{Value Per Share}}{\text{Earnings Per Share}}$

Illustration II-10

Assume 1. several comparable businesses which have established market prices, have an average price per share of \$100 and earnings per share of \$10 and 2. the business to be valued has earnings per share of \$200. The calculation then would be:

$$\text{VPS} = \frac{100}{10} \times 200 = \$2{,}000$$

In this example, the VPS (estimated value per share) for the business interest would be \$2,000.

It can be confusing to talk in the same terms of a capitalization rate and of an earnings multipler calculated from price/earnings ratios. Because the capitalization rate is a divisor, it can be expressed as a percentage or in decimal form. The earnings multiplier can be expressed as a whole number. Comparatively, the higher the capitalization rate percentage is, the lower the earnings multiplier will be. For example, if the capitalization rate is 5 percent, the multiplier will be 20; but if the capitalization rate is 20 percent the multiplier will be 5. In other words, a capitalization rate of 8 percent is the same as a price/earnings ratio of 12.5 to 1. Chart II-2 displays this.

Chart II-2
COMPARISON CHART

Capitalization Rate	Price/Earnings Ratio
3.5%	28.57/1
4.0%	25.00/1
5.0%	20.00/1
6.0%	16.67/1
7.0%	14.29/1
8.0%	12.50/1
9.0%	11.11/1

Chart II-2 (*Continued*)

Capitalization Rate	Price/Earnings Ratio
10.0%	10.00/1
11.0%	9.09/1
12.0%	8.33/1
13.0%	7.69/1
14.0%	7.14/1
15.0%	6.67/1
16.0%	6.25/1
17.0%	5.88/1
18.0%	5.56/1
19.0%	5.26/1
20.0%	5.00/1
25.0%	4.00/1
30.0%	3.33/1
35.0%	2.86/1

The 8, 10, 15 and 20 percent capitalization rates or their comparable P/E ratios have in the past been the ones most frequently used. The current trend of generally high interest rates in the money market should make higher figures more common.[61]

§2.20 —Estate Planning and Capitalization Rate

You should realize that changes in the rate of capitalization have a dramatic effect on the valuation of assets.

Illustration II-11

Assumptions	
Asset's Earnings	$250,000
Capitalization Rates:	
Option (1)	10%
Option (2)	12.5%
Calculations:	
(1) $\frac{250,000}{.10}$ = $2,500,000	
(2) $\frac{250,000}{.125}$ = $2,000,000	

The estimated value of the asset at a 10% capitalization rate is $2,500,000, while the estimated value of the asset at a 12.5% capitalization rate is $2,000,000.

A change of 2.5 percentage points in this illustration caused a 20 percent decrease in the value from 10 percent to 12.5 percent, or a 25 percent increase in the value from 12.5 percent to 10 percent. Therefore, the appraiser has the discretion to substantially affect valuation under this technique. Depending upon whether you want a higher or a lower value, your determination of the capitalization rate will be significant.

61 *See* Jensen, *Stock Valuation Formulas for Estate and Gift Taxes,* 117 Tr. & Est. 239, Table I (1978).

§2.21 Income Flow Determination

The determination of the net income flow may be a difficult task. First, you often must project a hypothetical future income flow based primarily on past experience. Second, even past experience may be inadequate. For example, past data may not be useful where the property is producing no income but is capable of producing income, the property is producing less income than it should because of the owner's failure to exact the full limits of the market, or the past income figures available are inaccurate because of accounting discrepancies (e.g., management expenses that are understated or excessive).[62] Also see the discussion of income flow under income capitalization techniques for specific types of assets.[63]

The rate of capitalization is also difficult to determine because it is only an estimate of what the asset's income should be. This determination requires you to compare a large number of market factors.[64] For example, you must consider going rate of interest for money in the general economy. This amount probably constitutes the bottom for the rate of capitalization. In addition, the risk of the particular asset involved is important. Some income-producing assets are far riskier than others, and consequently the rate of return on such an asset must be higher than that of a safer endeavor. The first consideration is less variable and more easily determinable than the second. The risk factor of any single asset is a particularly difficult figure to determine. The deciding factors include the general condition of the economy, the industry and the asset's position therein, the financial strength of the asset, and the quality of its management.

Where comparable assets are traded on an active market, the preferred technique is to use market rates of return.

An additional complexity to this problem is that a capitalization rate determination requires the making of one of two assumptions. Either the income will remain static (capitalization in perpetuity), or the income is related to the productivity of the wasting asset and thus should include recapture of part of the investment (capitalization for a finite period).[65] When capitalization in perpetuity is employed, the rate will not vary and does not anticipate recovery of the capital investment. It is purely related to the risk of the investment in the market place and corresponds to the rate of return for other comparable investments. It constitutes the interest component of a capitalization rate.

When your asset has a wasting aspect to it, the return on the investment should include a return of the investment as well. This is referred to as recapture of the investment. The techniques for determining recapture are dependent on the wasting asset's expected economic life. There are three basic methods recognized for determining recapture rates:

---

62 I.R.S. Tax Law Course, 21-10.

63 *See* §**4.5** Capitalization of the Business Interests' Earnings, §**5.14** The Income Approach to Real Property Valuation, §**7.4** The Income Method of Mineral Interest Valuation.

64 I.R.S. Tax Law Course, 21-12.

65 Cox, *Income Approach to Value,* Encyclopedia of Real Estate Appraising 47-52 (E. Friedman 3d ed. 1978).

1. Straight Line Method: The straight line method attributes an equal rate per year to recapture, depending on the number of years that the asset will remain productive. In other words, if an asset is expected to be productive for forty years, the recapture rate would be 2.5 percent per year.

2. Hoskold Method: The sinking fund or Hoskold method determines a rate by combining the ordinary rate of return on capital with a safe compound interest rate on an assumed sinking fund that will equal the value of the asset when the asset is exhausted.[66] This method assumes that the owner of the asset does not have access to all of the net income. Although this method is no longer used for most capitalization purposes, there are a few areas where reference to it is still made.[67] Tables are available to provide calculation factors.[68]

3. Annuity Method. The third system is the annuity method.[69] It is similar to the sinking fund method, but does not anticipate that the recapture part is placed in a sinking fund at compound interest. This method assumes that it is paid periodically to the investor. The rate factors attributable to this technique are determinable from precalculated tables.[70]

§2.22 Tax Shelters and Rates of Return

Some investments can be used to shelter income from tax. Although the term "tax shelter" has different meanings to different people, it basically refers to the asset owner's ability to deduct items that are not out-of-pocket expenses. The most common examples of such deductions are depreciation and depletion. The most common assets providing tax shelters are improved commercial real estate, oil and mineral interests and investments and all other depreciable investment. Although investment tax credits are similar, they do not have the same tax shelter effect; because they benefit all taxpayers on a dollar basis, they do not have the same effect on investments as do the deductions.

The particular tax benefits of any tax shelter investment varies depending upon the tax status of the investor. With our progressive tax rates, it is clear that high-bracket taxpayers benefit more from the deductions than lower-bracket taxpayers do.

Because of this tax savings phenomenon, tax-sheltered investments are clearly more attractive to your clients who have a higher rate of tax liability. Consequently, the effect of tax saving is relevant in determining the rate of return for these kinds of investments to these investors. Most financial analysis materials about tax-sheltered investments

---

66 A. Ring, The Valuation of Real Estate 273-74 (2d ed. 1970).

67 *See, e.g.,* **§7.4** The Income Method of Mineral Interest Valuation.

68 *See, e.g.,* I.R.S. Tax Law Course, 25-21.

69 A. Ring, The Valuation of Real Estate 274-76 (2d ed. 1970).

70 *See* **§2.17** Valuation Mathematics.

discuss and incorporate the tax-saving aspects of these investments into their calculations.[71]

The following illustrates one technique for recognizing the tax savings potential for some investments:

Illustration II-12

Assumptions	
1. Price of Asset	2,000,000
2. Loans and mortgages	1,600,000
	30 years
	12%
3. Cash investment	400,000
4. Gross income	400,000
5. Vacancy and operating expenses	175,000
6. Net operating income	225,000
7. Reserves	16,000
8. Debt payment	197,494
9. Cash flow	11,500
10. Interest on debt	191,688
11. Depreciation (First year)	
Building ($1,600,000-ACRS-15 yrs)	192,000
Personal property ($120,000-ACRS-5yrs)	18,000
12. Property put in service	January 1
13. Taxpayer's marginal income tax rate	50%

Calculations	
14. Profit and loss	
Net operating income	225,000
Less debt interest	−191,688
Less depreciation	−210,000
Taxable profit (loss)	(176,688)
15. Tax savings attributable to the loss	
50% × loss =	88,344
16. Rate of return on cash flow and tax savings	

$$\frac{\text{Cash flow} + \text{Tax savings}}{\text{Cash investment}} = \text{Rate of return}$$

$$\frac{11{,}500 + 88{,}344}{400{,}000} = \frac{99{,}844}{400{,}000} = .25 = 25\%$$

The rate of return on cash flow alone would only be three percent. Because depreciation

[71] *See* Real Estate Review, Financial Analysis of Real Estate Investment, Portfolio No. 7 (1975).

can shelter income, the tax shelter capabilities of the depreciation clearly makes an investment like this desirable. If the asset is actually appreciating rather than depreciating, which is often the case, this type of investment is even more attractive. The "loss" due to depreciation is purely a paper loss. There is also a positive cash flow: in other words, the income from the asset is sufficient to cover the actual out-of-pocket-costs. Consequently, this investment has another advantage.

All depreciable assets have a tax-sheltering capability though the results are not always so dramatic.

Although it might be speculative to subjectively incorporate tax shelter considerations into capitalization rate determination, the effect of tax sheltering will ordinarily be objectively reflected in the data showing rates of return on comparable sales of comparable property. This data should reveal whether tax shelter considerations are affecting fair market value. This analysis is only valid if the properties are really comparable.

The practical result is that appraisers commonly rely primarily upon capitalization rates and price/earnings ratios on comparable assets actively traded in recognized markets. However, even rates and ratios found from the traded assets should be adjusted. For example, capitalization rates are ordinarily higher, and price/earnings ratios lower, for close corporations and other forms of nontraded business interests than for publicly-traded corporations.

Since valuation factors are as discretionary as capitalization rates are, the I.R.S. will always have a significant influence over the determination, because I.R.S. determinations are presumed valid.

§2.23 Actuarial Calculations

Precalculated tables, based on actuarial assumptions, are used to calculate the value of assets such as annuities, life estates, reversions, life insurance, and interests in pension and profit-sharing plans. These tables are prepared by expert actuaries, professionally trained in the science of compound interest, probability and mortality distribution and other aspects of insurance and annuities.[72] In order to prepare the actuarial tables and calculations, the actuary must estimate future uncertainties that affect the valuations to be made. These estimates are called actuarial assumptions; they deal with mortality, rates of interest and any other factors that relate to the particular purpose for which the actuarial table is being prepared. For pension plans, for example, additional relevant factors include future levels of compensation, plan withdrawals not caused by death, and the plan's investment performance.[73]

Actuarial tables provide you with calculations that divide less than full present and future interests into actuarially-set decimalized factors. You can choose appropriate factors from the tables and can multiply them by the market value you have determined

72 E. Spiller, Financial Accounting—Basic Concepts 413 (1977).

73 Haneberg, The Actuarial Process, 36-S N.Y.U. Inst. Fed. Tax'n 225, 229 (1978).

for the asset as a whole. These calculations provide you with the present value of the various interests. For example, the tables permit you to calculate the respective values of both a life and a remainder interest in the same asset.[74]

In its Regulations and Revenue Rulings, the I.R.S. has prepared several actuarial tables. These tables are mandated for use in certain noncommercial transactions; they are not used otherwise. More specifically, the I.R.S. has actuarial tables concerning mortality,[75] life insurance (P.S. 58) rates[76], and the valuation of annuities, life estates, and remainders. The latter tables are calculated assuming both a three and one-half percent rate of return for transactions prior to January 1, 1972[77] and a six percent rate of return for transactions after December 31, 1970.[78] These same Regulations also provide compound interest tables for three and one-half and six percent annuities, terms certain, and remainders.

Consult the relevant subject headings for an explanation of how to use these tables.[79]

§2.24 Exceptions to Use of Actuarial Tables

Because actuarial tables are based upon average assumptions, not on actual facts, it is sometimes argued that they should not be applicable for all purposes. These arguments can be summarized as follows:

1. The mortality assumptions are not applicable to the specific case because of known circumstances
2. The interest rate assumptions are not applicable due to the actual interest rate experience or anticipated return of the fund involved
3. Human actions are uncertain, and therefore render the tables unreliable.

Despite these objections, the general rule is that the tables are applicable and you must use them. The justification for the rule is:[80]

1. Valuation decisions must be based on facts available at the valuation date; post-valuation date events are not relevant
2. The acturial tables are calculated to take unusual fact patterns into account.

There are exceptions to the general rule, however:

---

74 *See* **§11.5** Future Interests Valuation.
75 Reg. §1.72-9.
76 Rev. Rul. 55-747, 1955-2 C.B. 228; Rev. Rul. 66-110, 1966-1 C.B. 12; reproduced in Appendix C.
77 Regs. §§20.2031-7(f), 25.2512-5(f).
78 Regs. §§20.2031-10(f), 25.2512-9(f); reproduced in Appendix B.
79 For annuities, *see* **§8.8** Annuity Valuation; for life insurance, *see* **§§8.5–8.7;** and for life estates, remainder interests, terms certain and other future interest tables, *see* **§§11.5** and **11.6.**
80 *See* Rev. Rul. 66-307, 1966-2 C.B. 429.

1. If the life tenant, whose interest is being valued, is "afflicted with a fatal and incurable disease in its advanced stages, and that he cannot survive for more than a brief period of time," the mortality assumptions in the relevant table are not determinable and valuations must be made on the real facts[81]
2. The tables are not applicable to the life interest passing in the transferor's will where the beneficiary and the transferor die simultaneously[82]
3. Deviation from the tables because of a different rate of interest can be justified only if the specific assets in the fund involved earn a different rate of interest, and no change in this investment or the rate is possible[83]
4. The tables are not followed to support deduction where the actuarial art is unable to deal with a contingency involving human acts or motivation to a significant extent[84]
5. The life interest tables are not applicable to value a minor's life interest in a trust for purposes of the $10,000 gift tax exclusion under §2503(b) where the transferred trust property continually operates at a loss.[85]

For the practical lawyer, several observations on the above exceptions deserve mention. Mere poor health on the part of the person on whose life expectancy the interest is being valued does not cause the tables to be inapplicable.[86] Unless the first exception applies, death soon after the valuation date is not determinative of the applicability of the tables either. In addition, the interest rate set in the table will be held to apply in almost all situations. The conditions of the exception are too restrictive and do not have great applicability in practice. Finally, with regard to the exceptions concerning human volition and motivation, the I.R.S. position is, even if an interest in an asset cannot be valued with sufficient accuracy to support a charitable income tax deduction, the asset is not necessarily without an ascertainable value for gift and estate tax purposes.[87]

The types of human volition and motivation contingencies referred to include: a) The requirement of having "descendants," "children" or "issue" survive or of dying without issue; and b) The contingency of marriage or remarriage of the person whose interest is being valued. The American Remarriage Tables prepared by the Casualty Actuarial Society of America have been used to value an interest when the nonmortality contingencies of marriage have been involved.[88]

Whether the tables are applicable is not always the question. Often, the proper question is whether the asset has any value at all due to the conditions in the transfer.

---

81 Rev. Rul. 66-307, 1966-2 C.B. 429.

82 *See* Estate of Lion v. Commissioner, 438 F.2d 56 (4th Cir. 1971), *cert. denied,* 404 U.S. 870 (1971).

83 *See* Estate of E. Gooel, 68 T.C. 504 (1977); Rev. Rul. 77-195, 1977-1 C.B. 295.

84 Commissioner v. Estate of Sternberger, 348 U.S. 187 (1955).

85 Maryland Nat'l Bank v. United States, 609 F.2d 1078 (4th Cir. 1979); *cf. also* Rev. Rul. 77-358, 1977-2 C.B. 342.

86 Robinson v. United States, 632 F.2d 822 (9th Cir. 1980).

87 Rev. Rul. 61-88, 1961-1 C.B. 417.

88 *See, e.g.,* Rev. Rul. 71-67, 1971-1 C.B. 271; Commissioner v. Maresi, 156 F.2d 929 (2d Cir. 1946).

There are several cases that agree with the taxpayers that conditions deprive assets of value.[89]

Remember that, despite the availability of exceptions for some valuations, you must use the I.R.S. actuarial tables for the reversionary interests under I.R.C. §2037(b) (transfers taking effect at death) or under §2042(2) (reversionary interest in life insurance), regardless of the actual facts concerning the reversion.[90] This is because Congress is said to have created a rule of administrative convenience that requires their application.

§2.25 Statistical and Regression Analysis

The advent of relatively inexpensive computers and sophisticated calculators have changed some very complex valuation techniques into simple ministerial procedures. Consequently there has been a resurgence of statistical and regression analysis as a supplemental technique for making valuations.[91] Where at one time you would have needed an advance degree in mathematics and statistics to make certain calculations, today the same calculations can be made easily by entering a list of numbers into a computer or calculator.

These methods are usually only supplemental, and are not to be used to the exclusion of other valuation efforts. Used as a supplement, they offer an additional analytical approach, and can be helpful in resolving some uncertainties. On the other hand, the supposed accuracy of these techniques should not be exaggerated. Notwithstanding their mathematical precision, they still constitute only estimates. A human judgment factor always remains. Use these techniques to improve judgment, not substitute for it.

Only the most cursory explanation of statistical and regression analysis can be given here. If you are interested in more detail, an excellent, readable and understandable explanation may be found in Brown, *Statistics and Regression Analysis in Real Estate Appraisal,* Encyclopedia of Real Estate Appraising, 153-78 (Friedman 3d ed. 1978). Although this book deals with real estate appraising, most of the concepts and techniques described are also applicable to other valuation situations. In its most elementary sense, statistical analysis is a valuation technique that uses graphic presentations, special symbols (vocabulary) and algebraic equations.

Statistical analysis often makes liberal use of graphic information. Common devices include tables outlining the relevant statistics used and various charts that reveal comparison of the statistics. Three types of charts are frequently used to show the relationship between two variables. The first is the "bar chart" that shows bars running horizontally from the left hand margin (or vertically from the bottom). Another chart, the "histogram," conveys the same type of information in a vertical chart of laterally connected bars or blocks. The last common type of chart is a "line graph," which

---

[89] *See, e.g., In re* Hill's Estate, 193 F.2d 724 (2d Cir. 1952). *See* **§1.1** Introduction.

[90] Rev. Rul. 67-307, 1966-2 C.B. 429.

[91] Allison, *Appraisal Theory and Practice in the Computerized Age,* Encyclopedia of Real Estate Appraising 15-18 (E. Friedman 3d ed. 1978).

graphs the data according to two known variables using dots connected by lines. See examples below:

Chart II-3

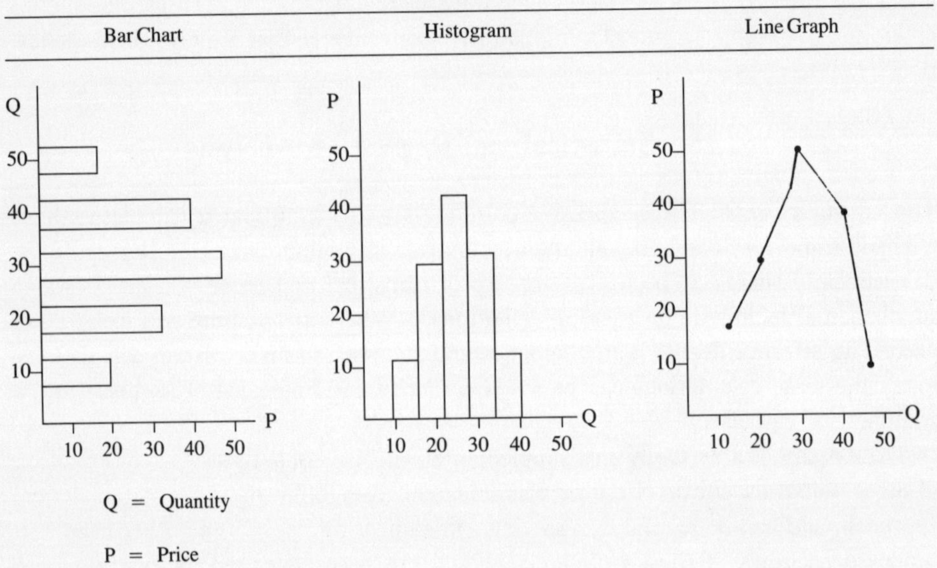

You will find it helpful if you gain a basic understanding of some of the terminology. Here are several very commonly used terms.

A "variant" is one item in a group that makes up the "population." With the population, one may be able to refine a group of variants that equal a "sample."

It may be necessary to determine and measure the "central tendency" or typical variant in the population. Several determinations may have to be made. The "mean" is the average, or the sum of the figures of the variants divided by the total number of variants. This calculation is very important to the valuation determination and is used constantly in these endeavors. Sometimes a weighted average is required.[92] Another common calculation is the "median." The median is the figure that has an equal number of variants both above and below it. The "mode" is the figure with the most variants in the population. Under different circumstances, you may determine that either the mean, the median or the mode constitutes a more accurate representation of the central tendency.

In addition to determining the central tendency of the population, you may also find it desirable to determine the extent that values in the population or sample differ from one to another[93]—that is, to measure the "dispersion." Several different calculations are relevant to this measurement. The "range," is the difference between the highest

92 *See* **§2.27** Weighting of Valuation Techniques.

93 L. Kazmier, Basic Statistics for Business and Economics 34-39 (1979).

and lowest values in the population or sample. The range determination is sometimes modified by eliminating portions (e.g., ten percent) of the two valuation ends of the population or sample to calculate the middle 80 percent range. The range provides an obvious description of the outside limits of the population or sample.

From a statistical reference standpoint, however, the "variance" and the "standard deviation" are more significant determinants of dispersion. The variance for a population is determined by subtracting the mean from each value in the population, squaring that result and adding all of the squares of the differences. The sum of the squares is then divided by a denominator equal to the number in the population. The standard deviation for a population is determined by calculating the square root of the variance. The variance and standard deviation calculations for a sample require an adjustment in this above calculation. To adjust for bias caused by sampling, the above denominator is calculated by subtracting 1 from the number in the sample.

Because the variance is a squared measure of the dispersion, the square root of the variance or standard deviation is used more often. The standard deviation can be an accurate measure of dispersion. Ordinarily, the range of one standard deviation above and below the mean will include approximately 68 percent of the values in the population or sample. Two standard deviations will include approximately 95 percent.

The following illustration presents an example of these calculations for a population:

Illustration II-13
EXAMPLES OF MEAN-MEDIAN-MODE-RANGE-VARIANCE-STANDARD DEVIATION FOR A POPULATION

	Sales Prices for Eleven Comparable Sales			
	X	(X−m)	$(X-m)^2$	Analysis
1.	$20	−5	25	
2.	20	−5	25	Mean (m) = 275 ÷ 11) = 25
3.	23	−2	4	Median = #6 = 26
4.	23	−2	4	Mode = ##3, 4 and 5 = 23
5.	23	−2	4	Range = (30 − 20) = 10
6.	26	+1	1	Variance = $\frac{(X-m)^2}{N} = \frac{114}{11}$ = 10.36
7.	27	+2	4	Standard Deviation = $\frac{(X-m)^2}{N}$
8.	27	+2	4	= $\frac{114}{11}$ = 10.36 = 3.22
9.	28	+3	9	
10.	28	+3	9	
N = 11	30	+5	25	
TOTAL	$275		114	

§2.26 Linear and Multiple Regression Analysis

Linear regression analysis is a mathematical process that permits you to determine the value of one unknown variable from the value of a known variable. For example, the unknown value of an asset may be estimated from the known value of similar assets that have a homogenous or common variable. Thus, the unknown sales price of the apartment you want to value might be determinable from the known sale prices of other apartments by making a linear regression analysis of the known sale prices as they relate to the square footage of both the apartments whose prices are known and the subject apartment. However, this is only possible if there is a linear relationship. The latter relationship can be shown by plotting the variables on a line graph. If a straight line results, then linear regression analysis may be relevant.

Basically, multiple regression analysis is similar to linear regression analysis but more complex, because there is more than one independent variable. Because multiple regression analysis is time-consuming, computers or programmable calculators should be used. You should use multiple regression analysis only under strict circumstances: it requires clear uniformity and similarity between assets being analyzed. Plotting a graph is also helpful.

In practical terms:

1. Statistical and regression analysis is not necessary for all appraisals
2. When statistical and regression analysis is necessary, an expert appraiser is usually required
3. Great care should be taken in presenting statistical and regression analysis to lay bodies such as juries: experience says that triers of fact do not like complex tables and computations
4. Despite the apparent accuracy of statistical and regression analysis, the final products are still only estimates
5. Because many of the numbers used to calculate statistical and regression analysis are subject to the discretion of the valuator, contesting parties may produce differing valuations using the same formulas and techniques
6. Because of the ready availability of sophisticated computers, appraisals will more frequently employ statistical and regression analysis. You should therefore gain an understanding of the strengths, weaknesses and planning potential of these techniques.

Remember these valuation techniques may prove to be advantageous to your client. However, the above constitutes only the briefest of discussions of the various techniques for statistical and regression analysis. Before using these techniques, thorough knowledge of their uses and abuses is essential.

§2.27 Weighting of Valuation Techniques

Often, you will want to use more than one technique to determine the value of an asset. When multiple valuation techniques are relevant, you often will find it desirable to compare and weigh their significance. If the valuation techniques are considered equal in significance, the value of the asset may be determined by averaging the values set by all of the techniques. When several valuation techniques are not equal in degree but are all relevant, it may be useful to attribute a weight to the values of each of the techniques.

Weighting is a process that uses a mathematical formula to accord greater significance to one factor than to another. The weighting process may be accomplished in several ways. One method (the percentage technique) divides 100 percent into a determined number of segments or shares equal to the number of factors that are to be weighted. The relevant valuations are then multiplied by these segments or shares. The sum of the resultant calculations equal market value. The following example will show how this process works:

Illustration II-14

Valuation Method	Valuation		Percentage of Segment		Total
Book Value	$100,000	×	20%	=	$20,000
Earnings	150,000	×	50%	=	75,000
Dividends	90,000	×	30%	=	27,000
Total Weighted Market Value			(100%)		$122,000

Another method (the weighted unit technique) multiplies each valuation by various selected units. The sum of all the multiplication results is divided by the sum of the multipliers.

Illustration II-15

Valuation	Unit or Multiplier		Total
$10	2	×	20
20	3	×	60
	5		80 ÷ 5 = 16

Total weighted market value equals 80 divided by 5, or $16.00.

The first technique has gained popularity in valuing business interests.[94] The second technique is commonly employed in situations such as the valuation of actively traded stock when there are no sales on the date of valuation but there are sales within a reasonable time before or after, or both.[95]

It is important to note that the averaging and weighting processes may be employed at various stages in the valuation process. For example, to value actively traded stocks, one might first have to average the high and low market prices on two particular days, and they, depending on the date spread, weight those averages.

INTERNAL REVENUE SERVICE PROCEDURE

§2.28 I.R.S. Valuation Explanation

Taxpayers of estate and gift taxes frequently complained that the I.R.S. set different values for assets included in tax returns, and did not explain these values. Congress provided that, under specified circumstances, the I.R.S. must provide a statement giving specific information about a value it has set.[96] The stated purpose for this requirement is to give both parties full information on how each arrived at its valuation.[97] Since the taxpayer submitted valuation data with the return, the requirement that the I.R.S. do the same is intended to equalize the situation between the antagonists somewhat. The hope, of course, is that value differences may be more easily resolved, and that litigation will be avoided.

The valuation statement requirement applies to determined or proposed valuations or proposed valuations of assets made by the I.R.S. with regard to estate, gift, and generation-skipping taxes.[98] It is necessary only where the I.R.S.' determination is different from that submitted by the taxpayer on the appropriate return.[99]

To get this valuation statement, the appropriate person may file a written request with the District Director's office that has audit jurisdiction over the return involved.[1] The request must be made by the executor (estate tax valuations), by the donor (gift tax valuations) and by the person required to file the return (generation-skipping transfers). This filing must be made before the statutory period for assessment of the tax expires.

The I.R.S. must furnish the statement within 45 days after the date of a proper

---

94 *See* **§4.19** Weighting of Business Interest Valuation Factors.

95 *See, e.g.,* **§3.3** Valuation of Stocks; Illustration III-2.

96 I.R.C. §7517.

97 H.R. Rep. 94-1380, 94th Cong., 2d Sess. 61, reprinted in 1976 U.S. Code Cong. & Ad. News 3415.

98 I.R.C. §7517.

99 Reg. §301.7517-1.

1 *Id.*

request, or the date of the I.R.S.' determination or proposed determination, whichever is later.[2] The statement must include the following information:[3]

1. The I.R.S.' basis or method on which the valuation was determined or proposed
2. Any computations used in arriving at the asset's value
3. A written copy of any expert appraisal made by or for the I.R.S.

Although this valuation statement is intended to encourage valuation settlements, neither the value determination nor the method used in arriving at such a value is binding on the I.R.S.[4] Presumably, however, the I.R.S. seldom changes its stated values or methods except to compromise with the taxpayer. The statement should provide the taxpayer with a reasonable basis for deciding whether to litigate a valuation disagreement.

§2.29 Documentation for Federal Tax Returns

Although there is no authority, logic and experience tell us that the more carefully prepared and comprehensive the documentation of a value included with the appropriate tax return is, the less likely the value will be questioned by the I.R.S. Unfortunately, taxpayers often determine value hastily and without investigation just to complete a tax return and file it on time. It is not until after the I.R.S. questions the value that the taxpayer will attempt, post facto, to obtain data that justifies the value on the return. This is sometimes a very difficult and unfruitful endeavor.

Although you cannot and should not obtain expensive appraisals of all assets that must be valued for tax purposes, consider obtaining an appraisal from a qualified expert of assets whose tax significance is considerable.[5] Obtaining an appraisal before filing the return, and including the appraisal report with the return, may save you a significant amount of time, headaches and money after the return is filed.[6]

Although the I.R.S. requires certain documentation to be filed with the form, the tax form preparer has substantial discretion as to the degree of documentation. Again, an ounce of prevention is worth a pound of cure.

The documentation requirements for the estate tax Form 706 are much more specific those for most other returns.[7]

For real estate, the grounds for the value used on the return must be stated. Copies of any appraisals should be included. Appraisals should be prepared by qualified appraisers. Unless the cost of a private appraisal is prohibitive, probate court appraisals should not be used, because the I.R.S. frequently refuses to accept them. Significantly,

---

[2] I.R.C. §7517(a).

[3] *Id.* at (b).

[4] *Id.* at (c).

[5] *See* **§§2.3–2.7** on APPRAISALS.

[6] *See generally,* Harnack, *Techniques in Preparing a Valuation Case,* 30 N.Y.U. Inst. Fed. Tax'n 163-84 (1972).

[7] *See* I.R.S., Instructions for Form 706 (Rev. 6-82).

the cost of an appraisal is a deductible expense of administration.[8]

Market prices of traded securities are ordinarily a matter of public knowledge. When not readily available, attach copies of documents (letters are sufficient) indicating the source and applicable quotations. If a blockage discount is taken on the return, include complete data supporting the discount.[9]

Attach all financial and other data relevant to the determination of value of closely-held businesses. This includes the balance sheet nearest to the valuation date, and those for each of the five immediately preceding years. You should attach:

1. All other balance sheets
2. Statements of net earnings or the result of operations
3. Records of the dividends paid.

For assets with no or nominal values, attach all information, including appraisals and market data, showing that certain assets have no value, or nominal value.

When life insurance is in the estate, attach Form 712 prepared by the issuing company for all policies. For any asset that is included on Form 706 as a jointly owned asset and that would require documentation of value if individually owned, attach the same documentation. For example, the return that includes jointly owned real property should include copies of any appraisal made on the property.

If an appraisal has been obtained, attach a copy of it to the gift tax return. Also attach any other documents related to value. The gift tax instructions are more specific in some regards.[10]

Include a full statement on the basis by which any real estate was valued with the gift tax return. If the basis is included in an appraisal, the appraisal, of course, should be attached.

For a close corporation or an inactive stock, attach the business' balance sheets, including the one nearest to the date of the gift. Also include the statements of the business' net earnings or operating results and dividends paid out by the business for each of the previous five years. Similar data is necessary for other types of business interests, too.

For life insurance, include a Form 712, completed by the issuing company, with the return; or file it as soon as it is obtained.

Remember that any asset whose value cannot readily be obtained should be appraised, and the appraisal included with the gift tax return.

Because many valuation issues arise for income tax purposes, it is difficult to be very specific about documentation. Generally, the rules for documentation are the same for income tax returns, as for estate, and gift tax returns. As a rule of thumb, if the determination of value is important for income tax purposes, you should have as much documentation as possible: any appraisals made, and any other relevant data concern-

---

[8] Reg. §20.2053-3(d).

[9] Reg. §20-2031-2(e). *See* **§3.5** Blockage Discount for Traded Securities.

[10] *See* I.R.S., Instructions for Form 709 (Rev. 6-77).

ing value. For example, consider the valuation of in-kind gifts to charities for purposes of taking an income tax charitable deduction. The I.R.S. has outlined the documentation requirements for this issue. Basically, the taxpayer must state the kind of property contributed and the method used to determine the fair market value on the date of valuation.[11] If an appraisal has been made, you should include it, too.[12] Presumably, other valuation issues for income tax purposes would be treated similarly.

---

[11] Reg. §1.170A-1(a)(7).

[12] Rev. Proc. 66-49, 1966-2 C.B. 1257.

PART II

A TO Z GUIDE TO VALUING ASSETS

CHAPTER 3

HOW TO VALUE TRADED SECURITIES

§3.1 Introduction to Traded Securities Valuation

This Chapter deals with securities that are actively traded on an established market.[1] Although the frequency of transactions may vary from one every few seconds to one every year or so, it must be sufficient to make market price relevant to a determination of market value. Clearly, the frequency of trading affects the method of calculation and the weight to be given to the market price. If a security is traded infrequently and no trading has occurred near the date of valuation, market price data will not be considered conclusive. Other methods such as those discussed in Chapter 4, How to Value Business Interests, must be used to determine the value of the security.

[1] *See* §3.2 Terminology and Concepts.

There are several reasons for using market price as the test of market value. First, the determination of market value for actively traded securities is seldom difficult. It requires only a simple mathematical calculation using readily available market price data. Because this is efficient and convenient, the use of market price data is justifiable from a practical standpoint. Second, market price is an objective standard that, in most situations, is preferable to any attempt to establish an asset's subjective value. Consequently, the courts have found that an adjusted market price is presumptive evidence of value.[2]

There are several situations where market price is not determinative of a traded security's market value. Two situations, discussed in this book occur when: 1. the number of shares of a particular security involved is so high that the market could not absorb the shares at current market price if sold concurrently; and 2. the shares to be valued are restricted in their resale by the Securities Exchange Commission.[3]

A worksheet is provided at the end of this Chapter for the purpose of calculating market value from market price information.[4] This worksheet can be used for all types of traded securities and has separate calculation procedures for the various methods of reporting market price. The I.R.S. worksheet for traded securities is also included.

The I.R.S. specifically recognizes that, under certain circumstances, the selling or the bid and asked prices may not properly reflect the market value of the traded securities. Some "reasonable modification" or other data is relevant to determining the fair market value.[5] Although taxpayers have urged the application of this rule, they have received only limited success.[6] For example, it has been urged that the market price data is not properly determinative of market value under one or more of the following circumstances:

1. The market is in a boom or depressed state
2. The market is being manipulated by particular sellers
3. The market is misinformed or uninformed about relevant economic factors concerning the stock.

Court decisions concerning these matters have relied upon the facts of the particular case; they do not have a great deal of precedential value.[7]

Generally, these factors have not been considered relevant unless the market price data is so sporadic or lacking as to raise a serious question of its validity, or the stock involved is a restricted SEC stock or covered by the blockage discount concept.[8]

---

2 Estate of L. McKitterick, 42 B.T.A. 130 (1940).

3 *See* **§3.5** Blockage Discount for Traded Securities, **§3.8** Restricted and Control Securities Discount.

4 *See* **§3.15** Worksheets for Traded Securities.

5 Regs. §§20.2031-2(e), 25.2512-(2)(e).

6 *See* Krahmer & Henderer, *Valuation of Shares of Closely Held Corporations,* 221 T.M. A-16 to -32 (1978).

7 *See, e.g.,* Estate of L. McKitterick, 42 B.T.A. 130 (1940).

8 *See, e.g.,* G. Johnson, 74 T.C. 89 (1980). The latter two issues, blockage discount and restricted stock will be discussed in **§3.5** Blockage Discount for Traded Securities, and **§3.8** Restricted and Control Securities Discount, respectively. The method of determining value for nontraded securities is discussed in Ch. 4, How to Value Business Interests.

The fact that traded securities are pledged, held by a broker, or purchased on margin does not affect the determination of market value for federal estate tax purposes.[9] You must still value such traded securities at their fair market value according to the appropriate techniques discussed above. In addition, any debt or obligation is treated as a separate deduction for estate tax purposes under I.R.C. § 2053.

§3.2 Terminology and Concepts for Traded Securities

Several of the valuation terms and concepts used in this Chapter were explained previously:

§2.9 Fair Market Value
§2.10 Market
§2.8 Proof of Value
§2.11 Sales of the Asset
§2.27 Weighting of Valuation Techniques

Other valuation terms are relevant to securities.

"Bid" and "asked prices" are used to determine purchase and sale price of over-the-counter securities and some other investments.[10] The bid price (lower than the asked price) is the price the dealer will pay to buy the security; the asked price is the price at which the dealer is willing to sell the security. The spread between the two prices constitutes the dealer's profit, and is equivalent to a broker's commission in an ordinary exchange transaction for securities.[11]

Although most price quotations for traded securities are carried in eights, for federal tax purposes market values must be figured to sixteenths (to at least four decimal places in some cases).[12] For example, if the low quotation for a bond or stock is 12 1/8 (which equals 12.125), the high quotation of the day is 13 6/8 (which equals 13.750), the total equals 25.875 which, divided by 2, equals 12 15/16 or 12.9375. You must use this four-decimal figure for tax valuation purposes rather than rounding it to the closest eighth or to two or three decimals. Some bond price quotations, in particular Treasury Bonds, are carried in thirty-seconds. You must figure the value of such bonds to sixty-fourths or to at least six places when necessary.

Only the actual trading days before and after the valuation date are considered when the weighting of days for value purposes is important.[13] Generally, Saturdays, Sundays and recognized or legal holidays are not trading days and do not enter into the calculations.

When sales price data before or after, or both, the valuation date must be used, the

---

[9] Reg. §20.2031-2(g).

[10] G. Christy & J. Clendenin, Introduction to Investments 204-05 (7th ed. 1978).

[11] *See* **§3.3** Valuation of Stocks, **§3.11** Valuation of Bonds.

[12] Rev. Rul. 68-272, 1968-1 C.B. 394.

[13] *See* **§2.27** Weighting of Valuation Techniques; Regs. §§20.2031-2(b), 25.2512-2(b).

sales must be within a reasonable period of time near the valuation date.[14] Although the term "reasonable period" is not defined by the Regulations, the I.R.S.' basic approach is to determine whether general economic conditions materially changed between the valuation date and the date or dates of the relevant price quotation data.[15] If the general economic conditions have changed, then the sale price information does not come from within a reasonable period. Despite the economics of the matter, if the intervals before and after the valuation date are a few days long, the market price calculations will ordinarily be appropriate.

A "traded security" is a stock, bond, or other security that is regularly traded either on a recognized market such as an exchange, or an "over-the-counter" system.[16] For securities that appear on more than one exchange, the reporting services give stock listings including quotations from the New York Stock Exchange and the American Stock Exchange. The I.R.S. now recognizes the validity of composite reporting if the principal exchange on which the traded security is dealt is not available in a listing or publication of general circulation.[17]

Stocks reported by the National Association of Securities Dealers and the Instinet System also get composite quotes.[18]

STOCK VALUATION

§3.3 Valuation of Stocks

Traded stock securities are probably today's most common vehicle for accumulated wealth. For valuation purposes, actively traded stocks can be divided into two categories (depending on the market situation and the type of stock involved): 1. stocks for which the market data include actual sale price quotations that list the high and low prices for the stock on the particular trading day or days involved[19] and 2. stocks for which the market data include only bid and asked price information on the particular trading day or days involved.[20] In both situations, market price value must be properly fractionalized.[21]

Reporting services typically carry the highest, lowest, and closing quoted selling prices for stocks traded on a trading day. For a listed or an over-the-counter stock for which actual sales occurred on the valuation date, the fair market value is the average or mean between the highest and lowest selling price quotations of that stock on that

---

14 Regs. §§20.2031-2(b), 25.2512-2(b).
15 *See* I.R.S. Tax Law Course, 22-22.
16 Regs. §§20.2031-2(b), 25.2512-2.
17 Regs. §§20.2031-2(b)(1), 25.2512-2(b)(1).
18 *See* W. Sharpe, Investments 583 (1978).
19 Regs. §§20.2031-1(b)(1), 25.2512-2(b)(1).
20 Regs. §§20.2031-2(c),(d), 25.2512-2(c),(d).
21 *See* **§3.2** Terminology and Concepts.

date.[22] For example, if on the date of valuation, the relevant stock is traded at a high of $12 and a low of $10, the market value for tax purposes is the mean of these two prices.

Illustration III-1

$$(12 + 10) \div 2 = 22 \div 2 = 11$$

The fair market value equals $11.00 per share.

When no sales of the relevant listed or over-the-counter stock occurred on the date of valuation, but sales occurred a reasonable period of time both before and after the date of valuation, a different formula is used to determine the stock's market value. Basically, the formula is a weighted average.[23] Consequently, the fair market value of the stock is determined by taking the mean between the highest and lowest prices on each of the trading dates and inversely weighting the day spread between the trading dates and the valuation date in calculating an average of those two means.[24] In other words, the number of trading days between the valuation date and the relevant trading date after the valuation date is multiplied by the mean price on the date prior to the valuation date. At the same time, the number of trading days between the valuation date and the relevant trading date before the valuation date is multiplied by the mean price on the trading date after the valuation date. The sum of these two calculations is then divided by the sum of the number of trading days before and after the date of valuation.[25]

Although this sounds confusing and complex, the calculations are relatively easy to make. For example, if two trading days before the date of valuation the mean price is $10 and three trading days after the date of valuation the mean price is $12, the calculation is as follows:

Illustration III-2

$$\frac{(3 \times 10) + (2 \times 12)}{3 + 2} = \frac{30 + 24}{5} = \frac{54}{5} = 10.8$$

The fair market value is $10.80 per share.

---

[22] Regs. §§20.2031-2(b)(1), 25.2512-2(b)(1).

[23] *See* **§2.27** Weighting of Valuation Techniques, Illustration II-14.

[24] Regs. §§20.2031-2(b)(1),(3), 25.2512-2(b)(1),(3).

[25] Regs. §§20.2031-2(b)(3) (Example 1), 25.2512-2(b)(3) (Example 1).

On the valuation date, the fair market value equals the average or mean between the bona fide bid and asked prices.[26]

For trading dates a reasonable period before and after the valuation date, the market value equals a weighted average of the bid and asked prices.[27]

When dividends of traded stocks are declared on one date but not paid until a later date, the value of traded stocks may require adjustment for the dividends.[28] When stocks are transferred, four dates are generally used to determine whether the old or the new owner is entitled to declared dividends:[29]

1. declaration date
2. ex-dividend date
3. stockholder of record date
4. payment date.

This type of dividend information may be obtained in Standard and Poors Annual Record.

For federal estate tax purposes, each date has its own rule:

1. From the date of declaration up to the ex-dividend date, the market price value of traded stock reflects the value of the dividend to be paid at a later date. No adjustment to the stock's market price value is necessary.
2. If the valuation date is on or after the ex-dividend date but before the stockholder of record date, the security's market price no longer reflects the value of the dividend. The dividend must be added to the market price value of the traded security on that date.[30] If the valuation date falls on a weekend and a stock begins selling ex-dividend on the following Monday, the dividend must be added to the mean of the stock price quotations on that Monday.[31]
3. If the valuation date occurs on or after the stockholder of record date but before the date of payment, the value of the dividends must not be added to the value of the stock on the valuation date. It must be added to the value of the federal taxable gross estate as a separate item.
4. Finally, if the valuation date occurs on or after the payment date, it is assumed that the dividend is an estate asset.

For federal estate tax purposes, the same problems may occur when the alternate valuation date is selected.[32]

---

26 *See* Illustration III-1.

27 Regs. §§20.2031-2(c), 25.2512-2(c). See description of calculation in **§3.3,** Illustration III-2.

28 Regs. §§20.2031-2(i), 20.2031-8(b).

29 I.R.S. Tax Law Course, 22-13.

30 Rev. Rul. 54-399, 1954-2 C.B. 279. *See* Butala, *Valuation of Securities Generally,* 14 W. Reserve L. Rev. 182 (1963).

31 Rev. Rul. 68-610, 1968-2 C.B. 405.

32 Rev. Rul. 60-124, 1960-1 C.B. 368.

The problems with regard to accrued dividends and ex-dividend accretions occur primarily for federal estate tax valuations, although they may occur in the context of state estate valuation, too.

§3.4 —Valuation of Investment Company and Mutual Fund Stock

Basically, investment companies are business organizations that use the proceeds of the sale of their own securities to invest and manage a diversified portfolio of other securities.[33] The two most common types of investment companies are the closed-end type and the open-end type (mutual fund). The latter type represents almost 90% of all investment company resources.

Closed-end investment companies are similar to other typical corporations. Their securities are bought and sold on the ordinary securities markets, and investors have no right to request the investment company to redeem their shares or to sell them more shares. The fair market value of such securities, therefore, will be determined in the same manner as the market value of other actively traded securities.[34]

Open-end investment companies or mutual fund companies operate in a different manner.[35] These companies offer new shares for sale, and have agreed with their shareholders to redeem existing shares in cash at a shareholder's request. Consequently, in effect there is only one seller and one buyer. Although the securities for such funds are listed on a bid and asked price basis, in practice the bid price is the only price that a shareholder receives on redemption. On the other hand, a buyer pays the asked price. The difference between the bid and asked prices actually constitutes the mutual fund's "load" or market fee.

It is well established that the fair market value for open-ended mutual fund securities is their redemption or bid price.[36] When no public redemption price is available on the date of valuation, the last public redemption price, quoted by the mutual fund on the first day preceding the valuation date, is treated as the fair market value.[37]

The ex-dividend problem is applicable to all investment company and mutual fund securities.[38]

§3.5 Blockage Discount for Traded Securities

The blockage discount derives from the economic observation that, if a seller markets an abnormally large quantity of identical items (particularly traded securities) within a short period of time, the price that will be received necessarily will be lower than the

---

[33] G. Christy & J. Clendenin, Introduction to Investments 523-25 (7th ed. 1978).
[34] *See* **§3.3** Valuation of Stocks.
[35] G. Christy & J. Clendenin, Introduction to Investments 525-26 (7th ed. 1978).
[36] United States v. Cartwright, 411 U.S. 546 (1973); Reg. §20.2031-8(b).
[37] I.R.S. Tax Law Course, 22-15 to -16.
[38] Regs. §§20.2031-2(i), 20.2031-8(b). *See* **§3.3** Valuation of Stocks.

price that would be received under ordinary circumstances. This economic fact has its primary application here in valuation determinations for large blocks of all types of traded securities for federal tax purposes (e.g., income, gift, and estate taxes).[39] It has been held applicable to other assets, such as real estate, as well.[40]

Although the I.R.S. recognizes that a blockage discount is potentially permissible, it has been very reluctant to recognize its actual applications.[41] This is probably because a blockage discount is merely hypothetical: actual sales do not ordinarily occur. Consequently, the I.R.S. has adopted several restrictive guidelines and requirements that the courts generally have accepted.

1. The blockage discount does not apply where the security has no public market and no established market price.[42]
2. Even when applicable, the blockage discount is only available "in certain exceptional cases."[43] The I.R.S. and the courts strongly prefer that the security's prevailing market price be used.[44]
3. The burden is on the taxpayer, to prove the application and scope of the blockage discount.[45] Experience has shown that it is difficult for taxpayers to overcome the presumption of correctness of I.R.S. determinations. Consequently, a blockage deduction is improper unless the discount can be substantiated. The courts have even rejected the testimony of expert witnesses who failed to indicate the basis of their judgment.[46]
4. You may not assume that the hypothetical sale is to be made on one day, but must assume that the sale of the block will be spread over a reasonable period of time.[47] "A reasonable time" has not been defined, and must be determined on a case-by-case basis.[48]
5. It must be assumed that the sale will be conducted by a broker who is reasonably skilled in dealing with the security in number and kind.[49] In determining a blockage discount you must consider the use of all technical facilities available for marketing such a block of securities.[50]
6. With respect to the application of the blockage discount to gifts, the gift to

---

39 *See generally,* Hocky, *Blockage,* 248 T.M. (1979).
40 Estate of T. Folks, 51 T.C.M. (P-H) ¶82,043 (1982).
41 Regs. §§20.2031-2(e), 25.2512-2(e). *See* I.R.S. App. Off., 15-1 to -20.
42 Schnorback v. Kavanagh, 102 F. Supp. 828 (W.D. Mich. 1951).
43 Regs. §§20.2031-2(e), 25.2512-2(e).
44 St. Joseph Bank & Trust Co. v. United States, 48 A.F.T.R. 1561 (N.D. Ind. 1953).
45 I.R.S. Tax Law Course, 22-6; Estate of T. Prell, 48 T.C. 67 (1967).
46 Estate of Ridgely v. United States, 180 Ct. Cl. 1220 (1967).
47 Bull v. Smith, 119 F.2d 490 (2d Cir. 1941).
48 *See, e.g.,* H. DuPont, 2 T.C. 246 (1943), *nonacq.* 1943 C.B. 30 (90 days); Groff v. Munford, 150 F.2d 825 (2d Cir. 1945) (several months); Estate of A. Larson, 13 T.C.M. (P-H) ¶44,168 (1944) (longer than several months).
49 Bull v. Smith, 119 F.2d 490 (2d Cir. 1941); I.R.S. Tax Law Course, 22-3.
50 Richardson v. Commissioner, 151 F.2d 102 (2d Cir. 1945), *cert. denied,* 326 U.S. 796 (1946).

each donee is treated separately.[51] Consequently, although the gift tax is calculated on the total value of all the gifts, the blockage discount must be calculated as if each gift were made separately and at a different time.

7. Finally, where a large block of a security constitutes actual or constructive control of a corporation, the block of securities may be subject to "inverse blockage," having greater value than its ordinary market price.[52]

§3.6 —Determination of the Blockage Discount

Neither the courts nor the I.R.S. have developed adequate criteria for determining when and how a blockage discount will be applied. Its application, consequently, must be determined on a case by case basis. The I.R.S. has stated "each block of stock is to be valued, as in the case of unlisted securities, depending on the facts in each case."[53] In addition, the blockage discount has often been combined with the restricted security discount.[54]

Nonetheless, it is clear that the blockage discount is composed of two deductions.[55] The first deduction includes all extraordinary distribution expenses that would be involved in a hypothetical block sale. These expenses may be deducted even though the security is not otherwise reduced in value, and therefore may be the only deduction allowed.[56] Deductible expenses include, for example, the many expenses (including underwriting fees) incurred in making "a secondary offering" of the large block of stock. The total expenses for such an offering generally run from two percent to more than eight percent of the sale proceeds.[57] Significantly, the above deductible expenses do not include ordinary brokerage fees that would be incurred in any sale of a security.

The second element of the blockage discount is the market reduction necessary in order to sell a large number of securities. The I.R.S. has identified the following nine factors that must be considered in making this determination.

1. **The Size of the Block:** One of the most important factors is the size of the block of securities as compared to the total number of tradable securities outstanding.[58]

---

[51] Rushton v. Commissioner, 498 F.2d 88 (5th Cir. 1974).

[52] Regs. §§20.2031-2(e), 25.2512-2(e), *See* Estate of M. Brush, 32 T.C.M. (P-H) ¶63,186 (1963); Wiley, *Valuing Large Holdings of Publicly Traded Stock: The "Blockage" Problem,* 8 U. Miami Inst. Est. Plan. ¶74.801, at 8-4 (1974).

[53] I.R.S. App. Off., 15-20.

[54] *See* Estate of A. Little, 51 T.C.M. (P-H) ¶82,026 (1982); **§3.9**—Calculating the Discount for Restricted Securities.

[55] I.R.S. App. Off., 15-8.

[56] *See* Phipps v. Commissioner, 127 F.2d 214 (10th Cir. 1942), *cert. denied,* 317 U.S. 645 (1942).

[57] I.R.S. App. Off., 15-9; I.R.S. Tax Law Course, 22-7.

[58] Badger, *Blockage as a Valuation Problem,* 20 N.Y.U. Inst. Fed. Tax'n 91 (1962).

Obviously, the greater the percentage that a block constitutes of the whole, the greater the potential for applicability of the blockage discount.

2. **Current Trading Activity Data:** Probably the most important factor is the size of the block of securities as compared to the number of shares traded daily on the relevant market. If it appears that the block could easily be consumed within a short period of time as a part of the daily trading, it is unlikely that a blockage discount will be granted. The reverse is also true. The I.R.S. has indicated that it will scrutinize any blockage discount taken on a block of stock smaller than the average number of shares of that security traded in a three-month period.[59]

3. **The Dollar Value of the Block:** By itself, this factor is probably one of the least important. It is by no means true that a block with a higher value is always harder to market than one with a lower value.

4. **The Price Level Per Share:** Like factor 3, this factor is not very important in itself; but it is interrelated to all the other factors. It can also be important because of the market's sensitivity to an attempt to sell a large number of shares of the same security. Higher-priced securities may be more susceptible to price decline if their tradable numbers increase significantly and unexpectedly.

5. **Control:** The block owner's opportunity to change or control the corporation will have the effect of eliminating the blockage discount, and could add a premium to the security's value.

6. **The Market and Industry Trends:** In determining whether a market is capable of absorbing the sale of a block of stock, the trends of the market and of the particular industry involved are very relevant. A blockage discount is difficult to justify in a rising market. Similarly, if the future for the particular industry involved is bright, the blockage discount argument is going to have less chance of success. Market or industry decline would have a contrary effect, and might justify a blockage discount. Significantly the courts deciding the availability of a blockage discount have been willing to weigh the effect of market data occurring after the valuation date.[60] Courts are not required to close their eyes to subsequent market information that demonstrates the correctness of a particular valuation urged by the Commissioner or taxpayer.

7. **The Security's Earnings:** Because earnings are an important factor in setting market value price, the earnings of the company must be considered. If earnings of the

---

[59] I.R.S. App. Off., 15-20.

[60] Mott v. Commissioner, 139 F.2d 317 (6th Cir. 1943).

security are adequate, a blockage discount is harder to justify because investors will be interested in buying such a security. Conversely, if earnings are inadequate and the future is not bright, the blockage discount argument may have additional force and effect.

8. **S.E.C. Registration Requirements:** Because of expense and delay, the necessity of registering a block of securities with the S.E.C. is a recognized justification for a discount from the market price value of the security.[61] The actual amount of a discount is determinable by reference to the other factors, however; no set percentage or amount is recognized.

9. **The Dividend History of the Security:** The company's policy, history, and present capacity for paying dividends are directly related to the earnings factor already discussed. The better the dividend history and capability, the more likely that a block of a security will be easily absorbed in the market place and the less likely a blockage discount will be allowed. Facts to the contrary, of course, would have the opposite effect.

These factors provide only limited guidance for making a blockage valuation decision.[62]

In the trading of securities several special types of marketing techniques have developed for marketing large blocks of listed securities outside the usual market channels. The most common of these techniques include private placements, special offerings, exchange distributions, and secondary distributions and offerings.[63] Each varies in its particular requirements, application, complexity, and cost. Referred to by some as the security's "wholesale" market, these techniques raise the possibility of a discount because of additional high expenses involved and special factors that lower the price.[64] Although the I.R.S. regulations specifically recognize the merit and relevance of such special marketing techniques, the I.R.S. has taken the position that discounts based on the use of such methods are only additional evidence to be considered when all the facts require their use.[65]

The following illustration shows how a blockage discount is taken. It does not imply how one is to be calculated:

---

61 *See* **§3.8** Restricted and Control Securities Discount.

62 *See* Hocky, *Blockage,* 248 T.M. A-17 (1979).

63 *See* G. Christy & J Clendenin, Introduction to Investments 198-99, 202-03 (7th ed. 1978).

64 Wiley, *Valuing Large Holdings of Publicly Traded Stock: The "Blockage" Problem,* 8 U. Miami Inst. Est. Plan ¶74.801 at 8-4 (1974).

65 I.R.S. Tax Law Course, 22-7; *see also,* Regs. §§20.2031-2(e), 25.2512-2(e).

Illustration III-3

Assumptions		
Market Price Value Per Share of Stock in Estate		$50.00
Number of Outstanding Shares	100,000	
Number of Tradable Shares	90,000	
Number of Shares Held by Estate	10,000	
Monthly Trading Volume of Shares	1,000 or less	
Discount Determinations		
Deductible Expenses (Assume 10% of Market Value of Stock)		$ 50,000.00
Blockage Discount (Assume 10% of Market Value of Stock)		$ 50,000.00
Total Discount		$100,000.00
Calculation		
Market Value of Block of Stock		$500,000.00
Less Total Discount		−100,000.00
Estimated Market Value of Block of Stock		$400,000.00

§3.7 —Blockage Discount Strategies and Presentations

Because there are no fixed or formula deductions, the blockage discount problem is difficult. This Chapter outlines strategies and the type of information necessary to substantiate a blockage discount. Your first strategy is "plan ahead." Do not make an eyeball estimate. Gather all relevant information before the blockage discount is taken on the relevant tax return. Post-facto efforts to substantiate a blockage discount are generally unsuccessful; neither the I.R.S. nor the courts give much credence to those efforts. The assistance of one or more experts in security analysis is almost always essential. Potential experts include brokers, market analysts and investment counselors; sometimes bankers are useful.[66]

Your goals in assembling documentation are:

1. To put together sufficient facts to show that the block of securities involved could not be traded on the market in a normal manner, within a reasonable time using all of the relevant technical facilities, without causing the price to be below the current relevant market price

---

66 *See* §§**2.3-2.7** on APPRAISALS, §**2.8** Proof of Value.

2. To establish the amount of the deduction.

These are questions of fact; the more relevant facts that substantiate them, the better. Your documentation for a blockage discount should contain at least the following information:

1. The qualifications of all the experts employed
2. The total number of outstanding issues of the security
3. The number of outstanding issues that are freely tradable
4. The number of the issues in the block of securities involved
5. The appropriate market price on the date of valuation of the security involved
6. Daily statistics for a month before and after the valuation date, indicating the number of issues of the security traded and the relevant market price
7. Weekly statistics for up to a year before and after the valuation date, indicating the average number of shares traded and relevant average market price
8. The average of the number of shares traded in each of the four three-month periods before the valuation date and the three month period available after the valuation date
9. The security's price-earnings ratio on the valuation date
10. The conditions of the market in general and in the relevant industry
11. The company's financial condition
12. An itemized list of the extraordinary costs attributable to any special market technique needed to market the shares
13. A description of any S.E.C. restrictions on the sale of the security
14. Any other relevant information (e.g., the effect of other large-volume sales of the security within a reasonable period of time near the valuation date on the market).

When you are considering whether to attempt to use and justify a blockage deduction, you must give careful consideration to the relative costs versus the expected benefits from such a discount. It must be emphasized again that many of these items are hypothetical. The shares of the block in question have not been sold, and probably will never be sold, as a block. From the I.R.S. standpoint, the deduction is discretionary.

On the cost side you must remember the increased likelihood of an I.R.S. audit and potential litigation over the issue. Even on the benefit side, the tax savings from taking the discount only apply to the marginal tax rate against each dollar of the discount taken. Furthermore, additional costs due to taking the discount (unless deductible for tax purposes), affect the taxpayer on a dollar-for-dollar basis, not on a marginal rate basis.

In the final analysis, this is not to imply that a blockage discount should never be considered. When deciding whether to take a blockage discount, be aware that the tax saving advantages must be compared against the possible additional costs and delay.

§3.8 Restricted and Control Securities Discount

The federal securities laws and the regulations of the S.E.C. prohibit certain securities from being lawfully distributed to the general public until a registration statement relating to the security's issuer has been filed with the S.E.C.[67] Frequently, the issuing company has securities of the same class or quality being actively traded on one or more of the security markets. The valuation problem involves the extent of the discount from market price that should be accorded the securities whose immediate public sale is restricted.

To determine the potential applicability of a discount due to a security's restricted resale, you must understand the why security is restricted and the situations that exempt the security from the resale restrictions. Remember that the discount does not apply to securities that are exempt from or are not affected by resale restrictions. The amount of any discount will also be affected by the scope of partial exemptions.

This discussion of the scope and requirements of the law of securities regulation is necessarily cursory. That effort is left to the principal treatises on that subject and to expert assistance from those fully cognizant of S.E.C. matters.

There are basically two types of securities that have resale restrictions: "restricted securities" and "control securities."[68] Restricted securities are "acquired directly or indirectly from the issuer thereof, or from an affiliate of such issuer, in a transaction or chain of transactions not involving any public offering . . .."[69] Control securities are held by persons in a control relationship with the issuer.[70] The terms "affiliate" and a "control person" have basically the same definition. They refer to a person who "directly, or indirectly through one or more intermediaries, controls, or is controlled by, or is under common control with," the issuer of the securities.[71] The concept of "control" is generally defined to mean "the possession, direct or indirect, of the power to direct or cause the direction of the management and policies of a person whether through the ownership of voting securities, by contract, or otherwise."[72] Although the determination or identification of a "control person" is a question of fact, officers, directors or substantial stockholders (holding ten percent or more) of the issuer are generally treated as coming within the term.[73] A restricted or control security is ordinarily restricted in its resale until a registration statement disclosing material information about the issuer is, in effect, filed with the S.E.C., and a statutory prospectus is sent or made available to investors.

---

67 *See* H. Bloomenthal, Securities and Federal Corporate Law §1.02, at pp. 1-16.38-.41 (1982).

68 S. Goldberg, Private Placements and Restricted Securities §7.1 (1979).

69 S.E.C. Rule 144(a)(e).

70 S. Goldberg, Private Placements and Restricted Securities §7.2(b) (1979).

71 S.E.C. Rule 144(a)(1).

72 S.E.C. Rule 405.

73 S. Goldberg, Private Placements and Restricted Securities §8.2(b) (1979).

Revenue Ruling 77-287 explains the underlying philosophy behind the discount. Because the acquirer is purchasing a security that may not be resold (or may be sold only in a limited market and under limited circumstances), the funds used by the purchaser to buy these securities are, in a sense, frozen. The issue then is how much the seller will be required to discount the security to attract purchasers willing to tie up or freeze their funds. This discount must be weighed against the expenses that the seller saves by not having to register the security.

Several exemptions from these resale restrictions also deserve mention. The exemptions are best understood by distinguishing between a restricted security and a control security.

The source of the exemptions are: section 4(1) of the Securities Act of 1933[74] and S.E.C. Rule 144.[75]

The section 4(1) exemption states that restricted securities held by a person other than an issuer, underwriter, or dealer are exempt from the registration requirements.[76] Although the terms "issuer" and "dealer" are easy to identify, the term "underwriter" under the Act has been given a broader and less clear definition. It is generally agreed that whether one is an underwriter depends upon the security holder's mental state at the time of the acquisition. If the holder intended to hold it for investment, he or she is exempt; if the holder intended to hold it for subsequent distribution, he or she is an underwriter and not exempt.[77]

Consequently, in order to assure the exemption, three particular steps were commonly taken. First, at the time of purchase, the buyer was required to sign a letter stating that he or she took the stock not with a view toward public resale, but with an intent to hold the stock as an investment.[78] Actually, investment intent might more properly be called nondistributive intent.[79] Second, a restrictive legend was placed on the certificate setting forth the security's restricted character.[80] Third, advice was obtained from the S.E.C.'s staff, that because the transaction appeared to be in compliance with the S.E.C. regulation, the S.E.C. would take no action against the contemplated transaction when it took place. This was called a "no-action" letter.[81] However, when it adopted Rule 144 in 1972, the S.E.C. announced that it would no longer issue "no-action" letters with respect to resales of securities.[82] Consequently, although the first two steps are still feasible, the practical efficacy of a section 4(1) exemption is questionable since one can no longer obtain a "no-action" letter.

In order to qualify for a Rule 144 exemption, four requirements must be met. The four requirements are:

---

[74] 15 U.S.C. §77(b)(1) (1976).

[75] 17 C.F.R. §230.144.

[76] Securities Act of 1933, §4(1).

[77] *Id.* at §11.

[78] S. Goldberg, Private Placements and Restricted Securities, Chs. 2, 7, and 8 (1979).

[79] *Id.* at §2.5(a), p. 2-90.

[80] *Id.* at §2.6, 2-96 to -98.

[81] *Id.* at §2.10, 2-112.6 -.7.

[82] S.E.C. Securities Act Release No. 5223.

1. Public disclosure of certain information
2. A manner of sale for the securities
3. A holding period for the securities
4. A limitation on the amount of securities to be sold.[83]

Although the public disclosure requirements must be satisfied in all situations, the other three have exceptions that will be noted.

1. Public Disclosure. Rule 144(c) provides that "adequate current public information with respect to the issuer of the securities" must be available.[84] The Rule itself defines the type of information necessary to satisfy this requirement.[85]

2. Manner of Sale Requirements. Generally, public sales under the exemptions of Rule 144 must be made either in "brokers' transactions" within the meaning of section (4) of the Securities Act of 1933 or in transactions directly with a "market maker" as that term is defined in section 3(a)(38) of the Securities Exchange Act of 1934.[86] In both situations, the person selling the security is not permitted to solicit, or arrange for the solicitation of, orders to buy the securities in anticipation of, or in connection with, such transactions, or to make any payment in connection with the offer or sale of the securities to any person other than the broker who executes the order to sell the securities. Subject to these limitations, a broker in a "brokers' transaction" may execute the order or orders to sell the securities, receive the usual and customary broker's commission, ask other brokers who have indicated an interest in the securities within the preceding sixty days, ask his customers who have indicated an unsolicited bona fide interest in the securities within the ten previous business days, and publish bid and ask quotations for the security in an inter-dealer quotation system so long as special requirements are met.[87]

A very important exception to the limitations on the manner of sale is that they do not apply to decedents' estates nor to beneficiaries of decedents' estates, so long as they are not control persons or affiliates of the issuer.[88]

Even if a Rule 144 exemption is applicable, the application of the marketing limitations may justify a discount for the restricted security. The limitation on solicitation, for example, may make it difficult to sell the securities at their ordinary market price, because a lower sale price will be necessary to attract purchasers.[89] On the other hand,

---

[83] S. Goldberg, Private Placements and Restricted Securities, §8.2 at p. 8-10 (1979).
[84] S.E.C. Rule 144(c).
[85] *Id.* at (c)(1) and (2).
[86] S.E.C. Rule 144(f).
[87] *Id.* at (g).
[88] *Id.* at (f).
[89] Comment, *Restricted Securities Need Not Be Restricted When Valuing for Federal Estate and Gift Tax Purposes,* 31 Tax. Law. 492 (1978).

the 1978 amendment to the rule permitting transactions with market makers should make it easier to sell restricted securities, and thereby enable the holder of the securities to obtain a better price. If this is the case, then any discount taken because of a limitation on manner of sale must be reduced.

3. Holding Period for Restricted Securities. Generally, restricted securities, but not control securities, must be held by the owner for a specified period of time.[90] The holding period is two years. However, certain holding periods may be combined (or tacked on) in order to meet the requirements.[91] The most relevant tacking situations include:

a.) Donees may tack on the time held by their donors[92]
b.) Trusts may tack on the time held by their settlor[93]
c.) Estates subject to the holding rule may tack on the time held by their decedents.[94]

It is important to note, however, that estates and estate beneficiaries are only subject to the holding period requirement if they are considered to be control persons or affiliates.

Although control securities are not subject to this limitation, under certain circumstances control securities may be treated as restricted securities. For example, when a control person sells his control secruities in a private transaction, the securities are treated as restricted securities in the hands of a purchaser. Control securities may at the same time be restricted securities, and thus the holding period is applicable.

4. Limitation on Amount of Securities. With several exceptions, Rule 144 limits the aggregate number of securities that may be sold within the preceding three month period to the greater of:

a.) One percent of the shares of other units of the class outstanding
b.) The average weekly reported volume of trading during the four calendar weeks preceding the filing of notice of intention to sell, or preceding the placing of an order to execute the sale with a broker
c.) The average weekly volume of trading in such securities reported through the consolidated transactions reporting system.[95]

This statement reflects significant amendments made to this section in September, 1978. The three-month requirement permits periods to begin and end as each sale of the

---

[90] S.E.C. Rule 144(d).
[91] S. Goldberg, Private Placements and Restricted Securities §8.5(e), at pp. 8-82 to -247 (1979).
[92] S.E.C. Rule 144(d)(4)(v).
[93] *Id.* at (d)(4)(vi).
[94] *Id.* at (d)(4)(vii).
[95] *Id.* at (e)(1).

restricted security is made.[96] Other sales made by the person within the three-month period are aggregated; so are sales under attribution rules made by certain other persons (including relatives, spouses, control corporations, and trusts and estates in which the person or his relatives or spouse have either a ten percent beneficial interest or serve as trustee or executor).[97] The amendments that changed the period from six months to three months and the aggregate number of securities from the lesser to the greater should increase the usefulness of this exemption significantly.

Although the above limitations apply generally to both control and restricted securities, a special, more liberal limitation was adopted in 1979 for restricted securities only.[98] This new rule removes any limitation on the amount of securities that can be sold under two specified circumstances, if the person for whom these securities is being sold is not an affiliate during the preceding three months. First, the quantity limitations are not applicable if the securities have been beneficially owned by the person for a period of at least three years prior to the sale, and are part of a class that is either listed on a national securities exchange or quoted on NASDAQ. Nor do the quantity limitations apply if the securities have been beneficially owned by the person for a period of at least four years prior to their sale, and the securities' issuer is in compliance with the information requirement of paragraph (c)(1) of Rule 144. These special exceptions to the quantity limitations should significantly increase the amount of securities to which the Rule 144 exemption will be applicable. However all other requirements must be satisfied unless another exemption is available.

Another important exception to the quantity limitation is that it does not apply to estates or their beneficiaries if they are neither affiliates nor control persons.[99]

§3.9 —Calculating the Discount for Restricted Securities

In Revenue Ruling 77-287, the I.R.S. tried to give some guidance on the factors relevant in determining the discount for restricted and control securities:

1. All automatic or mechanical solutions to the valuation of such securities must be rejected
2. The discount must be determined on a case by case basis
3. All relevant facts and circumstances must be taken into account.

Beyond these principles, the Ruling merely presents a list of variable factors that the I.R.S. considers relevant to the discount.

Using a study published in 1971 by the S.E.C., the Ruling sets out four relevant factors for determining the amount of a discount allowed for restricted and control

---

96 S. Goldberg, Private Placements and Restricted Securities §8.6(a)(1), at p. 8-250 (1979).

97 S.E.C. Rule 144(a)(2); *see* S. Goldberg, Private Placements and Restricted Securities §8.6(a)(2), at pp.8-250 to -251 (1979).

98 S.E.C. Rule 144(e).

99 *Id.* at (e)(3)(b).

securities.[1] First, because earnings apparently have the greatest effect on determining an investment's degree of risk, they have a significant influence on the size of the discount. Second, the dollar amount of sales of the company is very influential. For example, a high discount may be justified when low dollar amounts of sales are involved. Third, the particular market on which the security is traded is also influential. The Ruling states that discounts are lower for securities listed on the New York Stock Exchange, higher for those listed on the American Stock Exchange, and highest for those securities traded over-the-counter. Fourth, any resale agreement between the issuer and the purchase is also important. The ruling lists six provisions in such an agreement that will reduce the discount, and one that will increase the discount. The six reducing provisions are:

1. The issuer agrees to include the buyer's securities in any subsequent registration statement filed with the S.E.C. ("piggyback" option)
2. The buyer holds an option to require registration at the issuer's expense
3. The buyer has a right to receive continuous disclosure information from the issuer or seller
4. The buyer holds a power to select one or more of the issuer's directors
5. The buyer holds an option to purchase additional securities from the issuer
6. The buyer holds a contingent power to have a greater voice in operations depending upon the issuer's operation performance.

The one positive factor, which may have no affect on the discount (and might in fact increase it) is that the buyer holds an option to require registration at the *buyer's* personal expense.

Although the Revenue Ruling attempts to explain the weighting of the various facts and circumstances, its attempt is not very revealing. Earnings are said to be a primary consideration, particularly for manufacturing, producing and distributing companies, but subordinated to net asset values for investment or holding companies. The Ruling states the obvious when it indicates that the longer the buyer must wait to liquidate the security, the greater the discount, and that a piggyback provision would have the effect of reducing the discount. No guidelines concerning how much the discount should be increased or decreased are provided. Finally, the Ruling recites again that the particular market on which the security is listed may have an effect on the amount of the discount.

One of the I.R.S.' more definitive references to an appropriate discount states that "hot" or "investment letter" securities (colloquial terms for restricted and control securities) traded in a public market ordinarily command a substantial discount (in excess of 25 percent).[2] Such a discount is not to be permitted, however, for restricted blue-chip or high-quality investment securities. A recent tax court decision allowed a 12 percent discount from the market price of a restricted security for registration and

---

[1] S.E.C., Institutional Investor Study Rep. (1971). The relevant parts of this S.E.C. study are reproduced in Appendix D.

[2] I.R.S. Tax Law Course 22-13.

distribution costs including the risk of price change during the registration period.[3] Another decision recognized a 60 percent combined blockage and restricted security discount.[4] Even the I.R.S. appraiser in that case agreed to this discount. A court of claims decision adopted a 43 percent discount for restricted stock, a 40 percent discount for six percent long-term nonconvertible notes, and a 42 percent discount for six percent short-term nonconvertible notes.[5] This decision relied primarily on the S.E.C. study mentioned above.[6]

§3.10 —Restricted Securities' Discount Strategies and Presentations

Determining a discount when a restricted or control security is involved is like determining a blockage discount.[7] Consequently, the suggestions and information provided in that section should be consulted for use here.

Significantly, many restricted securities also involve a blockage discount.[8] It is therefore necessary to coordinate the determination efforts for the two discounts. Sometimes the two types of discounts totally coincide and therefore are accumulative. At other times, only one discount is applicable to some of the securities, the other discount is, or both discounts are, applicable to the remaining number of securities involved.[9] The following illustration reveals this problem:

Illustration III-4

Assumptions	
Per-share Market Price Value of Stock in Estate	$ 50
Number of Outstanding Shares	100,000
Number of Tradable Shares	90,000
Number of Shares Held by Estate	10,000
Number of Shares Held by Estate that are Restricted Securities	10,000
Number of Shares Held by Estate that are Exempt under Rule 144	2,000

3 Estate of W. Piper, 72 T.C. 1062 (1979).
4 Estate of A. Little, 51 T.C.M. (P-H) ¶82,026 (1982).
5 Campbell v. United States, 48 A.F.T.R.2d ¶81-5068 (Ct. Cl. 1981).
6 S.E.C., Institutional Investor Study Rep. (1971). (See Appendix D).
7 *See* §3.7—Blockage Discount Strategies and Presentations.
8 *See* Estate of A. Little, 51 T.C.M. (P-H) ¶82,026 (1982).
9 Comment, *Restricted Securities Need Not Be Restricted When Valuing for Federal Estate and Gift Tax Purposes,* 31 Tax Law. 482 (1978).

Illustration III-4 (*Continued*)

Discount Determinations	
Restricted Securities Discount (Assume 25% of Market Value of Stock not exempt) (8,000 × 50 × .25)	$100,000
Deductible Expenses (Assume 10% of Market Value of all Stock)	50,000
Blockage Discount (Assume 10% of Market Value of all Stock)	50,000
Total Deductions	$200,000
Calculation	
Market Value of Block of Restricted Stock	$500,000
Less Total Deductions	−200,000
Estimated Market Value of Block of Restricted Stock	$300,000

Revenue Ruling 77-287 lists several documents and facts that should be a part of any discount analysis:

1. Any agreement or document relating to the restricted security
2. Any document showing offers to buy or sell or indications of interest in buying or selling the restricted security
3. The company's latest prospectus
4. The company's annual report for three to five years preceding the valuation date
5. Trading prices and trading volumes of the actively-traded issues of the restricted security for one month preceding the valuation date
6. The relationship of the party to any agreement concerning the restricted security (including the party's familiar relationships and positions with the company)
7. Whether the block of the restricted security represents a majority or minority ownership.

Because you will need to substantiate any discount taken, it is essential to develop the strongest case possible. The facts and information above cannot be relied on exclusively. Expert appraisals are essential.

BOND VALUATION AND MISCELLANEOUS SECURITIES

§3.11 Valuation of Bonds

For tax purposes, actively-traded bonds are usually valued in the same way as actively-traded stocks. However, there are four kinds of actively-traded bonds, depending on the market situation and the type of bond involved. The first category includes bonds whose market data include actual sales price quotations. This category is subdivided into two groups: bonds whose sales price quotations list the high and low prices on the particular trading day involved,[10] and bonds whose sales price quotations list only the bond's closing price on the particular day involved.[11] The second category includes bonds whose market data includes only bid and asked price information.[12] The third category includes federal government bonds covered by special rules.[13] Finally, the fourth category includes "flower bonds" (another type of federal government bonds).[14] In all categories, the market price value must be properly fractionalized.[15]

For sales on the valuation date, the fair market value of a listed or an over-the-counter bond having actual sales on the value date is the average or mean between the bond's highest and lowest selling price quotations on that date.[16]

The fair market value of a listed or over-the-counter bond that was traded on dates within a reasonable period before and after the valuation date is determined by taking the mean between the highest and lowest prices on each of the trading dates and inversely weighting the day spread between the trading dates and the valuation date in calculating an average of those two means.[17]

For actual sales within a reasonable period before or after the valuation date (not both), the bond's fair market value equals the mean or average between the highest and lowest sales price quotations on either date available.[18]

For sales on valuation date and the trading date before valuation date, the bond's fair market value equals the mean between the two quoted closing selling prices.[19] For

---

10 Regs. §§20.2031-2(b)(1), 25.2512-2(b)(1).

11 Regs. §§20.2031-2(b)(2), 25.2512-2(b)(2).

12 Regs. §§20.2031-2(c),(d), 25.2512-2(c),(d).

13 Rev. Rul. 55-278, 1955-1 C.B. 471.

14 Rev. Rul. 69-489, 1969-2 C.B. 172.

15 *See* §**3.2** Terminology and Concepts.

16 Regs. §§20.2031-2(b)(1), 25.2512-2(b)(1). *See, e.g.,* §**3.3** Valuation of Stocks, Illustration III-1.

17 Regs. §§20.2031-2(b)(1), 25.2512-2(b)(1). The same calculation is explained in §**3.3** Valuation of Stocks, Illustration III-2; *see* Regs. §§20.2031-2(b)(3) (Example 6), 25.2512-2(b)(3) (Example 5).

18 Regs. §§20.2031-2(d), 25.2512-2(d).

19 Regs. §§20.2031-2(b)(2), 25.2512-2(b)(2).

example, the only selling quotation price available on the valuation date is the closing selling price of $10, and on the immediate preceding trading day the only sales price available is the closing sales price of $12, the fair market value is calculated as follows:

Illustration III-5

$$\frac{10 + 12}{2} = \frac{22}{2} = 11$$

The fair market value equals $11.00 per bond.

For sales on valuation date and reasonable period before valuation date (no sales on the immediately preceding trading date), the bond's fair market value equals the mean between the two quoted closing selling prices, weighted in favor of the closing price on the valuation date.[20] For example, if the valuation date closing price is $11, the closest preceding trading day on which sales were made is three trading days before the valuation date, and on that date the closing selling price is $15, the market value of the bond is calculated as follows:

Illustration III-6

$$\frac{(3 \times 11) + (1 \times 15)}{3 + 1} = \frac{33 + 15}{4} = \frac{48}{4} = 12$$

The fair market value equals $12.00 per bond.

For sales on date of valuation (no sales within a reasonable period before the valuation date), fair market value is the closing price on the valuation date.[21]

If there were no actual sales on the valuation date, but actual sales on dates within a reasonable period before and after the valuation date, the fair market value equals the weighted mean between the quoted closing selling prices on these two dates.[22]

If the bid and asked prices on the valuation date are the only data available, the fair market value equals the mean between the bona fide bid and asked prices on the valuation date.[23] For example, if the bid price is $10 and the asked price is $12, the calculation is as follows:

Illustration III-7

$$\frac{10 + 12}{2} = \frac{22}{2} = 11$$

The fair market value equals $11 per bond.

---

20 *Id.*

21 *Id.*

22 *Id.* This requires the calculation explained in **§3.3** Valuation of Stocks, Illustration III-2.

23 Regs. §§20.2031-2(c), 25.2512-2(c).

Where other bid and asked prices are available: for trading dates occuring a reasonable period before and after the valuation date, the bond's fair market value equals a weighted mean of the bid and asked prices calculated as in §3.3, Illustration III-3;[24] for trading dates occuring a reasonable period before or after the valuation date (not both), the bond's fair market value equals the mean between the bona fide bid and asked price quotations on either date available.[25]

§3.12 —Valuation of Certain United States Government Bonds

Because Series E and the new Series EE United States Bonds are nontransferable in a market sense, and therefore have no market value, these bonds are valued at their redemption price as of the valuation date for most purposes, including estate and gift tax purposes.[26]

For estate tax purposes, the market value of these bonds is the redemption price on the date of death—whether the personal representative elects the date of death or the alternate valuation date.[27] For estate tax purposes, it is important to answer the question whether bonds from these series are included in the decedent's gross estate.

For gift tax purposes, the question is whether and when the actual gift occurred. There are many rules and differing situations that may affect the answers to these questions.[28] The answer to the estate tax question is typically dependent on who contributed the funds that were used to purchase the bonds. The answer to the gift tax question typically depends upon the form in which the ownership of the bond is registered. The cited Revenue Ruling discusses a series of situations in an attempt to answer most of these questions.

Series E and EE bonds do not pay interest in the ordinary sense. They increase in value by specific fixed amounts after the passage of certain time periods, usually months. However, for estate and gift tax purposes, the proper value of such bonds is the redemption value on the valuation date. The increment, however, is income; that which is earned before the valuation date is income in respect of a decedent (estate situation) or income attributable to the donor (for gift purposes).[29] This increment is reduced, of course, by any amounts that the taxpayer has properly declared as income in previous years.

---

24 *Id.*

25 Regs. §§20.2031-2(d), 25.2512-2(d).

26 Rev. Rul. 55-278, 1955-1 C.B. 471; 31 C.F.R. §§351.1 -.12 (1980).

27 I.R.S. Tax Law Course, 22-18.

28 *See* Rev. Rul. 68-269, 1968-1 C.B. 399.

29 Rev. Rul. 55-278, 1955-1 C.B. 471.

The value of series H and HH bonds for estate and gift tax purposes is different. These bonds are issued at par and bear interest payable at six-month intervals. Although they can be redeemed at par at any time, the interest payments terminate at the end of the preceding interest preceding the redemption.

When an owner of such bonds dies between interest intervals, no interest is includable in the decedent's estate.[30] The same rules applies to such bonds includable in an estate although co-owners exist. Because the interest is made to the survivor on reissue, the decedent's estate has no right to any interest accrued between the last interest interval and the date of death.[31]

Certain U.S. Government bonds, issued before March 31, 1971 (commonly called "flower bonds"), contain the provision that if they are used to pay federal estate tax for the deceased owners estate, they are redeemable at par plus accrued interest. Because they may be redeemed at par value in order to pay the estate tax, to the extent that they are so redeemed and used (or even could have been redeemed and used), their fair market value for estate tax purposes equals par value plus interest accrued to the date of death.[32] For other purposes, to the extent that the flower bonds exceed the federal estate tax, the fair market value of flower bonds is calculated like that of other bonds traded in the market. It equals the mean between their highest and lowest quoted selling prices on the date of death plus interest accrued to that date. The interest earned between the date of death and the redemption date is income to the estate, and is not part of the gross estate.

The bonds, which are qualified for par value redemption, must meet three requirements.[33] First, they must have been owned by the decedent at the time of his or her death. Second, they must constitute part of his or her estate. Special rules come into play when the bonds are owned in joint ownership, in a partnership or by a trust. Third, no transactions involving changes of ownership may occur after the owner's death except specific permitted transactions (e.g., transferring the bonds from the name of the decedent to the name of the representative of decedent's estate).

All Federal Reserve Banks have lists of the Treasury Bonds that are qualified to be redeemed at par. These lists change because older issues mature and are retired. The market price for the bonds available is listed in many daily newspapers under the heading "Government Security." The issues available at this writing are displayed in Chart III-1.

In practical terms, because the rate of return is very low compared to current interest rates, it is seldom worthwhile to own such bonds for an extended period. Your best tax planning situation is to buy them when your client is terminally ill or his or her death is imminent. Purchases of these bonds by an attorney-in-fact have been allowed although the decedent was incompetent at the date of purchase.[34] In this case, under state

---

[30] *See* Estate of W. King, 18 T.C. 414 (1952), *acq.* 1953-1 C.B. 5.

[31] Letter Rul. 8114058.

[32] *See* Estate of E. Simmie, 69 T.C. 890 (1978), *aff'd,* 632 F.2d 93 (9th Cir. 1980); Rev. Rul. 69-489, 1969-2 C.B. 172.

[33] 31 C.F.R. §306.28.

[34] United States v. Estate of Manny, 645 F.2d 163 (2d Cir. 1981).

Chart III-1
CURRENTLY AVAILABLE FLOWER BONDS

Issue	Dated	Redeemable on Call and After[a]	Due
3-1/4% Bond of 1978-83	5/1/53	6/15/78	6/16/83
3-1/4% Bond of 1985	6/3/58		5/15/85
4-1/4% Bond of 1975-85	4/5/60	5/15/75	5/15/85
3-1/2% Bond of 1990	2/14/58		2/15/90
4-14% Bond of 1987-92	8/15/62	8/15/87	8/15/92
4% Bond of 1988-92	1/17/63	2/15/88	2/15/93
4-1/8% Bond of 1989-94	4/18/63	5/15/89	5/15/94
3% Ror Bond of 1995	2/15/55		2/15/95
3-1/2% Bond of 1998	10/3/60		11/15/98

[a] *Although these bonds may be called for redemption after the date shown at the option of the Secretary of the Treasury, none of the bonds have been called in the past.*

law the agent's acts were voidable not void. The repeal of carryover basis for estates has also made the flower bonds somewhat more attractive: there would be no capital gain on redemption by the personal representative or other fiduciaries responsible for paying the federal estate tax.[35]

§3.13 Miscellaneous Securities

There are a significant number of types of securities other than stocks and bonds that deserve mention. The tax methods for calculating the valuation of such securities, like those for stocks and bonds, depend on how prices are quoted.

Chart III-2

Type of Security	Price Quotation Method	Section
Future prices	High and low quotations	§3.3
Less active futures market	Settlement price (closing price)	§3.11
London metal exchange prices	Bid and asked	§3.3
Foreign Markets (selected issues)	Closing prices	§3.11
Listed options	Closing prices	§3.11

[35] The I.R.S. has set out specific procedures for redemption of flower bonds. Rev. Proc. 69-18, 1969-2 C.B. 300; *see also* Rev. Rul. 69-489, 1969-2 C.B. 172; Rev. Rul. 53-156, 1953-2 C.B. 253.

Some foreign markets list their prices in their own currency. These prices must be converted to American dollars.[36]

§3.14 Alternative Valuation Techniques for Traded Securities

Although the I.R.S. and courts who deal with tax cases give lip service to other valuation techniques in unusual cases, most rulings and decisions in valuation cases dealing with traded securities clearly prefer the specific calculations related to market price discussed in this Chapter.[37] Even in situations where the blockage discount or the restricted resale discount is applicable, the results clearly show a reluctance to deviate from the market price calculations.[38]

Other valuation techniques have developed when valuation issues arise in nontax situations. Two of the most important nontax situations are litigation of dissenters' stock buy-out rights, and corporate reorganizations pursuant to the bankruptcy law.[39]

Dissenter buyout statutes apply in the situation where a minority of shareholders disagree with a fundamental or organic change in the corporation. These statutes accord the dissenting shareholders certain rights to be bought out by the corporation.[40] Nearly every state has such a statute, but they vary significantly in substantive rights and procedures for exercising those rights. Generally, these statutes recognize the practical effect a material organic change in a corporation has on its existing dissenting shareholders: their stock will not be readily tradable either privately or on an open market.

Ordinarily, dissenter buyout statutes give the dissenting shareholders appraisal rights, a procedure for satisfying those rights and a standard such as "fair market value," "fair value," or "value," for determining the value of the shares to be purchased by the corporation. The valuation controversy often ends up being determined by a court. The courts in these cases go beyond "market price," the most prevalent tax factor, in determining the value of the shares.[41] Although market price is considered, it is no longer predominant. It has been said that the courts attempt to determine the shares' "intrinsic value."[42]

Just as the statutes vary, so do the courts' decisions as to the relevant factors to consider for valuation. The best example for our purposes is the Delaware courts' technique for dealing with their dissenter buyout statute. Although the Delaware

---

36 *See* **§11.2** Cash and Currency Valuation.

37 *See* Richardson v. Commissioner, 151 F.2d 102 (2d Cir. 1945), *cert. denied,* 326 U.S. 796 (1946).

38 *See* Zanuck v. Commissioner, 149 F.2d 714 (9th Cir. 1945).

39 *See* Banks, *Measuring the Value of Corporate Stock,* 11 Cal. W.L. Rev. 1 (1974).

40 Comment, *The Dissenting Shareholders Appraisal Remedy,* 30 Okla. L. Rev. 629 (1977).

41 *See* Annot., 48 A.L.R.3d 430 (1973).

42 *See* Rams, *Judicial Valuation of Dissenting Shareholder Interests,* 8 Lincoln L. Rev. 74 (1973).

technique is not exclusive, it is by far the most comprehensively developed and respected among all the other state courts.[43] The Delaware courts have developed a variable formula using calculations that estimate the value of each share of stock under each of three or four separate factors. The value as determined by each factor is then weighted according to its relevance and applicability to the security at hand.[44] The three primary factors are net asset value, earnings value, and market price value. Sometimes dividend value is calculated and given weight as a balancing or negative factor. Weighting of the various factors is a subjective matter, depending on the type of business involved, the corporation's financial position, and the condition of the market.[45]

A simple example will more clearly explain the technique involved:

Illustration III-8

Assumptions

Relevant Factor	Per Share Value	Weight of Factor
Asset Value	$10.00	20%
Earnings Value	$12.00	30%
Market Price Value	$11.50	40%
Dividend Value	-0-	10%

Calculation

Asset	$10.00 × 20% =	$2.00
Earnings	$12.00 × 30% =	$3.60
Market	$11.50 × 40% =	$4.60
Dividend	$ 0.00 × 10% =	$0.00
	Per Share Value	$10.20

If the dividend factor had not been weighted at 10%, and if its weight of 10% had been added to the asset value, the weighted asset value would have been increased by $1.00, and the total value for each share of stock would have been $11.20 rather than $10.20.

Some commentators have argued that this system provides a more reliable value

43 *See, e.g., In re* Olivetti Underwood Corp. 246 A.2d 800 (Del. Ch. 1968). Comment, *The Dissenting Shareholders Appraisal Remedy,* 30 Okla. L. Rev. 641 (1977).

44 *See* §2.27 Weighting of Valuation Techniques.

45 *See* Note, *Valuation of Dissenters' Stock Under Appraisal Statutes,* 79 Harv. L. Rev. 1453, 1471 (1966).

than that calculated under the tax law market price techniques.[46]

It may also be necessary to determine the value of an enterprise that is going through a corporate reorganization pursuant to the bankruptcy act.[47] The valuation issue is whether the bankrupt firm's going-concern value is greater than total corporate liabilities, or whether it is less than the corporate liabilities. The answer to the question helps decide who will become the new stockholders in the reorganized business. If the going-concern value is above total corporate liabilities, old stockholders may seek and obtain shares in the reorganized corporation. If it is lower, creditors will probably consume all of the new shares. The debate then centers on calculation of the going-concern value.[48]

There are several possibilities; one technique that has been approved deals with estimating future earnings.[49] This technique is based on a financial theory that attempts to calculate the value of a business by its projected income. Three so-called guesses must be made:[50]

1. An estimate of the business' future annual income
2. The length of time or probable life of the business as a going concern after reorganization
3. The proper rate at which to capitalize the projected earnings.

The future-earnings approach has been mandated by two Supreme Court decisions.[51]

The future-earnings valuation technique is complex. It does not have a large following in valuation determination for traded securities, but it does exist as a potential alternative valuation technique that may be useful in some cases, and that may support other valuation techniques in other cases.[52]

§3.15 Valuation Worksheets for Traded Securities

Instructions: Find the type of market price data available for the traded security to be valued in the Headings and complete calculation using that data.

I. Actual Sales on Valuation Date

1. Highest quoted (Bid) selling price ____________

2. Add lowest quoted (Asked) selling price ____________

---

[46] Banks, *Measuring the Value of Corporate Stock,* 11 Cal. W.L. Rev. 1, 59 (1974).

[47] Id. at 53-55.

[48] Blum, *The Law and Language of Corporate Reorganization,* 17 U. Chi. L. Rev. 565 (1950).

[49] *See* 5 Collier on Bankruptcy ¶1129.03, at 69-71 (15th ed. 1980).

[50] Blum, *The Law and Language of Corporate Reorganization,* 17 U. Chi. L. Rev. 565, at 573-75 (1950).

[51] Protective Committee v. Anderson, 390 U.S. 414 (1968); Consolidated Rock Prods. Co. v. Du Bois, 312 U.S. 510 (1941).

[52] *See* **§7.4** The Income Method of Mineral Interest Valuation, **§9.2** Patent Valuation.

3. Divide total by 2 ________ ÷ 2

4. Market value ________

II. Actual Sales Made on Dates that are a Reasonable Time Before and After the Valuation Date and Highest and Lowest (or Bid and Asked) Prices Quoted

Sales Before Valuation Date

1. Highest quoted (Bid) selling price ________
2. Add lowest quoted (Asked) selling price ________
3. Divide total by 2 ________ ÷ 2
4. Mean Price ________
5. Multiply 4. by number of trading days after valuation date × ________
6. Total ________

Sales After Valuation Date

7. Highest quoted (Bid) selling price ________
8. Add lowest quoted (Asked) selling price ________
9. Divide total by 2 ________ ÷ 2
10. Mean price ________
11. Multiply 10. by number of trading days before valuation date × ________
12. Total ________
13. Add 6. and 12. ________
14. Divide by total of 5. and 11. ÷ ________
15. Market value ________

III. Actual Sales Made on Valuation Date and on Immediately Preceding Trading Date But only Closing Prices Quoted

1. Closing quoted selling price on date of valuation ________

2. Add Closing quoted selling price on preceding trading date ________

3. Divide total by 2 ________ ÷ 2

4. Market value ________

IV. Actual Sales Made on Valuation Date and on Date a Reasonable Period Before Valuation Date but not on Immediately Preceding Trading Date But Only Closing Prices Quoted

1. Closing quoted selling price on date of valuation ________

2. Multiply 1. by number of trading days between the valuation date and the preceding date of sale × ____

3. Total ________

4. Closing quoted selling price on date prior to date of valuation ________

5. Multiply 4. by 1 × 1

6. Total ________

7. Add 3. and 6. ________

8. Divide 7. by total of 2. and 5. ÷ ____

9. Market Value ________

V. Actual Sales Made on Dates that are a Reasonable Time Before and After the Valuation Date But Only Closing Prices Quotes

1.	Closing quoted selling price prior to valuation date	______
2.	Multiply 1. by number of trading days after valuation date	______
3.	Total	______
4.	Closing quoted selling price on date after valuation date	______
5.	Multiply 4. by number of trading days before valuation date	× ______
6.	Total	______
7.	Add 3. and 6.	______
8.	Divide 7. by total of 2. and 5.	÷ ______
9.	Market Value	______

FORM **7308**
(REV. APRIL 1977)

DEPARTMENT OF THE TREASURY - INTERNAL REVENUE SERVICE

SECURITIES VALUATION

☐ ESTATE TAX
☐ GIFT TAX

NAME OF ESTATE/DONOR

VALUATION DATE

EXHIBIT

DATE OF DEATH OR DATE OF QUARTERLY GIFT TAX RETURN

ITEM NO. (a)	QUOTATIONS HIGH (b)	LOW (c)	MEAN (d)	NUMBER OF SHARES (e)	EXTENSION* (*Cols. (d) x (e)*) (f)	VALUATION PER RETURN (g)	ADJUSTMENTS INCREASE (h)	DECREASE (i)	ACCRUED DIVIDENDS OR INTEREST (j)	REMARKS (k)
			TOTALS →							

**If column (d) quotation not used, see explanation in column (k)*

FORM **7308** (REV. 4-77) **Page** ______

CHAPTER 4

HOW TO VALUE BUSINESS INTERESTS

INTRODUCTION

§4.1 Introduction to Business Interest Valuation

This Chapter covers all business interests for which market price is not an overriding determinant of value. This situation arises either because the subject business interests are not traded on recognized markets, or they are so traded, but not in sufficient number or frequency. All forms of business interests will be discussed, including sole proprietorships, partnerships, close corporations, and public corporations not actively traded on a recognized market.

Because the same valuation techniques are used for all forms of businesses, explanations of these techniques are separated from the discussion of the various forms of business interests. Several special issues are also discussed separately; goodwill, majority and minority interest problems, sophisticated corporate structures and private restrictive agreements concerning resale of corporate interests.

From the volume of literature on this subject, the valuation of a nontraded business interest is clearly of great significance to estate practitioners. There are several reasons for this. First, those who own such business interests are excellent clients for estate planning: generally, they have accumulated substantial assets, and therefore have serious tax problems. Second, their business interests, which ordinarily constitute the greater part of their estates, are particularly difficult to value both from lifetime and post-mortem planning standpoints. Third, the underlying reasons for which a valuation must be made are numerous and varied e.g., income, inheritance, gift and estate tax determinations, buy-sell agreement provisions, and various pension and employee stock benefit plans.

No two businesses are alike. Each one will, therefore, require separate consideration of the appropriate valuation techniques. What is most relevant in one situation may not be in another. Obviously, different types of businesses may justify or even require different approaches to valuation. For example, earnings capitalization may be the most important valuation technique for a manufacturing business.[1] Other techniques may be more important for other types of businesses. For example, adjusted book value is often considered paramount for an investment holding company.[2] Such differences of approach may even be necessary among businesses of the same type. For example, a new business may deserve different treatment than an old established business of the same type.

When using the same valuation techniques, variations between businesses may also demand different approaches. For example, under the comparable traded business approach, comparative analyses between the relevant comparable businesses may require that different factors be compared. Thus, one comparable traded firm may be more comparable with regard to sales statistics, whereas another might be more comparable on corporate structure. Both comparable traded businesses may be relevant to the untraded business interest's estimated market value.

To say that the state of the art of valuing nontraded business interests is in a state of confusion and disarray is to understate the problem.

From a practical standpoint, valuation of a business interest is difficult because all of the facts surrounding a particular business can be obtained only in the rare cases. Consequently, most valuation analyses must be made on the basis of incomplete and inadequate information.[3] Furthermore, from the facts obtainable, there are too many variable factors relevant to each situation.[4] Finally, not only are the variables too numerous, but clear formulas defining the relative merit or weight to be given to each of these factors are also absent. In fact, the tendency has been to shy away from attempting to develop such valuation tools.[5]

The situation is not hopeless, however. By necessity, valuation decisions must be made; and usually they must be made as of a particular date. Consequently, from a realistic standpoint, valuation determinations will be made, and even those under dispute will eventually be resolved.

If litigation or other major dispute over value is reasonably anticipated, it will ordinarily be necessary to employ an expert appraiser, or at least someone who is especially familiar with appraising techniques, for the purpose of valuing a business interest.[6] Three frequently reoccuring reasons for this are:

---

[1] *See* **§4.5** Capitalization of the Business Interest's Earnings.

[2] *See* **§4.4** Adjusted Book Value of the Business Interest.

[3] L. Bernstein, The Analysis of Financial Statements 253 (1978).

[4] *See* Englebrecht, *Valuation of Closely Held Corporations for Estate and Gift Tax Purposes,* P-H Est. Plan.—Ideas and Methods, ¶4014.2 at 4105 (1977).

[5] *See* Rev. Rul. 59-60, §1, 1959-1 C.B. 237.

[6] *See* **§2.3** Significance of Appraisals and Expert Testimony.

1. The owner's variety of accounting techniques, peculiar accounting method, or both, require a reconstruction of the business financial statements including the balance sheet and income statements
2. Some of the modern valuation techniques require the use of information not readily available to the lay person
3. The appraiser may be essential as an evidentiary factor in the litigation.

The above discussion should convey the frailty of any valuation determination for an untraded business interest. Even the I.R.S. recognizes that the range of possible values is very wide, and that in the typical case the relevant factors do not yield a single conclusive value.[7] Consequently, whenever there is a dispute over value, the disputing parties must allow some give and take. Clearly, you have significant control over value determinations due to the discretionary nature of most of the valuation factors. These judgment factors must be tempered by reasonableness.

In general, valuation of a business interest employs a two-step process. First, you determine a normal value for the business interest via one or more of the relevant valuation techniques. Second, after normal value is determined, you subtract the appropriate discounts and add the appropriate premiums to that normal value. Your ultimate goal is to make a reasonable estimate of the business interest's fair market value.[8]

§4.2 Checklists for Business Interest Valuation

The following information should be obtained:

1. Description of the type and scope of the business involved
2. All legal documentation of the form and terms of the business
3. List of owners and their relative interests
4. Relationships of the owners
5. History of the business
6. Statistics on operations including volume of business, trend of operations, acquisitions or mergers and all other similar relevant information
7. Balance sheets for the business for the last five to ten years
8. Income statements for the business for the last five to ten years
9. List and description of all significant assets not used in the business' operations
10. List and description of all sales of the business interest for the previous five or ten years
11. Status of the traded securities market

[7] I.R.S. App. Off., 7-19.

[8] *See* **§2.9** Fair Market Value.

12. List and description of all comparable businesses that have their stock actively traded on a securities market
13. All information available relevant to 6.—11. above for the comparable businesses listed in 12. above
14. Economic studies of the industry involved, from whatever source
15. Economic studies of the condition of the country, industry and of the business involved.

Once the information has been gathered, there are some helpful guidelines for its presentation:

1. More recent economic and accounting data are more significant and of greater weight than older data
2. Nonrecurring economic and accounting data should be discounted or ignored
3. The data gathered should be analyzed to determine the degree of risk of the business
4. An economic prognosis of the economy, industry and the particular business must be made
5. The quality and indispensability of the current management should be determined
6. Adjustments to the balance sheet and/or income statement must be incorporated, and their effect calculated
7. The business' earnings distribution capacity must be calculated
8. The business' nonfinancial advantages and benefits must be valued and weighed
9. The business' structure and ownership must be analyzed and explained
10. The companies whose traded securities are comparable to those of the business interest must be analyzed.

More specifically, if the interest is not publicly traded, the evaluation process is as follows:

1. Identify type of interest (sole proprietorship, partnership or corporation)
2. Itemize the composite assets of the interest within reasonable groupings (e.g., real estate, buildings, equipment, inventory, securities)
3. Determine the existence, validity, and effect of any buy-sell agreements
4. Determine adjusted book value of composite assets, individually and as a whole
5. Determine the interest's adjusted earnings for the last five to ten years
6. Determine the interest's dividends and dividend capacity
7. Collect data on contemporaneous sales of interest

8. Collect extrinsic data that may may affect value of interest e.g., relevant economic, historic, industrial, and legal matters)
9. Identify and make comparative analysis of similar traded interests
10. Calculate estimated market value using all techniques (adjusted book value, income, contemporaneous sales and comparative analysis)
11. Calculate and deduct applicable discounts (e.g., marketability, minority interest, loss of key person)
12. Calculate and add applicable premiums (e.g., majority interest)
13. Add value of any relevant non-operating assets
14. Prepare substantiating appraisal.

§4.3 Revenue Ruling 59-60 and Progeny

Although valuation determinations must be made for many reasons, tax reasons are the most common. The methods and requirements set by the I.R.S. are, therefore, of predominate importance. Fortunately, the I.R.S. has issued a relatively detailed set of criteria in Revenue Ruling 59-60, as modified and elaborated upon by Revenue Ruling 65-193 and Revenue Ruling 68-609. These rulings apply to income tax valuations as well as to gift and estate valuations.[9]

The principal Ruling initially introduces the reader to the I.R.S. valuation philosophy.[10] This philosophy recognizes that value determination is basically a question of fact, that there is no pervasive formula, that differences of opinion are very common, and that, therefore, it is not an exact science. The valuation recipe is said to be composed of relevant facts, common sense, informed judgment, and reasonableness mixed in varying quantities under varying circumstances. It is then conceded that valuation of close corporation securities is "in essence, a prophecy as to the future" made as of a particular valuation date.

The Ruling instructs the valuator concerning the scope of the data base to be used. It states that a valuation determination must be made upon "all available financial data" and "all relevant factors affecting the fair market value." Valuations based on less may be deficient.[11]

The Ruling then lists eight nonexclusive but essential factors necessary for any careful valuation analysis:[12]

1. The nature of the business and the history of the enterprise from its inception
2. The economic outlook in general and the condition and outlook of the specific industry in particular
3. The book value and the financial condition of the business

---

[9] Rev. Rul. 68-609, 1968-2 C.B. 327.

[10] Rev. Rul. 59-60, §3, 1959-1 C.B. 237.

[11] *See, e.g.* Rev. Rul. 78-367, 1978-2 C.B. 249.

[12] Rev. Rul. 59-60, §4.01, 1959-1 C.B. 237.

4. The earning capacity of the business
5. The dividend-paying capacity
6. The existence or nonexistence of goodwill or other intangible values
7. Sales of the stock and the size of the block of stock to be valued and
8. The market price of stocks of corporations engaged in the same or a similar line of business whose stocks are actively traded in a free and open market, either on an exchange or over-the-counter.

Revenue Ruling 59-60 elaborates on the meaning and content of each of the above factors. Consequently, a thorough perusal of this Ruling is essential for anyone attempting to value a nontraded business interest. The full text of this Ruling is reproduced in Appendix A.

Unfortunately, none of the relevant Rulings provides an all-purpose formula for the valuation of nontraded business interests. The valuation process, then, must be performed on a case-by-case basis. As previously stated, the process is clearly subjective and subject to a great deal of discretion by all parties involved.

One of the most important steps is to gather all the facts relevant to the task. As Revenue Ruling 59-60 indicates, this not only requires that you properly identify and apply valuation techniques, but also that you consider the nature and history of the particular business and the general and specific outlook for the economy. You cannot value a business without these facts. Each business has its own peculiar features. Consequently, both the valuation techniques and their application may vary depending upon the type of business involved.

A series of checklists and worksheets is included in this Chapter to aid your determinations:

§4.2 Checklists for Business Interest Valuation
§4.35 I.R.S. Analysis Worksheets for Business Interests
§4.34 I.R.S. Stock Valuation Inquiry Worksheet
§4.32 Outline of Sample Memorandum of Valuation of a Business Interest
§4.36 Comprehensive Worksheet for Business Valuation.

TERMINOLOGY AND CONCEPTS

§4.4 Adjusted Book Value of the Business Interest

Although some contend that little attention should be paid to book value, there are situations when reference to an adjusted book value is useful and a few situations when it is the determinative factor.[13] In addition, the I.R.S.' magnum opus on the valuation of business interests, Revenue Ruling 59-60, specifically lists book value as a fundamen-

[13] *See generally* **§2.12** Book Value (Asset Value).

tal and necessary factor in any analysis of valuation of such an asset.[14] The relative importance of book value in the court decisions on such matters is apparently subject to interpretation, however.[15]

Usually, you must adjust the book value found on the last balance sheet of the business to reflect current value more closely. The most common adjustments that you may be required to make include:

1. Adjusting depreciation schedules to reflect the actual situation of the principal assets
2. Deducting surplus funds that are properly distributable
3. Appraising all fixed assets at current market value
4. Discounting accounts receivable to reflect uncollectibles
5. Adjusting inventory values to reflect market value
6. Making the above adjustments to the book value of subsidiaries of the business interest
7. Combining all the adjustments with the other unchanged facts to calculate an adjusted book value.

Adjusted book value per common share is calculated by subtracting the current value of all liabilities (as adjusted if necessary) and the par value of any outstanding senior securities from the adjusted value of all the business interest's assets. The result of this calculation is then divided by the total number of common shares.

Illustration IV-1

1.	Adjusted Book Value		$500,000
2.	Total Adjusted Liabilities	$100,000	
3.	Par Value Preferred Stock	100,000	
4.	Subtract Total Deductions (2) and (3)		−200,000
5.	Result Equals Entity Market Value		$300,000
6.	Divide by the Number of Outstanding Common Shares		÷ 3,000
7.	Estimated Market Value Per Common Share		$100

14 *See* §**4.3** Revenue Ruling 59-60 and Progeny.

15 *Compare* Butala, *Valuation of Closely Held Corporations,* 7 U. Miami Inst. Est. Plan., ¶73.1402, 14-8 (1978) ("No discernible relationship between book values and tax court values can be observed.") *with* Englebrecht, *Valuation of Closely Held Corporations for Estate and Gift Tax Purposes* P-H Est. Plan.—Ideas and Methods, ¶4101.3(2), 4107 (1977) ("The author examined twenty-five years of Tax Court cases and found that book value was the most important guideline variable.")

There are specific situations in which book value as adjusted is clearly relevant to the valuation determination of a nontraded business interest.

1. The business is an investment or real estate holding company[16]
2. All assets are relatively new[17]
3. The entire business interest is a new interest and has been recently organized[18]
4. The liquidation of the business is contemplated[19]
5. The business interest is suffering large deficits[20]
6. Some form of merger may occur with another firm[21]
7. The business is a finance company[22]
8. The corporation is a mere receptacle for purposes of accumulating earnings.[23]

It is not suggested that you use adjusted book value as the sole method to value the business interest; other techniques should also be used for purposes of comparison and adjustment.

It should also be mentioned that adjusted book value may not be determinative in all circumstances. For example, if you are valuing a close corporation interest held by minority shareholders who cannot force liquidation, liquidation values have little relevance. In addition, adjusted book value may only be applicable to some of the business interest's assets. Consequently, adjusted book value would be only one valuation method to be used in conjunction with other relevant valuation techniques for other parts of the business interest. In these situations where different criteria are used for different parts of the business interest, you must exercise great care to avoid including the value of an asset twice in the calculation. A careful determination of adjusted book value is also essential as a guide to the forecast of earning power when capitalization of future earnings valuation is used.[24]

Finally, adjusted book value determinations are also relevant when valuations are to be calculated by reference to traded securities of comparable companies.[25] Here, a price/adjusted book value ratio is calculated for the comparable traded security to determine a price per share for the business interest to be valued.[26] This system calls

---

[16] Rev. Rul. 59-60, §5(b), 1959-1 C.B. 237; Butala, *Valuation of Closely Held Corporations,* 7 U. Miami Inst. Est. Plan. ¶73.1402, 14-9 (1978).

[17] Schreier & Joy, *Judicial Valuation of "Close" Corporation Stock: Alice in Wonderland Revisited,* 31 Okla. L. Rev. 862 (1978).

[18] *Id.*

[19] Butala, *Valuation of Closely Held Corporations,* 7 U. Miami Est. Plan. ¶73.1402, 14-9 (1978).

[20] *Id.*

[21] *Id.*

[22] *Id.* at 14-10.

[23] Starkey, *Valuation of Closely-Held Corporation Stock: Book Value v. Capitalization of Earnings,* 2 Est. Plan. 38 (1974).

[24] 1 J. Bonbright, Valuation of Property 264 (1937).

[25] Krahmer & Henderer, *Valuation of Shares of Closely Held Corporations, 221 T.M. A-45 (1978).*

[26] *See* **§4.17** Traded Securities Comparative Analysis

for an adjusted book value for both the subject business interest and the traded security. Adjustments might be necessary to both determinations. The formula using the price/adjusted book-value ratio is as follows:

Traded Security(ies)		Subject Business Interest
$\frac{\text{Per Share Market Price}}{\text{Adjusted Book Value Per Share}}$	=	$\frac{\text{VPS}}{\text{Adjusted Book Value Per Share}}$

Illustration IV-2

Assumptions

Traded Security (or Averages of Several Securities)	
Market Price Per Share	$56.00
Adjusted Book Value Per Share	42.00
Subject Business Interest	
Price Per Share	VPS
Adjusted Book Value Per Share	21.00

Calculation

$$\frac{56}{42} = \frac{\text{VPS}}{21}$$

$$\text{VPS} = \frac{21 \times 56}{42} = \frac{1176}{42} = 28$$

The estimated value per share estimate for the subject business interest is $28.00.

When adjusted book value is used as a determinant of market value, discounts have been recognized as applicable.[27] The I.R.S. has stated that, when an appraisal relies upon liquidation value as its valuation method, operating expenses and liquidation costs should be considered.[28] The issue of whether selling commissions and potential capital gains taxes should be deducted from the asset value of personal holding companies has not been finally determined at this point, however.[29]

---

[27] Obermer v. United States, 238 F. Supp. 29 (D. Hawaii 1964).

[28] Rev. Rul. 59-60, §5(b), 1959-1 C.B. 237.

[29] *Compare* Estate of Cruikshank, 9 T.C. 162 (1947) with Obermer v. United States, 238 F. Supp. 29 (D. Hawaii 1964)

§4.5 Capitalization of the Business Interest's Earnings

In the business and financial world, it is well settled that a significant factor in determining an asset's value is the earnings that the asset will return to the investor. This statement is particularly applicable to the determination of value of a business interest. When you invest money in a business enterprise, almost by definition, you expect to receive an adequate return on your investment. The amount of that return, of course, depends upon the risk of the enterprise and the ordinary rate of return in the economy.[30]

It is no surprise, then, that earnings of a business interest are significant in determining its valuation both for tax and other purposes. The I.R.S. takes the position that when a business interest sells products or services to the public, earnings may be the most important criterion of value.[31] The I.R.S. notes an exception to this view for the value of radio and television broadcasting stations held as nontraded businesses. For such businesses, the I.R.S. states that the best valuation determinator is total revenue rather than earnings.[32]

"Earnings" is an accountancy concept that is very important to the valuation of many business interests. Although it may refer to the firm's total revenue, most commonly it refers to the income or profit of the firm (total revenues less total expenses including taxes).[33] Total revenue and total expense data, of course, are readily available on any income statement prepared for a business interest. If the figures on the income statement could be trusted in all cases, the calculation would obviously be very simple to make. Unfortunately, the figures on occasion require adjustment. If circumstances require, an audit of the business may be necessary.

You may be required to make adjustments for a variety of reasons including:[34]

1. Accounting principles governing the determination and measurement of earnings may provide alternate methods for dealing with financial data that affect earnings
2. The purposes for the financial statements may differ, affecting their content
3. Those in control may manipulate the data to produce a desired result.

These factors sometimes make it very difficult to determine the "true earnings" of a business interest. They also show the discretionary nature of many of the factors

---

[30] *See* **§2.19** Capitalization of Income.

[31] Rev. Rul. 59-60, §5(a), 1959-1 C.B. 237.

[32] Rev. Proc. 75-39, 1975-2 C.B. 569.

[33] *See* S. Davidson, C. Stickney & R. Weil, Accounting; The Language of Business 25, 33, 50 (4th ed. 1979).

[34] L. Bernstein, The Analysis of Financial Statements 173-75 (1978).

involved in business interest valuation determinations. Control over these factors means control over value to the extent they affect earnings.

Some of the problematic items on financial statements that you must examine and that you may need to adjust up or down, are:[35]

1. All costs that may be varied according to the discretion of the management (e.g., salaries, maintenance and repairs, advertising, research and development costs, matters such as employee training programs)
2. The stated valuation of assets in the business interests—e.g., the values attributed to inventories (FIFO, LIFO), the valuation techniques used for all non-inventory assets, and the value of accounts receivable (are there any large bad debts?)
3. Unusual reported gains and losses (to determine whether they are random, nonreoccuring and erratic in nature and should be excluded, or if they are sufficiently stable and regular to justify consideration)
4. All liabilities that may not have been indicated on the financial statement (e.g., liability for employee pensions with respect to past service, for accrued wages, and for product warranties)
5. If not previously considered, all transactions including salaries, loans, and other business deals between the business interest and its owners, to assure that they are of an arm's length nature.

With adjusted earnings in hand, two additional steps must be completed. You must identify the future flow of income and the proper rate of capitalization. These figures can be determined either statistically or nonstatistically. Probably because of lack of experience with statistical techniques, most valuators have opted for a nonstatistical approach and the courts approve.[36]

Commonly, the future flow of income has been determined by reference to the business interest's adjusted earnings for one or more years immediately preceding the date of valuation.[37] Usually, the preceding five to ten years of earnings are considered, with a clear preference for the five more recent years.[38] The standard practice is to average the earnings for the years selected. Where more recent years seem to be more appropriate and relevant, they may be weighted more heavily.[39] For example, if the earnings during the previous five years are used and it is appropriate to weight the more recent years more heavily, you might use the following weighting calculation:

---

[35] *See generally, Id.* at 224-26, 231-37.

[36] Jensen, *Stock Valuation Formulas for Estate and Gift Taxes,* 117 Tr. & Est. 248 (1978).

[37] Rev. Rul. 59-60, §4.02(d), 1959-1 C.B. 237.

[38] Butala, *Valuation of Closely Held Corporations,* 7 U. Miami Inst. Est. Plan. ¶73.1405, 14-15 (1978); Krahmer & Henderer, *Valuation of Shares of Closely Held Corporations,* 221 T.M. A-34 (1978).

[39] *See* §**2.27** Weighting of Valuation Techniques.

Illustration IV-3

Year	Earnings	Weight	Result
19X1	$10,000	1	$ 10,000
19X2	$11,000	2	$ 22,000
19X3	$11,000	3	$ 33,000
19X4	$15,000	4	$ 60,000
19X5	$14,000	5	$ 70,000
Totals	$61,000	15	$195,000

The average weighted earnings for the five year period equal $195,000 ÷ 15, or $13,000. The average unweighted earnings for the same period equal $61,000 ÷ 5, or $12,200.

However, averaging of prior years' earnings is not satisfactory where there is a clear trend in the business interest's earnings: the annual earnings are either steadily increasing or decreasing in amount.[40] Even the weighted averaging is not satisfactory. Although weighting accords greater weight to the most recent years, it makes no attempt to project either reductions or increases in the earnings calculated for future years.

Despite recognition of the problem, neither the I.R.S. nor the courts have developed an adequate solution. The general tendency has been to emphasize the more recent years as indicators of the business interest's earning power. In addition, when other valuation factors are also being used, there might be a slight tendency to deemphasize the earnings capitalization technique.

The determination of the rate of capitalization is no easy matter either.[41] This rate of capitalization is usually taken from one of three sources:

1. I.R.S. guidelines[42]
2. Comparable actively-traded securities[43]
3. Informed judgment on the rate of return on alternate forms of investment.

Historically most rates of capitalization fell between eight and 20 percent.[44] Riskier businesses carried a rate of capitalization of 20 or more percent. Today's high, erratic

40 Rev. Rul. 59-60, §4.02(d), 1959-1 C.B. 237.
41 *See* **§2.19** Capitalization of Income.
42 *See* Rev. Rul. 68-609, 1968-2 C.B. 327, for examples.
43 Rev. Rul. 59-60, 1959-1 C.B. 237.
44 Kascle, *Valuation of Closely Held Corporations,* 43 Taxes—The Tax Magazine 454 (1965).

interest rates clearly require higher rates. It would not be unreasonable to argue for rates at least two to three times higher, depending upon the risk of the business. Chart IV-1 suggests possible rates that might be set under generalized situations and the assumptions behind them.

The value of an untraded business can also be computed by reference to a price/earnings ratio.[45] Because the price/earnings ratio (or earnings multiplier) is merely the reciprocal of the capitalization rate, the same issues and answers apply. When using price/earnings ratios, it has been suggested that the following guidelines be used:[46]

1. If earnings are increasing: 12-1
2. If earnings are stable: 10-1
3. If earnings are declining: 6-1.

Like capitalization rates, these price/earnings ratios need to be adjusted for today's interest rate uncertainty. Of course, you will want to reduce the multiplier: dividing the above multipliers by two of three may be appropriate.

Notwithstanding the obvious relevance and importance of earnings capitalization as a valuation factor, it will seldom be the only factor considered. Ordinarily, you will want to compare, average, or weigh it in different proportions with the other major relevant valuation techniques such as asset value and dividend capacity value.[47]

§4.6 Dividends and Dividend Capacity of the Business Interest

Basically dividends are the return on the stockholder's investment in the corporate form of ownership.[48] Under limited circumstances, the stockholders of a corporation have the power to demand and require payment of profits as dividends. For a publicly traded corporation, its dividend paying record is a significant factor in determining its market price. For a close corporation, however, the significance of dividends to valuation is not as clear or direct.

Although the managers of publicly traded corporations want to set their dividend rates high enough to attract capital investors, the small groups of owner-managers of close corporations do not have the same motivation. In fact, because of the double taxation consequences of dividends, many close corporations do not want to pay any dividends at all. The goal is to pay out as much as allowable in salaries (items deductible by the corporation), and to retain in the corporation and reinvest as much earnings as is permitted without triggering the accumulated earnings tax on the corporation.[49]

---

[45] *See* **§2.19** Capitalization of Income.

[46] Lamson, *Factors That Will Substantiate the Valuation of a Closely Held Corporation,* 34 J. Tax'n. 227 (1971).

[47] *See* **§4.4** Adjusted Book Value of the Business Interest, **§4.6** Dividends and Dividend Capacity of the Business Interest.

[48] W. Fletcher, Cyclopedia of Corporations §5318 at p. 603 (1971).

[49] Butala, *Valuation of Closely Held Corporations,* 7 U. Miami Inst. Est. Plan. ¶73.1404, 14-11 to -12 (1978); Krahmer & Henderer, *Valuation of Shares of Closely Held Corporations,* 221 T.M. A-42 to -43 (1978).

Chart IV-1[a]
SUGGESTED RATES OF CAPITALIZATION FOR VALUING THE SHARES OF CLOSELY-HELD COMPANIES

Predictability of Future Earning Power —Qualitative Characteristics	Estimated Growth Potential	Capitalization Rate	Multiplier	Illustrative Industries
All organizations, large and small whose future earnings are predictable with a relatively high degree of accuracy. Past earnings have been quite stable, special talents on the part of management not required, finances good, the element of risk low.	Above average growth prospects	4-6.25%	25-16	Dairy products, electric power
	Less than average growth prospects	6.25-8.33%	16-12	Banks, telephone
Medium-sized organizations whose future earnings are predictable with a fair degree of accuracy. Past earnings have fluctuated moderately over the business cycle, requires average management ability, operates in a highly competitive environment, finances fair, the element of risk moderate.	Above average growth prospects	5.56-8.33%	18-12	Cement, electrical equipment, paper
	Less than average growth prospects	7.69-11.11%	13-9	Department store, finance
Small industrial organization whose earnings are predictable with little degree of confidence. Past earnings have fluctuated widely over the business cycle, requires no special managerial skill, little capital required, operates in a highly competitive environment, fair finances, the element of risk high.	Above average growth prospects	7.14-12.5%	14-8	Air conditioning, television and radio
	Less than average growth prospects	11.11-20%	9-5	Textiles, vegetable oils

Chart IV-1 (*Continued*)

Predictability of Future Earning Power —Qualitative Characteristics	Estimated Growth Potential	Capitalization Rate	Multiplier	Illustrative Industries
Medium and small industrial organizations whose earnings are predictable with little degree of confidence. Past earnings have fluctuated widely over the business cycle, requires unusual managerial skill and ability, operates in a highly competitive environment, fair finances, the element of risk very high.	Above average growth prospects	10-20%	10-5	Rare metals
	Less than average growth prospects	16.67-33.33%	6-3	Machine shops, motion pictures
Personal service businesses whose future earnings are unpredictable. Little capital investment required, no organization, no transferable goodwill.		25-100%	4-1	Insurance agency, theatrical agency

[a] Source: Adolph Grunewald, *Stock Valuation in Federal Taxation* (East Lansing: Bureau of Business and Economic Research, Michigan State University, 1961), p. 87. Reproduced from Herbert L. Jensen, Stock Valuation Formulas for Estate and Gift Taxes, 117 Trusts and Estates 238, at 239, Copyright 1978 by Communications Channels, Inc.; Trusts and Estates, 6285 Barfield Road, Atlanta, GA 30328.

The lack of relationship between dividends paid and valuation of close corporations prompted the I.R.S. to deemphasize dividends actually paid and to emphasize "dividend-paying capacity" in Revenue Ruling 59-60.[50] By "dividend-paying capacity," the I.R.S. means the amount earned by the corporation that is capable of being paid out as a dividend, less a reasonable portion of the profits retained in the corporation in order to meet competition. Even with this rephrasing, however, the I.R.S. does not consider dividend-paying capacity a material element when the value of an actual or effective controlling interest of a corporation is being determined.

The end result is that dividends or their hypothetical cousin, dividend-paying capacity, are relevant to the valuation of an interest in a close corporation only when the interest is not an actual or effective controlling interest—in other words, a minority interest. However, no distinction is made between minority interests that form a part of the control group and outside minority interests. In the former situation, dividend-paying capacity may be a justifiable factor in valuation. For those in the latter group, the record of dividends actually paid is more relevant. Because such shareholders cannot change the dividend rate, the economic value of their shares depends on the actual dividends paid.[51]

Despite the limited usefulness of dividends or dividend-paying capacity as a valuation determinator, you should prepare some form of dividend analysis in any appraisal of a close corporation. First, where high dividends are paid, the I.R.S. has argued that they constitute a prime consideration in a valuation determination.[52] Second, the courts have occasionally objected to valuation analysis that failed to consider dividends.[53] Finally, the I.R.S. expects dividends paid or dividend-paying capacity analysis to be submitted, at least when minority interests are being valued.[54]

The process of determining dividend-paying capacity is very similar to that for determining a business interest's earnings. Consequently, the data to be gathered and the adjustments to be made are also similar.[55]

When dividends paid or dividend-paying capacity is determined, you must convert these dividends into a per-share value for the close corporation. This requires capitalizing the dividends at an appropriate capitalization rate. Because some profits must be retained for purposes of growth and to meet competition, your capitalization rates for dividends will be significantly lower than capitalization rates of earnings. The following illustration shows how this operates:

---

[50] Rev. Rul. 59-60, §4.02(e).

[51] Butala, *Valuation of Closely Held Corporations,* 7 U. Miami Inst. Est. Plan. ¶73.1404, 14-12 (1978).

[52] *See* O'Bryan Brothers v. Commissioner, 127 F.2d 645 (6th Cir. 1942), *cert. denied,* 317 U.S. 647 (1942).

[53] Louis v. United States, 369 F.2d 263 (7th Cir. 1966).

[54] Rev. Rul. 59-60, §4.02(e), 1959-1 C.B. 237.

[55] *See* **§4.5** Capitalization of the Business Interest's Earnings.

Illustration IV-4

Assumptions	
Adjusted Earnings Per Share	$100
Dividends Per Share	$ 50
Percent of Earnings Retained	50%
Capitalization Rate for Earnings	16%
Capitalization Rate for Dividends	8%

Calculation

Dividends ÷ Dividend Capitalization Rate = Estimated Market Value

$50 ÷ .08 = 625

The estimated market value per share equals $625.

In the above llustration, the same value is found by capitalizing the adjusted earnings by the capitalization rate for earnings. However, it is assumed in this Illustration that the rate of dividends paid or payable is comparable to the rate of dividends paid by the industry and the economy.

As previously indicated, if the subject business interest is a minority interest without control over the declaration of dividends, the actual dividend rate of return may be much less than the normal rate. To properly estimate the value of a business interest of this nature using the dividend capitalization technique, you should capitalize the dividends paid by the normal dividend rate of return, not by the actual dividend rate of return:

Illustration IV-5

Assumptions	
Adjusted Earnings Per Share	$100
Dividends Paid Per Share	$ 25
Percent of Earnings Retained	75%
Capitalization Rate for Earnings	16%
Capitalization Rate for Dividends (Normal)	8%
Capitalization Rate for Dividends (Actual)	4%

Calculation

Dividends Paid ÷ Normal Dividend Rate = Estimated Market Value

$25 ÷ .08 = $312.50

The estimated market value per share equals $312.50. Had the dividends paid been capitalized by the actual dividend rate, the per-share market value would equal $625, the figure determined in Illustration IV-4.

When comparable actively-traded companies are used to make a valuation decision, the dividends of these companies may become a separate valuation factor. One approach is to divide the average dividends of the close corporation by the average dividend yield of the comparable traded corporation or corporations.[56] The dividend yield is calculated by dividing the average market price per share into the average dividends per share. An illustration may more clearly explain this technique.

Illustration IV-6

Assumptions
1. The close corporation had average annual dividends per share equal to \$4.00;
2. The comparable traded corporation paid \$5.00 average annual dividends per share; its relevant share price per share was \$100.00.
Calculation (Value Per Share)
$\text{Value Per Share} = \frac{\$4.00}{\$5.00 \div 100} = \frac{\$4.00}{\$.05} = \$80.00$

Under this system, the estimated value per share for the close corporation equals \$80.00.

§4.7 Goodwill (Unidentified Intangible Assets)

One of the eight key factors of Revenue Ruling 59-60 is the possibility that a nontraded business interest may have "goodwill or other intangible value."[57] For valuation purposes, goodwill or the unidentified intangible assets are defined as the excess of the market value of an operating business interest over the fair market value of all of the business' tangible assets.[58] Only the additional value attributable to the unidentified intangible assets is considered to be the goodwill.[59] Goodwill is said to exist when the rate of return of the business being valued exceeds the normal industry-wide rate of return.

The most obvious examples of unidentified intangible assets include above average: 1. customer relations, 2. efficiency in operation, 3. utilization of advertising, 4. clientele or customer lists, 5. brand name identification, 6. location. 7. creditor preferences, 8. higher employee morale, 9. preferred or respected business name, and 10. any other factor that puts the business a cut above the competition.[60]

---

56 *See* L. Bernstein, The Analysis of Financial Statements 13 (1978).

57 Rev. Rul. 59-60, §4.01(f).

58 I.R.S. Tax Law Course, 24-13.

59 E. Spiller, Financial Accounting—Basic Concepts 231 (1977).

60 I.R.S. App. Off., 6-3 to -4; Comment, *Depreciability of Going Concern Value,* 122 U. Pa. L. Rev. 485 (1973).

However, the value attributable to specifically identifiable intangible assets (e.g., patents, copyrights, formulas, and trademarks), is not considered to be goodwill, because these assets may be valued individually and are treated the same as tangible assets.[61]

The I.R.S. has conveniently provided one of its few formulas[62] when a goodwill premium adjustment is necessary. You merely need to follow the following procedure:

1. Calculate the average annual value of the tangible asset investment for at least the preceding five years
2. Calculate the average annual earnings on the assets in 1. for the same period of time
3. Multiple 1. by the proper rate of capitalization for tangible assets:
   (a) Eight percent for businesses with a small risk factor
   (b) Ten percent for businesses with a high risk factor
   (c) Prevailing rate in the particular industry
4. Subtract the result of the calculation in 3. from the amount in 2.; the result equals the average annual excess earnings from the business intangible assets
5. Divide the result of the calculation in 4. by the proper rate of capitalization:
   (a) Fifteen percent for businesses with a small risk factor
   (b) Twenty percent for businesses with a high risk factor
   (c) Prevailing rate in the particular industry;
6. Add the result of calculation in 5. to the amount in 1.

The total derived in 6. equals the fair market value of the business including the value of the goodwill. This amount, of course, may be divided by the number of outstanding shares to determine the fair market value for each share.[63]

The following illustrates the above procedure:

Illustration IV-7

Assumptions	
Rate of Return—Business is a low risk operating company	8% and 15%
Five year average annual value of business' tangible assets	$750,000

61 *See* **§9.2** Patent Valuation, **§9.3** Trademark and Tradename Valuation, **§9.4** Copyright Valuation.
62 Rev. Rul. 68-609, 1968-2 C.B. 327.
63 *See* **§4.36** Comprehensive Worksheet for Business Interest Valuation, Part VI Goodwill.

Illustration IV-7 (*Continued*)

Assumptions (*Continued*)			
Five year average of business' annual earnings			$ 75,000
Calculation			
1. Tangible Asset Value	$750,000		$750,000
2. Average Earnings		$ 75,000	
3. Proper Rate of Return (Multiply 1. by proper rate)	.08		
Result	$ 60,000		
4. Excess Earnings (Subtract result of 3. from 2.)		−60,000	
Result		$ 15,000	
5. Capitalize the Goodwill Earnings (Divide result of 4. by proper rate)		÷ .15	
Result		$100,000	
6. Total Values (Add result of 5. to 1.)			$100,000
Result			$850,000

The total estimated value of the business interest including goodwill equals $850,000.

However, you should be aware that the relevance and application of any goodwill adjustment premium are very limited. First, the I.R.S. takes the position that the goodwill formula calculation should only be used in a situation where "there is no better basis therefor available" for determining the value of intangibles.[64] "Better basis" could mean valuations determined by any recognized method that takes into account excess earnings, including earnings capitalization, dividend capacity, comparative security analysis, or a combination of these techniques. Second, goodwill could only be applicable if adjusted book value is the sole basis of valuation. Third, goodwill applies only to operating companies and not to investment companies. Business interests of the latter type do not have unidentified tangible assets value.

Current I.R.S. policy makes goodwill a minor factor in valuation; it has been aruged that the concept should be totally abandoned in all valuation cases.[65] One cannot assume, however, that goodwill premium adjustment will never have any application.

[64] Rev. Rul. 68-609, 1968-2 C.B. 327.

[65] Butala, *Valuation of Closely Held Corporations,* 7 U. Miami Inst. Est. Plan. ¶73.1403, 14-11 (1978).

In a perplexing illustration, the I.R.S. has suggested that a goodwill adjustment might be appropriate if a solid and respected operating business has suffered losses in earnings during the last few years before valuation. Here, the position of the I.R.S. is that the preferred method of valuing the business would be to take the higher adjusted book value and add a premium for goodwill.[66] The formula is difficult to apply in this situation. If the business has been losing money, it probably has not received above-average excess earnings. In other words, you cannot capitalize a loss under the formula.

Nonetheless, because goodwill continues as one of the eight primary factors listed in Revenue Ruling 59-60, those preparing valuations should take goodwill into account, whether by indicating that goodwill is inapplicable or by determining its value when applicable.

For a full understanding of business valuation, it is helpful to review several of the valuation terms and concepts that were explained before, including:

§2.3 Appraisals and Expert Analysis
§2.12 Book Value (Asset Value)
§2.19 Capitalization of Income
§2.14 Discounts and Premiums
§2.9 Fair Market Value
§2.11 Sales of the Asset
§2.27 Weighting of Valuation Techniques

TYPES OF BUSINESS INTERESTS

§4.8 Valuing Sole Proprietorships

Even in an age where complex business arrangements are the rule rather than the exception, the quantity, quality and size of sole proprietorships in existence today would astound most people. The family farm, the sole practitioner in a profession, and the small retail outlet are common examples of the types of business interests that are held as sole proprietorships. Estate planners must be able to deal with and value such business interests.

Because there may be no package of assets, such as there is in a corporation or a partnership, valuation techniques must adjust accordingly. Frequently, your valuation is merely the process of valuing the sole proprietorship's individual assets as if it were undergoing liquidation.[67] Each asset valuation, of course, must use the appropriate valuation techniques. When the business interest is small and divisible, and when the

---

66 I.R.S. App. Off., 6-3.

67 Chalmers, *Valuation of Real Estate,* 299 T.M. A-17 (1978).

income-earning assets can be treated like an investment, not a business, the asset-by-asset valuation technique should be adequate.

To determine whether the assets can be individually valued, you must answer the following questions:

1. Do the assets constitute an identifiable package of assets rather than individual investments?
2. Will this package of assets have a continuing existence or need for a continuing existence after the valuation date (e.g., the sole proprietor's death or retirement)?

If the answers to both questions are affirmative, individual asset valuation is ordinarily inadequate.

Many sole proprietorships are not properly valued as individual assets. This is true if there exists an obvious package of assets dedicated to the business and the successors-in-interest want or need to continue the operation of the business after the sole proprietor leaves it because of sale, death, or retirement. This package of assets, although not a partnership or a corporation, has the same attributes as those business forms and requires use of similar valuation techniques.

A common approach to valuing a sole proprietorship as a package or as a unified business entity is to convert the available accounting data into the form used for a nontraded corporation. Methods used to value this type of corporation are then used to value the hypothetical corporation. The two most important financial alternations that you should make in order to complete the conversion are the deduction of:

1. The estimated salaries for hypothetical corporate officers, and,
2. The hypothetical income taxes that would be paid if the business were a corporation, from the earnings of the sole proprietorship.

§4.9 Valuing Partnerships

The generally recognized technique for valuing partnerships is anomalous. Despite the fact that in many situations partnership interests are unsalable, market values must be determined for them for tax purposes.[68] In addition, despite obvious factual and financial differences, the regulations of the Internal Revenue Code treat partnership interests and close corporation stock similarly.[69]

Basically, the I.R.S. suggests that you convert the partnership accounting informa-

---

[68] Korner, *Issues and Problems in Valuing Closely Held Business Interests for Estate Tax Purposes, Especially Partnership Interest,* 30 N.Y.U. Inst. Fed. Tax'n 202-07 (1972).

[69] Regs. §§20.2031-3, 25.2512-3; Rev. Rul. 65-192, 1965-2 C.B. 259 (applying provisions of Rev. Rul. 59-60 to partnerships).

tion to a hypothetical corporation format.[70] For example, you must adjust the partnership's accounting methods for treating taxes and salaries of partners to conform to the same methods used for corporations. Once you make these financial adjustments, the valuation of a partnership interest becomes very similar to the valuation of a close corporation interest.

The appropriateness of the analogy to close corporation stock may depend on the nature of the partnership agreement, however. If the partner whose interest is being valued cannot transfer his or her rights either to the specific partnership or to participate in the management of the partnership, the only interests that he or she may transfer are the rights to future income and to a ratable share of the assets in the event of dissolution.[71] In this situation a more refined and appropriate valuation technique requires you to compare the value of a partnership interest to a similar nonvoting common stock interest. A minority interest characteristic would be applicable in this situation, too.[72] Limited partnership interests that cannot compel dissolution and liquidation of the limited partnership, and that have no voice in the management of the partnership have been held to be entitled to a minority interest discount.[73]

Partnerships evoke other difficulties similar to the valuation problems of close corporations: the occasional need to determine the value of goodwill and the effect of private restrictive resale agreements among the partners, for example.

Naturally, if the partnership terminates and must be liquidated, the individual assets in the partnership must be valued. This, in effect, constitutes the partnership's liquidation value. Extraordinary costs of liquidation would be a deduction from the liquidation value.

§4.10 Valuing Close Corporations

The term "close corporation" is related to many other terms including "closed corporation," "closely held corporations," "family corporation," "chartered partnership," "incorporated partnership," and "a corporation de jure and partnership de facto." Depending on how they are used, these terms may be synonymous, differentiable or complementary concepts.[74]

For purposes of reducing confusion and for consistency, this Handbook uses the term "close corporation" exclusively when reference is made to a corporation that does not list or trade its stock over a recognized securities exchange market.

Ordinarily, corporations of this nature have one or more other common attributes including:

---

70 I.R.S. App. Off., 8-6.

71 Korner, *Issues and Problems in Valuing Closely Held Business Interests for Estate Tax Purposes, Especially Partnership Interests,* 30 N.Y.U. Inst. Fed. Tax'n 202-06 (1972).

72 *See* Comment, *Estate and Gift Tax Valuation: Discounts of Partnership Interests,* 59 Neb. L. Rev. 750-52 (1980).

73 Estate of B. Bischoff, 69 T.C. 32 (1977).

74 *See* O'Neal, Close Corporations Law and Practice, Ch. 1 (2d ed. 1971).

1. There are only a few shareholders
2. Their shareholders are family members or close business associates
3. All or most of the shareholders are active in the business and serve in official capacities
4. There are restrictions or limitations on the sale of the stock
5. The business policies of the corporation are greatly influenced by tax considerations.

Although most close corporations are relatively small in the sizes of their business operations, number of employees and net worth, size is not generally a distinguishing feature between close corporations and corporations traded on recognized securities exchanges. In any case, your valuation considerations and techniques are the same regardless of the particular size of the close corporation.[75]

§4.11 Valuing Public Corporations (Not Actively Traded)

The vast majority of corporations that have "gone public" are not traded actively enough so that their market prices, if there are any, are determinative of their market values.[76] In its Regulations, the I.R.S. recognizes that sometimes market value price does not reflect fair market value and that "some reasonable modification of that basis or other relevant facts and elements of value are [to be] considered in determining the fair market value."[77] In these situations, the most usual approach is to use techniques similar to those used to value close corporations.

§4.12 Sophisticated Business Interest Structures

Because the world of finance and business is, to say the least, very complex, business arrangements have become equally complex in operation, legal formation, and structure. From concepts such as "freezing the value of an estate" to the technical rules of funding employee stock ownership plans (ESOPs), there has developed an increasing use of more sophisticated business structures. The close corporation with only one class of stock or the general partnership arrangement is no longer the only business interests one finds or creates. For example, close corporations with two or more kinds of stock, and partnerships with both general and limited partners are becoming more and more common.

Sophisticated business structures share certain issues that concern the bundle of rights of ownership. In a stock or a general partnership this bundle of rights is in the hands of stockholders and partners. The bundle includes three basic rights:

---

75 *See generally,* Annot., 22 A.L.R. Fed 31 (1975).
76 *See* **§3.2** Terminology and Concepts for Traded Securities.
77 Regs. §§20.2031-2(e), 25.2512-2(e).

1. To determine and receive profits of the business
2. To control management and operations of the business
3. To cause and share in the proceeds of liquidation.

These rights usually center around the right to vote or power to control.

In sophisticated arrangements, these bundle of rights are separated and spread over the various forms of ownership. For example, preferred stock may have a preference for dividends and under liquidation but have no voting power to declare dividends or cause liquidation. The common stock, in turn, has the power to vote but gets only secondary preference to the distributions made.

Allocation of rights among the various forms of ownership has a significant effect on the value of each of the forms. For example the power to vote, particularly if it constitutes control of the business, may add to the value of an interest.[78] More frequently, however, the effect of the division of the bundle of rights is a negative factor or creates a disability that causes the interest to be valued at a lower than normal value or to be subject to a discount.[79]

Frequently, rights are divided for reasons directly related to valuation issues. The "freezing the value of an estate" technique is an example. The technique, in its basic form, is to create multiple forms of interests. Rights are allocated so that one of the forms includes the primary portion of the entire business interest's market value but will not increase in value; the other forms includes the business' potential growth in value. This technique is commonly used today both with preferred/common stock arrangements and with limited/general partnership arrangements. Thus, the preferred stock or limited partnership interest holds the basic, unchanging value of the business currently; the common stock or general partnership holds the potential future growth value. This is only a brief description of the simplest example.

When you use the above arrangements, be sure that the values are properly divided among the interests so that the values in fact exist.

Significantly, the aggregate value of all of the forms of ownership should add up to the full market value of the business interest.[80] This means that if one of the types of interests is improperly valued, the correction will affect the other types. For example, if a preferred stock or limited partnership interest is valued too high, the correction would cause value to be added to the common stock or general partnership interest. This domino effect is important for estate planning purposes.

The valuation process of the various sophisticated business interest structures is similar but not identical to the more ordinary type of business interest. The same factors and concepts are applicable. For example, to value preferred stock or a limited partnership, one would look to its book value, its dividend or earnings pay-out capacity, the underlying business' earnings capacity, its comparison to comparable traded securities or a combination of these techniques.

From another standpoint, the valuation process is different. Because these arrange-

---

78 *See* **§4.25** Majority Interest Premium.

79 *See* **§4.23** Minority Interest Discount.

80 This statement does not consider the potential relevance of discounts on the value. *See* **§4.23** Minority Interest Discount.

ments typically do not carry voting rights, their owners generally lack control over the operation and managements of the particular business interest. The perquisites of control are missing. Therefore, the valuation process is somewhat similar to the valuation of notes and bonds, using the rate of return and the risk of nonpayment.[81]

To deal with these special circumstances, it is necessary to adjust the valuation process. One suggestion when dealing with nonvoting preferred stock is to calculate that stock's coverage ratio of earnings over preferred stock dividends and its coverage ratio of assets over preferred redemption values.[82] The following illustrates the proper calculations:

Illustration IV-8
PER-SHARE DATA ON COMPARABLE TRADED PREFERRED STOCK

Assumptions			
Net Earnings After Taxes			$100
Interest Expense			50
Current Assets			125
Current Liabilities			40
Long Term Debt			60
Redemption Value of Stock			20

Calculations			
Earnings Coverage			
1. Net Earnings After Taxes			$100
2. Add Interest Expense			50
3. Available Interest and Preferred Dividends			150
4. Preferred Dividend Paid			$25
5. Add Interest Expense Paid			50
6. Total Preferred Dividend and Interest Paid			75
7. Divide 3. by 6.		3.	150
		6.	÷ 75
8. Earnings Coverage Ratio			2.0/1
Net Current Asset Coverage			
1. Current Assets			$125
2. Subtract			
Current Liabilities	$40		
Long Term Debt	60		
			−100
3. Available Current Assets			25
4. Redemption Value			20
5. Divide 3. by 4.		3.	25
		4.	÷ 20
6. Net Current Asset Coverage Ratio			1.25/1

[81] S. Koffler, 47 T.C.M. (P-H) ¶78,159 (1978). See §**8.2** Note, Mortgage and Nontraded Bond Valuation.
[82] *See* Martin & Sandford, *Applying Fair Market Value Appraisal Techniques to Closely Held Preferred Stock,* 56 Taxes—The Tax Magazine 108-15 (1978).

The same calculations are also to be made for the subject business interest. Because these two ratios are significant factors in the determination of market price for actively traded nonvoting preferred stocks, it is contended that these ratios for such traded stock should be compared with the ratios for the subject nontraded preferred stock. By selecting the most economically similar traded preferred stocks, a comparable dividend yield rate can be estimated that shows what an investment such as the subject preferred stock should produce.[83] The earnings or dividends of the subject preferred stock are then divided by this yield rate to arrive at the valuation of the subject preferred stock. Depending upon the preferred stock's dividend paying history and other economic factors, the identification of comparable traded preferred stocks will vary. Because traded preferred stocks are rated as to risk, and the nonpayment of dividends is relevant to this risk, it should be possible to find reasonably comparable traded preferred stocks. However, subjective considerations will necessarily be a part of the process.

After normal value is determined, it is still necessary to determine whether discounts or premiums are applicable. Nonvoting preferred stocks and limited partnership interests with little possibility of affecting business management or policy might deserve a minority interest discount.[84] A discount for lack of marketability is often applicable.[85] When voting or other control features are present, a control premium may be applicable. Depending on the situation, a discount for the loss of a key manager or owner may also be applicable.[86]

§4.13 Nonoperating Investments in the Business Interest

The I.R.S. contends that when a business interest's working capital, exclusive of any investments, is otherwise satisfactory, large nonoperating investments of the business interest should be valued separately from the interest's operating assets.[87] This is called a "segregated approach" to business interest valuation. The nonoperating investments are valued at their individual market values and this value is added to the otherwise determined value of the operating assets.

The "segregated approach" is only applicable when the rate of capitalization is different for the nonoperating investments and the operating assets. Even when applicable, this approach should be used only where the business interest clearly has other adequate working capital.

---

[83] *See* Estate of E. Goodrich, 47 T.C.M. (P-H) ¶78,248 at p. 1062 (1978); *see* **§4.6** Dividends and Dividend Capacity of the Business Interest.

[84] *See* **§4.23** Minority Interest Discount. *See* Estate of B. Bischoff, 69 T.C. 32 (1977).

[85] *See* **§4.26** Lack of Marketability Discount. *See* S. Koffler, 47 T.C.M. (P-H) ¶78,159 (1978).

[86] *See* **§4.27** Loss of Key Manager/Owner Discount.

[87] I.R.S. App. Off., 14-4 to -9.

MATHEMATICAL TECHNIQUES

§4.14 Ratios and Other Tools of Financial Analysis

When market price is not determinative of market value, it is often necessary to use financial analyses to set the value of business interests. Various techniques have been employed to make such financial analyses, including financial ratios, multiple year financial statement analysis, and trend analysis.[88] Each of them will be discussed in this section, with emphasis on ratio analysis.

Financial analysis tools are useful for valuation determinations in at least two ways. First, they indicate the financial health of the business interest to be valued. The existing financial status of the business interest on the date of valuation is very material to the eventual determination of estimated market values. Second, financial analysis tools are used to identify the traded business interest most comparable to the interest to be valued. The valuator calculates the value of the untraded business interest from the market price of the traded business interest.[89]

The basic purposes of financial analysis are:

1. To determine the financial condition of the interest for purposes of loans, purchase, valuation, etc.
2. To juxtapose the business interest in a range of similar interests
3. To weigh comparisons between similar business interests
4. To use known established values for some business interests to value other business interest whose values have not been established.

Ratio analysis is the technique most commonly used for financial analysis. By definition, a ratio uses an equation to determine a relationship between two quantities. Ratios are most often expressed as a relationship of one number to another—for example, two to one or 2:1. Sometimes the ratio is expressed as a percentage. For example, 2:5 equals two divided by five, or 40 percent.

Probably, an infinite number of ratios could be developed for financial analysis.[90] Fortunately, only a few ratios are essential for any one purpose. Ratios by themselves have no significance: the ratio chosen must be appropriate for the purpose for which it is used.[91] For our purposes, they must be relevant either to basic valuation determinations or comparison identification.

Ratios require financial data. Therefore, in order or use ratio analysis, it is necessary to gather the relevant financial data. For most business interests, this includes the balance sheets and income statements for the last five or ten years and the most recent

---

[88] *See* L. Bernstein, The Analysis of Financial Statements 4-15 (1978).

[89] *See* **§4.17** Traded Securities Comparative Analysis.

[90] J. Van Horne, Financial Management and Policy 715 (5th ed. 1980).

[91] L. Bernstein, The Analysis of Financial Statements 1-11 (1978).

information of this type. This information is available from many sources. For the business interest to be valued, it should be obtained from the interest's accountants. For other comparable business interests, it may be obtained directly from the interests or from well-known publications that include such information.

Ratios are used to compare the business interest to be valued:[92]

1. With past ratios of the same interest
2. With ratios of other similar business interests
3. With some predetermined business standard.

Some ratios will have the necessary relationship in nearly all situations. Other ratios are very specialized, and can only be used in particular circumstances.

Many kinds of ratios are used in business analysis. Although not universal, the following categorizations are reasonably appropriate for valuation purposes:

1. Liquidity ratios (used to test the interest's ability to meet short-term obligations)
2. Debt, coverage or leverage ratios (used to test the interest's security with respect to creditors)
3. Performance ratios (used to test the interest's profitability in relation to operations and investment)
4. Activity or utilization ratios (used to test the interest's use of its assets)
5. Market measure ratio (used to test the interest's status with regard to its marketability).

The following ratios are representative of the typical ratios used for this kind of financial analysis:

Chart IV-2
COMMON USEFUL RATIOS

Major categories of ratios	Method of computation
Liquidity ratios:	
Current ratio	Current assets / Current liabilities
Acid test	Current Assets - Inventory / Current liabilities
Coverage ratios:	
Net worth to total debt	Net worth / Total liabilities

92 *Id.* at 12.

Chart IV-2 (*Continued*)

Major categories of ratios	Method of computation
Net worth to long-term debt	$\frac{\text{Net worth}}{\text{Long term debt}}$
Net worth to fixed assets . . .	$\frac{\text{Net Worth}}{\text{Fixed assets}}$
Times interest earned	$\frac{\text{Income before interest and taxes}}{\text{Interest expenses}}$
Performance ratios:	
Return on total assets	$\frac{\text{Net income}}{\text{Total assets}}$
Gross margin ratio	$\frac{\text{Gross profit (margin)}}{\text{Sales}}$
Operating profits to sales . . .	$\frac{\text{Operating profit}}{\text{Sales}}$
Pretax income to sales	$\frac{\text{Pretax income}}{\text{Sales}}$
Net income to sales	$\frac{\text{Net income}}{\text{Sales}}$
Utilization ratios:	
Sales to cash	$\frac{\text{Sales}}{\text{Cash}}$
Sales to account receivables .	$\frac{\text{Sales}}{\text{Accounts receivable}}$
Sales to inventories	$\frac{\text{Sales}}{\text{Inventories}}$
Sales to working capital (Current assets - Current liabilities) . . .	$\frac{\text{Sales}}{\text{Working capital}}$
Sales to fixed assets	$\frac{\text{Sales}}{\text{Fixed assets}}$
Sales to total assets	$\frac{\text{Sales}}{\text{Total assets}}$
Market ratios:	
Price/Earnings ratio	$\frac{\text{Market price}}{\text{Earnings per share}}$

Chart IV-2 *(Continued)*

Major categories of ratios	Method of computation
Price/Dividend ratio	$\frac{\text{Market price}}{\text{Dividends per share}}$
Price/Book value ratio	$\frac{\text{Market price}}{\text{Book value per share}}$

§4.15 Comparative Financial Statements

Taken by themselves a business interest's financial statements for a single year are seldom sufficient without analyzing their relationship to the figures of a previous year or years.[93] Obviously, comparing several years of financial statements enables the valuator to identify important economic trends. For example, sales, costs, and net income trends may be very important to the valuation of the business interest.

Comparative financial statements are normally set out on a one- or two-year basis. For example, the most recent year of financial data available will be compared to the previous year. Ordinarily, the changes from one year to the next will be shown in dollars and percentages. The earlier year is used as the base year for these comparisons.

There are a few rules for calculating a percentage change. When the base year shows a negative amount for an item and the most recent year shows a positive amount, percentage change is not meaningful and should not be indicated. This is also true if the base year amount is zero and the recent year's amount is positive. However, when the base year figure is positive and the most recent year's figure is zero, there is a 100% decrease. Percentage change is not meaningful when a base-year positive amount changes to a recent-year negative amount.

Another comparative financial statement that may be useful is an average of several years for each factor. The average is compared to the most recent data for similar factors. The use of these averages has the benefit of smoothing out erratic or unusual fluctuation in the raw data, but emphasizes unusual factors in the most current year.

The common-size financial statement is another useful tool.[94] This technique takes various major headings on the balance sheet and income statement and expresses them as percentages of the whole. On a balance sheet, total assets equal 100%. The subcategories (cash, accounts receivable, inventory, etc.) would be compared to that 100%. The same approach can be used to break down liabilities and net worth or to break down the income statement. Subcategories can be broken down into further common-size analyses, a technique sometimes referred to as "vertical" analysis.

Common-size analysis is basically an analysis of the internal structure of a business interest's financial statements. Used on a balance sheet, it allocates the business' total

93 *Id.* at 5-7.

94 *Id.* at 8-10; J. Van Horne, Financial Management and Policy 748-52 (5th ed. 1980).

assets, liabilities, and net worth by percentages. For example, a common-size balance sheet shows what percentage of total assets accounts receivable constitute, or how much of total liabilities and net worth are in the form of long-term debt. Similar insight can be obtained from a common-size income statement. Sales constitutes the base, and the components of this amount can easily be observed. We can determine, for example, the percentage of sales allocable to the cost of goods sold, or earnings before or after taxes.

Because common-size statements do not reflect the variation in the size of businesses, they constitute a very useful analysis tool for intercompany comparison. In addition, a business' common-size statements are useful to compare with industry-wide, common-size, composite statistics. These comparisons, then, are useful to determine the business' financial strength and identify comparable traded businesses for direct valuation analysis.

As with all comparisons between selected business interests or between business interests and industry statistics, great care must be exercised in deriving conclusions. Variations between the selected businesses or between individual businesses and the industry in general may require adjustments before the comparisons will be valid. Adjustment is solely within the reasonable discretion of the valuator. As always in such matters of judgment, the opinions of experienced persons or experts are often very helpful.

Index-number trend analysis is another technique used to analyze a business interest's data over a period of three or more years.[95] Under this valuation analysis technique, a base year is determined for all balance sheet and income statement items. This base year is usually three or more years before the most current year for which data is available, though any year can be chosen. All items in the base year are considered to equal 100.0 for that year. The amounts for subsequent years are compared to this index. For example, if the actual amount of an item in the base year equals $20,000 and the comparable item in a subsequent year equals $25,000, the index for the subsequent year would equal 125.0. If, on the other hand, the item in another subsequent year equals $15,000, the index equals 75.0. Index-number trend analysis is referred to as "horizontal" analysis.

It is not necessary to prepare index-number trend comparison for all items on the financial statement: only the most significant items need to be indexed. Index-number analysis is similar to year-to-year comparative change analysis. However, it offers an ability to observe the changes in a balance sheet or income statement over a greater number of years. This has the benefit of providing the valuator or financial analyst with information concerning the trend of the business or industry. Index-number trend analysis may be very useful for identifying various philosophies, policies and other attributes of the management of the business.

Index-number trend comparison, like other matters of financial analysis, can be prepared both for individual business interests or for industries in general.

Because index-number trend analysis does not reveal the actual amounts involved,

---

[95] L. Bernstein, The Analysis of Financial Statements 7-8 (1978); J. Van Horne, Financial Management and Policy 750-52 (5th ed. 1980).

distortions can occur due to the price alterations in the market. The more years used in this trend analysis, the greater the potential distortion.[96]

§4.16 Financial Data For A Fictitious Business

Illustration IV-9
XENON CHEMICAL CORPORATION
Balance Sheet
(in thousands)

Assets	19X1	19X2	19X3	19X4
Cash	$ 2.33	$ 3.65	$ 8.97	$ 12.47
Accounts receivable	69.94	71.47	76.34	92.49
Inventory	75.43	80.13	85.47	101.15
Other current assets	5.94	5.44	6.04	5.59
Current assets	153.64	160.70	174.84	211.72
Fixed assets-net	75.11	89.76	96.54	111.72
Other long-term assets	4.19	4.84	5.94	5.14
Total assets	$232.95	$255.31	$279.32	$328.59
Liabilities and Net Worth				
Accounts payable	$ 34.55	$ 30.11	$ 36.33	$ 57.34
Notes payable	19.43	24.33	13.55	16.63
Other current liabilities	9.99	6.97	7.75	14.33
Current liabilities	63.98	61.42	57.64	88.30
Long-term debt	.77	.89	1.19	2.00
Total liabilities	64.76	62.32	58.84	90.31
Preferred stock			.50	1.89
Common stock	11.79	15.15	22.10	26.45
Capital surplus	37.43	39.53	41.44	45.77
Retained earnings	118.18	153.45	156.43	164.16
Net worth	$168.18	$192.98	$220.48	$238.28
Total liabilities and net worth	$232.95	$255.31	$279.32	$328.59

[96] L. Bernstein, The Analysis of Financial Statements 8 (1978).

Illustration IV-9 (*Continued*)

Income Statement
(in thousands)

	19X1	19X2	19X3	19X4
Sales	$319.48	$335.44	$385.67	$475.07
Cost of goods sold	(130.34)	(141.34)	(171.76)	(201.58)
Gross profit	189.13	194.10	213.91	273.49
Selling expenses	72.34	96.99	97.54	96.11
General and administrative expenses	43.77	42.43	47.79	53.32
Total Expenses	(116.11)	(137.43)	(145.33)	(149.43)
Gross profit less total expenses	73.02	54.67	68.57	124.06
Other income	1.14	3.34	4.21	3.10
Earnings before interest and taxes	74.16	58.01	72.79	127.16
Interest expense	(2.97)	(4.01)	(2.13)	(3.00)
Taxes	(32.62)	(22.09)	(30.62)	(54.49)
Earnings after interest and taxes	$ 38.56	$ 31.90	$ 40.03	$ 68.67

Common-Size Balance Sheet

Assets

	19X1	19X2	19X3	19X4
Cash	1.0%	1.4%	3.2%	3.8%
Accounts receivable	30.0	28.0	27.3	28.1
Inventory	32.4	31.4	30.6	30.8
Other current assets	2.6	2.1	2.2	1.7
Current assets	66.0	62.9	63.3	64.4
Fixed assets-net	32.2	35.2	34.6	34.0
Other long-term assets	1.8	1.9	2.1	1.6
Total assets	100.0%	100.0%	100.0%	100.0%

Liabilities and Net Worth

	19X1	19X2	19X3	19X4
Accounts payable	14.8%	11.8%	13.0%	17.4%
Notes payable	8.3	9.5	4.9	5.1
Other current liabilities	4.3	2.7	2.8	4.4
Current liabilities	27.5	27.0	20.7	26.9
Long-term debt	.3	.4	.4	.6
Total liabilities	27.8	24.4	21.1	27.5
Preferred stock	0	0	.2	.6
Common stock	5.1	5.9	7.9	8.0
Capital surplus	16.1	15.5	14.8	13.9
Retained earnings	51.1	54.2	56.0	50.0
Net worth	72.2	75.6	78.9	72.5
Total liabilities and net worth	100.0%	100.0%	100.0%	100.0%

Illustration IV-9 (*Continued*)

Common Income Statement

Sales	100.0%	100.0%	100.0%	100.0%
Cost of goods sold	40.8	42.1	44.5	42.4
Gross Profit	59.2	57.9	55.5	57.6
Selling expenses	22.6	28.9	25.3	20.2
General and administrative expenses	13.7	12.7	12.4	11.2
Total expenses	36.3	41.6	37.7	31.4
Gross profit less total expenses	22.9	16.3	17.8	26.1
Other income	.3	1.0	1.1	.7
Earnings before interest and taxes	23.2	17.3	18.9	26.8
Interest	.9	1.2	.6	.6
Taxes	10.2	6.6	7.9	11.7
Earnings after interest and taxes	12.1%	9.5%	10.4%	14.5%

Indexed Balance Sheet

Assets

	19X1	19X2	19X3	19X4
Cash	100.0%	156.5%	384.7%	534.7%
Accounts receivable	100.0	102.2	109.2	132.3
Inventory	100.0	106.2	113.3	134.1
Other current assets	100.0	91.6	101.7	94.2
Current assets	100.0	104.6	115.1	137.8
Fixed assets-net	100.0	119.5	128.5	148.7
Other long-term assets	100.0	115.6	141.8	122.8
Total assets	100.0%	119.6%	119.9%	141.1%

Liabilities and Equities

Accounts payable	100.0%	87.1%	105.1%	165.9%
Notes payable	100.0	125.2	69.8	85.6
Other current liabilities	100.0	69.8	77.6	143.4
Current liabilities	100.0	96.0	90.1	138.0
Long-term debt	100.0	115.9	154.5	258.4
Total liabilities	100.0	96.2	90.9	139.4
Preferred stock	0.0	0.0	100.0	379.0
Common stock	100.0	128.5	187.4	224.3
Capital surplus	100.0	105.6	110.7	122.3
Retained earnings	100.0	129.0	131.5	138.0
Net worth	100.0	114.7	131.1	141.7
Total liabilities and net worth	100.0%	109.6%	119.9%	141.1%

Illustration IV-9 (*Continued*)

Indexed Income Statement

	19X1	19X2	19X3	19X4
Sales	100.0%	105.0%	120.1%	148.7%
Cost of goods sold	100.0	108.4	131.8	154.7
Gross profit	100.0	102.6	113.1	144.6
Selling expenses	100.0	134.1	134.8	132.9
General and administrative expenses	100.0	96.9	109.2	121.8
Total expenses	100.0	120.1	125.2	128.7
Gross profit less total expenses	100.0	74.9	93.9	169.9
Other income	100.0	292.8	369.7	271.9
Earnings before taxes	100.0	78.2	98.2	171.5
Interest	100.0	135.0	71.7	101.0
Taxes	100.0	67.7	93.9	170.1
Earnings after interest and taxes	100.0%	82.7%	103.8%	178.1%

Ratio Analysis

Major categories of ratios	Method of computation	Ratio for 19X4
Short-term liquidity ratios:		
Current ratio	$\frac{\text{Current assets}}{\text{Current liabilities}} = \frac{21,172}{8,830} =$	2.4:1
Acid test	$\frac{\text{Current assets - Inventory}}{\text{Current liabilities}} = \frac{21,172 - 10,115}{8,830} = \frac{11,057}{8,830} =$	1.25:1
Capital structure and long-term solvency ratios:		
Net worth to total debt	$\frac{\text{Net worth}}{\text{Total liabilities}} = \frac{23,828}{9,031} =$	2.64:1
Net worth to long-term debt	$\frac{\text{Net worth}}{\text{Long-term debt}} = \frac{23,828}{200} =$	119.14:1
Net worth to fixed assets	$\frac{\text{Net worth}}{\text{Fixed assets}} = \frac{23,828}{11,172} =$	2.13:1
Times interest earned	$\frac{\text{Income before interest and taxes}}{\text{Interest expenses}} = \frac{12,716}{300} =$	42.39:1

Illustration IV-9 (*Continued*)
Ratio Analysis (*Continued*)

Major categories of ratios	Method of computation	Ratio for 19X4
Return on investment ratios:		
Return on total assets	$\frac{\text{Net income}}{\text{Total assets}} = \frac{6,867}{32,859} =$	21%
Operating performance ratios:		
Gross margin ratio	$\frac{\text{Gross profit (margin)}}{\text{Sales}} = \frac{27,349}{47,507} =$	58%
Operating profits to sales	$\frac{\text{Operating profit}}{\text{Sales}} = \frac{12,406}{47,507} =$	26%
Pretax income to sales	$\frac{\text{Pretax income}}{\text{Sales}} = \frac{12,716}{47,507} =$	28%
Net income to sales	$\frac{\text{Net income}}{\text{Sales}} = \frac{6,867}{47,507} =$	14%
Asset-utilization ratios:		
Sales to cash	$\frac{\text{Sales}}{\text{Cash}} = \frac{47,507}{1,247} =$	38.09:1
Sales to accounts receivables	$\frac{\text{Sales}}{\text{Accounts receivable}} = \frac{47,507}{9,249} =$	5.14:1
Sales to inventories	$\frac{\text{Sales}}{\text{Inventories}} = \frac{47,507}{10,115} =$	4.7:1
Sales to working capital (Current assets—current liabilities) . .	$\frac{\text{Sales}}{\text{Working capital}} = \frac{47,507}{12,342} =$	3.85:1
Sales to fixed assets	$\frac{\text{Sales}}{\text{Fixed assets}} = \frac{47,507}{11,172} =$	4.25:1
Sales to total assets	$\frac{\text{Sales}}{\text{Total assets}} = \frac{47,507}{32,859} =$	1.45:1

§4.17 Traded Securities Comparative Analysis

When time and expense permits, one of the best methods for estimating the market value of an untraded business interest is to compare the market value and all available financial data for actively traded securities that are factually and financially close to the subject nontraded business interest.[97]

The following Chart lists some of the sources of information for making comparisons:

Chart IV-3

PRINCIPAL SOURCES OF INFORMATION ON COMPARABLE TRADED BUSINESSES

Publication	Content
Federal Government Publications:	
Standard Industrial Classification Manual	Categorizes industries into groups and assigns them Standard (SIC) Codes.
Securities and Exchange Commission, Directory of Companies Required to File Annual Reports with the Securities and Exchange Commission (G.P.O. March 31, 1980).	Lists companies required to file annual reports under the Security Exchange Acts.
U.S. Department of Commerce; Census of Business	These publications include summary statistics and ratios on various industry matters.
Department of the Treasury; Statistics of Income, Corporation Income Tax Returns	Same as above.

[97] Schreier & Joy, *Judicial Valuation of "Close" Corporation Stock: Alice in Wonderland Revisited,* 31 Okla. L. Rev. 863-64 (1978).

Chart IV-3 (*Continued*)

Publication	Content
Private Professional Publications:	
Dun and Bradstreet, Inc., Business Economics Division, Dun's Review	Key operating and financial ratios for 125 lines of businesses (71 manufacturing and construction lines, 30 wholesale lines and 24 retail lines). Five-year summaries are presented in lower quartile, median, half and upper quartile ranges.
Moody's Investor Service, Moody's Manual	Multi-volume service including detailed descriptions of selected publicly-held corporations; descriptions are divided into Bank & Finance, Industrials, OTC Industrials, Public Utilities and Transportations.
Robert Morris Associates, Annual Statement Studies	Contains eleven financial and operating ratios for about 156 lines of business based on information obtained from Robert Morris Associates' number banks
Standard & Poor Corporation, Cooperation Records	Multi-volume service including detailed description of selected publicly-held corporations: SIC Code is used
Standard & Poor Corporation, Register	List of public-traded corporations under SIC Code.

There are also many specialized publications relating to a particular industry[98] or to a particular geographic region.[99] Information may also be obtained directly from relevant corporations whose existence may be discovered on a personal or local basis.

Obviously, the greater the similarity between the actively-traded corporation and the nontraded business interest, the more relevant any comparison of financial data for the two entities will be. When searching for comparables, the full range of financial information is important. You should seek publicly-traded corporations that are similar in product or service line, size of business, facilities, marketing area, growth, profitability, overhead, competitive position, and all other factors related to the general financial condition, diversification and capital structure.[1]

The most typically used sources of this data are the respective balance sheets and income statements of the various identified business interests. From these materials, comparable ratios, trends, and analyses can be produced and compared.[2] Adjustments must be made when, as in the usual case, exact comparability is not found. The adjustment process is similar to that made for the market approach to valuing real property.[3]

Although this technique can produce a very accurate estimated value for a nontraded business interest, it is also the most difficult to use. It not only requires an enormous amount of information concerning the business, other similar businesses, and the entire industry, but it also requires comprehensive analysis of that information. The average estate planner lacks the desire, time, and resources to search out all of the necessary information and the expertise to evaluate and analyze the information. For most purposes, then, valuations using traded securities comparative analyses will be left to the expert appraiser. By using his or her experience and accumulated resources, the expert appraiser can usually produce a valid, usable appraisal with this technique.

Because of the complexities of this technique, even some courts have shied away from its use.[4] Although they reaffirm its relevance and usefulness, there is clearly a tendency to rely on other techniques unless it is possible to identify very similar traded securities.

However, if it is possible to easily and quickly identify an actively traded security that is a close facsimile to the subject business interest, valuation determinations may be significantly reduced in complexity. Under these circumstances the technique may

---

98 *See* L. Bernstein, The Analysis of Financial Statements 23-24 (1978).

99 *See* S. Pratt, Valuing a Business—The Analysis and Appraisal of Closely-Held Companies 131 (1981).

1 *See* I.R.S. App. Off., 7-1, 12-1 to -3.

2 *See* **§4.14** Ratios and Other Tools of Financial Analysis.

3 *See* **§5.11** The Market Approach to Real Property Valuation.

4 *See, e.g.,* F. Meijer, 79 T.C.M. (P-H) ¶79,344 (1979).

be very efficient and reliable.[5] However, you must be sure that actual comparability is present.[6]

It is almost guaranteed that there will be differences between the traded corporations and the subject business interest. Although differences do not destroy the efficacy of the comparability technique, they make the valuator's job more complex. The differences may relate to arbitrary decisions based on taste rather than on definable judgment. Making a decision is even more difficult than it is in the market approach for determining the value of real property. Most real property being valued is clearly marketable. Untraded business interests, on the other hand, are clearly much less marketable or totally unmarketable.

There must be discretion exercised in choosing this technique and applying it. Because a vast amount of relevant data is available and analysis is complex, full use of this technique should be limited to situations where it has significant results. This will normally only be true if the untraded interest has one or more of the following attributes:[7]

1. It is very large
2. Its value is very high
3. Its value is very important to the purpose for which the valuation is being made.

Consequently, from a practical estate planning standpoint, this technique is better suited to larger untraded businesses, those that have a value over $10,000,000. It will be much easier to identify comparable traded securities for the larger untraded business than for the smaller ones. Issues of size, corporate structure, earnings, liabilities and diversification are more likely to be comparable.

Limited use of this technique might be helpful if traded securities relatively similar to the subject business interest can be identified quickly. Less than full employment of the technique runs a greater risk of distortion, and thus must be used only with extreme care. The procedure is similar to the use of short form valuation techniques for real property.[8]

This technique is sometimes inapplicable: for example, where the subject business interest is highly diversified. In this situation, it is unlikely that reasonable comparables can be identified unless the diversified divisions are separable for valuation purposes.

The I.R.S. has identified several common errors in the use of comparative analysis for valuation purposes:[9]

1. Careless selection of comparables

---

[5] Schreier & Joy, *Judicial Valuation of "Close" Corporation Stock: Alice in Wonderland Revisited,* 31 Okla. L. Rev. 863-64 (1978).

[6] *See* I.R.S. App. Off., 12-1 to -22.

[7] *See* I.R.S. App. Off., 12-22.

[8] *See* **§5.4** Short Form Valuation Techniques for Real Property.

[9] I.R.S. App. Off., 12-1 to -21.

2. Lack of comparability in growth rate
3. Noncomparable capital structure
4. Size differentials between the comparables.

Generally, the I.R.S. recognizes the difficulty of the use of this method when it indicates that judgment must be carefully exercised concerning its use.

Once one or more comparable traded securities are identified, numerous comparisons may be made between the traded and untraded business interest. The following is a nonexclusive list of some of the factors you may use in such a comparison:[10]

1. Price/earnings ratios
2. Price/dividend ratios
3. Price/book value ratios.

If a sufficiently comparable traded corporation has a price/earnings ratio of 6:1, then it would probably be valid to multiply the earnings of the nontraded business interest by six to arrive at the value of that business.[11] When three out of four factors in two comparable ratios are known, it is not difficult to determine the unknown factor.

In calculating the various ratios of the publicly traded securities, the information used to create the ratio should ordinarily be averaged. In other words, price per share, earnings, dividends, or book value of the traded securities should be averaged over a period of time (usually five years).[12] The following illustrates:

Illustration IV-10

Assumptions: Comparable Traded Security Data

Annual Averages Per Share	Market Price	Adjusted Earnings
19X1	42.00	10.50
19X2	30.00	4.50
19X3	37.00	7.50
19X4	40.00	8.00
19X5	35.00	8.40
Totals	184.00	38.90
Divide Totals by Number of Years of Data Used	÷5	÷5
Averaged Data on Comparable	36.80	7.78

[10] Schreier & Joy, *Judicial Valuation of "Close" Corporation Stock: Alice in Wonderland Revisited,* 31 Okla. L. Rev. 862 (1978).

[11] For other examples, *see* **§2.19** Capitalization of Income, Illustration II-10; **§4.4** Adjusted Book Value of the Business Interest.

[12] *See* **§4.36** Comprehensive Worksheet for Business Interest Valuation, Part IV. Comparative Security Analysis.

Illustration IV-10 *(Continued)*

Assumptions: Subject Business Interest Data

Annual Averages Per Share	Adjusted Earnings
19X1	7.50
19X2	6.75
19X3	8.00
19X4	5.45
19X5	9.80
Totals	37.50
Divide Total by Number of Years of Data Used	÷5
Averaged Data on Subject Business Interest	7.5

Calculation

Traded Security	Subject Business Interest

$$\frac{\text{Market Price Value}}{\text{Averaged Earnings}} = \frac{\text{VPS}}{\text{Averaged Earnings}}$$

$$\frac{36.80}{7.78} = \frac{\text{VPS}}{7.5}$$

$$\text{VPS} = \frac{36.80 \times 7.5}{7.78} = \frac{276}{7.78} = 35.48$$

The estimated comparable traded security per-share value for the subject business interest equals $35.00 (rounded). Similar calculations can be made with adjusted book value and dividend rate.

When multiple comparables are identified, the relevant information may be used in several ways. First, the relevant ratios may be calculated for each comparative security. Because of differences among the comparables, particular ratios of one or more of the comparables may be isolated for comparison to the nontraded business interest.[13] You must, however, be careful that distortion does not occur due to improper isolation.

A second technique, when comparative analysis is made, averages the relevant information and/or ratios for all of the comparables.[14] The averaged information or

[13] I.R.S. App. Off., 6-8 to -9.

[14] Schreier & Joy, *Judicial Valuation of "Close" Corporation Stock: Alice in Wonderland Revisited,* 31 Okla. L. Rev. 862 (1978).

ratios are then used to calculate the nontraded business interest's value. This technique has the advantage of smoothing out individual differences, but carries the risk of deemphasizing similarities.

The information gathered may also be used in combination with other valuation techniques. For example, the rate of return of the comparable traded security may be determinative or influential in determining the rate of capitalization under the capitalization of earnings technique.[15] The information may also be helpful in determining dividend-paying capacity.[16]

§4.18 —Charts for Comparative Analysis

Chart IV-4

STEPS TO COMPARATIVE SECURITY ANALYSIS

1. Determine the traded securities that are most comparable to the subject business interest considering:
- **(a)** Basic industry and economic statistics of the business involved[17]
- **(b)** Ratio analyses[18] and
- **(c)** Other financial analysis techniques.[19]

2. Using the most comparable traded securities, weigh the relative positions of the traded business interest with the subject business interest considering:
- **(a)** Risk (Creditor security)
- **(b)** Profitability and payout (Owner protection and return)
- **(c)** Performance (Asset utilization)
- **(d)** Growth and development (Future potential).

3. On a per-share basis, determine and adjust the applicable market measure ratios:
- **(a)** Price/earnings ratio
- **(b)** Price/dividend ratio
- **(c)** Price/adjusted book value ratio.

4. Calculate the estimated market value for the subject business interest, using the appropriate market measure ratios.[20]

The following Charts may be useful in making valuation determinations using comparative traded securities.

Chart IV-5 can be used to gather relevant industry and financial data concerning potential comparative traded securities. Any number of similar businesses may be compared: merely use additional charts. In addition, the data used may represent

---

[15] *See* **§4.5** Capitalization of the Business Interest's Earnings.

[16] *See* **§4.6** Dividends and Dividend Capacity of the Business Interest.

[17] *See* Chart IV-1.

[18] *See* Chart IV-2.

[19] *See* Chart IV-1.

[20] *See* Part IV Comparative Traded Security Analysis in **§4.36** Comprehensive Worksheet for Business Interest Valuation.

Chart IV-5

INITIAL COMPARABILITY ANALYSIS

Data for Single year/ / or Multiple years/ / # yrs./ /

	Comparable Traded Securities				
Comparable Factor	1	2	3	4	Subject Business Interest
Product or Service Line					
Size—Net Worth					
Facilities—Plant					
Marketing Area					
Competitive Position					
Diversification					
Profitability					
Capital Structure					
Growth Rate					
Working Capital					
Sales					
Gross Income					
Net Income					
Number of Employees					
Management Capabilities					
Price Per Share: Common Stock					
Preferred Stock					
Earnings Per Share Common Stock					
Preferred Stock					
Dividends Per Share Common Stock					
Preferred Stock					
(Adjusted) Book Value Per Share Common Stock					
Preferred Stock					

Chart IV-6

COMPARATIVE RATIO ANALYSIS

Data for Single year/ / or Multiple years/ / # yrs./ /

	Comparable Traded Securities				
Ratio Analysis	1	2	3	4	Subject Business Interest
Current Ratio					
Acid Test					
Net Worth to Total Liabilities					
Net Worth to Long Term Debt					
Net Worth to Fixed Assets					
Times Interest Earned					
Return on Total Assets					
Gross Margin Ratio					
Operating Profits to Sales					
Pretax Income to Sales					
Net Income to Sales					
Sales to Cash					
Sales to Accounts Receivable					
Sales to Inventories					
Sales to Working Capital					
Sales to Fixed Assets					
Sales to Total Assets					
Dividends to Net Income					

information for a single year (usually the latest) or for a multiple-year period such as the last five years.

Chart IV-6 contains additional comparable data dealing with financial ratios. It is usually preferable to use this chart after an initial screening is accomplished by way of Chart IV-3.[21] Ratio analysis is the most important process of comparability.

The ratios listed in Chart IV-7 under Market Ratio Analysis are, of course, applicable to the traded security for which there is a market price. This data from the most comparable traded securities or securities is used to calculate estimated market value for the nontraded subject business interest.

Chart IV-7
MARKET MEASURE RATIOS

Market Ratio Analysis	1	2	3	4	Composite or Average Figures
Price/Earnings Ratio					
Dividend/Price Ratio—Common					
Dividend/Price Ratio—Preferred					
Price/(Adjusted) Book Value Ratio					

There is an obvious overlap between the valuation of traded securities and the valuation of nontraded securities or business interests. Consequently, it is sometimes argued that traded securities should get the same in depth analysis as nontraded securities receive. The degree of success for this argument is low. Market price is king and, with only a few recognized exceptions, will reign over intrinsic value.

Although the market price will not be determinative when valuing nontraded securities, there are situations where market price will clearly be a significant influence on the valuation determination. Examples of such situations include: when many similar businesses are actively traded and the securities of the one in question could be too; and, when there is a market for such businesses by way of merger, acquisition, etc.

The position of the I.R.S. concerning sales prices for nontraded business interests is relatively clear. Because market price does not conclusively equal market value, the Service takes the position that the prices received from sales of stocks are merely one of many factors to determine and weigh in making evaluation decisions.

Within the above limitation, the prices you obtained from actual sales of the business interest or security may be a strong indication of fair market value. Although not rejected totally as a valuation factor, sales between family members, and particularly

21 *See* §**4.14** Ratios and Other Tools of Financial Analysis (including Chart IV-2).

sales of minority interests by the majority interest owner to family members or close business associates, will be put under close scrutiny.[22]

§4.19 Weighting of Valuation Factors

Despite the I.R.S.'s admonition against averaging of factors, several cases have recognized the advantages of attributing varying weight to the several relevant valuation factors. The typical valuation factors in such a weighting process include adjusted book value, earning capacity, and dividend capacity. The basic approach is to determine the value of the business interest using each of the relevant factors separately. The values of each of these factors then are weighted by percentage. The sum of the weighted factors equal the business interest's market value. The amount of weight given each factor varies from case to case.[23] Some writers contend that this is the best judicial approach to valuation.[24] The following example shows how this process works:

Illustration IV-11

Valuation Method	Valuation		Percentage of Segment		Total
Book Value	$100,000	×	20%	=	$20,000
Earnings	150,000	×	50%	=	75,000
Dividends	90,000	×	30%	=	27,000
Total Weighted Estimated Market Value			100%	=	$122,000

Several features of this approach deserve mention. First, courts have not unanimously adopted the technique. In fact, only three decisions have primarily relied upon it.[25] This means that taxpayers are not going to be able to rely upon its analysis alone, and will have to be prepared to justify valuation on a variety of bases. Second, this technique resembles that developed by state courts for dissenting shareholder buy-out situations;[26] before using such a technique, it would be wise to peruse the cases concerned with that valuation issue.

---

22 Rev. Rul. 59-60, §4.02(g), 1959-1 C.B. 237. See **§2.15** Replacement and Reproduction Costs.

23 *See generally* **§2.27** Weighting of Valuation Techniques.

24 Schreier & Joy, *Judicial Valuation of "Close" Corporation Stock: Alice in Wonderland Revisited,* 31 Okla. L. Rev. 882-85 (1978).

25 Righter v. United States, 439 F.2d 1204 (Ct. Cl. 1971); Central Trust Co. v. United States, 305 F.2d 393 (Ct. Cl. 1962); Bader v. United States, 172 F. Supp. 833 (S.D. Ill. 1959).

26 *See* **§3.14** Alternative Valuation Techniques for Traded Securities.

DISCOUNTS AND PREMIUMS

§4.20 Discounts and Premiums in General

In the literature dealing with the valuation of close corporations and other nontraded business interests, the application and determination of certain discounts or premiums are significant topics. More specifically, the most important discounts apply if there is:

1. A lack of marketability
2. A minority interest
3. The loss of a key person.

The one premium commonly encountered that may have to be added to the normal market value due to the ownership of a majority interest or effective control of the business by the relevant person or estate. One or more of these valuation adjustments are involved in almost every situation where a nontraded business is being valued.[27]

It is important to emphasize, however, that although the issue is frequently raised and litigated, neither the I.R.S. nor the courts have established any firm procedures or guidelines for determining the proper valuation adjustments. The lack of firm and settled rules means that valuators have a great deal of discretion. Even expert appraisers will almost always disagree on the precise value of a discount or premium.

§4.21 Determination of Minority or Majority Interests

The issue of whether an interest represents a minority or a majority may become very difficult when close corporations are involved, and when majority interest owners create minority interests by gifts of stock to one or more persons. According to the I.R.S., control of a close corporation interest may exist either in actuality or in effect.[28]

Actual control presumably means that the owner owns or controls a sufficient percentage of the corporation to control its operations (including liquidation). Typically, the question of actual control is merely a mathematical calculation: anything more than 50 percent of the voting shares of the corporation. Occasionally, state law or private contract requires a greater percentage: for example, to force the liquidation of a close corporation.[29]

The question of control "in effect" is one of fact, and would have to be determined on a case-by-case basis. One important factor is the number of other minority owners. The more there are, the more important a substantial minority interest becomes for

---

[27] *See* **§4.36** Comprehensive Worksheet for Business Interest Valuation.

[28] Rev. Rul. 59-60, §4.02(g), 1959-1 C.B. 237.

[29] Krahmer & Henderer, *Valuation of Shares of Closely Held Corporations,* 221 T.M. A-52 (1978).

purposes of determining control. For example, a person with a 30 percent interest could effectively control a business if no one else owned more than one percent. Relevant to any determination of de facto control would be evidence of the exercise of such a power by the minority interest owner. It follows that if an interest is not a controlling interest in actuality or in effect, it is a minority interest.

When estate tax values have been involved, the courts have ordinarily employed the mathematical test.[30] The estate is considered to control a minority interest if it is found to hold 50 percent or less of the voting stock being valued, and a majority interest if it controls more than 50 percent.

Several cases have approved discounts even if the taxpayer owns 50 percent of the business interest.[31] In the *Obermer* case,[32] the husband-donor and the wife each owned 50 percent of the business. In the *Estate of Lee* case,[33] the decedent wife's and her husband owned 80 percent of common stock and 100 percent of the preferred stock as community property.[34]

Interests that have been donated in contemplation of death or within three years of death, and thus are considered part of the gross estate under I.R.C. §2035, and all of the business interest owned by decedent at the time of his death and included under I.R.C. §2033 are treated as under the estate's control. They must be treated as one block to determine whether the decedent's interest in the business constitutes a minority or majority interest.[35] Whether this blocking technique is also applicable to other interests that become part of a decedent's gross estate (including transfers with retained life estates under I.R.C. §2036, transfers taking effect at death under I.R.C. §2037, revocable transfers under I.R.C. §2038, joint interests under I.R.C. §2040 and powers of appointment under I.R.C. §2041) has not been specifically determined by the I.R.S. One could reasonably expect that the I.R.S. will contend that all interests that become a part of the gross estate, no matter for what reason, should be blocked for minority or majority determination purposes.

The issues get more complex when gifts of minority or majority interests are involved. Much of the confusion in this area derives from the failure to treat gift tax valuation of assets consistently from the standpoint of the transferor and not the transferee. The federal gift tax is a transfer tax on the donor, not an inheritance tax on the transferee (although the tax may have to be paid by the transferee if the transferor does not pay it). Consequently, valuations of gifts should be treated solely from the standpoint of the value of the gift in the transferor's hands.[36] If this approach

---

30 *Id.* at A-57 to -58.

31 Obermer v. United States, 238 F. Supp. 29 (D. Hawaii 1964) (33% discount); Estate of W. Lee, 33 T.C. 1064 (1960) (10-15% discount); *see also* Estate of Bright v. United States, 658 F.2d 999 (5th Cir. 1981).

32 Obermer v. United States, 238 F. Supp. 29 (D. Hawaii 1964).

33 Estate of W. Lee, 33 T.C. 1064 (1960).

34 *See* Treanor & Johnson, *Valuation of Community Property Minority Interests Reflect Judicial Inconsistancies,* 52 J. Tax'n 356 (1980); Smith, *Court Decisions Now Recognize Valuation Discounts for Community Property Interests,* 53 J. Tax'n 28 (1980).

35 Rev. Rul. 79-7, 1979-1 C.B. 294.

36 Butala, *Valuation of Closely Held Corporations,* 7 U. Miami Inst. Est. Plan. ¶73.1407, 14-20 (1978).

were adopted, there would be much less confusion and debate with regard to the value of minority interests for gift tax purposes.

If anyone is to be blamed, it might be the I.R.S., which successfully contended that several contemporaneous gifts of a traded security could not be aggregated to take a blockage discount, because each gift must be valued separately.[37] When the I.R.S. found itself working the other side of the street, the Tax Court was not very sympathetic.[38] The facts of *Estate of Heppenstall*[39] are that the taxpayer held a majority interest before the gifts were made. The taxpayer then made several simultaneous gifts to several people. After these gifts, the taxpayer no longer held a majority interest; no donee held a majority interest, and even the aggregated ownership of the donees did not equal a majority interest. Citing the *Phipps* case,[40] the Tax Court held that each gift was entitled to a minority interest discount.

From a policy standpoint, both the *Phipps* and *Heppenstall* cases are in error; the value of gifts should have been analyzed from the transferor's standpoint, not the transferee's. In *Phipps,* the taxpayer should have been entitled to the blockage discount, because the hypothetical market value of those traded shares at the time of the simultaneous gifts should reflect the reduction in price that would be necessary to market such a large block of stocks. The fact that each individual gift would not cause a blockage problem is irrelevant. If an attempt was made to market all of the shares at the same time, the market would treat them as a block and not individually. By the same token, the taxpayer in the *Heppenstall* case should not have received a minority discount. Because the taxpayer in *Heppenstall* held a majority interest at the time of the gift, the transferor could have marketed those shares as a majority interest. The transferor created minority interests by a voluntary act: this should not entitle him to a discount for gift tax purposes.[41]

The courts have not yet accepted the above argument. They continue to determine minority and majority interest by the status of the transferee. Subsequent cases have either affirmed or compounded the problem. For example, in *Whittemore v. Fitzpatrick,*[42] a federal district court in Connecticut expressly held that several gifts, which separately equaled minority interests but which in aggregate equaled a majority interest, were to be treated as three separate gifts of minority interests.

---

37 *See* **§3.6**—Determination of the Blockage Discount; L. Phipps, 43 B.T.A. 1010 (1941), *aff'd,* 127 F.2d 214 (10th Cir. 1941), *cert. denied,* 317 U.S. 645 (1942).

38 Estate of C. Heppenstall, 18 T.C.M. (P-H) ¶49,034 (1949); *cf.* Clark v. United States, 36 A.F.T.R. 2d ¶75-6417 (E.D.N.C. 1975).

39 Estate of C. Heppenstall, 18 T.C.M. (P-H) ¶49,034 (1949).

40 L. Phipps, 43 B.T.A. 1010 (1941), *aff'd,* 127 F.2d 214 (10th Cir. 1941), *cert. denied,* 317 U.S. 645 (1942).

41 *See* Krahmer & Henderer, *Valuation of Shares of Closely Held Corporations,* 221 T.M. A-58 (1978); Butala, *Valuation of Closely Held Corporations,* 7 U. Miami Inst. Est. Plan. ¶73.1407, 14-20 (1978).

42 Whittemore v. Fitzpatrick, 127 F. Supp. 710 (D. Conn. 1954).

§4.22 —Taking Advantage of the Separate Gift Rule

Significant tax savings can be achieved when nonmajority gifts from majority owners are treated as gifts of minority interests subject to a minority interest discount. The basic scheme is to make periodic *inter vivos* gifts of nonmajority interests in a nontraded business interest to several donees. Each gift will be treated separately and each gift will be entitled to a minority interest discount. Fully carried out, the scheme contemplates gifts of the business interest to continue until the donor no longer owns a majority interest. At this point no single person or entity owns a majority interest. All interests are entitled to a minority interest discount. When the donor dies, the retained minority interest in the estate will be able to take a minority interest discount from its estate tax valuation.

The practical effect of this technique is to change a majority interest, which might be subject to a premium valuation, to a minority interest which could be entitled to a substantial minority interest discount. In the estate planning profession, this technique has been referred to as the "Disappearing Wealth Syndrome," and has been persuasively criticized from a tax policy standpoint.[43]

Several disadvantages of this scheme deserve mention:

1. The owner loses control of the interest if gifts cause the retained interests to fall below control percentages
2. The estate may lose the redemption and tax postponement elections[44]
3. The I.R.S. may question the scheme.

The I.R.S.' response is a peripheral attack on this tax avoidance technique. The consequences are that the decisions have gone from bad to worse. An estate tax case and an income tax case imply that nonmajority transfers to one who had, or will have because of the transfer, a majority interest, may be valued for tax purposes at a higher value than comparable gifts to persons who do not and will not have control.[45] Except for the few dollars in taxes collected, there is little justification for imposing estate, gift, or income taxes on transfers on the basis of the transferred assets' intrinsic value to the transferee.

A more direct attack on the disappearing wealth syndrome is to argue that gifts to family members should be aggregated on a basis similar to family attribution rules. Although this argument has been successful in at least two cases, the facts in both of the cases were particularly favorable to the I.R.S.[46] In both cases there was clear evidence that, although only minority interests were donated, it was known and intend-

[43] *See* Fellows & Painter, *Valuing Close Corporations for Federal Wealth Transfer Taxes: A Statutory Solution to the Disappearing Wealth Syndrome,* 30 Stan. L. Rev. 895 (1978).

[44] *See* **§1.8** Estate Tax Considerations.

[45] Slimp's Estate, 48 A.F.T.R. 1572 (W.D. Tex. 1954); R. Turner, 23 T.C.M. (P-H) ¶54,142 (1954), *aff'd.,* 343 F.2d 150 (4th Cir. 1955)(Income Tax).

[46] Blanchard v. United States, 291 F. Supp. 348 (S.D. Iowa 1968); Driver v. United States, 38 A.F.T.R.2d ¶76-6315 (W.D. Wis. 1976).

ed that majority control would be exercised or available. Notwithstanding, these two decisions serve as a clear warning against abuse of this estate planning technique. This is particularly true where control of a business interest has not actually been fragmented but, in fact or practically speaking, has merely been shifted. The I.R.S. has now stated that unless "there is evidence of family discord or other factors indicating that the family would not act as a unit in controlling the corporation," minority discounts will not be allowed "with respect to transfers of shares of stock among family members where, at the time of the transfer, control (either majority voting control or de facto control) of the corporation exists in the family."[47]

The aggregation or family attribution rule should not be automatically extended to all family business interests, however.[48] The theory that family members will normally act in concert definitely has its limitations. Even among close families, many financial considerations will cause the minority family owners to express and exercise different motivations in the operations of the business interest. Common examples include differences in their income tax situation, capital gain or loss situation, and general financial and personal commitment to the business. The aggregation and family attribution rule should be limited to the situations indicated in the two cases recognizing it. This rule requires that the court find an intent, either actual or implied, that control was not actually being dispersed. When so applied, the attribution and aggregation concepts will not prove unfair to unprotected minority interests.

A recent federal circuit court decision agrees with this conclusion.[49] The court held that for estate tax valuation purposes "family attribution should not apply to lump a decedent's stock with that of related parties."[50] In addition, the court held that the attribution concept itself is inconsistent with the willing buyer-seller valuation rule in the Regulations.[51]

§4.23 Minority Interest Discount

A well-recognized but still controversial discount is the discount for minority interests in a nontraded business interest. The controversy centers around two issues: the applicability of the discount and its amount or value. Although the I.R.S. specifically recognizes a discount for a fractional minority interest, it also states that such a discount is not automatic. Considering the amount of litigation on the issue, it is willing to fight over it.[52]

Although both the minority interest discount and the lack of marketability discount stem from the fact that such interests are difficult to sell at prices obtainable for comparable traded interests, the lack of marketability discount is more pervasive. It applies to all business interests that are not actively traded.

---

47 Rev. Rul. 81-253, 1981-43 I.R.B. 10.

48 *But see* Letter Rul. 8010017.

49 Estate of Bright v. United States, 658 F.2d 999 (5th Cir. 1981).

50 *Id.* at 1005.

51 *Id.; see* Reg. §20.2031-1(b).

52 Schreier & Joy, *Judicial Valuation of "Close" Corporation Stock: Alice in Wonderland Revisited,* 31 Okla. L. Rev. 864 n.46 (1978).

The minority interest discount, however, only applies to noncontrolling interests in businesses. For example, a 15 percent discount was allowed against the normal value of a limited partnership in a real estate holding company on this ground.[53] A minority interest in a nontraded business is usually much more difficult to sell than a majority interest in the same business. Often, the only true potential purchasers may be other owners in the business. Consequently, if properly analyzed, a minority interest discount should be separate from and in addition to the lack of marketability discount.[54] As indicated, this has not always been recognized by the parties or courts.[55] The financial disabilities of a minority interest in a nontraded business interest are that the minority interest owner may be powerless to:

1. Select directors
2. Select officers
3. Determine officers' salaries
4. Determine dividends
5. Force liquidation or
6. Require dissenter's rights appraisal procedures.

If all of the above disabilities are present, and if there is an identifiable majority owner or block of owners who absorb the earnings as salaries and pay no dividends, and who do not intend to go public, the minority interest's value is low. In such a situation, a minority discount of 90 percent or more would be in order.[56] Despite the I.R.S.'s position on this matter, it is little consolation that majority interests owe a fiduciary obligation to minority interests.[57] From a legal, economic and practical standpoint, this obligation is of little value.[58]

However, if by stockholder agreement or otherwise, the minority interest owner discards one or more of the above disabilities and becomes more than a mere nuisance to the controlling interest, then clearly the discount must be less. The discount would depend upon the circumstances. At the other end of the spectrum where, by agreement or other authority, significant powers are given to minority interest owners, a minority interest discount may not be justified at all.

Begrudgingly, the I.R.S. has recognized that a minority interest may be entitled to a discount from normal value.[59] Until recently, a discount from five to 15 percent was the maximum that the I.R.S. would recognize. Prodded probably by some recent court decisions, the I.R.S. has begun to recognize larger discounts, in the 20 to 25 percent range.[60]

---

[53] Estate of B. Bischoff, 69 T.C. 32 (1977).

[54] Whittemore v. Fitzpatrick, 127 F. Supp. 710 (D. Conn. 1954); Estate of T. Folks, 51 T.C.M. (P-H) ¶82,043 (1982).

[55] *See* Lyons & Whitman, *Valuing Closely Held Corporations and Publicly Traded Securities with Limited Marketability: Approaches to Allowable Discounts From Gross Values,* 33 Bus. Law. 2217-18 (1978).

[56] *Id.*, at 2218.

[57] *See* I.R.S. App. Off., 11-4.

[58] H. O'Neal, Close Corporations Law and Practice, §3.03, 59-62 (2d ed. 1971).

[59] I.R.S. Tax Law Course, 24-21.

[60] Coolidge, *Fixing Value of Minority Interest in a Business: Actual Sales Suggest Discount As High As 70%,* 2 Est. Plan. 138 (1975).

If a minority interest is in fact involved, in most cases the I.R.S. will accept a 20 percent discount without argument. This I.R.S. action is probably a counterattack against recent literature advocating much larger discounts, ranging from 50 to 90 percent. Although a high discount may be justifiable and sustainable, one should expect to fight "every inch of the way" in order to prevail. Although the I.R.S. recognized a combined discount for lack of marketability and a minority interest of 50 percent in a 1975 case,[61] claimed discounts above 20 percent will receive very close scrutiny on any gift or estate tax return.

Recent commentary on the discount for minority interest has urged a much higher discount than has ordinarily been recognized in the past, on the grounds that minority interests have been overvalued.[62] It is contended that such interests in fact have very little marketability; a substantial discount would have to be recognized in order to market such an asset.

As proof of the argument, reference has been made to published findings of the discounts at which certain investment companies have purchased "letter stock."[63] Using a thirty-case sampling, the data indicates that the discount on most letter stock exceeds the typical 20 to 25 percent discount the I.R.S. allows for minority interests.[64] From these cases, several interesting statistics are apparent. The average discount is 36.1 percent; 56 percent of the discounts ranged from 30 to 78 percent; and 56 percent of the discounts ranged from 20 to 49.9 percent.

The status of letter stock is somewhat like the status of a minority interest in a business interest. They both suffer from a restriction on marketability. The difference is that letter stock is nonmarketable because of a restriction on the access to a recognized market, whereas the minority interest is nonmarketable because of a lack of control over the business. Notwithstanding, a thoroughly prepared appraisal using the letter stock sample as a reference should be able to justify a discount in the 35 percent range.

§4.24 Record of Courts on Allowing Discounts for Minority Interest

Chart IV-8 reveals and analyzes court holdings concerning minority discounts between 1920-75. Chart IV-9 updates the information to mid-1982.

---

61 Estate of E. Kirkpatrick, 44 T.C.M. (P-H) ¶75,344 (1975).

62 *See* Arneson, *Minority Discounts Beyond Fifty Percent Can Be Supported,* 59 Taxes—The Tax Magazine 97 (1981); Moroney, *Most Courts Overvalue Closely Held Stocks,* 51 Taxes—The Tax Magazine 144 (1973); Gelman, *An Economist-Financial Analyst's Approach to Valuing Stock of a Closely-Held Company,* 36 J. Tax'n. 353 (1972).

63 *See* **§3.8** Restricted and Control Securities Discount.

64 Coolidge, *Fixing Value of Minority Interest in a Business: Actual Sales Suggest Discount As High as 70%,* 2 Est. Plan. 139-41 (1975).

Chart IV-8[a]

RECORD OF COURTS ON ALLOWING DISCOUNT FOR MINORITY INTEREST

(Dollar amounts are in thousands except when stated per share)

Case	Tax and Asset Being Valued	Percentage of Ownership	Taxpayer	Valuation I.R.S.	Court	Percentage Discount
1920-1929						
Ray Consolidated Copper Co., 268 U.S. 373 (1925)	Excise—Corp. Stock	100%	\$34,803	\$103,905	\$103,905	None
Cook, 2 BTA 126 (1925)	Estate—Interest in bus. trust	9/14ths	\$100	\$210	\$101	None
Estate of Barclay, 2 BTA 696 (1925)	Estate—Undivided interest in real estate	½	\$211	\$234	\$234	None
Estate of Baer, 3 BTA 881 (1925-26)	Estate—6 parcels realty; corp. stock	100%	\$419	\$610	\$610	None
Couzzens, 11 BTA 1040 (1928)	Income—Ford Motor Co. Stock	10.9%	\$9,849/sh	\$3,548/sh	\$10,000/sh	None
Estate of Andrews, 13 BTA 651 (1928)	Estate—Undivided interest realty	½	\$64	\$95	\$88	Not clear
Estate of Sanderson, 16 BTA 1022 (1929)	Income-Partnership interest	½	\$125	None	None	None
1930-1939						
Estate of McColgan, 10 BTA 958 (1930)	Estate—realty	¼	\$165	\$207	\$207	None
Estate of Pitts, 19 BTA 288 (1930)	Estate—Partnership	32½%	\$38	\$51	\$38	None
Laird, 29 BTA 196; 38 BTA 926 (1933)	Estate—Corp. Stocks	Less than 7% in each	C.S. \$800/sh DRL \$781/sh GL \$340/sh	\$1,761/sh \$15,067/sh \$397/sh	\$1,000/sh \$8,500/sh \$397/sh	None stated

Chart IV-8 (*Continued*)

Case	Tax and Asset Being Valued	Percentage of Ownership	Taxpayer	Valuation I.R.S.	Court	Percentage Discount
Estate of Staunton, 29 BTA 376 (1933-34)	Estate—Stock and land	18% ¼	$100/sh $20/Front Ft.	$857/sh $73/Fr. Ft.	$150/sh $20/Fr. Ft.	None stated
Estate of Stewart, 31 BTA 201 (1934)	Estate—Stock; Land parcels	Not stated 3/10 & 1/3	$127/sh 40% discount	$191/sh No disc.	$165/sh 15% disc.	14% 15%
Cravens, 10 F. Supp. 94 (DC Cal., 1935)	Income—Stock in Realty Co.	20%	No disc.	Disc.	Disc.	Not clear
Brown, DC Kans., 7/30/35	Estate—Stock in Realty Co.	33%	Not stated	$71	$29	None
The George D. Harter Bank, Ex'r, 38 BTA 387 (1938)	Estate—Stock in Hoover Co.	4% Pfd. 8% Com.	$50/sh $5/sh	$95/sh $15/sh	$83/sh $9/sh	Not stated
Weber, 101 F.2d 62 (CA-2, 1938)	Estate—Stock in Realty Co.	20.7%	$100/sh	$183/sh	$183/sh	Not stated
Second Nat'l Bank & Trust Co., 39 BTA 1242 (1939)	Estate—Corp. Stock	HDC 5% WBC 10% DSC—	$75/sh $100/sh No value	$671/sh $1,002/sh $66/sh	$140/sh $350/sh No value	33% 25% NA
1940-1949						
Estate of Gregory, 41 BTA 1340 (1940)	Estate—interest in leased fee & realty	35/90 35/90	$125 $43	$194 $49	$194 $49	15% 15%
Estate of Vail, 42 BTA 1478 (1940)	Estate—Pf'd units in ranch	100% Pf'd but not control	$53/unit	$152/unit	$53/unit	Not stated
Hooper, 41 BTA 114 (1940)	Estate—Mfg. Co.	35%	$10-20/sh	$100/sh	$45/sh	Not stated
Estate of Kaffie, 44 BTA 843 (1941)	Estate—P'ship	½	$97	$171	$97	None
Forbes, 38 F. Supp. 62 (DC Mass., 1941)	Estate—Stock in Realty Co.	21%	No value	$7/sh	$6/sh	15%

Estate of Brittingham, 46 BTA 1278 (1942)	Estate—Stock	19.1%	$423/sh	$625/sh	$625/sh	6%
Estate of Johnson, TCM, 6/2/43	Estate—interest in realty	½	$133	$225	$150	Not stated
Blackard, 62 F. Supp. 234 (DC Okla., 1944)	Estate—Stock in family corp.	23½%		Book value	25% disc.	25% discount
Estate of Henry, 4 TC 423 (1944)	Estate—parcels of real estate	1/3	$111	$139	$125	11%
Campanari, 5 TC 488 (1945)	Estate—parcels of realty	1/3	$548 less 12½%	$569	$548	12½%
Richardson, 151 F.2d 102 (CA-2, 1945)	Gift—Stock in family corp.	5.1%	Not stated	$96/sh	$96/sh	None
Estate of Cruikshank, 9 TC 162 (1947)	Estate—Stock in family corp.	26.31%	$211/sh	$225/sh	$225/sh	None
Pabst, TCM, 10/31/47	Gift—Stock in PHC	2¼%	$152/sh	$266/sh	$212/sh	None stated
Estate of Schroeder, 13 TC 259 (1949)	Estate—Stock in corp.	7½%	$20/sh	$42/sh	$25/sh	None stated
1950-1959						
Estate of Helmers, TCM, 6/20/50	Estate—Stock in family corp.	17 1/3%	$500/sh	$1,000/sh	$900/sh	None stated
Estate of Smith, TCM, 10/17/50	Estate—Stock in family corp.	21.94%	$3,500/sh	$7,318/sh	$5,700/sh	Not stated
Bishop Trust Co., Ltd., Adm'r., DC Haw., 4/28/50	Estate—Stock in family corp.	12.4%	$285/sh	$485/sh	$323/sh	Not clear
Goss, 97 F. Supp. 765 (DC Conn., 1951)	Estate—Stock in family corp.	14%	$60/sh	$106/sh	$60/sh	43%
Estate of Garrett, TCM, 10/7/53	Estate—Stock in family corp.	12½%	$60/sh	$286/sh	$286/sh	None
		12½%	$49/sh	$82/sh	$56/sh	Not stated
Estate of Herter, TCM, 3/31/54	Estate—interest in realty	29%	$191	$224	$191	15%
Whittemore, 127 F. Supp. 710 (DC Conn., 1954)	Gift—Three 23.8% blocks stock in family corp.	71.4%	$1,000/sh	$3,228/sh	$1,056/sh	50% + 16%

Chart IV-8 (*Continued*)

Case	Tax and Asset Being Valued	Percentage of Ownership	Taxpayer	Valuation I.R.S.	Court	Percentage Discount
Estate of McGinn, DC Ore., 12/31/54	Estate—interest in business trust	5/24	$109	$160	$109	20%
Bartram, 157 F. Supp. 757 (DC Conn., 1957)	Gift—Stock in family corp.	1.8%	$114/sh	$163/sh	$130/sh	20%
Bader, 172 F. Supp. 833 (DC Ill., 1959)	Income—Stock in auto agency	Minority	$416/sh	$1,250/sh	$585/sh	10%
Tishman, 207 F. Supp. 830 (DC Va., 1959)	Estate—interest in real estate	½	$34	$40	$34	15%
1960-1969						
Blackburn, DC Ind., 7/20/60	Estate—interest in realty	¼	$25	$30	$18	None
Dean, TCM 1960-54	Gift—Stock in family corp.	11%	$425/sh	$884/sh	$640/sh	20%
Estate of Tompkins, TCM 1961-338	Estate—Stock in family corp.	28.6%	$1,920/sh	$8,000/sh	$5,500/sh	Not stated
Worthen, 192 F. Supp. 727 (DC Mass., 1961)	Estate—Stock in family corp.	18.6%	$100/sh	$175/sh	$104/sh	15%
Central Trust Co., 305 F.2d 393 (Ct. Cls., 1962)	Gift—Two blocks stock in family corp.	27½%	$8/sh	$24/sh	$16/sh	15-20%
Drybrough, 208 F. Supp. 279 (DC Ky., 1962)	Gift—Stock of 4 corps. & real estate	40% 40%	$109 $24	$462 $64	$140 $30	35% 15%
Estate of Leyman, 40 TC 100 (1963)	Estate—Stock in family corp.	18% Pf'd 12.5% Com.	$195-536/sh	$850-700/sh	$630/sh	26%

Messing, 48 TC 502 (1967)	Gift—Stock in close corp.	3%	$10/sh	$30/sh	$13/sh	Not stated
Estate of Katz, TCM 1698-171	Estate—Stock in ad agency	19.1%	$290/sh	$800/sh	$300/sh	Not clear
Estate of Maxcy, TCM 1969-158 1970-1975	Estate—Stock in family corp.	14%	15% & 26% discs.	Zero & 25% discs.	15% & 26% discs.	15% & 26%
Estate of Dooly, TCM 1972-164	Estate—Stock in two ranch corps.	Both minority	$4/sh $5/sh	$20/sh $23/sh	Under $4/sh $5/sh	Not stated
Hicks, 335 F. Supp. 474 (DC Colo., 1971)	Estate—Stock in two corps.	52% 49%	$14/sh $126/sh	$37-42/sh $450-306/sh	$42/sh $306/sh	None None
Estate of Hayes, TCM 1973-236	Estate—Stock in family corp.	15.6%	25% disc.	20% disc.	25% disc.	25%
Estate of Cotchett, TCM 1974-31	Estate—Stock in family corp.	20.2%	$66-50/sh.	$80/sh	$66/sh	34%
Estate of Pinkerton, TCM 1974-71	Estate—Stock in 4 newspapers	Minority interests	$4,394/sh $169/sh $1,714/sh $3,519/sh	$9,500/sh $900/sh $3,500/sh $8,000/sh	$5,400/sh $400/sh $2,200/sh $4,500/sh	Not stated
Estate of Thalheimer, TCM 1974-203	Estate—Stock in closely held co.	Less than 10%	44-46% discs.	14-19% discs.	34-37% discs.	34-37%
Bollenbach, TCM 1974-270	Gift—Stock in family co.	Minority interests	$131-170/sh	$450-1,400/sh	$300-600/sh	15-20%
Gallun, TCM 1974-284	Gift—Stock in family co.	9%	$396/sh	$661/sh	$520/sh	55%
Estate of Heckscher, 63 TC 485 (1974)	Estate—Stock in family co.	2%	$60/sh	$113/sh	$100/sh	48%

[a] Reproduced from Thomas W. Dant, Courts Increasing Amount of Discount for a Minority Interest in a Business, 43 The Journal of Taxation 104, at pp. 106-08 by permission from The Journal of Taxation published by Warren, Gorham and Lamont, Inc., 1633 Broadway, New York, N.Y. 10019. Copyright © 1975, Tax Research Group.

Chart IV-9

SUPPLEMENTAL RECORD OF COURTS ON ALLOWING DISCOUNT FOR MINORITY INTEREST

Case	Tax and Asset Being Valued	Percentage of Ownership	Taxpayer	Valuation I.R.S.	Court	Percentage Discount
Estate of Stoddard 44 T.C.M. (P-H) ¶75-207	Estate—stock in newspaper corp.	20%	$22/sh	$70/sh	$37	33 1/3% (combined with lack of marketability discount)
Estate of Kirkpatrick, 44 T.C.M. (P-H) ¶75,344	Estate—stock in closely held corps.	43%	$216/sh	$500/sh	$300/sh	Not stated
		6.5%	$171/sh	$650/sh	$250/sh	Not stated
Lagrew, 45 T.C.M. (P-H) ¶76,310	Income-stock of closely held land corp.	41%	Not Income	$5974/sh	$3545/sh	25%
Estate of Bischoff 69 T.C. 32 (1977).	Estate—limited partnership	10% and	$78,797	$86,000	$73,100	15%
		15%	$76,700	$125,000	$106,250	15%
Estate of Brown, 46 T.C.M. (P-H) ¶77,085	Estate—partnership in real estate	25%	$1,143,567	$1,983,373	$1,360,000	10%
Estate of Tully, 78-1 U.S.T.C. ¶13,228 (Ct. Cl. 1978)	Estate—stock of closely held construction corp.	50%	$1.00/sh	$280/sh	$164/sh	None

Koffler, 47 T.C.M. (P-H) ¶78,159	Gift-common stock in closely held corp.	Minority interests created	$1,200/sh	$2,000/sh	$1,250	30% (combined with lack of marketability discount)
Meijer, 48 T.C.M. (P-H) ¶79,344	Gift—stock of closely held corp.	Minority interests created	$44.50/sh $46/sh $38-40/sh	$72/sh $78/sh $78/sh	$49/sh $52/sh $47/sh	None stated
Estate of Grootemaat, 48 T.C.M. (P-H) ¶79,049	Estate—closely held real estate corp.	10%	$1,150/sh	$4,466/sh	$2,750/sh	25%
Maris, 49 T.C.M. (P-H) ¶80,444	Gift—closely held corp.	Minority interests created	$2,318/sh $2,318/sh	$7,745/sh $9,566/sh	$5,111/sh $5,149/sh	30% (combined with lack of marketability discount)
Estate of Folks, 51 T.C.M. (P-H) ¶80,043	Estate-stock in closely held investement company	16.5%	[Not given]			50%

§4.25 Majority Interest Premium

Most authorities and authority agree that majority ownership or control of a business interest may justify a premium valuation.[65] This opinion is not unanimous, however.[66] Agreement in principle has not led to agreement in practice. Two of the most significant problems that arise are what constitutes control and when is a premium appropriately added to a properly determined normal value.[67]

The sole fact that an owner of a nontraded business interest possesses control of that interest does not automatically justify the addition of a premium. If the techniques used to determine this normal value fully take into account the intrinsic value of the interest, a premium on that value would be unjustified and a duplication of the value determinators. When the normal value is based upon liquidation value, or even on the price for which minority interest could be sold, however, a premium should be added for the additional value purchasers would pay for a controlling interest.[68]

Generally, a premium for control is expressed as a percentage of the normal value of the business interest in question. Thus, this percentage of the normal value is then added to the normal value. There is no authority indicating whether the percentage of premium varies depending upon whether the ownership interest ranges from mere 50 plus 1 percent or minimum control, whichever is greater, to 100 percent ownership control.

Estate of J. Salsbury, cited above, demonstrates the relevance and application of the premium in an estate tax valuation situation. There were two classes of voting common stock in the corporation involved. Class A common stock had a par value of, and redemption right to, $1.00 per share and a six percent cumulative preferred dividend right. Class B common stock had no preference either on dividends or liquidation, but would receive a pro rata share of the remaining assets of the corporation on liquidation after all preferred classes were satisfied. Class B stock, in other words, received the growth value of the corporation.

The estate owned 372,152 shares of Class A stock, which represented 51.8 percent of the voting power of the corporation. With this voting interest, the owner could, by way of voting control, elect the entire board of directors, control the business affairs of the corporation, control the declaration of dividends, remove all corporate officers and fix their salaries. The normal value for these preferred stock shares was conceded by all to equal their $1.00 par value. The issue was the relevance of adding a premium for the voting power.

Significantly for our purposes, the *Salsbury* decision rejected several other contentions. It rejected a premium adjustment based on the ability of a majority owner to obtain excessive compensation, because such a premium is purely speculative. It also rejected a premium based on a percentage of the aggregate value of the Class B stock

---

[65] *E.g.,* Rev. Rul. 59-60, §4.02(g), 1959-1 C.B. 237; Butala, *Valuation of Closely Held Corporations,* 7 U. Miami Inst. Est. Plan ¶73.1407, 14-21 (1978).

[66] Arneson, *The Case for No Majority-Control Premium,* 59 Taxes—The Tax Magazine 190 (1981).

[67] Krahmer & Henderer, *Valuation of Shares of Closely Held Corporations,* 221 T.M. A-57 (1978).

[68] Estate of J. Salsbury, 44 T.C.M. (P-H) ¶75,333 (1975).

that was held by a particular class of minority shareholders. The court held that a premium is limited to the shares currently under consideration. Finally, it rejected, again as mere speculation, a premium based on the possibility that a hypothetical purchaser would be able to obtain additional earnings participation in a reorganization of the corporation by relinquishing voting control to the remaining owners.

In arriving at its determination, the decision selectively accepted the opinion of three expert appraisers. It held that a premium of 38.1 percent should be added to the normal value of the stock. This percentage came from one of the appraisers whose research showed that average premiums above normal market prices were being paid in a relevant year in connection with mergers and acquisitions involving majority stock interests. The *Salsbury* case is an excellent example of the importance of carefully and thoroughly prepared expert appraisals and testimony.

The basic concept behind this technique has been recognized by another source as well.[69] In a study of twenty-six original cash tender offers made for controlling interests in publicly traded corporations, the average cash premium above market price was 32.228 percent. As a starting point this percentage should be halved for nontraded business interests.

Although the *Salsbury* court did not reduce the premium percentage as suggested, the premium approved in that case should be considered to be the maximum for most situations. Even given a premium for a majority interest, the nontraded business interest should also receive some form of a marketability discount. Majority interests in traded securities are far more marketable than are those of nontraded business interests and would, consequently, deserve a higher premium.

The meager quantity of authority on this point indicates that when valuing a majority interest, you may need to consider a majority interest premium in the 16 to 38 percent range.

§4.26 Lack of Marketability Discount

The lack of marketability problem is inherent in the valuation of all business interests that are not actively traded on recognized markets. The poor marketability of nontraded business interests stems from several factors. First, most of these businesses are small family-owned and -run operations. Such businesses run great risk of failure; The greater the risk, the lower the value. Second, these interests lack liquidity. There is no large pool of potential buyers for these interests when they come on the market. The longer it takes to sell an asset, the lower the value will be as compared to more actively tradable assets. Such a business interest must be sold at a substantial discount in order to attract buyers, as recognized by court decisions.[70] The actual amount of the discount, of course, will vary from situation to situation.

Because this discount is frequently meshed with other relevant discounts, a separate

---

[69] Maher, *An Objective Measure for a Discount for a Minority Interest and a Premium for a Controlling Interest,* 57 Taxes—The Tax Magazine 451 (1979).

[70] Central Trust Co. v. United States, 305 F.2d 393 (Ct. Cl. 1962).

discount for lack of marketability is not always available. If, for example, a minority interest in a close corporation is valued, the clear tendency of the litigants and determinators is to lump any lack of marketability discount with the minority interest discount. In addition, the reduction in value for a restrictive resale agreement ordinarily includes consideration for the discount based on lack of marketability.[71] There is a strong argument, however, that these discounts are different and should be calculated separately.[72]

When the lack of marketability discount has not been integrated into the initial valuation process or considered a part of other relevant discounts, the amount to be deducted has frequently been set as the cost of a primary public offering or secondary offering.[73] These costs run from 2.3% to 19.3% for primary offerings, and from 3.4% to 12.7% for secondary offerings, all dependent upon the size of the offering. Primary offerings are the preferred technique; because most business interests involved here are small (i.e., $500,000 or less) and carry a very high risk, the discount under this approach might range as high as 20 percent.

The discount for lack of marketability could also be considered comparable to the discount required to attract mutual fund purchasers for restricted or control common stock.[74] The discounts, under this approach, are determined by comparing the mutual fund's costs for the restricted shares to the market value of the same company's unrestricted securities of the same class on the acquisition date. According to the underlying study made, the appropriate mean discount would equal 35 percent. This 35 percent discount, it is argued, would not include a justifiable additional discount due to the valuation of a minority interest. There is judicial authority for a discount of this magnitude.[75] However, others looking at the same data and study have concluded that the nonmarketability discount should range from 30 to 35 percent.[76] A recent discussion argues that, considering all of the relevant costs, the discount should start at 50 percent, subject to adjustment up or down.[77]

Although it is clear that most nontraded business interests qualify for a lack of marketability discount, it is not so clear what that discount should be. The range from 15 to 50 percent is not very precise. Because there is a broad range of possibilities, the importance of thorough and competent expert analysis increases. The party with the

---

71 Baltimore Nat'l Bank v. United States, 136 F. Supp. 642 (D. Md. 1955).

72 *See* Maher, *Discounts for Lack of Marketability for Closely Held Business Interests,* 54 Taxes—The Tax Magazine 571 (1976).

73 Butala, *Valuation of Closely Held Corporations,* 7 U. Miami Inst. Est. Plan ¶73.1406, 14-17 to -18 (1978).

74 Maher, *Discounts for Lack of Marketability for Closely Held Business Interests,* 54 Taxes—The Tax Magazine 565-71 (1976).

75 Estate of Pinkerton, 43 T.C.M. (P-H) ¶74,071 (1974).

76 Lyons & Whitman, *Valuing Closely Held Corporations and Publicly Traded Securities with Limited Marketability: Approaches to Allowable Discounts From Gross Values,* 33 Bus. Law. 2216 (1978).

77 Arneson, *Nonmarketability Discounts Should Exceed Fifty Percent,* 59 Taxes—The Tax Magazine 31 (1981).

best expert analysis will be victorious.[78] Between equals, courts will naturally have a tendency to split the difference between the contentions.[79]

§4.27 Loss of Key Manager/Owner Discount

Many small businesses are significantly dependent upon the ability, initiative and judgment of a single person. The loss, for whatever reason, of that person may have significant economic consequences to that business.[80] For example, such a loss may significantly affect the business' ability to earn money, to promote its product or service, or to obtain credit. Any one or more of these effects may harm the market value of the business. In line with this, the I.R.S. specifically recognizes that "the loss of the manager on the future expectancy of the business and the absence of management succession potential maladies are pertinent factors to be taken into consideration."[81]

Although it is clear that a discount is justified for the loss of a key person or central management figure, the amount of the discount is not calculable with any degree of exactitude.[82] It is another one of those nebulous, unscientific valuation factors, to be weighed with the others.

It has been contended that the true effect of a loss of a key man can be determined only some time after the loss. Unfortunately, for most valuation purposes, (e.g., income, gift and estate taxes) it is impossible to delay the determination for such post-loss data.

The most common mathematical method for calculating the key person loss discount is to determine a percentage discount from the normal value of the asset.[83] For example, if the key person loss discount is set at 10 percent and the otherwise appropriate market value of the business is \$100,000, the calculation is as follows:

$$\$100{,}000 - (\$100{,}000 \times .10) = \$100{,}000 - \$10{,}000 = \$90{,}000$$

Using this system, it has been estimated that a discount of from 10 to 15 percent may be appropriate for the loss of a key person in a business for which a competent successor manager may be obtained.[84] When a successor is not available, greater discounts (probably in the 20 to 30 percent range) should be taken. The extent of such discounts would depend upon the situation.

Another method used for recognizing the loss of a key person is to adjust either the expected rate of return or the capitalization factor.[85] This may have particular applica-

---

[78] *See* **§2.3** Significance of Appraisals and Expert Testimony.

[79] *See* **§1.4** How the Courts Look at Valuation.

[80] *See generally* Maher, *Application of Key Man Discount in the Valuation of Closely Held Businesses,* 55 Taxes—The Tax Magazine 377-80 (1977).

[81] Rev. Rul. 59-60, §4.02(B), 1959-1 C.B. 237.

[82] Newell v. Commissioner, 66 F.2d 102 (7th Cir. 1933); Estate of J. Huntsman, 66 T.C. 861 (1976), *acq.* 1977-1 C.B. 1.

[83] Estate of J. Huntsman, 66 T.C. 861 (1976), *acq.* 1977-1 C.B. 1.

[84] Lyons & Whitman, *Valuing Closely Held Corporations and Publicly Traded Securities with Limited Marketability: Approaches to Allowable Discounts From Gross Values,* 33 Bus. Law. 2221 (1978).

[85] *See* **§4.5** Capitalization of the Business Interest's Earnings.

bility where the rate of return, and/or the capitalization factor has been used to set the normal value for the business interest. This approach merely recognizes that the loss of a key person will raise the risk of the business. Consequently, the rate of return for a riskier business should be increased; at the same time, the capitalization multiplier factor should be reduced. For example, when a less risky business has a 10 percent rate of return and therefore a capitalization factor of ten, the riskier business will have a rate of return of 12.5 percent and a capitalization factor of eight.

When the normal value of the business has been determined by reference to adjusted book value, the discount can be used to adjust any goodwill premium added to the adjusted book value. If goodwill depends on the abilities of the key person, its premium value should be reduced (if not eliminated) by the loss of that person. In any case when the abilities and skills of the key person are important to the earning capacity of the business interest, any goodwill premium should be reduced by 20 to 30 percent.

There are some limitations on the use of the key person loss discount. You should not use it:[86]

1. Where the asset's value is set by liquidation value, liquidation value basically equals the lowest market value possible, and may not be reduced any further
2. When a private restrictive agreement discount has been taken because the agreement anticipates loss of a key person
3. When a minority discount is applicable because the key person ordinarily has control of the business.

On the other hand, you should be able to take the discount in combination with a lack of marketability discount.

§4.28 Miscellaneous Discounts

Several other discounts from ordinary value could be relevant, depending on the situation. For example, factors such as restricted financing capabilities, unaudited financial statements, or potentially high liability might justify a reduction in value. These factors, however, are probably preferably dealt with as a matter of risk determination or of the underlying asset's valuation.

The pyramid discount is another kind of discount applicable to a business interest that owns diversified assets.[87] It is supposed that such a business could be more difficult to sell. Even a majority interest has been accorded a discount under this approach.[88] Because it raises questions of marketability, the pyramid discount probably is seldom recognized separately, but is dealt with as part of the marketability discount.

A similar potential discount is the holding company discount, applicable when the

---

[86] *See* Lyons & Whitman, *Valuing Closely Held Corporations and Publicly Traded Securities with Limited Marketability: Approaches to Allowable Discounts From Gross Values,* 33 Bus. Law. 2221 n.32 (1978).

[87] F. Burke, Valuation and Valuation Planning For Closely Held Business 128 (1981); *see* Estate of G. Maxcy, 38 T.C.M. (P-H) ¶69,158 (1969).

[88] Estate of G. Maxcy, 38 T.C.M. (P-H) ¶69,158 (1969).

value of the underlying assets should be reduced because of the impairment caused by the insulating holding company.[89] This is only true for a minority interest in the holding company, and thus this discount is merely a special application of the minority discount concept.[90]

A variation on the holding company discount is the investment company discount. A recent case held that a discount of 40% from the net asset value was justified for an investment company under the circumstances of the case.[91] The factors considered in setting the amount of the discount included:

1. Illiquidity of assets
2. High demand notes payable
3. Significant contingent tax liabilities
4. Questionable significant notes receivable
5. Low interest rates on notes receivable
6. Below median net income on net asset value for investment companies
7. Loss of key person by death of decedent owner
8. The small relative size of the subject investment company to others.

No particular weight was given to any of these factors. The discount was based on the total effect of all of them. Significantly, the court agreed that the discount was separate from the lack of marketability discount.

Actually a discount of some degree may be justified for any reason that causes a business interest to be restricted in its resale.[92] For example, discounts have been recognized for such restrictions as a surviving spouses's homestead rights[93] and discovered criminal activity by agents of the business interest.[94]

PRIVATE RESTRICTIVE AGREEMENTS

§4.29 General Information on Restrictive Agreements

If is often useful in close corporations to include restrictions on the transfer of the corporation's stock. In any particular case one or more of the following situations may justify the use of such restrictions:[95]

---

89 F. Burke, Valuation and Valuation Planning For Closely Held Business 162 (1981).

90 *See* **§4.23** Minority Interest Discount.

91 Estate of T. Folks, 51 T.C.M. (P-H) ¶82,043 (1982).

92 For an explanation of this point and a list of discount situations, *see* Estate of H. Johnson, 77 T.C. 120 (1981).

93 Estate of H. Johnson, 77 T.C. 120 (1981).

94 Estate of Tully v. United States, 78-1 U.S.T.C. (CCH) ¶13,228 (Ct. Cl. 1978).

95 H. O'Neal, Close Corporations Law and Practice §7.02 (2d ed. 1971).

1. When it is desirable to choose one's future associates due to the presence of a close working arrangement
2. Similarly, when it is expected that shareholders will be active participants and not passive investors
3. When restrictions are necessary in order to avoid violation of a law or loss of a beneficial status for tax purposes
4. When continuity of ownership is desired in anticipation of disability or death of an owner.

Although subject to nearly infinite variation and combination depending upon the imagination, creativity and needs of the parties, the basic types of private restrictive agreements are classified as follows:[96]

1. Absolute or blanket prohibitions against transfers (limited in time only)
2. Transfers allowed only with the prior consent of shareholders or other designated persons
3. Transfers allowed only to specified buyer (e.g., relatives, employees), or prohibited to specified buyers (e.g., competitors)
4. Transfers allowed subject to first option powers in officers, directors, shareholders or other specified persons (e.g., first refusal rights)
5. Purchase option powers in the corporation's officers, directors, shareholders or in other specified persons on the happening of a specified event (e.g., on death, disability, bankruptcy, or change of residence)
6. Buy-sell agreements between current owners
7. Redemptions by corporation when a specified event happens
8. Unrestricted redemption power in corporation or directors.

It is also not uncommon to find restrictions of the first six types used in conjunction with partnership arrangements. Unless reference is made specifically to corporations and shareholders, the following discussion applies to these business arrangement as well.

In corporations, these restrictions may be found in the corporation's charter, bylaws, in a separate stock agreement, or a combination of one or more of those instruments.[97] In partnerships, they may be found in the partnership agreement, in a separate partner's agreement, or in both.

The most effective resale or transfer restriction provisions are included in all relevant documents. For corporations this means the relevant restrictive agreement should be set out or referred to in the articles of incorporation, the by-laws and the shareholder's agreement. Inclusion in the shareholder's agreement is not superfluous because it constitutes a binding contract between the parties, but the charter and by-laws are

---

[96] *Id.* at §7.05.
[97] *Id.* at §7.14.

alterable by the majority shareholders without constituting a breach of contract.[98] Consequently, minority shareholders would be subject to changes in the restrictions without significant legal recourse. For partnerships, the restrictive agreement should be made a part of the partnership agreement and any other relevant instruments.

The validity of these restrictions is tested by state law.[99] Although the validity under state law of a restriction or combination of restrictions is not determinative of value of the shares of stock, it is essential in order for the restriction to have any effect on marketability and therefore on the value of the corporation.

The I.R.S. indicates that the degree to which a restriction affects value may depend upon whether the restriction was created contemporaneously with the original creation of the interest or issuance of the shares, or was later created voluntarily.[1] The former is said to have greater effect than the latter. Apparently, the I.R.S. is fearful that subsequent voluntary agreements are subject to collusion among the owners and shareholders. If so, this distinction has little basis; in a partnership or close corporation, the owners or shareholders typically have as much control and collusive capabilities at creation or incorporation as they do after creation.[2]

The effects of private restrictions are varied. They may be determinative of market value, raise market value, lower market value or merely be one of many factors affecting market value. The particular effect depends upon many factors, including the type of restriction involved and the particular valuation issue. In addition, the effect of private restrictive agreements on valuation is influenced significantly by the presence or absence of price criteria in the agreement.

The effect of these restrictions is different for income, gift or estate tax cases:[3]

1. For income tax purposes, restrictive agreements may cause close corporation stock to be valued at zero, to merely postpone valuation or be one factor in determination of market value.
2. For estate tax purposes, restrictions on transfer may specifically set and determine the value of business interests or merely be one factor in determining market value.
3. For gift tax purposes, private restrictions on transfer ordinarily are only one factor in determining the market value for donated business interests.

It is very important that the parties make sure that this agreement will have the intended effect. The agreement must not only be effective against the parties involved, but also against the I.R.S. There have been cases where the agreement was valid as between the parties, but not against the I.R.S.[4]

---

98 *Id.*

99 *Id.* at §7.06.

1 Rev. Rul. 59-60, §8, 1959-1 C.B. 237.

2 Krahmer & Henderer, *Valuation of Shares of Closely Held Corporations*, 221 T.M. A-9 (1978).

3 *See Id.* at A-3 to -16.

4 *See* S. Kess, B. Westlin & R. Whitman, Financial and Estate Planning ¶745.45, 1121-3 (CCH).

§4.30 —Restrictions Where Price of Resale is Set

The terms of many restrictive agreements include a specific price or calculable price at which the restricted interests must be sold:[5]

1. Common purchase option powers given to specifically named persons, or to the corporation, on a first option or other basis
2. Buy-sell agreements
3. All redemption power provisions, for example.

When the agreement sets a designated price, the manner by which this price is to be determined is also ordinarily set in the agreement. The methods for this value determination may take any of the following forms:

1. Book value, adjusted book value or net asset value
2. Capitalization of earnings
3. Independent appraisal or arbitration
4. A fixed or alterable specified dollar figure.

The determination of when and how to make the above value decisions is typically set out in the agreement.[6] The effect of a designated price depends significantly on the particular tax issue involved.

In income tax cases, some price designations have been held to be determinative of value. In one case, the Supreme Court held that fair market value could not exceed par value when the stock was issued subject to an option to purchase at par value.[7] Similar holdings have been made in cases dealing with price designations in redemption agreements and specified buyer arrangements.[8]

For gift tax valuation purposes, the I.R.S. has successfully taken the position that restrictive agreements setting a price are never conclusive of the value of the business interest, even though they can set the estate tax value.[9] The explanation for this difference is that the estate, because the restrictive agreement is triggered by the death of the owner, is obligated to transfer the business interest at the agreed price on the valuation date, the donee is ordinarily not under a binding obligation to sell the interest at a price determined on the valuation date. In fact, the agreement is ordinarily not exercisable until the happening of another triggering event such as the death of the

---

[5] Butala, *Restrictive Agreements—Their Effect Upon the Tax Valuation of Corporate Stock,* 105 Tr. & Est. 15 (1966).

[6] *See* §**4.33** Sample Valuation–Setting Provisions for Buy-Sell Agreements.

[7] Helvering v. Salvage, 297 U.S. 106 (1936).

[8] *See, e.g.,* P. Kalech, 23 T.C. 672 (1955), *acq.* 1955-2 C.B. 7.

[9] Rev. Rul. 59-60, §8, 1959-1 C.B. 237; Rev. Rul. 189, 1953-2 C.B. 284.

donee. Consequently, the donee has the right to retain the business interest and its financial accoutrements, including dividends and other ownership rights.[10]

This means that for gift tax purposes restrictive agreements that set price affect, but are not determinative, of market value. The cases have indicated that this effect may run from being an indeterminable factor to constituting a substantial weighted factor.[11]

For estate tax purposes the I.R.S. has conceded that the price set in restrictive agreements may determine the business interests' market value if certain conditions are met.[12] The failure to satisfy any one or more of them may cause the I.R.S. to conclude that the set price is not determinative.

The requirements and conditions for a binding agreement are:

1. The price must be set (either fixed or determinable according to a formula)
2. The estate or successor in interest must be obligated to sell at the set determined or determinable price
3. The sale obligation at the set price must be as binding during the decedent's lifetime as it is after decedent's death[13]
4. The restrictive agreement must be the result of a *bona fide,* arm's length transaction
5. The specified purchaser under the agreement must be required to exercise the option, or at least have the power to exercise it
6. The restrictive agreement must be for an adequate consideration (Full and adequate in money or money's worth consideration apparently is not needed).[14]

Certain terms are unsatisfactory:

1. Voluntary purchase restrictions such as first refusal rights are not sufficient by themselves
2. Restrictions applicable only at death, but not during the lifetime, or vice versa, are insufficient
3. The transaction must not be a bequest to the specified purchaser.

The prohibition against restrictive agreements in bequests derives from the situation where a testator requires the consideration for a testamentary gift from the recipient, and consideration is much less than the asset's market value. In this situation, the testator, in effect, is making a gift of the difference between the consideration paid and the value of the gift. Because it is contended that the set value in this discussion determines market value, the I.R.S. justifiably wants to determine whether the restric-

---

[10] Butala, *Restrictive Agreements—Their Effect Upon the Tax Valuation of Corporate Stock,* 105 Tr. & Est. 15 (1966); *see* Baltimore Nat'l Bank v. United States, 136 F. Supp. 642 (D. Md. 1955).

[11] *Compare* Spitzer v. Commissioner, 153 F.2d 967 (8th Cir. 1946), *with* C. Chamberlin, 12 T.C.M. (P-H) ¶43,347 (1943) *and* L. McDonald, 13 T.C.M. (P-H) ¶44,096 (1944).

[12] Estate of L. Weil, 22 T.C. 1267 (1954), *acq.* 1955-2 C.B. 10.

[13] Reg. §20.2031-2(h).

[14] Estate of O. Littick, 31 T.C. 181 (1958), *acq.* 1959-2 C.B. 5.

tive agreement is actually a gift or a bona fide business transaction for adequate consideration.[15]

In addition, several nonmandatory considerations and factors deserve mention:

1. The restriction need not be reciprocal among all relevant parties. When it is unilateral, it is subject to closer scrutiny as to whether the restriction is a bona fide business arrangement.[16]
2. Purchasers may be other owners, third persons or the business interest itself.[17]
3. The purchase option by the designated purchaser does not have to be exercised.[18]
4. The restrictive set price need not be binding on the whole of the business interests in the estate, although the set price will only be determinative for the interest subject to the restriction.[19]

The following illustrates how this valuation process operates:

Illustration IV-12

Assumptions

1. Close corporation with two stockholders, A and B, each owning fifty percent of the stock;
2. Buy-sell agreement between the two stockholders that provides:
   (a) Each must sell to the other;
   (b) Sale obligation is binding both during stockholder's lifetime and at death; and
   (c) Price is set at the value of the average net earnings of the corporation for the five-year period prior to the date of valuation capitalized at 20 percent;
3. A dies and B seeks to exercise the agreement;
4. The average annual net earnings for the corporation for the last five years equals $200,000.

Calculation

$$\text{Five Year Average Net Earnings} \div \text{Capitalization Rate} \times \text{percentage of business} = V$$
$$(200{,}000 \div .20) \times .50 = V$$
$$1{,}000{,}000 \times .50 = V = 500{,}000$$

[15] *See* Corneel, *Valuation Techniques in Buy-Sell Agreements: Effect on Gift and Estate Taxes,* 24 N.Y.U. Inst. Fed. Tax'n 655-56 (1966).

[16] *See* Butala, *Restrictive Agreements—Their Effect Upon the Tax Valuation of Corporate Stock,* 105 Tr. & Est. 16 (1966); *cf.* Armstrong's Estate v. Commissioner, 146 F.2d 457 (7th Cir. 1944).

[17] Estate of A. Salt, 17 T.C. 92 (1951), *acq.* 1952-1 C.B. 4; Rev. Rul. 54-76.

[18] Butala, *Restrictive Agreements—Their Effect Upon the Tax Valuation of Corporate Stock,* 105 Tr. & Est. 17 (1966).

[19] Krahmer & Henderer, *Valuation of Shares of Closely Held Corporations,* 221 T.M. A-13 (1978); *see* Belser v. Edwards, 54-1 U.S.T.C. (CCH) ¶10,942 (M.D.Ga. 1954).

The estate tax value of the corporation under this buy-sell agreement equals $500,000.

A recent district court decision illustrates the value-reducing possibilities of buy-sell agreements that set the price, or give a formula for setting the the price, of the business interest.[20] The qualified buy-sell agreement set the price for the relevant business interest according to a formula that used previous years' earnings as the valuation determinant. Because the business had lost money during the relevant time period, the value of the interest according to the formula was zero. The court held that because the agreement met all of the I.R.S.' requirements for a valid buy-sell agreement, the formula price, zero, was the value of the interest for purposes of the deceased owner's estate tax return. The I.R.S.' argument that other valuation techniques showed the business interest had a much higher value, i.e., $144,319, was rejected by the court.

There are two qualifications to the rule that the set price will be determinative. First, the set option price should not be determinative when it can be shown that market value is less than the option price.[21] In this situation, unless the option was mandatory on the specified purchaser, it will probably not be exercised. Second, despite its very limited application, there is authority that if the set price makes reference to book value as the price formula, the value of the "goodwill" on the intangible assets may have to be added to the set price.[22]

§4.31 —Restrictions Where Price of Resale is Not Set

Although transfer restrictions that do not set price can never determine a set tax value for the business, they may have an important effect on their determination. The blanket restriction on resale in income tax cases presents a good example.

The economic theory that supports a discount from market value is that buyers will pay less for a stock subject to potential resale difficulty caused by resale restrictions.[23] Any interference with the speed or terms of alienability will have the economic effect of depressing the value of the asset.

Valuation problems of restricted stock in income tax cases arise generally in two situations. First, restricted stock may be issued in exchange, raising a capital gain or loss problem. Second, restricted stock may be issued as compensation for various services rendered to the corporation.

The absolute or blanket restriction of resale for a period of time is involved in most of the litigated cases. Courts in both of the above situations have held that, if the stock

---

[20] Roth v. United States, 48 A.F.T.R.2d ¶148,468, (E.D.Mo. 1981).

[21] Corneel, *Valuation Techniques in Buy-Sell Agreements: Effect on Gift and Estate Taxes*, 24 N.Y.U. Inst. Fed. Tax'n 654 (1966).

[22] Estate of G. Trammell, 18 T.C. 662 (1952), *acq.* 1953-1 C.B. 6; *but see* Butala, *Restrictive Agreements—Their Effect Upon the Tax Valuation of Corporate Stock*, 105 Tr. & Est. 15-17 (1966); Rev. Rul. 68-609, 1968-2 C.B. 327.

[23] Butala, *Restrictive Agreements—Their Effect Upon the Tax Valuation of Corporate Stock*, 105 Tr. & Est. 17 (1966).

issued is highly speculative, the value of the stock for the income tax purposes may be zero because it has no ascertainable fair market value.[24]

In these cases, the decision is often only a postponement, not a final determination. If the stock subsequently is valuable and transferred, it will be subject to taxation at least as a capital gain to the taxpayer.

In the estate and gift tax area, transfer restrictions that do not set the price have also been held to have an effect—though not a determinative effect—on valuation. For example, first refusal right in the corporation,[25] and first refusal right in shareholders if sale is to be made to other than specific persons,[26] have been held to be a value-depressing factor that must be weighed in valuing the stock. A similar conclusion was reached for shares valued for gift tax purposes.[27] In all of these cases, the party possessing the right of first refusal was permitted to purchase the shares at book value. The fact that the shareholders did not have to sell did not prohibit the availability of a discount. Although book value was not held to be determinative of the valuation issue, the restriction on transfer was held to depress the price from an otherwise higher market value.

It follows reasonably that any other restriction conditioning resale, although it does not set price, should have a depressing effect on market value. The amount of discount will depend upon the degree to which the restriction inhibits alienability.

Although it is well-recognized that a discount is appropriate for a business interest that is subject to private restrictive resale agreements, there is no formula or agreement as to the calculation of the discount. Consequently, the determination of the amount of the discount becomes a subjective matter to be determined on a case-by-case basis. The restriction is another those nebulous factors to be taken into account in determining the value of a business interest.[28] Expert appraisers will be essential in these situations and their opinions must be based upon sound economic analysis.

SUMMARY: COMBINING VALUATION TECHNIQUES

§4.32 Outline of Sample Memorandum of Valuation of a Business Interest

TO: ____________________

RE: Valuation of the ________

24 *See* Helvering v. Tex-Penn Co. 300 U.S. 481 (1937); M. Kopple, 35 B.T.A. 1056 (1937), *acq.* 1937-1 C.B. 14.

25 Worcester County Trust Co. v. Commissioner, 134 F.2d 578 (1st Cir. 1943).

26 Mathews v. United States, 226 F. Supp. 1003 (E.D. N.Y. 1964).

27 C. Chamberlin, 12 T.C.M. (P-H) ¶43,347, (1943).

28 *See* **§3.10** Restricted Securities Discount Strategies and Presentations for a discussion of a similar problem with restricted and control securities.

This memorandum reviews the operations of the ______________________ and establishes a value for [the shares] [the partnership] [the sole proprietorship]. This valuation is based upon the understanding that it will be used for purposes of [merger or acquisition] [a buy/sell agreement] [estate tax preparation] [gift tax preparation] [an employee stock benefit plan].

I. Valuation techniques employed

II. General information concerning

A. History

B. Description of the business

III. Operations of the business (last five years)

A. [Sales] [Gross revenues]

B. Net earnings

C. Anticipated future changes

IV. Assets

A. Real property

B. Plant(s) and equipment

C. Other assets

V. Management factors

A. Key officers and directors

B. Key employees

C. Anticipated future owners or employees

VI. Financial conditions

A. Balance sheet analysis

B. Income statement analysis

C. Other relevant factors

VII. Business comparables

A. Other closely held companies

B. Publicly traded companies

VIII. Value determination

A. Major factors

B. Calculations

§4.33 Sample Valuation-Setting Provisions for Buy-Sell Agreements

The following are samples of valuation processes for buy-sell agreements:

Set Price; Arbitration

1. For the purposes of this Agreement, as of the date of this Agreement, the value of each share of stock of the Corporation is ________ Dollars ($________). This price has been agreed upon by the Stockholders as representing the fair value of each share of stock including the goodwill of the Corporation. Within ____ days following the end of each [fiscal] [calendar] year, the stockholders agree to redetermine the value of each share of stock, and shall indicate such value by endorsement on Schedule A attached hereto and made a part of this Agreement. Such endorsement shall take the following form:

> "The undersigned mutually agree on this ________ day of ________, 19____, that for the purpose of this Stock Purchase Agreement each share of the Corporation has a value of ________ Dollars ($________).
>
> Signed ________ (,________) and ________."

2. If for any reason the stockholders fail to redetermine the value for a particular year, the last previously stipulated value shall control. Provided, however, that if no revaluation has been agreed upon within ________ months immediately preceding the death of a stockholder, or during the ________ year period during which the disabled stockholder was totally and continuously disabled, then the value of a deceased or disabled stockholder's stock shall be agreed upon by the representative of the deceased stockholder or the disabled stockholder and remaining stockholder(s).

3. If the representative of the decedent or the disabled stockholder and the surviving or remaining stockholder(s) do not agree upon the value within ____ days after the death or within ____ days after the disabled stockholder has been totally and continuously disabled for a period of ____ years, the value of the deceased or disabled stockholder's stock shall be determined by arbitration as follows: the surviving or remaining stockholder(s) shall name one arbitrator and the representative of the estate or the disabled stockholder shall name one arbitrator. If the two arbitrators do not agree upon the value of the stock within ________ days of their appointment, they shall appoint a third arbitrator and the decision of the majority shall be binding. In determining values by arbitration [life insurance proceeds] [cash surrender values] [disability income insurance proceeds] shall [not] be taken into account.

Book Value

Example 1

1. For the purposes of this Agreement, the value of each share of stock of the corporation shall be determined as follows:

(a) The Certified Public Accountant then in charge of the corporation's books of account shall determine the assets and liabilities of the corporation as of the end of the month preceding the month in which the death of the stockholder shall have occurred. All determinations of value shall be in accord with generally accepted accounting principles, except as herein provided.

(b) In making the computations he shall value goodwill at [$________.] [twice the average net profits of the business, before taxes, during the last three years.] He shall value buildings and machinery at the appraisal value as determined by the Certified Public Accountant.

(c) He shall determine the net assets by subtracting the liabilities and par value of preferred stock from the assets, as calculated above, and divide by the total number of common shares issued and outstanding, to arrive at the value of each common share.

2. The purchase price shall be the value of each share multiplied by the number of shares held by the executor.

3. The purchase price shall be fixed within ________ days after the qualification of the legal representative of the estate, but in no event later than ________ months after the date of death.

Example 2

1. For the purposes of this Agreement, the value of each share of the stock of the Corporation shall be determined by first valuing the entire assets of the corporation as of the first day of the month preceding the month in which the shareholder dies in the manner hereinafter prescribed:

(a) All real estate, machinery, equipment, furniture, and fixtures shall be taken at the valuation appearing on the books of the Corporation: that is, at cost less deduction of all reserves for depreciation of such items computed in the then most recent federal income tax return.

(b) Inventory of merchandise, raw materials, and supplies shall be computed at cost or market value, whichever is lower, and on a basis consistent with prior federal income tax returns.

(c) All accounts payable shall be taken at the face amount, less discounts deductible therefrom.

(d) All accounts receivable shall be taken at the face amount thereof, without reserve for bad debts, discounts, allowances, or adjustments to customers, except that accounts of debtors adjudicated bankrupt shall be excluded.

(e) The cash surrender value of the life insurance policy held by the corporation shall be included.

(f) Leased machinery, equipment, furniture, and fixtures and the obligations of the Corporation under such leases shall not be considered for any purpose.

(g) All taxes accrued as of the date of valuation shall be deducted as liabilities.

(h) All matters with respect to valuation, not provided for above, shall be determined in accord with generally accepted accounting principles.

2. The purchase price shall be the value of each share multiplied by the number of shares held by the executor.

3. The purchase price shall be fixed within sixty days after the qualification of the legal representative of the estate, but in no event later than six months after the date of death.

Earnings

Example 1

1. For the purposes of this Agreement, the value of each share of the stock of the Corporation shall be determined as follows:

(a) The executor of the deceased shareholder and the surviving shareholder shall each appoint one arbitrator, who, together, shall agree upon the value of the corporate assets. In the event the two cannot agree, they shall appoint a third arbitrator and the decision of the majority shall be binding on all parties.

(b) They shall compute the average yearly earnings by adding the net income, before taxes, as reported by the Certified Public Accountant for the last eight years and dividing said total by eight.

(c) The average yearly earnings in excess of 10% of the appraised value of the net assets shall be capitalized at 15%.

(d) The appraised value of the corporate assets shall be added to the capitalized value calculated in subparagraph (c.), and the total divided by the number of common shares issued and outstanding, to arrive at the value of each common share.

2. The purchase price shall be the value of each share multiplied by the number of shares held by the executor.

3. The purchase price shall be fixed within ________ days after the qualification of the legal representative of the estate, but in no event later than ________ months after the date of death.

Example 2

1. For purposes of this Agreement, the value of each share of the stock of the Corporation shall be determined as follows:

(a) The Certified Public Accountant shall compute the average yearly earnings before taxes for the past two years.

(b) The average yearly earnings shall be capitalized at 8%.

(c) The capitalized value shall be divided by the number of common shares issued and outstanding to arrive at the value of each common share.

2. The purchase price shall be the value of each share multiplied by the number of shares held by the executor.

3. The purchase price shall be fixed within ____ days after the qualification of the legal representative of the estate, but in no event later than ____ months after the date of death.

§4.34 I.R.S. Stock Valuation Inquiry Worksheet

U. S. TREASURY DEPARTMENT - INTERNAL REVENUE SERVICE

STOCK VALUATION INQUIRY

Please furnish the information requested in items 1 through 8 regarding your stock owned by taxpayer on valuation date shown on reverse.

1. ESTIMATED FAIR MARKET VALUE PER SHARE OF YOUR STOCK OWNED BY TAXPAYER *(If unlisted)*

COMMON	PREFERRED
$	$

2. NUMBER OF SHARES OWNED BY TAXPAYER	2A. COMMON	3 DIVIDEND PER SHARE DECLARED BUT UNPAID ON VALUATION DATE →	3A. AMOUNT *(Common)*	4. DATE BOOKS CLOSED *(Or stock became ex-dividend)*
	2B. PREFERRED		3B. AMOUNT *(Preferred)*	

5. If stock is listed	5A. Enter amounts under one of the three following alternatives:			5B. NAME OF EXCHANGE
	High - Low sale on valuation date	Bid or Asked price on valuation date	Sale or Quotation nearest valuation date	
	$ High	$ Bid	$ Sale	
	$ Low	$ Asked	Quot.	

6. If not listed	6A. SELLING PRICE, NEAREST VALUATION DATE *(Except to relative of taxpayer)*		6D. NAMES OF PARTIES TO TRANSACTION
	6B. DATE	6C. NUMBER SHARES	

7. Please furnish a copy of your balance sheet nearest valuation date, or, if unavailable, please complete below *(If stock is unlisted)*

7A. BALANCE SHEET AS OF: ______ DATE

☐ ATTACHED ☐ SUMMARIZED BELOW

ASSETS	AMOUNT	LIABILITIES	AMOUNT
(1) Cash	$	(1) Notes payable	$
(2) Notes receivable		(2) Accounts payable	
(3) Accounts receivable		(3)	
(4) Inventory			
(5) U. S. Gov't bonds and notes			
(6) Other securities not in subsidiaries		(4) Depreciation reserve	
(Market $)		(5) Depletion reserve	
(7) Subsidiaries *(List below)*		(6) Federal and other taxes	
(8) Deferred charges		(7) Mortgages payable	
		(8) Bonded debt	
		(9) TOTAL LIABILITIES	$
(9) Delivery equipment			
(10) Furniture and fixtures		**NET WORTH**	**AMOUNT**
(11) Machinery and equipment		(1) Preferred stock outstanding	
(12) Land		*(No. shares:)*	$
(13) Buildings		(2) Common stock outstanding	
		(No. shares:)	
		(3) Surplus *(earned)*	
(14) Patents, trade-marks, etc.		(4) Surplus *(paid in)*	
(15) Good will		TOTAL NET WORTH	$
(16) TOTAL ASSETS	$	TOTAL LIABILITIES AND NET WORTH	$

SUBSIDIARIES *(Please indicate (a) name, (b) address, (c) % of interest owned)*

8. SUMMARY OF CAPITAL, INCOME, & DIVIDENDS FOR FIVE YEARS PRECEDING VALUATION DATE *(If stock is unlisted)*

YEAR ENDED	INVESTED CAPITAL (Capital stock & surplus at beginning of year)	TOTAL SALES OR GROSS RECEIPTS	FEDERAL AND STATE INCOME AND CORPORATION TAXES	NET INCOME AFTER TAXES	DIVIDENDS PAID PER SHARE Preferred	DIVIDENDS PAID PER SHARE Common
	$	$	$	$	$	$

DATE	SIGNATURE AND TITLE OF PERSON PREPARING THIS FORM

U.S. GOVERNMENT PRINTING OFFICE : 1961 O—108103-8

FORM 867 (REV. 10-61)

§4.35 I.R.S. Analysis Worksheets for Business Interests

VALUATION OF CLOSELY HELD CORPORATION STOCK

1. ESTATE	2. VALUATION DATE	3. DATE OF DEATH
4. DONOR		5. DATE OF GIFT
6. NAME AND ADDRESS OF CORPORATION		
7. CITY AND STATE WHERE INCORPORATED		8. DATE INCORPORATED

9. BASIS FOR RETURNED VALUE

☐ VALUATION ☐ SALE ☐ OTHER (Specify)

10. NAMES OF PRINCIPAL STOCKHOLDERS AND THEIR HOLDINGS

11. SUMMARY

	NUMBER OF SHARES VALUED (a)	TOTAL SHARES OUTSTANDING (b)	RETURNED VALUE PER SHARE (c)	RECOMMENDED VALUE PER SHARE (d)
COMMON STOCK				
PREFERRED STOCK				

12. VALUATION DATA

YEAR (a)	BOOK VALUE COMMON (b)	BOOK VALUE PER SHARE (c)	PROFITS FOR COMMON (d)	PROFITS PER SHARE (e)	DIVIDENDS PER SHARE COMMON (f)	GROSS SALES (g)	OFFICERS' SALARIES (h)	CURRENT RATIO (i)
TOTALS								
AVERAGE								

U.S. TREASURY DEPARTMENT – INTERNAL REVENUE SERVICE

FORM 2543 (7-59)

13. DATE OF BALANCE SHEET ADJUSTMENTS

ASSETS (a)	BOOK VALUE (b)	ACTUAL VALUE (c)	BASIS FOR ADJUSTMENT (d)
TOTALS			
NET ADJUSTMENT			

14. FACTORS

AVERAGE EARNINGS CAPITALIZED @ % = PER SHARE

AVERAGE DIVIDENDS CAPITALIZED @ % = PER SHARE

ADJUSTED BOOK VALUE =

RECORD OF SALES

PRIOR ESTATE OR GIFT TAX VALUATION

OTHER FACTORS CONSIDERED THOUGH NOT DISCUSSED HEREIN IN DETAIL

FORM 2543 (7-59)

VALUATION OF INTEREST IN AN UNINCORPORATED BUSINESS

1. ESTATE	2. VALUATION DATE	3. DATE OF DEATH
4. DONOR		5. DATE OF GIFT

6. NAME AND ADDRESS OF THE BUSINESS

7. NATURE OF THE BUSINESS

8. NAMES OF OWNERS AND THEIR RESPECTIVE SHARES IN THE BUSINESS

NAME (a)	POSITION (b)	SALARY (c)	PERCENT INTEREST IN ASSETS (d)	PERCENT INTEREST IN PROFIT AND LOSS (e)

9. BASIS FOR RETURNED VALUE

☐ VALUATION ☐ SALE ☐ OTHER (Specify)

10. VALUATION DATA

YEAR (a)	BOOK VALUE (b)	EARNINGS (c)	PARTNERS' SALARIES* (d)	GROSS SALES (e)	CURRENT RATIO (f)
TOTALS					
AVERAGE					

* *If the business is operated as a partnership, state in item 13 whether a copy of the partnership agreement has been furnished, the salaries and interests of the owners, as stated above, are in accordance with such agreement, and the agreement contains a provision for determining the value of an owner's interest in the event of his death, withdrawal from the business, or other disposition of his interest.*

U. S. TREASURY DEPARTMENT – INTERNAL REVENUE SERVICE (Over) FORM 2542 (7-59)

11. DATE OF BALANCE SHEET ADJUSTMENTS

(a) ASSETS	(b) BOOK VALUE	(c) ACTUAL VALUE	(d) BASIS FOR ADJUSTMENT
TOTALS			
NET ADJUSTMENT			

12. FACTORS

A. AVERAGE EARNINGS CAPITALIZED @ % =

B. ADJUSTED BOOK VALUE =

C. RECOMMENDED VALUE OF (DECEDENT'S) (DONOR'S) INTEREST

13. OTHER FACTORS CONSIDERED THOUGH NOT DISCUSSED HEREIN IN DETAIL

GPO 876936

FORM 2542 (7-59)

§4.36 Comprehensive Worksheet for Business Interest Valuation

Instructions: Compute estimated market value by each of the following techniques:

I. Adjusted Book Value[29]

A. Book Value of Business Interest on Balance Sheet ______

B. Adjustments to Book Value—Additions and (Subtractions):

1. Depreciation ______
2. Appraisals of Fixed Assets ______
3. (Discounts for Uncollectables) ______
4. Inventory Values ______
5. (Current Distributions) ______
6. Other

______ ______

______ ______

7. Add or (Subtract) Total Adjustments To or From A. ______

C. Adjusted Book Value ______

D. Liabilities of Business Interest on Balance Sheet ______

1. Adjustments to Liabilities—Additions or (Subtractions): ______
2. Add or (Subtract) Total Adjusted Liabilities From C. ______

E. Adjusted Book Value Less Liabilities ______

---

[29] *See* **§4.4** Adjusted Book Value of the Business Interest.

F. Preferred Interests

1. Number of shares [or Percentage] of Preferred Interest ________

2. Par Value or E. × ________

3. (Subtract) Total Value of Preferred Interests From E. ________

G. Estimated Adjusted Book Value of Non-Preferred Interests ________

II. Capitalization of Earnings[30]

A. Total Earnings or Revenue from Income Statement ________

B. Adjustments to Earnings—Additions and (Subtractions):

1. ________________ ________

2. ________________ ________

3. Add or (Subtract) Total Adjustments From A. ________

C. Total Gross Adjusted Earnings ________

D. Total Expenses and Taxes on

Income Statement ________

1. Adjustments to Expenses—Additions or (Subtractions): ________

2. Adjustments to Taxes—Additions or (Subtractions): ________

3. Add or (Subtract) Total Adjusted Expenses and Taxes From C. ________

---

[30] *See* **§4.5** Capitalization of the Business Interest's Earnings.

E. Total Net Adjusted Earnings ____________

[Repeat the above steps for preceding five accounting years—use additional forms].

F. Future Flow Income Determination[31]

1. Year		Earnings	Weight	Result
________	– ________	________	× ________	= ________
________	– ________	________	× ________	= ________
________	– ________	________	× ________	= ________
________	– ________	________	× ________	= ________
________	– ________	________	× ________	= ________

2. Total of Results ____________

3. Divide 2. by Total Weight ÷ ____________

G. Weighted Average Earnings ____________

H. Rate of Capitalization

1. Divide G. by Capitalization Rate Decimal ÷ ____________

OR

2. Multiply G. by Price/ Earnings Ratio × ____________

I. Estimated Capitalized Income Value ____________

J. Add value of Nonoperating Investment[32] ____________

K. Total Estimated Value ____________

[31] *See* **§4.5** Illustration IV-3, for weighted nonstatistical method.

[32] *See* **§4.13** Nonoperating Investments in the Business Interest.

III. Dividend Capacity Value[33]

A. Total Net Adjusted Earnings (See II,E above) __________

B. Less Retained Earnings – __________

C. Distributable Dividends __________

D. Rate of Capitalization

1. Divide C. by Capitalization Rate Decimal ÷ __________

OR

2. Multiply C. by Price/ Dividends Ratio × __________

E. Estimated Capitalized Dividend Value __________

F. Add Value of Nonoperating Investment[34] __________

G. Total Estimated Value __________

IV. Comparative Traded Security Analysis[35]

Instructions:

Fill in data available on one of these forms for each relevant comparable traded security and for the subject business interest.

A. ____________________
Name of Comparable Security or Subject Business Interest

Data on (Comparable Traded Security) (Subject Business Interest)

---

[33] *See* **§4.6** Dividends and Dividend Capacity of the Business Interest.
[34] *See* **§4.13** Nonoperating Investments in the Business Interest.
[35] *See* **§4.17** Traded Securities Comparative Analysis.

Averaged Annual Data	a. Adjusted Earnings Per Share	b. Adjusted Dividends Per Share	c. Adjusted Book Value Per Share	d. Market Price
Year				
1.________	________	________	________	________
2.________	________	________	________	________
3.________	________	________	________	________
4.________	________	________	________	________
5.________	________	________	________	________

B. Totals a. ________ b. ________ c. ________ d. ________

C. Divide B. by Number of Years ÷________ ÷________ ÷________ ÷________

D. Averaged Comparable Data[36] a. ________ b. ________ c. ________ d. ________

E. Calculation Formula

Traded Security — Subject Business Interest

$$\frac{\text{1. Market Price Value—D.d.}}{\text{2. Average Data Figure—D. a., b. or c.}} = \frac{\text{VPS}}{\text{3. Known Figure Comparable to D.a., b., or c.}} =$$

$$\frac{1.\ \_\_\_\_\_\_\_\_}{2.\ \_\_\_\_\_\_\_\_} = \frac{\text{VPS}}{3.\ \_\_\_\_\_\_\_\_} =$$

$$\text{VPS} = \frac{(1.\ \_\_\_\_\_\_\_\_)\ (3.\ \_\_\_\_\_\_\_\_)}{2.}$$

VPS = ____________

[36] This analysis may be done for several comparable traded securities. The Averaged Comparable Data in D. for each security may then be computed, and overall averages determined. Because of dissimilarities between the comparable traded securities and the subject business interest, you may have to make adjustments to the above Averaged Comparable Data. Although these adjustments are discretionary in nature, they should only be made for the purposes of recognizing true economic realities.

F. Adjustment due to significant differences between comparables(s) and subject business interest (Calculate as a percentage) Add as premium or subtract as (discount) from VPS in E. × ________

G. Estimated Comparable Traded Security—Per-Share Value ________

[Go to Part VII. for calculation of marketability and other related discounts and premiums].

V. Weighting of Valuation Factors[37]

A. Valuation

	Estimated Value		Weight Percentage		Total
I. Adjusted Book Value	________	×	________ %	=	________
II. Adjusted Earnings Value	________	×	________ %	=	________
III. Adjusted Dividend Value	________	×	________ %	=	________
IV. Comparative Analysis Value	________	×	________ %	=	________

B. Total Weighted Estimated Market Value 100% = ________

VI. Goodwill[38]

A. Tangible Assets of Business Interest

---

[37] *See* **§2.27** Weighting of Valuation Techniques, Illustration II-14.

[38] *See* **§4.7** Goodwill (Unidentified Intangible Assets).

	Year	Adjusted Tangible Asset Value
1.	________ – ________	________
2.	________ – ________	________
3.	________ – ________	________
4.	________ – ________	________
5.	________ – ________	________

B. Total of Tangible Asset Values ________

C. Divide B. by Number of Years Used ÷ ________

D. Average Annual Tangible Asset Value ________

E. Annual Earnings of Business Interest

	Year	Adjusted Annual Earnings
1.	________ – ________	________
2.	________ – ________	________
3.	________ – ________	________
4.	________ – ________	________
5.	________ – ________	________

F. Total of Annual Earnings ________

G. Divide F. by
Number of Years Used ÷ ________

H. Result Equals the
Average Annual
Earnings ________

I. Multiply D. by proper
Rate of Capitalization D. ________

1. 8% for Small
Risk Business

OR

2. 10% for High
Risk Business × ________

OR

3. Prevailing Rate for
Particular Industry

J. Subtract Result of I.
from H. − ________

K. Result Equals the Average
Annual Earnings from Unidentified
Intangible Assets ________

L. Divide K. by Proper Rate of
Capitalization

1. 15% for Small Risk
Business

OR

2. 20% for High Risk
Business × ________

OR

3. Prevailing Rate for Particular Industry

M. Result Equals Value of Goodwill ____________

N. Add Adjusted Book Value of Business Interest (See I, G, above) to M. ____________

O. Result Equals Estimated Value of Business Interest Including Goodwill Value ____________

VII. Discounts and Premiums to Business Interest Valuation[39]

Instructions: Use only Discounts Applicable to Situation.

A. Estimated Market Value of Entire Business Interest ____________

B. Lack of Marketability Discount

1. Amount from A. ____________

2. Discount Percentage × ______

3. Discount Amount ____________

C. Minority Interest Discount

1. Amount from A. ____________

2. Discount Percentage × ______

3. Discount Amount ____________

D. Loss of Key Manager/Owner Discount

1. Amount from A. ____________

---

[39] *See* **§4.20** Marketability Discounts and Premiums.

2. Discount Percentage × ______

3. Discount Amount ______

E. Summary of Discounts

1. Marketability Discount ______

2. Minority Discount ______

3. Key Manager/Owner Discount ______

F. Subtract Total Discounts from A. ______

G. Estimated Market Value
of Business Interest
Less Discounts ______

H. Majority Interest Premium

1. Amount from A. ______

2. Premium Percentage × ______

I. Add Premium Amount to
A. or G. Whichever
Is Applicable ______

J. Estimated Market Value
Of Business Interest
Including Premium Adjustment ______

CHAPTER 5

HOW TO VALUE REAL PROPERTY

§5.1 Introduction to Real Property Valuation

The effort to determine the value of real property is a pervasive task in our society. Valuation determinations are necessary for tax purposes and for many other reasons; for example, all arm's length transfers and real property tax assessment determinations. Therefore, the processes for valuing real property constitute the most comprehensive, sophisticated, documented and developed system available for making valuations.

The determination of the value of real property is primarily a question of fact. The particular data that you must analyze depend almost entirely upon the type of property that is involved. For example, when valuing farm or ranch property, many of the physical characteristics of the property are very important (e.g., the quality and moisture content of the soil, the existence of timber or crops on the property, the possible existence of minerals on the property, draining and erosion conditions, and the location of other relevant economic physical features including the towns and highways).

Other types of assets are just as distinctive. For example, zoning restrictions may be very important in valuing commercial or potentially commercial property. Environmental control regulations may be particularly relevant to industrial properties and their potential uses. The variables are almost endless.

Real property must be studied from the standpoint of its personal peculiarities. The data gathered must be related to those factors. In the end, valuation must be derived from a consideration of all of the data and of the valuation techniques applied to that data. The more relevant data that is obtained and that can be usefully integrated into the valuation determination processes, the better the eventual valuation determination estimate will be.[1]

The admonition that the valuator must value an asset at its highest and best use value is very important for the valuation of real property.[2] This determination includes speculation about the use for vacant land and any other better uses for which improved property might legally be adapted or altered. Alternative uses, of course, must be physically, financially and legally feasible.

As with all rules, there is an exception. In the 1976 Tax Reform Act, Congress enacted I.R.C. §2032A, which recognizes that, under very particular circumstances, certain real property may be valued for estate tax purposes at its special use value rather than its highest and best use value.[3]

It is prudent to hire a qualified appraiser if a valuation determination of real property is important or if an unusual degree of accuracy is necessary.[4] Generally, appraisals run from relatively simple individual appraisals for assets such as personal residences to extensive and elaborate documented appraisals for income producing real property such as plants, ranches and farms. The latter appraisals are naturally more expensive.

---

1 *See* **§1.2** When and Where Valuation Determinations are Made.

2 *See* **§2.9** Fair Market Value.

3 *See* **§2.16** Special Use Value.

4 *See* **§2.3** Significance of Appraisals and Expert Testimony.

Although you may not feel personally qualified to make the appraisal, the following explanation of the primary valuation techniques for real property provides sufficient information to analyze and criticize the professional appraisers work product. This type of analysis is particularly useful when value negotiations or decisions to litigate are involved.

There are circumstances where the accuracy and importance of the valuation will not require an expert appraiser. For example, low-valued residential real estate in small probate estates may not require appraisal, and appraisal may be omitted for pre-death estate planning where only reasonable estimates are needed. In these situations, some of the short-form appraisal techniques might be appropriate.[5] It cannot be overemphasized, however, that these techniques must be used cautiously. All short-form techniques are fraught with potential error. By themselves, they would clearly not sustain a valuation in litigation.

There is a plethora of information about real property valuation. These reference materials are very detailed and include appraisal techniques for nearly any imaginable property asset.

Four useful collateral references are:

1. Encyclopedia of Real Estate Appraising (E. Friedman, 3d ed. 1978)
2. A. Ring, The Valuation of Real Estate (2d ed. 1970)
3. American Institute of Real Estate Appraisers (AIREA), The Appraisal of Real Estate (7th ed. 1978)
4. American Society of Farm Managers and Rural Appraisers, Inc., Rural Appraisal Manual (5th ed. 1979).

§5.2 —Checklist of Information to Gather for Real Property Valuation

The following information should be obtained:

1. Address and legal description
2. Approximate dimension of land including size, shape and area
3. Topography of land, if relevant
4. Description and location of easements, encroachments and rights of way
5. Description and source of tax or other liens and assessments against the land and improvements
6. Date of construction of all improvements on land
7. Appropriate dimensions of improvements
8. Description of improvements including style and use
9. Quality of all features of construction including materials and workmanship

---

[5] *See* **§5.4** Short Form Valuation Techniques for Real Property.

10. Location of improvements on land
11. Availability, existence and cost of relevant utilities including water, telephone, television, electricity, and natural gas
12. Approximate construction costs for improvements
13. Debts and terms of debts against the property including mortgages and other secured interests
14. Remaining economic life of improvements or other wasting assets on the land
15. Present and potential real property taxes on property
16. Present and potential uses of the property
17. Any gross income, including rents and earnings, from land and improvements
18. Vacancies in improvements and/or nonproductive segments of the land
19. All maintenance and operating expenses attributable to the land and/or its improvements
20. Reserves for replacements, if any
21. Proximity to relevant present and future transportation facilities including highways, rails, air services, and rapid transit
22. Supply and demand for the type of property
23. Financing possibilities
24. Climate and geological conditions and hazards
25. Economic and social character and quality of neighborhood and surrounding area
26. Economic and social trends in use of relevant surrounding property
27. Federal, state and local zoning, building, environmental, growth and other regulatory restrictions on present or potential use of land and/or improvements
28. Relevant demographic data concerning the property and surrounding area
29. International, national and local political and economic matters relevant to the property's value including wars, controls on wages, prices and rents, energy and other shortages, extraordinary economic inflation or deflation, and unemployment.

TERMINOLOGY AND CONCEPTS

§5.3 Classification of Real Property

Several of the valuation terms and concepts that were explained previously should be consulted for this Chapter including:

§2.13 Cost (Purchase Price)
§2.20 —Estate Planning and Capitalization Rate
§2.9 Fair Market Value
§2.10 Market
§2.8 Proof of Value
§2.15 Replacement and Reproduction Costs
§2.11 Sales of the Asset
§2.3 Significance of Appraisals and Expert Testimony
§2.16 Special Use Value
§2.25 Statistical and Regression Analysis
§2.17 Valuation Mathematics
§2.27 Weighting of Valuation Techniques.

Real property can be classified into an almost unlimited number of distinct categories. This number depends solely upon the degree to which distinctions are recognized. For our purposes, the most relevant characterizations relate to the subject real property's general use or potential use. Even these classifications are arbitrary, and may have to be refined if a distinction between similar-use real properties has an economic significance.

The following scheme constitutes a reasonable classification of real property by particular use. The second column indicates several special factors relevant to the type of use which should be considered when making a valuation determination for that type of use. The third column indicates the most frequently preferred valuation technique recognized as the primary determinative of value for the type of use indicated. It must be emphasized, however, that these preferences are not exclusive, and that the other methods may be used to corroborate or even supersede the valuation techniques listed.

Chart V-1

Classification of Real Property Use	Selected Special Characteristics	Preferred Valuation Technique
Residential (Non-Income Producing)	Aesthetics[6] and Amenities	Market[7]

6 *See* **§5.7** Amenities and Aesthetics.
7 *See* **§5.11** The Market Approach to Real Property Valuation.

Residential (Income-Producing)	Amenities Management Supply and Demand	Market and Income[8]
Office Facilities	Amenities Income Management Supply and Demand	
Store Properties	User Success Expectations Utility Flexibility	Market and Income
Shopping Centers	Tenants Trade Area Type	Income
Special Use Facilities	User Success Expectations Utility Flexibility	Income and Cost[9]
Industrial Properties	Accessibility Credit Capabilities of Users Obsolescence Type Utility Flexibility	Market and Cost
Rural Properties	Alternate Use Climate Irrigation Production Capacity Soil Quality Topography	Market
Subdivision Properties	Development Costs Absorption Rate	Development[10]
Mobile Home Parks	Amenities Management Supply and Demand	Income

§5.4 Short Form Valuation Techniques for Real Property

Several techniques are available for a quick estimate of the value of real property. Despite their general uselessness if subjective or detailed appraisals are necessary, they are useful for a sort of "eyeball" or objective estimate of value. They are also useful for getting a value that can be compared to values determined by other methods.

8 *See* **§5.14** The Income Approach to Real Property Valuation.

9 *See* **§5.17** The Cost Approach to Real Property Valuation.

10 *See* **§5.9** The Subdivision Approach to Real Property Valuation.

Basically, you take a known or determinable fact about the subject property (related to dimension, cost, or income) and multiply that fact by a carefully developed factor called a multiplier. The multiplier must evolve from current, local experience using comparable sales data. Unless great care is taken in determining the fact and the multiplier, the resultant valuations may not be accurate enough to use.

The principal short form techniques are:

1. **Gross Rent Multiplier.** Multiply the anticipated annual (monthly) gross rent or income of the subject real property by a current empirically-determined annual (monthly) multiplier. (Seven and eight are common annual multipliers)
2. **Net Rent Multiplier.** Multiply the anticipated annual (monthly) net rent or income of the subject real property by a current empirically-determined annual (monthly) multiplier
3. **Per-Square-or-Cubic Cost Multiplier.** Multiply the square or cubic footage of the subject real property by a current empirically determined cost figure per square or cubic foot. (The results for square feet and cubic feet may not be the same because costs for area may be different from costs for volume)
4. **Per-Rental-Unit Cost Multiplier.** Multiply the number of rental units in the subject real property by a current empirically-determined cost figure per rental unit
5. **Per-Acre Cost Multiplier.** Multiply the number of acres in the tract of the subject undeveloped or agricultural real property by the current empirically-determined cost figure per acre.

The following simple Illustrations show the basic calculations:

Illustration V-1

1. Gross Rent Multiplier

	Annual	Monthly
Gross Rent from Subject Property	$ 24,000	$ 2,000
Multiplier	× 7	× 84
Estimated Market Value	$168,000	$168,000

2. Net Rent Multiplier

	Annual	Monthly
Net Rent from Subject Property	$ 13,440	$ 1,120
Multiplier	× 12.5	× 150
Estimated Market Value	$168,000	$168,000

3. Per-Square- or Cubic-Foot Cost Multiplier

	Square Feet	Cubic Feet
Dimension of Subject Property	10,000	80,000
Multiplier — Cost Per Measurement	× 80	× 10
Estimated Market Value	$800,000	$800,000

Illustration V-1 (*Continued*)

4. Per-Rental-Unit Cost Multiplier	
Rental Units of Subject Property	10
Multiplier – Cost Per Unit	×$10,000
Estimated Market Value	$100,000

5. Per-Acre Cost Multiplier	
Acres of Tract of Subject Property	1,000
Multiplier – Cost Per Acre	× $500
Estimated Market Value	$500,000

§5.5 Assessment Offices and Assessed Valuation of Real Property

Most states have assessment offices where real property valuations are kept and maintained for purposes of real property taxes. The accuracy of these assessed values for general valuation determination purposes varies from state to state. They may or may not represent current estimates of value; they may or may not be updated periodically. They are almost always stated as a percentage of market value. Consequently, if used for market value purposes, you must convert the percentage assessed value to full market value.

The I.R.S. Regulations prohibit the use of assessed valuations as market value unless they represent the fair market value of the property.[11] A judge has expressed a similar sentiment.[12]

The assessed valuation is not totally irrelevant to a market value determination; even the I.R.S. considers it an excellent starting point.[13] The I.R.S. forewarns its attorneys to strive for amicable relations with assessment office personnel.[14]

Assessed valuation figures have also been consulted to determine the ratio of value between the land and its improvements. For example, if the total assessed value is $50,000, and this value is broken down into $10,000 for the land and $40,000 for the improvements, the proportion of 20 percent for the land and 80 percent for the improvements might be carried over to other valuation methods.[15] This ratio should only be used if it accurately reflects the proper division, however.

---

11 Reg. §20.2030-1(b).

12 S. Sochalski, 24 T.C.M. (P-H) ¶55,019 (1955).

13 I.R.S. Tax Law Course, 21-16.

14 *Id.*

15 Chalmers, *Valuation of Real Estate,* 299 T.M. A-10 (1978).

§5.6 Fractional Interest and Other Discounts for Real Property Valuation

When fractional interests in real property are valued for federal estate tax purposes, it has been argued that a discount should be subtracted from the ordinarily determined value of the fractional interest. The contention is that fractional interests are not freely marketable, justifying a reduction in value. Several specific marketability difficulties have been alleged and identified:

1. The inconvenience of dealing with several owners
2. The possibility and problems of minors owning an interest in the property
3. The possible expense and time for necessary partition suits
4. The general potential for disagreement among the several owners.

The applicability of the fractional interest discount depends solely on proof that a sale can be made only at the alleged discounted value. The cases go both ways; results depend upon the degree of proof offered by the contesting parties.[16] This requires investigation into the actual effect of fractional interests on sales in the particular market or community in which the real estate is located. Because the discount is not a matter of course, it is preferred that actual sales at discount be shown. In one case, where neither side could show the existence of the discount except that it was general practice in the community to recognize the discount, the court split the difference between the two contested valuations.[17] In a recent letter ruling, the I.R.S. refused to approve a discount sought by an estate for a 50 percent interest in a personal residence.[18] Recently, a court rejected for gift tax valuation purposes a fractional share discount for real property transferred into a trust, because the taxpayer failed to prove that the undivided interests had a fair market value of less than their proportionate share of the value of the entire property.[19]

In another court decision, the taxpayer was permitted to take a blockage discount from the normal value of the subject real properties.[20] At the time of his death, the decedent owned five lumber yards which constituted the largest single group owned by one person. The court held that a blockage discount applies "to an immediate oversupply of goods which demand (the Market) will not absorb at optimum prices."[21] The court allowed a 20 percent discount from normal fair market value of the properties.

Another discount that has been recognized is a lack of marketability discount. This discount is applicable when some factor is present that restricts the resale of the asset. For example, a court held that the gift tax value of timber land is affected by the

[16] I.R.S. Tax Law Course, 21-27 to -28; *see* Estate of M. Iacono, 49 T.C.M. (P-H) ¶80,520 (1980).
[17] Estate of S. Henry, 4 T.C. 423 (1944), *aff'd,* 161 F.2d 574 (3d Cir. 1947), *acq.* 1945 C.B. 4.
[18] Letter Rul. 8034005.
[19] W. Cullman, 50 T.C.M. (P-H) ¶81,666 (1981).
[20] Estate of T. Folks, 51 T.C.M. (P-H) ¶82,043 (1982). *See* **§3.5** Blockage Discount for Traded Securities.
[21] Estate of T. Folks, 51 T.C.M. (P-H) ¶82,043 at p.188 (1982).

existence of a long-term timber-cutting contract.[22] The court held that the land subject to such a contract should be given a lower value.[23] Although the court did not determine a specific percentage discount, it effectively set a discount by raising the capitalization rate applicable to the property's earnings.

§5.7 Amenities and Aesthetics

Amenities are basically the tangible and intangible non-monetary benefits that the owner of real property receives. The concept is like a nonbusiness, noneconomic analogue of goodwill. For residential property, amenities include nearby recreational or shopping facilities. Amenities are very difficult to value; appraisers are warned to be particularly careful. The consideration of amenities generally occurs in the context of single-family residential property, and sometimes for multiple-family dwellings such as duplexes, fourplexes, and condominiums.[24] This concept has similarities to the "value to the owner" concept. For tax valuation purposes, amenities are not given much weight.

Aesthetic considerations may also be relevant to particular buyers and sellers: for example, better neighborhoods or the best neighborhood, quality construction, and preferred architectural style might be relevant to valuation. Aesthetic factors should be and ordinarily will be incorporated into the normal methods of value determination but must be used with care. Aesthetic issues could arise for all types of improved real property, including commercial and residential properties.

§5.8 Livestock Carrying Capacity

Valuation determinations for large tracts of agricultural real property committed to raising livestock sometimes refer to the land's "livestock carrying capacity." This carrying capacity is stated in terms of an animal unit month (AUM). An AUM equals the number of animals that can be grazed on the land, usually per acre, during a month's time without injurious effect on the land's vegetation cover.

An animal unit is commonly defined as equal to one of the following:[25]

1. A mature beef animal or a dairy cow that produces two hundred pounds of butterfat per year
2. A two-year-old steer or range cow weighing 1,000 pounds or more
3. A fraction of one or both of the above.

---

22 Saunders v. United States, 48 A.F.T.R.2d ¶148,481 (M.D. Ga. 1981).

23 *Id.* at 6281; *see* **§4.26** Lack of Marketability Discount.

24 Anderson, *Appraisal of Residential Property,* Encyclopedia of Real Estate Appraising 217 (3d ed. E. Friedman ed., 1978).

25 American Society of Farm Managers and Rural Appraisers, Inc., Rural Appraisal Manual 35 (5th ed. 1979).

These standards are maintained regardless of the type of livestock is involved. For example, an adult sheep equals .2 or .25 AUM, and a horse equals 1.1 AUM.

Using AUMs, the value of the land is equal to the value attributed to each AUM times the number of AUMs the land will carry. This calculation requires estimations of both the value of an AUM and the land's carrying capacity. Because of the speculative nature of these two estimates, you should seldom if ever rely solely on carrying capacity valuation. It is used as a collateral and corroborative technique for the market and income approaches.

Where AUMs have a common local value, and carrying capacity of the land can be calculated relatively easily and reasonably accurately, carrying capacity valuations may constitute a type of short-form valuation.[26] As such, they possess all of the limitations and dangers inherent in the other short form techniques.[27]

§5.9 The Subdivision Approach to Real Property Valuation

As already stated, some real properties must be valued for purposes other than their current use. This is part of the highest and best use concept.[28] This is particularly true of undeveloped or vacant land suitable for subdivision.

If vacant land is suitable for subdivision, the ordinarily applicable market approach to valuation is sometimes inadequate. Consequently, an entirely distinct approach is necessary: the "subdivision" or "development" or "anticipated use" approach.[29] Sometimes it is used as the primary determinant of value; at other times it is used in combination with, or in corroboration of, the other relevant approaches.[30]

Basically, the sudivision approach attempts to estimate the present value of the vacant land as if the land were coverted into a subdivision and each of the individual lots were valued separately.

This general outline shows you how to make valuations under the subdivision approach:[31]

1. Develop a proposed plan that details the physical layout of the subdivision
2. Estimate the annual absorption rate (the rate at which the lots of the subdivision can be sold in the market) of the expected subdivision

---

26 *See* **§5.4** Short Form Valuation Techniques for Real Property.

27 *See* Davis, *Appraisal of Rural Real Estate,* Encyclopedia of Real Estate Appraising 583-602 (3d ed., E. Friedman ed., 1978).

28 *See* **§5.1** Introduction to Real Property Valuation.

29 Fuller, *Appraisal of a Proposed Residential Subdivision Development,* Encyclopedia of Real Estate Appraising 662 (3d ed., E. Friedman ed., 1978); American Institute of Real Estate Appraisers (AIREA), The Appraisal of Real Estate 147-48 (7th ed. 1978).

30 *See* Estate of E. Rabe, 44 T.C.M. (P-H) ¶75,026 (1975), *aff'd,* (9th Cir. 1977)

31 Fuller, Encyclopedia of Real Estate Appraising 661-69 (3d ed., E. Friedman ed., 1978).

3. Set the value of each individual lot in the subdivision using the market approach
4. Determine the annual gross proceeds derivable from anticipated sales of lots according to the absorption rate estimate
5. Estimate the annual direct costs (according to the absorption rate estimate) necessary to subdivide the land under the plan. Include costs due to development, construction, professional fees, license, permits, assessments, etc.
6. Estimate the annual indirect costs (according to the absorption rate estimate) necessary to subdivide the land under the plan. Include costs of financing, insurance, promotion, taxes, management, overhead, and developer's profit
7. Determine annual net proceeds for each year (according to the absorption rate estimate) by subtracting annual direct costs 5. and annual costs 6. from corresponding annual proceeds 4.
8. Determine the present value for each of the annual net proceed amounts, using an appropriate rate of return based on comparable investments
9. Add the present value calculations for each year to determine the market value for the entire subdivision.

Remember that the value determined under this approach is clearly hypothetical, calling for a great deal of speculation on the part of the valuator. Consequently, you should use this technique only if expert appraisers will be involved.

Sometimes the I.R.S. has used this approach for agricultural land in or near recreational and urban areas. The I.R.S. has been criticized for such use which helped prompt Congress to adopt I.R.C. §2032A.[32]

§5.10 Reuse Valuations

A reuse valuation deals with real property that has gone through a metamorphosis.[33]

For example, consider real property which began as vacant land, had improvements built on it, and now these improvements have been leveled. The land has returned to its original condition—i.e., vacant. The land must be valued as vacant land.

The market approach is the primary approach for valuing reuse property.[34] Urban renewal frequently causes valuation problems for reused land. When this is the case, favorable financing considerations may have to be treated in the valuation. Disadvantages (e.g., governmental interference, higher bid tendencies on building projects, limitations on resale, size of the land area and other marketability problems) also have to be considered.

---

32 *See* §**5.20** Special Use Valuation Generally.

33 Nelson, *Urban Renewal and Community Development,* Encyclopedia of Real Estate Appraising 323-57 (3d ed., E. Friedman ed., 1978).

34 *Id.* at 339-41; *see also* Rev. Proc. 79-24, 1979-1 C.B. 565.

VALUATION APPROACHES

§5.11 The Market Approach to Real Property Valuation

The most common, and some believe the most reliable, valuation technique for real property is to estimate value from sales of similar and comparable property.[35] When sales of similar properties are numerous and contemporary with the valuation date, the market approach is quite simple in application. It merely requires making minor adjustments to the sales prices of the most comparable properties.[36] This approach has been used often by the courts for tax valuation purposes.[37]

The first order of business for the market approach is to gather as much information as possible concerning sales of real property contemporary with the date of valuation. There are numerous sources for this information, including:[38]

1. Files of appraisers
2. Real estate concerns' listings and files
3. Records of Abstract or title insurance company records
4. Files of the tax assessor's office
5. Reporting services of real estate or financial newspapers
6. Other public records.

There are various factors that are useful in making a market comparison. The ideal situation would include the following:[39]

1. Knowledgeable buyers and sellers who are familiar with the local market
2. Numerous sales between such buyers and sellers
3. Sales concerned with properties comparable to the property to be valued
4. Terms of sale are similar
5. Contemporary sales.

With or without optimal data, the goal of the market approach is to decipher relevant information so that some reasonable estimate of value may be made. This effort requires analysis that may range from informal statistical information to computerized multiple regression analysis. Often, the effort will fall in between and employ a moderate

---

35 *See* Rev. Proc. 79-24, 1979-1 C.B. 565.

36 *See* 5 Am. Jur. Proof of Facts 2d, Market Value of Single-Family Residence—Market Comparison Appraisal 411 (1975).

37 Wolfsen Land & Cattle Co., 72 T.C. 1 (1979); Estate of D. Murphy, 50 T.C.M. (P-H) ¶81,489 (1947).

38 A. Ring, The Valuation of Real Estate 115 (2d ed. 1970); *see* **5.2**—Checklist of Information to Gather for Real Property Valuation.

39 Parvin, *Market Approach to Value,* Encyclopedia of Real Estate Appraising 23-24 (3d ed., E. Friedman ed., 1978).

statistical approach using linear regression analysis.[40] The purpose of statistical analysis is to discover some central tendency or frequency.

Almost every conceivable factual issue is comparable when the market approach is used. Comparability applies not only to the physical similarity between the properties, but also to all other relevant economic considerations. The following is a list of the most common comparable issues:

1. Type of property (is it residential, agricultural, business, manufacturing, etc.)
2. Physical characteristics in detail (including size, subparts, construction, etc.)
3. Location (the economic relevance of the particular surroundings of the subject property)
4. The land (including size, condition, content, etc.)
5. Legal restrictions (including zoning, convenants, taxes, assessments, etc.)
6. Terms of the sale (including assumable loan, cost of new financing, etc.).

In addition, it is particularly important to weigh relevant economic trends in the nation and in the particular community. These trends include such underlying factors as interest rates, construction costs, new starts, vacancy statistics, operating expenses and, of course, income.[41] Trends may indicate a downturn or an upturn in market values, and should be reflected in the estimated market value.

No two properties are exactly the same. Notwithstanding, the market approach is still a useful method to estimate the value of real property. The task of the appraiser, of course, is to make appropriate adjustments.

The more numerous and similar the comparable sales data are, the easier the derivation of a reasonable estimated value. When similarities and numbers decrease, the task is more difficult; it requires identification of the most comparable factors. This, in turn, requires that adjustments be made for economically important differences to the comparable sales. Such adjustments are often very arbitrary. Clearly, you have some degree of control over them. In the final analysis, the estimate of value that is most logical and best justified will be the one accepted when differences of opinion materialize.

The usual technique is to attempt to identify the most common denominators. Probably the most frequently used common denominator is the price-per-square-foot comparison. This may be particularly useful where the only difference is one of size. When other differences exist (and they usually do) a more refined approach may be necessary.

---

[40] *See* **§2.25** Statistical and Regression Analysis.

[41] Parvin, *Market Approach to Value,* Encyclopedia of Real Estate Appraising 35 (3d ed., E. Friedman ed., 1978).

§5.12 —Another Market Technique

Another common technique is to break the differences down into particular categories and to attempt to attribute some adjustment factor for each of the differences.[42] The adjustment factors are usually shown in one of the following manners:

1. In the form of a single lump-sum monetary adjustment
2. In monetary adjustments related specifically to the different component factors
3. By index or decimal adjustments, depending on the particular differences in the factors.

The following illustration summarizes these techniques:

Illustration V-2

LUMP SUM ADJUSTMENT

A. Comparable Sales	B. Sales Prices	H. Adjustment	J. Adjusted Value of Subject Property
1	$73,000	+$2,000	$75,000
2	$70,000	+$3,000	$73,000
3	$77,000	−$3,000	$74,000

COMPONENT MONETARY ADJUSTMENT

A. Comparable Sales	B. Sales Prices	C. Time	D. Location	E. Land	F. Improvements	G. Term of Sales	J. Adjusted Value of Subject Property
1	$73,000	−$2,000	+$2,000	—	+$2,000	—	$75,000
2	$70,000	—	−$1,000	+$2,000	+$1,000	+$1,000	$73,000
3	$77,000	—	−$2,000	+$1,000	−$1,000	−$1,000	$74,000

INDEX ADJUSTMENT

A.	B.	C.	D.	E.	F.	G.	I. Index of Comparability	J. (Rounded)
1	$73,000	.97	1.03	1.00	1.03	1.00	1.03	$75,000
2	$70,000	1.00	.99	1.03	1.01	1.01	1.04	$73,000
3	$77,000	1.00	.97	1.01	.99	.99	.96	$74,000

The Index of Comparability (I.) is calculated by multiplying the index numbers in columns C.—G. The index numbers in columns C.—G. roughly compare to the mone-

42 *Id.* at 31-34.

tary adjustments made in columns C.—G. under the Component Monetary Adjustment system.

The lump-sum adjustment method requires a thorough understanding of the market and of comparable factors. The index adjustment method is least desirable, because it requires an additional calculation that may change results. The component monetary adjustment method is most frequently used, because it is a compromise between the other two methods. It incorporates a degree of technical refinement without significantly increasing the complexity of the calculations.

Market approach analysis is also helpful in determining value according to either the cost approach or the income approach. For cost approach analysis, the market data technique is useful for obtaining data on the price of land, building materials, labor and other cost factors. For an income approach technique, market data may be referred to to determine the proper capitalization rate, or the proper anticipated income for new property.[43]

Several collateral matters deserve mention here: probate appraisals, unaccepted offers, sales at auctions, and comparable sales not at arm's length.

Probate court appraisals should not be relied upon unless qualified persons prepared them. There are situations, however, where such appraisals have been recognized. For example, they have been used successfully as corroboration for other expert appraisals, and have been relied upon when no other evidence has been presented.[44]

Similarly, unaccepted offers constitute evidence of value, but are not determinative of value. Rejected offers provide some inference that the seller believes the value is greater than the offer.[45] Unaccepted asking price offers imply that the property should not be valued above that amount. Again, it must be emphasized, these are evidentiary inferences, not conclusive presumptions; some courts, however, have relied heavily on rejected offers.[46]

Because a sale at an auction is typically considered a forced sale, auction sale prices are of little weight in determining market value.[47] This is also true of other involuntary sales including, for example, foreclosure sales, execution or attachment auctions, or even eminent domain compulsion sales.[48]

Comparable sales that are not made at arm's length are treated the same way. The clear inference here is that such sales do not necessarily constitute market value if familiar concerns have been injected into the bargaining process. When an arm's-length sale of the subject property occurs within a reasonable period of time before or after the valuation date, the sale price will be given significant weight in determining market value.[49] Obviously, the passage of time or the lack of arm's length dealing, or both, will raise the need for adjustment to the sale price.

---

[43] *Id.* at 28.

[44] *See* Chalmers, *Valuation of Real Estate,* 299 T.M. A-5-6 (1978); *see* **§2.7** Limitations on Appraisals and Expert Testimony.

[45] *See* Annot., 174 A.L.R. 386 (1948); Annot., 7 A.L.R.2d 781 (1949).

[46] C. Wilson, 5 B.T.A. 615 (1926), *acq.* VI-1 C.B. 6.

[47] Chalmers, *Valuation of Real Estate,* 299 T.M. A-4 (1978).

[48] Smith, *Issues and Problems in the Valuation of Real Estate,* 30 N.Y.U. Inst. Fed. Tax'n. 218 (1972).

[49] *See* **§2.11** Sales of the Asset; Rev. Proc. 79-24, 1979-1 C.B. 565; *see also* Chalmers, *Valuation of Real Estate,* 299 T.M. A-3 (1978).

§5.13 —Worksheet for the Market Approach to Real Property Valuation

ITEMS	COMPARABLES					SUBJECT PROPERTY
	1	2	3	4	5	
LAND Address						
Proximity						
Size						
IMPROVEMENTS Description						
Rooms						
Bedrooms						
Baths						
Other Rooms						
Size: Square Feet						
Year Built						
Construction Type						
Quality						
Condition						
Utility						
FINANCIAL Mortgage						
Terms of Sale						
Time of Sale						
Sale Price						
ADJUSTMENTS Time						
Location						
Land						
Improvements						
Terms						
Adjusted Value of Property						
Estimated Market Value						

§5.14 The Income Approach to Real Property Valuation

For most income-producing real property, it is essential that the valuator make use of the income approach of valuation even if one or more of the other approaches has also been completed.[50] Even with nonincome-producing property, the income approach may be useful, particularly if it is possible to justify hypothetical income for the property. The most typical cases of this kind are residential properties; a hypothetical income can be formulated using known rental income from comparable properties.

The basic technique of the income approach is to determine an appropriate annual net income, and to capitalize this income at an appropriate rate. The keys to this approach are obvious: determination of income and determination of the rate of capitalization.[51] Efforts to make these determinations run the gamut from cursory to extensive and complex, with most efforts falling somewhere in between.[52]

The first task is to determine what is sometimes called the "net operating income" by gathering data concerned with the financial operations of the income-producing real property. Preferably, three to five years of the financial statements and records of the property should be obtained and analyzed.[53] The goal is to estimate a future flow of income, using historical data as a base. If economic conditions indicate a future change of income, the past income figures must be adjusted.[54]

Information that must be extracted from this data includes:

1. The gross income estimate
2. Allowance for vacancies
3. Other income including, for example, parking fees and other concession services
4. Operating expenses including, for example, fixed expenses, amortization reserves for short-lived assets, and other expenses attributable to operations.

With the above figures, the net operating income can be determined, as the following simple example illustrates:

---

50 *See* Montrose Cemetary Co. v. Commissioner, 105 F.2d 238 (7th Cir. 1939), *aff'd,* 309 U.S. 622 (1940).

51 *See* **§2.19** Capitalization of Income.

52 *See generally* Cox, *Income Approach to Value,* Encyclopedia of Real Estate Appraising 41-43 (3d ed., E. Friedman ed., 1978); *see* 3 Am. Jur. Proof of Facts 2d, *Rental Value of Realty* 457 (1974).

53 *See* I.R.S. Tax Law Course, 21-10.

54 *See* **§4.5** Capitalization of Business Interest's Earnings, for a related discussion.

Illustration V-3

Assumptions	
Gross Income	$200,000
Vacancy Allowance	$10,000
Other Income	$5,000
Operating Expenses	$100,000

Calculation	
1. The gross income	$200,000
2. Less the vacancy allowance	−$10,000
3. Effective gross rental	$190,000
4. Add the other income	+$5,000
5. Effective gross income	$195,000
6. Less total operating expenses	−$100,000
7. Net operating income	$ 95,000

The care that must be taken in computing these figures cannot be overemphasized. All four must be carefully checked to insure accuracy. If the figures themselves are inaccurate, the valuator must develop a reasonable hypothetical figure. There is obviously a great deal of discretion that goes into their make-up, and thus ultimately into the estimate of value.

The determination of capitalization rates has been discussed before.[55] Further comment would not be made except that the determination process is probably more developed with respect to real property than with any other type of asset.

An important distinction that deserves immediate explanation relates to the practical observation that most income-producing improved real properties can be analyzed in two parts: the land without the improvement and the improvement. It can be assumed that each part contributes its share to the net income of the property as a whole. The two most important techniques for dealing with this distinction are direct capitalization and residual capitalization.

Direct capitalization takes a calculated overall rate of capitalization and computes it against total net operating income of the real property. No distinction is made between income attributable to the land and income attributable to the improvement.

Residual capitalization divides the rate of capitalization into two segments: one attributable to the income from the unimproved land, the other attributable to income from the improvements. A different rate of capitalization may be applied to each type of property.

Residual capitalization is often used where the net income and the value of one segment for the real property are known.[56] When this occurs, a fair interest rate is applied against the value of the known part, and the result of the calculation is

---

[55] *See* **§2.19** Capitalization of Income.

[56] *See* Saunders v. United States, 48 A.F.T.R.2d ¶148,481 (M.D. Ga. 1981).

subtracted from the net income. The income remaining, after the interest on the known segment is subtracted, constitutes the residual income which provides the name of the technique. The residual income is then capitalized at an appropriate rate to find the value of the unknown part. The sum of the value of the known segment and the capitalized value of the other segment constitutes the full market value of the real property. The following illustration exhibits this technique:

Illustration V-4

Assumptions	
Land value	$300,000
Net income	90,000
Remaining economic life of improvement	25 years
Amortization Method	Straight Line
Interest rate	.12

Calculation			
1. Land value			$300,000
2. Net income		$90,000	
3. Less apportionate income	$300,000 × .12		
	36,000	36,000	
		54,000	
4. Net income from improvement			
5. Interest rate	.12		
6. Recapture rate (1 ÷ 25 = .04)	.04		
7. Capitalization	.16		
8. 4. divided by 7.		÷ .16	
9. Improvement values			337,500
10. Total property value (1. plus 9.)			637,500
11. Total (Rounded)			$638,000

It is important to note that this method may be employed whether the value of the land segment is known or the value of the improvements segment is known.

§5.15 —How to Determine the Rate of Capitalization

The rate of capitalization is usually determined by one or more of the following five methods. No matter the method(s) used, the actual determination of the rate remains only an educated guess.

1. Market Method. This method calculates the rate of capitalization from sale prices and income figures of comparable income-producing real properties. The key to this technique is to find comparable properties, which requires an extensive market analysis and emphasizes the importance of the market approach to valuation.[57] For example if the most appropriate comparable property's sale price is $500,000, and that property's net operating income is $75,000, the rate of capitalization would equal the income divided by the sales price.

$$\frac{\$\ 75{,}000}{\$500{,}000} = .15$$

The rate of capitalization equals 15 percent.

2. Band of Investment Method. This method calculates the capitalization rate from a combination of factors. The typical factors include the rate of interest for primary and secondary financing of the property and the rate of interest desired by the purchaser on his or her equity. For example, if the property is to be financed by an 80 percent mortgage at 16 percent interest, and the purchaser wants to obtain a 14 percent interest rate on the equity, the calculations would be as follows:

Mortgage:	80 × .16 =	12.8
Equity:	20 × .14 =	2.8
Totals	100%	15.6

The rate of capitalization equals 15.6 percent.

3. Component Rate Method. This method is similar to the band of investment method, but uses different factors. Basically, it adds up the rates attributable to different factors including the ordinary U. S. Bond interest rate, the risk, potentiality of nonliquidity, and the cost of management of investment. For example, the rate might be calculated as follows:

U. S. Bond interest rate	13.00%
Risk factor	2.00%
Nonliquidity factor	.50%
Management of investment factor	.25%
Capitalization rate total	15.75%

Capitalization rate equals 15.75 percent.

4. Mortgage Equity Technique. The mortgage equity capitalization technique,

---

57 *See* **§5.11** The Market Approach to Real Property Valuation.

sometimes called the Ellwood method in honor of its creator, is a special technique for deriving an overall rate of capitalization.[58] Although difficult to understand and to apply if one began from scratch, the technique has been greatly simplified by precalculated tables.[59] This technique is now so simple and seemingly accurate that the I.R.S. fears its use discourages appraisers from using other techniques.[60] The theory behind mortgage equity capitalization is that the value of real property should be viewed from the standpoint of the investor. This technique is usually applied to income producing property. It is assumed that the investor who buys such property will ordinarily make a low down payment and borrow as much as possible to make the purchase. It is also assumed that, because of income tax considerations, the investor intends to hold the property for a limited period of time only. With these assumptions, it is assumed that the investor is concerned about three primary matters:[61]

1. The amount that he or she will have to invest
2. The rate of yield from the amount invested, and
3. The net amount recovered on sale of the asset.

The goal of this technique is to find an overall capitalization rate for the net income of the property. This requires, of course, a separate calculation of the net income, and determination of six variables that are built into the appropriate tables. These variables are:

1. The anticipated holding period
2. The ratio of loans anticipated
3. The term of the loan
4. The rate of interest of the loan
5. The anticipated appreciation or depreciation in value
6. The percentage of total yield on the purchaser's equity.

With the answers to the above variables, it is a simple task to turn to the appropriate table and to identify the proper capitalization figure.[62] This process may require complex analysis. In the area of real estate investment, there are popular systems that attempt to consider the effect of tax shelter possibilities on the yield of investments.[63]

The following illustration shows how this technique operates:

---

[58] Cox, *Income Approach to Value,* Encyclopedia of Real Estate Appraising 56-60 (3d ed., E. Friedman ed., 1978).

[59] A text that contains an excellent explanation of this technique is I. Johnson, Selling Real Estate by Mortgage-Equity Analysis (1976).

[60] I.R.S. Estate Tax Course, 21-14.

[61] I. Johnson, Selling Real Estate by Mortgage-Equity Analysis 1 (1976).

[62] *See* Chart V-2 in this section.

[63] *See* §**2.19** Capitalization of Income.

Illustration V-5
MORTGAGE-EQUITY CAPITALIZATION TECHNIQUE

Assumptions	
Net Annual Income	$10,000
Holding Period	Ten Years
Mortgage Data	
Loan Ratio	80%
Interest Rate	14%
Term of Years	Twenty Years
Appreciation (Depreciation)	40%
Equity Yield Rate	15%

Calculation

Net Annual Income ÷ Pre-calculated Overall Rate = Estimated Market Value

[Pre-calculated Overall Rate: Using the Chart V-2, the correct table is found by matching the holding period, yield rate, and loan ratio with the facts of the illustration. When these match, the factor is found by tracking down the first column under the term of years marked 20, passing to the next column on its right to the line under appreciation (depreciation) marked .40 and then moving along this line directly to the factor under the interest rate marked 14.0. The factor at that site is .121832]:

$10,000 ÷ .121832 = $82,080.24

The estimated market value for the real property under this technique is $82,000 (rounded).

Although the tables make the mathematics of the technique simple, the actual decision-making process with regard to the variables requires a significant amount of judgment. Assigning different amounts to the variables will result in different valuations. When two or more of the variables are changed, the effect on valuation will be even more significant. Consequently, in order to arrive at a fixed capitalization rate, the appraiser must arbitrarily select particular values for all the variables. In order to temper the arbitrariness, some suggest identifying a range of equity yields using several meaningful variables and then selecting a point among the range.[64]

5. The Gettel Technique. Another technique, the Gettel Method, has been recently suggested for determining the overall capitalization rate.[65] Recommended for investors, it is an offshoot of the Ellwood Method. It is actually less complex because it does not require the use of the tables that may be confusing or unavailable. The Gettel Technique

[64] The above constitutes only a brief and generalized explanation of the technique. A full explanation including illustrations of its application can be found in I. Johnson, Selling Real Estate by Mortgage-Equity Analysis (1976). Another full explanation of the system is found in L. Elwood, Tables for Real Estate Appraising and Financing, Part I-II (Compiled for the American Institute of Real Estate Appraisers by L. W. Ellwood) (3d ed. 1970).

[65] Gettel, *"Good Grief," ANOTHER Method of Selecting Capitalization Rates,* 46 Appraisal J. 90 (1978).

Chart V-2[a]

SAMPLE MORTGAGE EQUITY TABLE
(10.0 YEAR HOLDING PERIOD, .150 EQUITY YIELD RATE, .800 LOAN RATIO)

		INTEREST RATE												
TERM YEARS	APPR DEP	5.0	6.0	7.0	7.5	8.0	8.5	9.0	9.5	10.0	11.0	12.0	13.0	14.0
10	.40	.072720	.077477	.082362	.084851	.087372	.089924	.092506	.095119	.097762	.103138	.108630	.114236	.119953
	.30	.077646	.082402	.087287	.089776	.092297	.094849	.097431	.100044	.102687	.108063	.113555	.119161	.124879
	.20	.082571	.087328	.092212	.094702	.097222	.099774	.102357	.104970	.107613	.112988	.118480	.124086	.129804
	.10	.087496	.092253	.097137	.099627	.102148	.104699	.107282	.109895	.112538	.117913	.123405	.129011	.134729
	0.00	.092421	.097178	.102062	.104552	.107073	.109625	.112207	.114820	.117463	.122838	.128330	.133937	.139654
	–.10	.097346	.102103	.106988	.109477	.111998	.114550	.117132	.119745	.122388	.127764	.133256	.138862	.144579
	–.20	.102272	.107028	.111913	.114402	.116923	.119475	.122058	.124670	.127313	.132689	.138181	.143787	.149505
	–.30	.107197	.111954	.116838	.119328	.121848	.124400	.126983	.129596	.132239	.137614	.143106	.148712	.154430
	–.40	.112122	.116879	.121763	.124253	.126774	.129325	.131908	.134521	.137164	.142539	.148031	.153637	.159355
15	.40	.063325	.069106	.075070	.078119	.081211	.084344	.087519	.090734	.093988	.100608	.107372	.114271	.121296
	.30	.068250	.074031	.079996	.083044	.086136	.089269	.092444	.095659	.098913	.105533	.112297	.119196	.126221
	.20	.073175	.078957	.084921	.087969	.091061	.094195	.097369	.100584	.103838	.110459	.117223	.124121	.131146
	.10	.078100	.083882	.089846	.092895	.095986	.099120	.102295	.105509	.108763	.115384	.122148	.129047	.136072
	0.00	.083026	.088807	.094771	.097820	.100911	.104045	.107220	.110435	.113688	.120309	.127073	.133972	.140997
	–.10	.087951	.093732	.099697	.102745	.105837	.108970	.112145	.115360	.118614	.125234	.131998	.138897	.145922
	–.20	.092876	.098657	.104622	.107670	.110762	.113896	.117070	.120285	.123539	.130159	.136924	.143822	.150847
	–.30	.097801	.103583	.109547	.112595	.115687	.118821	.121995	.125210	.128464	.135085	.141849	.148748	.155772
	–.40	.102727	.108508	.114472	.117521	.120612	.123746	.126921	.130135	.133389	.140010	.146774	.153673	.160698
20	.40	.058770	.065101	.071636	.074975	.078360	.081787	.085257	.088766	.092312	.099512	.106841	.114286	.121832
	.30	.063695	.070027	.076561	.079900	.083285	.086712	.090182	.093691	.097238	.104437	.111766	.119211	.126757
	.20	.068620	.074952	.081487	.084826	.088210	.091638	.095107	.098616	.102163	.109362	.116692	.124136	.131683
	.10	.073545	.079877	.086412	.089751	.093135	.096563	.100032	.103541	.107088	.114288	.121617	.129061	.136608
	0.00	.078470	.084802	.091337	.094676	.098060	.101488	.104957	.108466	.112013	.119213	.126542	.133986	.141533
	–.10	.083396	.089727	.096262	.099601	.102986	.106413	.109883	.113392	.116938	.124138	.131467	.138912	.146458
	–.20	.088321	.094653	.101187	.104526	.107911	.111339	.114808	.118317	.121864	.129063	.136392	.143837	.151383
	–.30	.093246	.099578	.106113	.109452	.112836	.116264	.119733	.123242	.126789	.133988	.141318	.148762	.156309
	–.40	.098171	.104503	.111038	.114377	.117761	.121189	.124658	.128167	.131714	.138914	.146243	.153687	.161234

25	.40	.056146	.062834	.069731	.073251	.076814	.080418	.084061	.087740	.091451	.098965	.106585	.114292	.122074
	.30	.061071	.067760	.074656	.078176	.081739	.085343	.088986	.092665	.096377	.103891	.111510	.119218	.126999
	.20	.065996	.072685	.079582	.083101	.086664	.090269	.093911	.097590	.101302	.108816	.116435	.124143	.131924
	.10	.070921	.077610	.084507	.088026	.091590	.095194	.098837	.102515	.106227	.113741	.121360	.129068	.136849
	0.00	.075846	.082535	.089432	.092952	.096515	.100119	.103762	.107440	.111152	.118666	.126285	.133993	.141775
	–.10	.080772	.087460	.094357	.097877	.101440	.105044	.108687	.112366	.116077	.123591	.131211	.138918	.146700
	–.20	.085697	.092386	.099282	.102802	.106365	.109970	.113612	.117291	.121003	.128517	.136136	.143844	.151625
	–.30	.090622	.097311	.104208	.107727	.111290	.114895	.118537	.122216	.125928	.133442	.141061	.148769	.156550
	–.40	.095547	.102236	.109133	.112652	.116216	.119820	.123463	.127141	.130853	.138367	.145986	.153694	.161475
30	.40	.054483	.061428	.068578	.072221	.075904	.079624	.083378	.087163	.090975	.098674	.106453	.114296	.122189
	.30	.059408	.066353	.073503	.077146	.080829	.084549	.088303	.092088	.095901	.103599	.111378	.119221	.127114
	.20	.064333	.071278	.078428	.082071	.085754	.089474	.093229	.097013	.100826	.108524	.116303	.124146	.132039
	.10	.069258	.076204	.083354	.086996	.090680	.094400	.098154	.101938	.105751	.113449	.121228	.129071	.136964
	0.00	.074183	.081129	.088279	.091922	.095605	.099325	.103079	.106864	.110676	.118374	.126153	.133996	.141889
	–.10	.079109	.086054	.093204	.096847	.100530	.104250	.108004	.111789	.115602	.123300	.131079	.138922	.146815
	–.20	.084034	.090979	.098129	.101772	.105455	.109175	.112929	.116714	.120527	.128225	.136004	.143847	.151740
	–.30	.088959	.095904	.103055	.106697	.110380	.114101	.117855	.121639	.125452	.133150	.140929	.148772	.156665
	–.40	.093884	.100830	.107980	.111622	.115306	.119026	.122780	.126565	.130377	.138075	.145854	.153697	.161590

[a] Reproduced by permission of the publisher from Selling Real Estate By Mortgage-Equity Analysis by Irvin E. Johnson (Lexington, Mass.: Lexington Books, D. C. Heath and Company, Copyright 1976, D. C. Heath and Company).

uses a relatively simple formula that is composed of figures that most investors will already know or can reasonably estimate. The formula is:

Loan-to-Value Percentage × Annual Constant × Debt Coverage Ratio = Overall Capitalization Rate.

These terms are defined as follows: the loan-to-value percentage equals the anticipated percentage that the first mortgage loan constitutes of the total value of the property. The investor usually will know, or can find out from the relevant financial institution, what this percentage will be. The annual constant equals the percentage of the total loan that the total annual payments of the loan's interest and principal constitute. This figure is determinable from mortgage amortization schedules, if the investor knows the rate of interest and the term of years for the loan. The debt coverage ratio equals the percentage that the net operating income will constitute of the total annual payments of the loan's interest and principal. Although this figure may not be immediately available, it can be estimated by the investor as a matter of personal preference or from comparable market data.

The following illustration shows how this technique operates:

Illustration V-6

Assumptions	
Net Annual Income	$10,000
Mortgage Data—	
Loan-to-Value Percentage	80%
Interest Rate	14%
Term of Years	20 Years
Annual Constant	14.93%
Debt Coverage Ratio	1.15

Calculation

Loan-to-Value Percentage × Annual Constant × Debt Coverage Ratio = Overall Capitalization Rate

$.80 \times .1493 \times 1.15 = .137356$

Net Annual Income ÷ Overall Capitalization Rate = Estimated Market Value

$\$10{,}000 \div .137356 = \$72{,}803.52$

The estimated market value for the real property under this technique is $73,000 (Rounded).

§5.16 —Worksheet for the Income Approach to Real Property Valuation[66]

1. Gross Annual Rental Income $ ________

2. Subtract the Vacancy (Including Loss) Allowance
(________ %) −$ ________

3. Result Equals the Effective Gross Rental $ ________

4. Add Other Income $ ________

5. Result Equals the Effective Gross Income $ ________

6. Operating Expenses

(a) Management (________ %) $ ________

(b) Utilities $ ________

(c) General Repairs/Maintenance $ ________

(d) Salaries $ ________

(e) Cleaning and Supplies $ ________

(f) Advertising $ ________

(g) Professional Fees $ ________

(h) Reserves for Appliances $ ________

(i) Reserves for Heating/Cooling $ ________

(j) Reserves for Exterior $ ________

(k) Reserves for Interior $ ________

(l) Reserves for Roof $ ________

(m) Reserves for Carpet/Flooring $ ________

---

66 *See* **§5.14** The Income Approach to Real Property Valuation.

(n) Taxes $ ________

(o) Insurance $ ________

(p) ________ $ ________

(q) ________ $ ________

7. Subtract Total Operating Expenses from 5. −$ ________

8. Result Equals the Net Operating Income $ ________

9. Overall Rate of Capitalization Determination

(a) Market Method

i. Net Operating Income from Comparable Property ________

ii. Divide i. by Sale Price of that Comparable Property ÷ ________

iii. Rate of Capitalization by the Market Method . ________

(b) Band of Investment Method

Percentage Ratio × Rate = Composite

i. Mortgage ____ % × . ____ = . ____

ii. Equity ____ % × . ____ = . ____

iii. Add Composites for Total Rate of Capitalization by the Band of Investment Method . ________

(c) Component Rate Method

i. U. S. Bond Interest Rate . ________

ii. Risk Factor . ____________

iii. Nonliquidity Factor . ____________

iv. Management Factor . ____________

v. Add i-iv for Total Rate of Capitalization by the Component Rate Method . ____________

(d) Mortgage Equity Method[67]

Determine the Following:

i. Anticipated Holding Period ____________

ii. Ratio of Loan ____________

iii. Term of Loan ____________

iv. Rate of Interest on Loans ____________

v. Anticipated Appreciation (Depreciation) in Value ____________

vi. Desired Yield on Equity ____________

vii. Find Rate of Capitalization from Tables Using i.—vi. for Rate of Capitalization by the Mortgage Equity Method . ____________

(e) Gettel Method

i. Loan to Value (Percentage) Decimal ____________

ii. Annual Constant

[67] Requires use of precalculated tables; *see, e.g.,* table included in **§5.15** — How to Determine the Rate of Capitalization, Chart V–2.

(1) Annual Interest and Principal Payments ______

(2) Divide by Total Loan ÷ ______

iii. Result Equals Annual Constant × ______

iv. Multiply i. by iii. ______

v. Debt Coverage Ratio

(1) Net Operating Income ______

(2) Divide by Annual Interest and Principal Payments ÷ ______

vi. Result Equals Debt Coverage Rate × ______

vii. Multiply iv. by vi. Result equals the Rate of Capitalization by the Gettel Method . ______

10. Capitalization Calculations

Methods	9(a)	9(b)	9(c)	9(d)	9(e)
Net Operating Income 8.	______	______	______	______	______
Divide by Rate of Capitalization	÷. ______	÷. ______	÷. ______	÷. ______	÷. ______
Estimated Market Value of Real Property Using the Capitalization of Income Approach (Overall Rate)	______	______	______	______	______

§5.17 The Cost Approach to Real Property Valuation

The cost approach is considered a comparative valuation technique, and is not ordinarily used as a primary method for determining the market value for real property. The underlying theory of this approach is that potential purchasers will not pay more than reproduction cost to buy an asset. In determining whether it could be produced for less, it is necessary to consider costs due both to the physical reproduction of the asset and to the delay in having the asset reproduced.[68]

Although ordinarily relegated to secondary importance, the cost approach is definitely relevant in some situations.[69] First, it is commonly expressed that the cost approach sets the upper limit for market value; it offers a benchmark below which market value must be set. Second, it is also stated that the cost approach is the primary method for unique-purpose real property. (Unique-purpose real property includes schools, churches, funeral homes, unique or highly individualized structures and new or proposed structures.) Third, the cost approach may be referred to when the market and income approaches are not relevant or available.

Market value under the cost approach should be determined using the following procedure:

1. Determine the highest and best use value for the land as if vacant
2. Applying the appropriate cost data techniques, estimate the reproduction or replacement costs for each of the structures on the land
3. Estimate the value of all physical deterioration, functional obsolescence and economic obsolescence for each of the structures on the land
4. Subtract 3. from 2. to determine total present worth of all improvements
5. Add 4. to 1. to determine value of subject property. (Round off the amount in 5. so as to avoid the impression of precision.)

The following illustrates this procedure:

Illustration V-7

Assumptions	
Highest and Best Use Value of Land	$10,000
Reproduction or Replacement Cost	$ 75 (Per Square Foot)

[68] *See* **§2.15** Replacement and Reproduction Costs.

[69] *See generally* O'Flaherty, *Cost Approach to Value,* Encyclopedia of Real Estate Appraising 68–78 (3d ed., E. Friedman ed., 1978); *see* L. Scheidelman, 39 T.C.M. (PH) ¶70,070 (1970).

Illustration V-7 (*Continued*)

Assumptions	
Depreciation or Diminished Value	
Physical	$20,000
Economic	$10,000
Functional	$-0-
Improvement Size	2,000 Square Feet

Calculation

Real Estate—Cost Approach

1.	Highest and Best Use Land Value (Without Improvements)			$ 10,000
2.	Reproduction/Replacement Costs of the Improvement $75.00 × Sq. Ft. (2,000) =		$150,000	
3.	Subtract Depreciation or Diminished Value			
	a. Physical	$−20,000		
	b. Economic	−10,000		
	c. Functional	-0-		
	Total	$−30,000	−30,000	
4.	Add Net Cost of Improvements			120,000
5.	Value Using Cost Approach			$130,000

The cost approach requires that the land be valued separately from the improvements. Ordinarily, this is determined by the market approach.[70] Consequently, the value of the land is determined from comparable sales of the unimproved land. In valuing the land according to the market approach, it is necessary to value it at its highest and best use value. This might require valuing it for purposes other than those for which it currently used.

Appraisers use one or more of four techniques for estimating costs of new improvements.

1. The "quantity survey method" requires detailed analysis of the improvement. The improvements are broken down into individual components, and current prices are determined for each separate item. After the costs of all the items are determined, the costs of construction and collateral expenses (financing, architectural fees, profit, etc.) are added.
2. The "unit in place method" is similar to the quantity survey method, but places the costs in much broader categories including walls, floors, roofs, windows, foundations, etc. Eventually, this information is calculated into a

70 *See* Rev. Proc. 7924, 1979-1 C.B. 565.

cost per square foot or cubic foot. This makes it possible to calculate the comparable reproduction or replacement costs for any structure.

3. The "trade breakdown method" involves estimating the appropriate cost for major functional units of a structure. The cost of the entire structure is equal to the sum of the cost of the appropriate units. For example, cost will be attributed to excavation, foundation, concrete flatwork, exteriors, etc., until the whole structure is included. Direct costs including profit, overhead, architectural fees, etc., will be added to this figure.
4. The "comparative unit method" simply breaks down the cost of comparative units to a price per square foot. This figure is multiplied by the appropriate square footage of the particular structure to be valued.

The cost approach requires that, after the new costs are determined, the estimated value of the accrued depreciation be deducted. Accrued depreciation is not the same as depreciation taken for tax purposes. Accrued depreciation consists of three separate categories: physical deterioration, functional obsolescence, and economic obsolescence. Physical deterioration is self-descriptive. It may or may not be curable. Functional obsolescence refers to the structure's reduced utility from a capacity or performance standpoint. It also may be curable or incurable. Economic obsolescence refers to the structure's diminished utility due to outside economic forces. It ordinarily is not curable.

Techniques for determining accrued depreciation differ. They range from assumptions due to the estimated economic life to detailed analysis by engineers and other experts concerning the particular depreciation of the asset. The degree to which you should go to determine accrued depreciation depends on the importance of a cost approach appraisal.

§5.18 —Worksheet for the Cost Approach to Real Property Valuation[71]

1. Highest and Best Use Land Value (Without Improvements) $ __________

2. Reproduction/Replacement Costs of the Improvements

	Description	Size— ___. Ft.	Costs Per Unit	Costs
(a)	__________	__________	__________	$ __________
(b)	__________	__________	__________	$ __________

[71] *See* **§5.17** The Cost Approach to Real Property Valuation.

(c) ________ ________ ________ $________

(d) ________ ________ ________ $________

3. Total Reproduction/Replacement Costs $________

4. Depreciation or Diminished Value

(a) Physical Deterioration (Curable)*[a] $________

(b) Physical Deterioration (Incurable) $________

(c) Functional Obsolescence (Curable)*[a] $________

(d) Functional Obsolescence (Incurable) $________

(e) Economic Obsolescence $________

(f) Other Rehabilitation $________

5. Subtract Total Depreciation From 3. –________

6. Add Net Costs of Improvements to 1. ________

7. Estimated Market Value of Real Property Using the Cost Approach $________

[a]*Costs to cure deterioration or obsolescence.

§5.19 Correlation

Correlation constitutes the final step in the process of valuing real property. As previously discussed, real property valuation determinations generally employ three techniques: the market approach, the income approach and the cost approach. Correlation, then, attempts to identify the particular approach that is supported by a preponderance of the factual evidence.[72] It rejects the mere weighting or averaging of the values determined by the three approaches used.

Correlation involves five steps:

1. Comparison of the values determined separately according to the three approaches
2. Reconciliation and correction of inaccuracies in each of the three methods
3. Explanation of significant differences between the estimated values under the three approaches
4. Determination of the primary approach of value, and characterization of the other two approaches as secondary
5. Thorough documentation and explanation of the relative merit of the approaches.

Several generalities can be used to select a primary approach:

1. The market approach is usually the primary approach when there are a substantial number of sales of comparable properties
2. The income approach is usually the primary approach when comparable sales are not available, but significant information concerning the property income potential is available
3. The cost approach is usually the primary approach when the properties are new or unique purpose structures.

When two approaches arrive at the same value, it really does not make any difference

[72] Sarles, *Correlation, Analysis, and Conclusion as to Value,* Encyclopedia of Real Estate Appraising 181 (3d ed., E. Friedman ed., 1978).

which of the two is considered the primary approach, since the other will corroborate the estimated value.[73]

SPECIAL USE VALUATIONS FOR CERTAIN REAL PROPERTY

§5.20 Special Use Valuation Generally

Ordinarily, a cardinal benchmark of valuation determination is the highest and best use value of the asset being valued—the value that is tested in the marketplace. Consequently, concepts such as special use values have had little importance in valuation determinations particularly, for tax purposes. The recent alteration in this rule derives from I.R.C. §2032A, added by Congress in the 1976 Tax Reform Act and supplemented and clarified by the Economic Recovery Tax Act of 1981.[74]

Basically, this section permits a decedent's personal representative to elect a special use value for qualified real property. The special use value is related to its present use value and not to the qualified real property's highest and best use value. Several states have passed more or less similar provisions for their estate or inheritance taxes.[75] For example, California, Illinois, Kansas, Mississippi, New York, Tennessee and Virginia have provisions based on I.R.C. §2032A; Connecticut, Kentucky, Maryland and Oregon have provisions that are similar in effect to I.R.C. §2032A, but that are cast in their own form. Other states will probably follow suit in some form or other.

I.R.C. §2032A only applies to certain types of real property devoted to particular qualified uses. "Qualified use" is defined to include use as a farm for farming purposes, or use in any other trade or business.[76]

The term "farm" is specifically defined to include a long list of types of farms including, for example, ranches, orchards, and woodlands.[77] In the Internal Revenue Code Regulations, the term "trade or business" is limited to active businesses such as manufacturing, mercantile, or service enterprises as well as those related to agricultural or horticultural activities.[78] Passive rental real properties and nonprofit businesses do not qualify. Structures and other improvements regularly occupied or used for operat-

---

73 *See* A. Ring, The Valuation of Real Estate 350–51 (2d ed. 1970).

74 *See* **§2.16** Special Use Value.

75 *See* J. Kolb, Section 2032A: Special Valuation of Farm and Business Property, Ch. VIII (1981); D. Kelley & D. Ludtke, Estate Planning for Farmers and Ranchers §§17.21–.110 (1980).

76 I.R.C. §2032A(b)(2).

77 I.R.C. §2032A(e)(4).

78 Reg. §20.2032A3(b)(1).

ing purposes for the qualified real property do qualify within the meaning of these terms.[79] This would include, of course, a decedent's residence on a farm.

Under the Economic Recovery Tax Act of 1981, a special rule is adopted for timber. Before the Act, standing timber, like other growing crops, was not treated as part of the value of the qualified real property.[80] Under the Act, the personal representative may elect to specially value qualified woodland not as a crop but as part of the value of the qualified real property.[81] "Qualified woodland" is defined as any real property that is used in timber operations and is an identifiable area of land such as an acre or other area for which records are normally maintained in conducting timber operations. "Timber operations" means the planting, cultivating, caring for, or cutting of trees or preparation (other than milling) of trees for market.

If the standing timber in the qualified woodland is severed or disposed of, or the right to sever is disposed of, the disposition or severance is treated as a disposition of a portion of the qualified interest, and the recapture tax is imposed.[82]

I.R.C. §2032A sets out the special use techniques that must be used.[83] Basically, the techniques are divided into two systems. The first is used for valuing qualified farms under specified circumstances, and the second is for valuing qualified real property under all other circumstances. The first method is commonly referred to as a "Paragraph 7 valuation"; the second as a "Paragraph 8 valuation." These references come from I.R.C. §2032A(e).

§5.21 I.R.C. §2032A Pre-election Requirements

The general pre-election requirements for the special use value provision are as follows:

1. It is an election available only for a decedent's estate and therefore only for estate tax purposes
2. It is limited to decedents who are citizens or residents of the United States at the date of death
3. The qualified real property must be located in the United States
4. The estate must own qualified real property being used for a qualified use
5. The qualified real property must pass to a qualified heir
6. The qualified real property must have been owned and used for a qualified use by the decedent or member of decedent's family for periods aggregating five or more of the last eight years immediately prior to the decedent's death
7. Subject to special rules for surviving spouses, disabled persons and certain retired persons, the decedent or a member of decedent's family must have

---

79 Reg. §20.2032A3(b)(2).

80 Letter Rul. 8046012.

81 I.R.C. §2032A(e)(13).

82 I.R.C. §2032A(c)(2)(E).

83 I.R.C. §§2032A(e)(7), and (8).

materially participated in the operation of the qualified real property for periods aggregating five or more of the last eight years immediately prior to the decedent's death

8. The special use value is applicable only to the value of the qualified real property.

Most of the key terms used above are defined or explained in I.R.C. §2032A.[84]

It must be emphasized that you must read this section and its Regulations very carefully before any absolute determination of qualification is made. Currently, detailed analyses of this section are available in numerous publications dealing with estate planning or real property.[85]

§5.22 I.R.C. § 2032A Monetary Limitations

In order to make an election under I.R.C. §2032A, the estate must satisfy two threshold monetary criteria:[86]

1. The qualified real property and its accompanying personal property must, at its highest and best use adjusted value, equal 50 percent or more of the adjusted value of the gross estate
2. The highest and best use adjusted value of the qualified property alone must equal 25 percent or more of the adjusted value of the gross estate.

For these threshold qualification amounts, the properties are valued at their highest and best use value. The adjusted values are determined by subtracting unpaid mortgages or other indebtedness in respect of the property that are deductible under I.R.C. §2053(a)(4), from the highest and best use values of gross estate and the qualified property.[87]

If both threshold amounts and all other requirements are satisfied, the personal representative may elect to value the qualified real property portion of the estate at its special use value.

In no case may the reduction in value caused by the special use valuation exceed $500,000 for decedents dying through 1980, $600,000 for decedents dying in 1981, $700,000 for decedents dying in 1982 or $750,000 for decedents dying in 1983 and thereafter.[88]

The following Illustration may be helpful in understanding the monetary thresholds:

---

[84] *See* I.R.C. §2032A(e); Economic Recovery Tax Act of 1981, §421.

[85] *See e.g.*, J. Kolb, Section 2032A: Special Valuation of Farm and Business Property (1981); D. Kelley & D. Ludtke, Estate Planning for Farmers and Ranchers §§17.21–.87 (1980).

[86] I.R.C. §2032A(b)(1).

[87] I.R.C. §2032A(b)(3); §2053(a)(4).

[88] Economic Recovery Tax Act of 1981, §421(a), amending I.R.C. §2032A(a)(2).

Illustration V-8

I.R.C. § 2032A MONETARY QUALIFICATION

Assumptions

Assets	
1. Qualified Real Property	$300,000
2. Accompanying Personal Property	100,000
3. Other Property	300,000
4. Gross Estate (Total 1.—3.)	$700,000
Liabilities	
5. Mortgage on Qualified Property	$100,000
6. Security Liens on Accompanying Personal Property	50,000
7. Security Liens on Other Property	50,000
8. Unsecured Debts	50,000
9. Expenses and Claims	50,000
10. Total Liabilities (Total 5.—9.)	$300,000

Calculation

A. 50 Percent or More Threshold

$$\frac{\text{Qualified Property} + \text{Accompanying Personal Property} - \text{Relevant Secured Debts}}{\text{Gross Estate} - \text{Secured Debts}}$$

$$\frac{1.\ \$300{,}000 + 2.\ \$100{,}000 - [5.\ \$100{,}000 + \$50{,}000]}{4.\ \$700{,}000 - [5.\ \$100{,}000 + 6.\ \$50{,}000 + 7.\ \$50{,}000]} =$$

$$\frac{\$400{,}000 - \$150{,}000}{\$700{,}000 - \$200{,}000} = \frac{\$250{,}000}{\$500{,}000} = 50\%$$

B. 25 Percent or More Threshold

$$\frac{\text{Qualified Property} - \text{Relevant Secured Debts}}{\text{Gross Estate} - \text{Secured Debts}}$$

$$\frac{1.\ \$300{,}000 - 5.\ \$100{,}000}{4.\ \$700{,}000 - [5.\ \$100{,}000 + 6.\ \$50{,}000 + 7.\ \$50{,}000]} =$$

$$\frac{\$300{,}000 - \$100{,}000}{\$700{,}000 - \$200{,}000} = \frac{\$200{,}000}{\$500{,}000} = 40\%$$

Both thresholds are satisfied in the above illustration. Notice that the Unsecured Debts 8. and the Expenses and Claims 9. were not used in the calculations.

§5.23 I.R.C. §2032A Post-Election Rules

After an I.R.C. §2032A election has been made and approved by the I.R.S., there are additional factors that must be considered. First, within ten years after the death of the owner, there is the possibility of recapture of the tax or a part thereof due to an improper change in the use or disposition of the qualified property.[89] Second, qualified heirs will have either liens against the property or personal bonds against them to guarantee payment of the tax if recapture is ever applicable.[90] Consequently, despite the potential availability of an I.R.C. §2032A special use valuation election, the decision to make the election must be weighed against all of the costs and benefits applicable. The costs include, of course, the potential restraint on alienation, the loss of freedom in using the property, potentially higher capital gains tax on resale, the increased possibility of a full audit by the I.R.S., and the potential liability for the estate tax (plus interest if stepped-up basis is elected) under recapture. A full discussion of these matters is left to other works in the area.

§5.24 I.R.C. §2032A, Paragraph 7 Valuations

Qualified farm property may be valued for special use value purposes, either under Paragraph 7 or 8. When it is possible, however, it is usually desirable to calculate the special use value for farms under the Paragraph 7 technique.[91] This technique will ordinarily produce the lowest special use value, and is the easiest to calculate. The underlying approach is to capitalize a particular form of income flow.

The basic problems are to determine the amount of income and the capitalization rate. Paragraph 7 is very specific with respect to these determinations. It provides that the income to be capitalized equals the excess of the average annual gross cash rental income for comparable land over the average annual state and local real estate taxes for such comparable land. The comparable land must be used for farming purposes, and must be located in the same locality as the qualified farm. The rate of capitalization is defined as the average annual effective interest rate for all new federal land bank loans. Each of the average annual computations must be made on the basis of the five most recent full calendar years preceding the date of decedent's death.

For decedents who die after December 1, 1981, the Economic Recovery Tax Act of 1981 liberalizes the rules concerning what will qualify as cash rental income for comparable land. Under this Act, net share rentals may be substituted for cash rentals in the formula if the executor cannot identify actual tracts of comparable farm land rented for cash in the same locality as the decedent's farm property.[92] "Net share rental" is defined as the amount by which the value of the produce received by the lessor

---

89 *See* I.R.C. §2032A(c); Economic Recovery Tax Act of 1981, §421(c).
90 *See* I.R.C. §6324B.
91 I.R.C. §2032A(e)(7).
92 Economic Recovery Tax Act of 1981, §421(f).

of the land on which the relevant produce is grown exceeds the cash operating expenses of growing such produce paid by the lessor.

In many areas, this alternative valuation method will make it easier for many more farms to qualify under the Paragraph 7 technique. On the other hand, net share rentals should be significantly higher than cash rentals because of the added risk and uncertainity borne by the landowner.[93]

Regulation §20.2032A-4 imposes the following limitations on the use of the Paragraph 7 valuation technique:[94]

1. Cash rentals on the qualified farm do not qualify
2. Cash rentals from agreements not the result of arm's length transactions are not acceptable. This includes rentals from leases with the federal government or other governmental body, and from leases between family members that are lower than the commercial rate
3. Rents paid in any other manner other than cash are disqualified, including those payable wholly or partly in kind (such as crop shares)
4. Cash rentals calculated from area-wide averages complied by governmental agencies are not sufficient
5. Appropriate cash rental data must be obtained for each of the five calendar years preceding the decedent's death
6. Failure to satisfy the requirements of a Paragraph 7 valuation constitutes a waivcr or loss of the use of that technique, and requires valuation under Paragraph 8
7. Expenses and liabilities associated with the farm operation or with the lease must not be deducted
8. Leases may not be contingent upon production either
9. No amortization for perennial crops is allowed.

Regulation §20.2032A-4(d) goes into significant detail in defining "comparable farm property." It is said not to be a matter of mileage or political division; although the determination is conceded to be a factual one, the Regulation requires relatively detailed and specific documentation of comparability. This even includes the need to segment comparable properties into their most comparable parts for five full calendar years prior to death. The Regulation lists ten nonexclusive factors for determining comparability. These are:

1. The objective, scientifically-determined comparison of the soils and productivity studies of the soil
2. Comparable soil depletion from crops

---

93 Boehlje & Harl, *"Use" Valuation Under the 1976 Tax Reform Act: Problems and Implications,* 19 Jurimetrics J. 104 (1978).

94 *See generally* Dyer, *State Tax Savings and the Family Farm: A Critical Analysis of Section 2032A of the Internal Revenue Code,* 11 U.C.D. L. Rev. 8990 (1978).

3. Comparable soil conservation techniques
4. Comparable flooding potential
5. Comparable slope of the land
6. Comparable livestock operations on, and capacities of, the land
7. Comparable timber studies and information
8. Comparable contiguousness of multiple tracts of the lands
9. Comparable studies of the improvements and their economic advantages and disadvantages and
10. Comparable analysis of transportation convenience and proximity of properties.

Obviously, the above factors are not relevant in all situations and must be employed selectively. In most situations, comparability determinations will require expert analysis.[95]

The capitalization rate is defined as the average annual effective interest rate on new federal land bank loans. Regulation §20.2032A-4(e) states that this interest rate equals the average billing rate charged on new agricultural loans to farmers in the farm credit district in which the qualified property is located. If the rate of interest changes during a year, the rate must be weighted to reflect the appropriate rate charged during the various portions of the year. If rates differ as to the amount of the loan, the rate applicable to the average loan is selected.[96] Rates of interest must be computed to the nearest 100th of one percent.

Under the rules of the federal farm bank association, to get a loan, the borrower must purchase stock of the association equal to five percent of the gross amount of the loan. This purchase is a credit on the principal of the loan at retirement. Although a borrower only receives 95 percent of the principal of the loan, interest must be paid on its full value. Consequently, the billing rate must be adjusted to reflect the increased cost of borrowing caused by the stock purchase requirement.[97]

The Regulation provides that the applicable rates may be obtained from the district director. In response to this responsibility, the I.R.S. publishes annual revenue rulings listing the "average annual effective interest rates on new Federal Land Bank Loans to be utilized under I.R.C. §2032A(e)(A)(ii)."[98] Revenue Ruling 81–170 provides the average annual interest rates for each federal land bank district during the years 1977, 1978, 1979, 1980 and 1981. Revenue Ruling 82-104 adds the rates for 1982. The relevant rate is to be applied for decedents who die during those years. The states covered by each land bank district are also provided.

For a decedent dying during one of the years listed, the determination of the average annual effective interest rate merely requires selection of the proper rate listed in the

---

[95] J. Kolb, Section 2032A: Special Valuation of Farm and Business Property 187 (1981).

[96] Reg. §20.2032A4(e)(1).

[97] Reg. §20.2032A4(e)(2).

[98] Rev. Rul. 81-170, 1981-25 I.R.B. 18; Rev. Rul. 82-104, 1982-21 I.R.B. 7; *see also* Rev. Rul. 80-179, 1980-2 C.B. 253; Rev. Rul. 79-189, 1979-1 C.B. 293.

Ruling for the applicable year and the applicable federal land bank district. It can be assumed that the rates listed incorporate the normal calculations necessary, including the calculations for the weighted average billing rate, the stock purchase adjustment, and the five-year average.

The following reproduces the relevant parts of Revenue Rulings 81-170 and 82-104:

Table V-2

Federal Land Bank District in which property is located	Year of Death 1977	1978	1979	1980	1981	1982
Baltimore	8.65%	8.86%	9.04%	9.24%	9.66%	10.48%
Columbia	8.58%	8.79%	8.96%	9.17%	9.40%	9.81%
Houston	8.29%	8.48%	8.60%	8.76%	9.09%	9.74%
Louisville	8.64%	8.80%	8.88%	9.21%	9.53%	10.02%
New Orleans	8.26%	8.48%	8.72%	8.96%	9.33%	9.88%
Omaha	8.70%	8.92%	9.05%	9.25%	9.59%	10.17%
Sacramento	8.67%	8.82%	9.04%	9.35%	9.63%	10.12%
St. Louis	8.50%	8.71%	8.93%	9.20%	9.77%	10.37%
St. Paul	8.21%	8.47%	8.69%	8.95%	9.30%	9.84%
Spokane	8.63%	8.88%	9.10%	9.31%	9.60%	10.13%
Springfield	8.42%	8.55%	8.65%	8.81%	9.10%	9.52%
Wichita	8.52%	8.72%	8.88%	9.08%	9.56%	10.26%

Federal Land Bank Districts:

District	States
Baltimore	Delaware, District of Columbia, Maryland, Pennsylvania, Virginia, West Virginia.
Columbia	Florida, Georgia, North Carolina, South Carolina.
Houston	Texas.
Louisville	Indiana, Kentucky, Ohio, Tennessee.
New Orleans	Alabama, Louisiana, Mississippi.
Omaha	Iowa, Nebraska, South Dakota, Wyoming.
Sacramento	Arizona, California, Hawaii, Nevada, Utah.
St. Louis	Arkansas, Illinois, Missouri.
St. Paul	Michigan, Minnesota, North Dakota, Wisconsin.
Spokane	Alaska, Idaho, Montana, Oregon, Washington.
Springfield	Connecticut, Maine, Massachusetts, New Hampshire, New Jersey, New York, Rhode Island, Vermont.
Wichita	Colorado, Kansas, New Mexico, Oklahoma.

In order to determine the amount to be capitalized, the state and local real estate taxes on actual tracts of comparable real property in the same locality must be subtracted from the average annual gross cash rental for that comparable property.[99] Basically these are the same taxes that are deductible for income tax purposes under I.R.C. §164. The Regulations insist that the deductible amount be the same amount of tax that would be paid by the comparable real property used to determine the cash rentals. Current taxes on the qualified real property do not constitute the deductible amount.

It is not clear under the Regulations whether the amount deductible is the lowest possible tax payable, or the taxes actually paid. This issue becomes important in some jurisdictions where owners of farm properties can elect special provisions for local tax purposes. In California, for example, owners of farm land may have their land valued at its farm use value for local and state real estate taxes by agreeing to preserve the agricultural character of the property.[1] If the election is made, the real property taxes will be lower. The lower the tax, the higher the I.R.C. §2032A value under this calculation technique.

Numerous other questions also arise with respect to this issue. Must the lower tax rate be used? What if some of the comparable properties use the lower rate and some do not? Is it relevant whether the qualified farm takes advantage of the lower tax or not? There are no firm answers to any of these questions. Obviously, the I.R.S. will have to develop a policy on these matters.[2]

The effect of the amount of real estate taxes on the special use value is greater than one might at first realize. Each additional dollar of tax reduces the special use value by the capitalized rate of that dollar. For example, if the capitalization rate equals eight percent, each additional dollar of tax would reduce the special use value by $12.50. Consequently, the determination of the hypothetical real estate taxes may become an important issue.

The following example assumes the estate qualifies for a Paragraph 7 valuation.

Illustration V-9

Assumptions

State: Illinois

Federal Land Bank District: St. Louis

Year of Death: 1981

Average Annual Computations:

Year	Gross Rental	State & Local Real Estate Taxes
1979	$35,000	$3,750
1978	30,000	3,950
1977	32,000	3,650

99 Reg. §§20.2032A(4)(a),(c).

1 Cal. Gov't Code §§51200–95 (West Supp. 1977).

2 *See* Dyer, *State Tax Savings and the Family Farm: A Critical Analysis of Section 2032A of the Internal Revenue Code,* 11 U.C.D. L. Rev. 81 (1978).

Illustration V-9 *(Continued)*

Assumptions		
1976	37,000	3,600
1975	42,000	3,250
Five year Totals	$176,000	$18,200

Capitalization Rate for person dying in 1981: 9.77%[3]

Calculation

Five-Year Averages

$$\frac{\text{Five-Year Totals}}{5} = \text{Five-Year Average}$$

Gross Rental

$$\frac{\$176{,}000}{5} = \$35{,}200$$

Real Estate Taxes

$$\frac{\$18{,}200}{5} = \$3{,}640$$

Capitalization Rate

9.77%

§ 2032A, Paragraph 7 Valuation

$$\text{Average Annual Gross Rental} - \text{Average Annual State And Local Real Estate Taxes} \div \text{Average Annual Capitalization Rate} = V$$

$$\$35{,}200 - \$3{,}640 = \$31{,}560 \div .0977 = \$323{,}029.68$$

§ 2032A, Paragraph 7 valuation equals $323,000 (Rounded).

§5.25 I.R.C. §2032A, Paragraph 8 Valuations

Whenever the Paragraph 7 valuation technique does not apply, I.R.C. §2032A provides that the Paragraph 8 technique must be used to determine the special use value of any qualified real property.[4] Consequently, the Paragraph 8 technique will be very important in many cases. Even for qualified farms, Paragraph 8 techniques must be used if the Paragraph 7 gross cash rental requirement cannot be satisfied.

Because valuations under Paragraph 7 ordinarily are lower than valuations under Paragraph 8, the election on the estate tax return will include only a Paragraph 7 valuation for qualified farms. The I.R.S. may reject a valuation under Paragraph 7,

[3] *See* Rev. Rul. 81-170, 1981-25 I.R.B. 18.

[4] I.R.C. §2032A(e)(8).

however. In these situations, a Paragraph 8 valuation must be substituted. For efficiency and accuracy, personal representatives should obtain both Paragraph 7 and Paragraph 8 valuations for qualified farms, whichever is submitted on the return initially.

As of this writing, there are no Regulations or decisions explaining Paragraph 8 valuations. Consequently, we are left to the terms of I.R.C. §2032A itself.

Basically, the process is similar to other valuation techniques for tax purposes. The valuator must employ and analyze all factors relevant to the value of the qualified real property. In addition, however, I.R.C. §2032A includes four specific techniques that ostensibly must be used in all valuations under Paragraph 8 whether or not they apply. Probably the proper way to look upon these mandatory techniques is to analyze each from the standpoint of the qualified real property. A concise explanation of why one or more is inapplicable or irrelevant to a particular piece of qualified real property should be adequate, and should satisfy these requirements. This is true because several of the stated factors are only applicable to agricultural properties.

The four specific and mandatory valuation techniques are:

1. Capitalize the expected future income:
  - **(a)** receivable over a reasonable period of time
  - **(b)** assuming prudent management
  - **(c)** Using traditional cropping and perhaps other business techniques, and
  - **(d)** assuming comparable conditions and limitations

2. Capitalize the fair rental value of the land for similar purposes

3. Obtain the assessed land values under state law providing special use value for similar properties

4. Determine the market approach valuation:
  - **(a)** assuming comparable properties in the same geographical area, and
  - **(b)** assuming no significant price effect on agricultural properties caused by proximity to metropolitan or resort areas.

The section also provides that any other factor that values the qualified real property fairly must be applied.

Paragraph 8 valuations employ the ordinary valuation techniques used for real property, except that the highest and best use consideration must be eliminated in the calculations. In other words, if a qualified farm is being valued, that property should be analyzed as a farm, not as a subdivision or shopping center. Sales data and income analysis should be used accordingly.

The same technique would be applicable to nonagricultural qualified real property; the value of the superseding closely held business is very relevant to the value of the real property used in that business. If we are valuing a dry cleaning business for example, the underlying real property must be valued in relationship to the closely-held business, not separate from it. Presumably, the qualified real property may never be valued higher under special use values than the ordinary value of the closely-held business. Consequently, the capitalization of the earnings of the closely-held business would appear to be the most relevant valuation technique.[5] When the business is valued in this manner, the qualified real property should be valued at its estimated proportionate share of the business investment.

It is fair to state that, in many situations, Paragraph 8 valuations will be even more arbitrary and speculative than usual valuation determinations, because the market approach has basically been eliminated.

---

[5] *See* **§4.5** Capitalization of the Business Interest's Earnings.

CHAPTER 6

HOW TO VALUE AGRICULTURAL PERSONALTY

§6.1 Introduction to Agricultural Personalty Valuation

This Chapter is concerned with the determination of value for agricultural properties that are not real property but rather are classified as personal property or personal effects. This includes severed crops, livestock, farm machinery and equipment, portable buildings and other items of personal property. Crops before severance are in this category if they are not treated as part of the real property. Miscellaneous items of personal property, such as furniture and fixtures, are not considered here because they are discussed in Chapter 10 under personal effects.[1]

Such valuations must be made for many purposes: for example, sales, loans, tax assessments, decedents' estates, and income, gift and estate taxes.

The discussion here assumes that you need to make a separate valuation for these properties. In some cases this may not be necessary, however, because your values for these assets presumably are included within a value determination of the whole economic unit (e.g., the farm or agricultural corporation, partnership or sole proprietorship). When you have valued the entire business as a single economic unit, do not count the value of its personal assets in addition to the value of the business asset.

On the other hand, you may be required to value these personal properties to establish the entity's book value. In addition, an I.R.S. Regulation states that harvested and growing crops, livestock and farm machinery must ordinarily be itemized for estate

[1] *See* **§10.2** Household Effects Valuation.

tax purposes. A value for each item must be stated separately, apart from the value of the real property (except where all of such assets are valued as part of a business enterprise).[2]

Local custom and usage generally govern what is separate personalty and what is merely part of the realty.[3]

In making valuation determinations of all agricultural personalty, a systematic and comprehensive inventory is essential. Many of the items discussed in this Chapter use similar valuation techniques; consequently, a substantial amount of time can be saved if a proper inventory is prepared at the beginning.

The inventory must list all items that have a valuation significance. The list should also be as complete in description, quality, and other physical attributes of the property as possible. The more comprehensive the inventory is, the easier the task to value, and the more credible the valuation.

The steps to valuing agricultural properties are:

1. Determine type or kind of asset
2. Determine quantity, physical status (e.g., moisture content), unit (e.g., bushel, head), and weight
3. Determine the group, class and grade for the asset
4. Determine prices for the group, class and grade of asset both at the local and terminal markets
5. Determine all marketing expenses from storage to market.

Quantity, weight and grade determinations vary significantly, depending on the type of crop involved. Of course, these variables must be adjusted accordingly.

Several of the valuation terms and concepts that were explained previously should be consulted for this Chapter, including:

§2.9 Fair Market Value
§2.10 Market
§2.15 Replacement and Reproduction Costs
§2.11 Sales of the Asset
§2.3 Significance of Appraisals and Expert Testimony
§2.17 Valuation Mathematics.

§6.2 Crop Valuation

A common valuation problem for rural and agricultural lands is the value of the product of the land, including crops of all kinds. From a valuation standpoint, crops

---

[2] Reg. §20.2031-1(b).
[3] *See* D. Kelley & D. Ludtke, Estate Planning for Farmers and Ranchers §16.04, 587-88 (1980).

can be characterized into two different groups.[4] First, all crops that have not been severed or harvested are usually valued as part of the real property and do not have a separate valuation. Occasionally, it is necessary to value these crops separately: for example, when the real property is sold and the value of a crop in the ground must be determined for a crop sharing lessee, and for estate tax purposes if the farm assets are not valued as part of a business interest.[5] Second, crops that have been severed or harvested generally are considered personal property and must receive a separate valuation, even though the crops are merely cut and lying in the field.

When separate valuations are necessary for unharvested crops, the most revelant factors for valuation are:[6]

1. The variety of the seed
2. The stage of growth at the valuation date
3. The typical costs in the surrounding community of seed bed preparation, planting and cultivation to the valuation date
4. The stand and thrift of the crops to be valued
5. The possibility of damage to the crops due to insects, disease, floods, hail, freezing, and drought
6. The predicted sales price of the crop at harvest or market date.

In using the above factors, it is usual to distinguish between two situations. One valuation technique concerns crops that have not reached a point-of-yield projection; the other technique concern crops that have reached a point of predicted yield.

The valuation of a crop before its yield can be projected is basically a determination of the cost of planting. Cost includes all inputs including supplies, seed and labor. Unless greater cost can be justified, the usual cost of the particular community involved is used. Projected sales prices and return are not used at this point in the valuation process.

After the crop has matured to the point where its yield can be projected, a different valuation technique is employed. The first calculation is to determine the projected yields from the crop, and to multiply these yields by the projected sales price for the crop. The second calculation is to subtract the estimated value of all costs that will occur between the time of sale back to the date of valuation. As indicated, these costs are determined backwards, from projected sale until date of valuation.

The third calculation is the present value of the second calculation.[7] The discount amount would be determined depending on several factors including the uncertainties of market price and the hazards of production. Due to the significant effect of many factors including the fortuitous advent of certain weather conditions at strategic times, the determination of the yield and grade of unharvested crops is very difficult to make

---

[4] Doane, Rural Appraisal Handbook 712 (1947).

[5] Reg. §20.2031-1(b).

[6] Doane, Rural Appraisal Handbook 712 (1947).

[7] *See* **§2.17** Valuation Mathmetics.

if not speculative. Notwithstanding, the best, most reasonable estimates of these matters must be made as of the appropriate date. Clearly, the opinions of persons experienced in this area or of other identifiable experts, if available, is recommended.[8]

Because there is assumably a market for such an asset, your best source of market value is to determine what a severed or harvested crop can receive in the market place. Your best source of the value in the market place is from the local elevator, livestock dealer or other marketer that is in close proximity to the crop. Spot market prices are usually available and noncontroversial.[9] In order to derive a net realizable value, you would ordinarily subtract from market price costs incurred in bringing the crop to market.

Because market prices can only be attributed to comparable crops, it is necessary to determine the quality of the crops involved.[10] Nearly all crops have some system of setting standards for them. The United States Department of Agriculture has established standards for many types of crops. These standards should be consulted before valuation is attempted. The following lists the standardized crops and the source of the standards:

Chart VI-1

Crop	Citation (References to Sections in 8 C.F.R. (1981))
Beans	68.101-.122
Cottonseed	61.101-.104
Hay	57.1-.13
Lentils	68.601-.611
Peas (Split)	68.501-.510
Peas (Whole and dry)	68.401-.410
Rice (Brown)	68.251-.264
Rice (Milled)	68.301-.316
Rice (Rough)	68.201-.213
Straw	57.50-.52

§6.3 Timber Valuation

Growing timber, like other crops, is valued as part of the land. Basically, the same processes are used as are used for other real property valuations.[11] Because it is

[8] *See* §2.3 Significance of Appraisals and Expert Testimony.

[9] D. Kelley & D. Ludtke, Estate Planning for Farmers and Ranchers §16.05, 588 (1980).

[10] *See* Doane, Rural Appraisal Handbook 712 (1947).

[11] Stuart, *Appraisal of Timber and Timberland,* Encyclopedia of Real Estate Appraising 607-16 (3d ed., E. Friedman ed., 1978); *see* Chapter 5 for an explanation of real property valuation.

necessary to employ special techniques in order to value growing timber on real property, a professional forester or other qualified appraiser must be consulted.[12]

Severed timber becomes personal property, of course, and is valued at its merchantable value. The most common approach used to determine the value of severed timber is to extrapolate market value from sales of comparable timber. The following factors are considered in determining comparability:

1. Species of tree
2. Size of the timber
3. Grain (quality) of the timber
4. Class or utility (use) of the timber
5. Volume in board feet (usually thousand board feet or MBF) of the timber
6. Costs of getting it to market.

The federal income tax law contains several rules that treat the commercial aspects of timber in special ways favorable to the taxpayer, particularly with respect to capital gains and losses.[13] One special rule permits the appropriate taxpayer to elect to treat the cutting of timber as a sale or exchange in the year of the cutting.[14] The election applies even though the actual sale of the timber will not occur until subsequent tax years. The election is potentially advantageous to some taxpayers, who would otherwise have to treat the proceeds on the sale of the timber as ordinary income rather than as capital gains or losses.[15] The election is available even to those whose trade or business concerns timber, and to those who have a contract right to cut timber.[16] It is applicable only to timber that has been held by the taxpayer for more than one year, however.

Basically, the election operates as follows: first, the taxpayer determines the fair market value of the timber on the first day of the taxable year in which the timber is cut according to criteria set out in the Regulations.[17] Second, the taxpayer deducts the depletion allowance from this fair market value, and treats the result as capital gain or loss.[18] The consequence of this calculation is that the above-determined fair market value becomes the taxpayer's income tax basis for purposes of computing income in the year of the sale. Although there is no income unless the sales receipts exceed this basis, any income is ordinary income.

Before a taxpayer exercises this election, its benefits and detriments must be determined. If a capital gain is recognized during the year of the cutting, it will be taxable to the taxpayer even though payment for the timber is not received until years later. On the other hand, the election creates a high basis for the timber and converts what ordinarily would be ordinary income to the taxpayer in the year of the sale to capital gain income in the year of cutting.

---

[12] *See* **§2.3** Significance of Appraisals and Expert Testimony.

[13] C. Breeding, F. Burke & G. Burton, Income Taxation of Natural Resources, Ch. 22 (1977).

[14] I.R.C. §611.

[15] *See* N. Harl, Agricultural Law §27.03[9][b] (1982).

[16] Reg. §1.631-1(a)(4).

[17] *See* Reg. §1.611-3(f)(1).

[18] *See* N. Harl, Agricultural Law §§29.09[1],[5].

The following simple example illustrates how this election operates:

Illustration VI-1

Assumptions

1. Without an election the net profits from the sale of the timber would constitute ordinary income to taxpayer.
2. Taxpayer's marginal rate of tax on ordinary income equals 50%.
3. The taxpayer owns 100,000 feet of standing timber.
4. The timber is cut on July 1, 19X1.
5. Taxpayer has held the timber for more than a year before cutting.
6. Taxpayer's basis for the timber equals $12.00 per MBF.
7. The fair market value of the timber on January 1, 19X1 is $45.00 MBF.
8. The timber is sold for $50.00 MBF on July 1, 19X2.

Calculations

1. Fair market value of timber on January 1, 19X1 $45.00 × (100,000 ÷ 1,000) =	$4,500
2. Less adjusted basis of timber $12,00 × (100,000 ÷ 1,000) =	−1,200
3. Capital gain reported for tax year 19X1	3,300
4. New basis for timber for subsequent sale	4,500
5. Sale price $50.00 × (100,000 ÷ 1,000) =	5,000
6. Ordinary income for tax year 19X2	$ 500

Tax Comparisons

1. If election is exercised	
(a) Capital gain tax 19X1 (20%) 20% × $3,300 =	$ 660
(b) Ordinary income tax 19X2 50% × $500 =	250
Total Taxes Due	$ 910
2. If no election is exercised Ordinary income for year 19X2 50% × ($5,000 − $1,200 = 3,800) =	$1,900

Taxpayer saves $990 of taxes, but had to pay $660 in a year prior to the receipt of income.[19]

The Regulation that specifies how the fair market value is to be determined sets out very typical criteria.[20] The following is a composite list of the matters mentioned:

1. The value of the property shall be determined according to the condition of the property on the date of valuation
2. Concomitantly, subsequent changes including changes in surrounding circumstances, methods of exploitation and utilization, are not to be considered unless approved by the District Director on audit
3. The character and quality of the timber, including its species, age, size, condition and any other relevant matters, must be determined
4. The per acre and total quantity of the timber must be determined
5. The location of the timber and its juxtaposition with other timber must be considered
6. The accessibility and exploitation of the timber must be considered
7. The cost of getting the timber to important markets must be estimated.

The Regulation also lists a large number of important evidentiary factors. It emphasizes that the subjective value of the timber involved, not the general average value of timber in the region, is important, although it recognizes the relevance of regional values. The Regulation then states that consideration will be given to any and all facts and evidence having a bearing on market value (including costs, actual sales and transfers of similar properties, the margin between the cost of production and the price realized for timber products, market value of stock or shares, royalties and rentals, valuation for local or state taxation, partnership accountings, records of litigation in which the value of the property has been involved, the amount at which the property may have been inventoried or appraised in probate or in similar proceedings, disinterested appraisals by approved methods and other factors).[21]

The regulation does not add anything new to valuation determination techniques. Although preference is given to comparable sales data, other valuation attempts and actions are also relevant.[22] Finding sufficiently comparable timber sales is the typical problem. Obviously, the taxpayer needs to gather as much information on valuation as possible in order to anticipate the possibility of an audit. In situations where value is high and very important, expert appraisals should be obtained.

---

19 *Id.* at §27.03(9)(b), pp. 27-80 to -87.

20 Reg. §1.611-3(f).

21 Reg. §1.611-3(f)(2).

22 C. Breeding, F. Burke & G. Burton, Income Taxation of Natural Resources, ¶¶22.14, 22.15 (1977).

§6.4 Livestock Valuation

The valuation of livestock depends upon a large number of factors.[23] The United States Department of Agriculture (U.S.D.A.) has developed a comprehensive set of factors for most types of livestock.[24] The most important of these and other factors are as follows:

1. Age
2. Conformation
3. Grade (e.g., prime, choice)
4. Health
5. Heredity
6. Kind or type
7. Management
8. Physical appearance (e.g., fatness, maturity, muscular development)
9. Productivity (e.g., dairy cattle production)
10. Sex condition
11. Use
12. Weight.

Clearly, no neophyte will want to make decisions and consider all of these factors.

The most common valuation technique, of course, is to assimilate the relevant information on the above factors and to determine the market price for the most comparable animals in the most relevant and closest market. If only a small number of one type of animal is involved, the individual value for each animal must ordinarily be derived from the market prices. If large numbers of sales are involved, the animals are usually valued as part of reasonable groupings depending upon the relevant standards.

The U.S.D.A. first divides cattle by age. Vealers and calves are segregated from cattle in general.[25] Vealers are usually less than three months of age, calves are usually between three and eight months of age, and all of the rest are cattle. Vealers and calves are primarily distinguished by the type of feed (milk versus roughages), degree of maturity and age. Within the veal and calf categories, these animals are subclassified by sex condition—steers, heifers and bulls.[26] Finally within the above two classifications, animals are graded by a composite of conformation and fatness, maturity and other factors responsible for differences in quality of the lean flesh.[27] In addition to the actual physical characteristics of the animal, heredity and management factors are also

---

23 *See* Doane, Rural Appraisal Handbook 713-14 (1947).

24 *See* 7 C.F.R., Pt. 53.

25 *Id.* at §53.120.

26 *Id.* at §53.121.

27 *Id.* at §53.122.

relevant.[28] The five specific grades recognized for vealers and calves are prime, choice, good, standard and utility.

The U.S.D.A. sets out three basic criteria for classifying cattle other than vealers and calves: use—slaughter and feeder; class—sex condition; and grade—apparent relative excellence and desirability of the animal for its particular use.[29] Generally, slaughter cattle are those that are set for slaughter immediately or in the very near future. Feeder cattle are set for slaughter after a period of feeding. The relevant classes of cattle by sex condition are: steers, bullocks (males less than twenty-four months old), bulls, cows, and heifers. The U.S.D.A. uses a rather complex system to further classify the cattle. For slaughter cattle, subclassifications employ both grading (eight grades) based on quality and grading based on age and yield (five yield grades). Quality grades are "based on an evaluation of factors related to the palatability of the lean."[30] Yield grades are based primarily on muscling and fatness of the cattle.[31] Older cattle (thirty to forty-two months, and over forty-two months) receive lower quality grades. Heredity and management are also relevant factors for quality grade determination.[32]

The U.S.D.A. establishes three classifications for swine: slaughter or feeder, class—sex condition, and grade.[33] The slaughter-feeder distinction is the same as it is for cattle. There are five class distinctions based on sex conditions: barrow (male swine castrated before maturity); gilt (young female swine), sow, boar, and stag (male swine castrated after some degree of maturity).[34] The grades vary depending on whether slaughter or feeder swine are involved. For slaughter swine there are four grades: U.S. No. 1; U.S. No. 2; U.S. No. 3; and U.S. No. 4.[35] These grades are basically predicated on the basis of the quality of the lean, and the expected combined carcass yields of the four lean cuts (ham, loin, picnic shoulder and Boston butt). The classifications are usually based on the average backfat thickness in relation to carcass length or live weight. There are some differences between the grading of slaughter barrows and gilts versus slaughter cows. Feeder swine are graded on their logical slaughter potential and their thriftiness.[36] Thriftiness is a determination of a pig's apparent ability to gain weight rapidly and efficiently. Heredity and management are relevant factors that are only determinable through experience.[37]

Ordinarily, swine are sold by groups, and thus individual valuation is less important. The market price is set by determining the price for comparable classes and grades set at the terminal markets, less marketing expenses.

The U.S.D.A. establishes four classifications for market sheep: Use—slaughter or feeder; class—sex condition; age group; and grade—apparent relative excellence and

---

28 *Id.* at §53.122(f).
29 *Id.* at §53.201.
30 *Id.* at §53.203(b)(1).
31 *Id.* at §53.203(c).
32 *Id.* at §§53.204-05.
33 *Id.* at §53.150.
34 *Id.* at §53.151.
35 *Id.* at §53.152(d).
36 *Id.* at §53.158.
37 *Id.* at §53.152(j).

desirability of the animal for its particular use.[38] The slaughter-feeder distinction is the same as it is for cattle. There are five categories of sheep based on sex condition and age: ram; ewe; wether (male sheep castrated prior to maturity); lamb (under fourteen months of age); yearling (between one and two years of age) and sheep (over twenty-four months of age). For slaughter ovines, standards are divided between slaughter lambs and slaughter yearlings and sheep. There are five grades: prime, choice, good, utility and cull. Sheep cannot be prime, however. There are also five yield grades numbered one through five; number one is the best. Grades are based generally on conformation and quality. Quality relates to fatness, maturity and often involves indicators relating to the palatability of the meat.[39] Yield grades are based primarily on leg conformation and degree of fatness. An additional factor for sheep is that market value may depend on the value of both meat and wool. For goats, the primary consideration is the market price for mohair. The market price is set by determining the price for comparable classes and grades set at the terminal markets, less marketing expenses.

Horses are ordinarily valued according to height, weight, purpose and conformation. Mules are classified according to their purpose or use. Within these classes, considerations dealing with quality, condition, soundness, conformation and quality grades are most important. Valuation of these animals depends upon their market price in the most relevant or closest market. Again, the goal is to identify market prices from the most comparable animals sold. The U.S.D.A. does not set standards for horses and mules.

Poultry and animal specialities are classified as to type, class and grade. Unless error in valuation would occur, valuations will be made by groupings. Market value is determined in the same manner as it is for swine. The U.S.D.A. sets out grading standards for poultry and rabbit carcass products but not for such live animals.[40]

§6.5 Valuation of Other Farm Property

Farm machinery and equipment are so diverse in type, kind and quality that it would be impossible to list all valuation techniques. Only generalities will be provided here.[41]

The valuation of most farm machinery and equipment requires individual appraisal, unless reasonable groupings are justified by sufficient similarities. All items must be graded by quality and condition, either individually or as a group. Common grades are excellent, good, medium, fair or scrap.

There are basically three valuation techniques. One common method is to determine the replacement cost of the item minus actual depreciation. This technique is useful for very specialized items that do not suffer much loss of economic value.

---

38 *Id.* at §53.130.

39 *Id.* at §53.132(c).

40 *Id.* at §§2870.200-.332. The valuation process is the same as described in **§6.1** Introduction to Agricultural Personalty Valuation.

41 *See* Doane, Rural Appraisal Handbook 714 (1947). For valuation of common motor vehicles such as trucks, see **§10.5** Vehicles Valuation.

The second, and most common, technique is to determine market value from sales of comparable property in the market place. Information of this sort may be obtained from dealers who handle such used items, wholesale price books on the item or from known sales of similar items. Price information from each of these sources may require adjustment due to dissimilarities either in time, place or kind. The third technique is concerned with items that have no useful value or utility. This junk or salvage value is determined by what the item will return as scrap.

When presenting valuations of such property, it is desirable to include information concerning the following:

1. Detailed descriptions of the item including brand, type, and other identification matters
2. Year of purchase
3. Purchase price
4. Condition or quality
5. Market value.

Portable buildings and significant unattached agriculturally-related fixtures are normally valued at their replacement cost.[42] Relevant considerations include the kind and type of asset, its size, construction, age, and conditions. Economic depreciation must also be taken into account. Replacement costs for many of these items can be found in farm equipment and farm implement catalogs.

A vast array of other produce of agricultural properties may also require valuation. This includes dairy products, milk, cheese, and eggs, and the carcasses of slaughtered livestock. As for crops and livestock, there are markets from which market prices can be determined.[43] Because of the relatively perishable nature of these assets, they must be marketed frequently and thus the sales price received for the asset will ordinarily constitute the most important indicia of value.

The United States Department of Agriculture has established standards for the following agricultural properties:

Chart VI-3

Property	Citation [References to sections of 7 C.F.R. (1981)]
Beef (Carcasses)	2853.102-.107
Eggs	2856.200-.234
Lamb, Yearling and Mutton (Carcasses)	2853.122-.127
Pork (Carcasses)	2853.132-.137

42 *See* **§2.15** Replacement and Reproduction Costs.

43 Again, the valuation problem is the same described in **§6.1** Introduction to Agricultural Personalty Valuation.

Chart VI-3 (*Continued*)

Property	Citation [References to sections of 7 C.F.R. (1981)]
Poultry (Ready-to-Cook)	2870.200-.271
Rabbits (Ready-to-Cook)	2870.300-.332
Veal and Calves (Carcasses)	2853.112-.117

There may be a substantially large number of miscellaneous nonproduce items that will also require valuation for agricultural properties:[44] feeds, silage, fuel, building materials, fertilizer, and veterinary supplies and equipment. If there is a ready market (there is for feeds, silage and fuels), market prices in that market should be employed. The other types of property require the identification of a market as well as market prices. If a market and market prices are not available, then replacement costs less depreciation could be used in valuation.

Obviously, in valuing all similar types of items, careful inventory is essential. Quality determination is also essential, whether or not the item has a special grading system. Items should be inventoried according to kind, quality and container. Homogeneous items may be put into groupings. When inventories show substantial quantities and consequently substantial value, care must be taken to properly segregate and identify appropriate units. Some of these items may be spoiled, obsolete, or nonworking and consequently have nothing more than a junk value. At other times, because of transportation costs, many of these items may actually have a negative value.

[44] Doane, Rural Appraisal Handbook 715 (1947).

CHAPTER 7

HOW TO VALUE OIL AND MINERAL INTERESTS

§7.1 Introduction to Oil and Mineral Interest Valuation

Setting the value of oil and mineral interests involves all aspects of valuation determinations: income, gift and estate tax, real property taxation, eminent domain, lender security and, of course, sale or transfer.

Valuation techniques for oil and mineral interests are basically the same as they are for other forms of real property. Consequently, the discussions in Chapter 5 concerning the techniques for valuing real property are relevant here.[1] Only special attributes of oil and mineral interests as they relate to these valuation techniques will be discussed here.[2]

The primary techniques used to value oil and mineral interests are the market approach, the cost approach, the income approach, and the sales of the asset approach. The income approach in this area is frequently referred to as the "analytical appraisal approach." The technique calls for identifying a future income flow and determining its present value.

The most common problem in making valuations of these types of assets is the determination of the nature and scope of the asset. Each mineral interest must be

[1] *See* §**5.11** The Market Approach to Real Property Valuation; §**5.14** The Income Approach to Real Property Valuation; §**5.17** The Cost Approach to Real Property Valuation; and §**5.19** Correlation.

[2] *See* §**1.2** When and Where Valuation Determinations Are Made.

carefully identified and described.[3] Concomitantly, valuation determinations must be made for each segregatable mineral interest. Each interest is said to be unique and to require individual valuation consideration.[4]

Another related problem that must be recognized is what might be called the engineering problem—the obvious technical nature of mineral development. Valuing mineral interests requires experience with, and knowledge of, very technical terms and techniques; use of expert appraisers and specialists is highly suggested and in some cases essential to proper valuation determination. Usually, appraisers in this specialized field have engineering or geological experience or education. The quality of the appraiser is very important and will weigh heavily if litigation occurs.[5]

When oil and mineral interests are valued, other valuation issues often arise. For example, the valuation of existing oil or mineral interests may be the most important valuation determination for the real property on which or in which the oil or mineral interest is located. In this situation, the valuation determination for the oil or mineral is merely a specialized valuation effort for the real property.

When oil and/or mineral interests are a part of a business interest, the valuations for these interests may be only a part of the process of valuing the business interest as a whole. It may or may not be appropriate to segregate the effort of valuing the oil or mineral interest, depending upon the significance of these interests to the business interest in general. Frequently, the oil or mineral interest asset will constitute the predominant part of the business interest, and thus will require separate consideration.

Another special valuation situation deals with the oil or mineral interest that is divided into working and nonworking interests.[6] The most common example of a non-working interest is the royalty interest held by the landowner in the production of the oil and mineral properties. Sometimes valuation determination must attempt to define the value of the royalty interest alone, which ordinarily requires valuation of the whole interest of which the royalty interest is only a part.[7]

There are several other discussions concerning the valuation of mineral interests that should be consulted if additional information is desired. The following are suggested.

1. Fiske, *The Valuation of Oil and Gas Properties in Estates and Trusts,* 2 Rocky Mountain Mineral Law Institute 371-86 (1956)
2. Oberbillig, *Appraisal of Mineral Property,* Encyclopedia of Real Estate Appraising 617-30 (3d ed., E. Friedman ed., 1978)
3. R. Parks, Examination and Valuation of Mineral Property (4th ed. 1957)
4. Parks, *Valuation of Mineral Property,* Real Estate Appraiser 37-46 (May-June 1972)

---

[3] *See* Reg. §§1.611-1(d)(1), 1.611-2(e)(1).

[4] Oberbillig, *Appraisal of Mineral Property,* Encyclopedia of Real Estate Appraising 620-21 (3d ed., E. Friedman ed., 1978).

[5] *See* **§2.3** Significance of Appraisals and Expert Testimony, and **§2.8** Proof of Value.

[6] *See* **§7.2** The Composition of a Mineral Interest.

[7] *See* Estate of Frankel v. United States, 512 F.2d 1007 (5th Cir. 1975).

5. Tippit & Phipps, *Valuation of Mining Properties,* 4 American Law of Mining §§26.1-.3, at pp. 567-88 (1963)

Because there are no significant differences between the valuation techniques for oil interests and those for other mineral interests, the discussion will be general. In addition, the term "mineral interest" will be used to refer to all types of natural resource interests, including oil interests.[8]

Because of the technical and complex nature of valuing mineral interests, the opinions of persons experienced and knowledgeable in the field are frequently sought.[9] Although these persons are not professional appraisers, if they have information about actual sales of similar properties, their valuation estimates may be given great weight when other forms of market value evidence and information are unavailable. They may also be useful to corroborate estimated market values determined through the other techniques.

Several of the valuation terms and concepts that were explained previously should be consulted for this Chapter, including:

§2.19 Capitalization of Income
§2.13 Cost (Purchase Price)
§2.9 Fair Market Value
§2.8 Proof of Value
§2.11 Sales of the Asset
§2.3 Significance of Appraisals and Expert Testimony
§2.17 Valuation Mathematics.

§7.2 The Composition of a Mineral Interest

Valuing mineral interests is typically more complex than valuing the real property in which the mineral interest is located. This brief explanation of the divisibility of a mineral interest is significantly generalized in substance, and is not a substitute for careful study of those matters when necessary. In addition, hard mineral interests and oil and gas interests are lumped together, although they may be severable and distinct under specific circumstances and laws.[10] Differences between hard minerals and oil and gas are mentioned only if valuation determinations are affected.

Generally, the ownership of the surface of real property and the ownership of the mineral interests in that property are severable.[11] This means that a landowner can convey a mineral estate (in any mineral, including oil or gas) separate and distinct from his or her surface ownership. This is usually done by lease. Both estates are considered

---

[8] *See* Reg. §1.611-1(d)(5).

[9] Fiske, *The Valuation of Oil and Gas Properties in Estates and Trusts,* 2 Rocky Mtn. Min. L. Inst. 383 (1956).

[10] 2 American Law of Property, § 10.4 at 510 (A. J. Casner ed. 1952).

[11] 1 E. Kuntz, Oil and Gas §3.1 (1962); Martz, Carrell & Kirgis, *Conveyancing and Status of Mineral Interests,* 3 Am. L. of Min., tit. 15, §15.13 at 71-223 (Rocky Mtn. Min. Legal Fdn. ed. (1960); Swenson, *Solid Mineral Leases,* 5 Am. L. of Min., tit 30, §30.11 at 301-84 (Rocky Mtn. Min. Legal Fdn. ed. 1967).

real property.[12] The relationship between the separate estates has been characterized as adjoining landowners rather than cotenants.[13]

The scope and extent of the mineral estate is very broad and basically parallels that of the surface estate.[14] A deed for a mineral estate may contain any of the following limitations:

1. Limit enjoyment and/or duration
2. Separate different minerals or separate oil and gas from other minerals
3. Separate or be precise as to strata or location of the interest
4. Create co-ownership interests.

From a valuation standpoint, it may be necessary to value the mineral estate separate from the surface estate.

The "mineral lease" is the instrument in which the working interest in the minerals is created.[15] Typically, the term of the lease is set for a specifically stated period of time called the "primary term."[16] During this term, the lease is kept active either by royalty payments or by drilling or other mining activity on the subject land. Some provision in the lease is made for termination of the lease if production does not occur within the primary term or its expressed alternative requirements. After the primary term lapses, the lease usually includes a clause that provides for its continued validity so long as certain events continue. The typical event necessary in order to continue the lease is production in paying quantities. So long as the paying quantities are produced, the lease will continue for an unlimited length of time thereafter. A lease of this nature has been construed to create in effect a fee simple defeasible in the lessee, with the lessor retaining a possibility of reverter.[17]

The "working interest," or what is sometimes called the "operating interest," is the interest held by the person who has the exclusive right to exploit the minerals in or on the land.[18] Economically, it equals the mineral interest minus the royalty interest. The landowner's royalty interest usually equals one-eighth or one-sixth; thus the working interest equals either seven-eighths or five-sixths. The working interest is burdened with the cost of development and operations of the property. The owner of the working interest may transfer other interests out of this interest in various ways, including the transfer of overriding royalty interests.

Several important terms for commercial transactions dealing with mineral interests include "bonus," "royalty," "overriding royalty," and "production payments." Basically, they deal with the lease of a mineral interest and the various types of payments

[12] 1. E. Kuntz, Oil and Gas §3.1 (1962); Helmick & Tippit, *Royalty Interests and Ore Payments,* 3 Am. L. of Min., tit 17, §17.2 at 431-82 (Rocky Mtn. Min. Legal Fdn. ed. 1967).

[13] 1. E. Kuntz, Oil and Gas §3.2 (1962).

[14] *Id.* at §3.1; Martz, Carrell & Kirgis, *Conveyancing and Status of Mineral Interests,* 3 Am. L. of Min., tit 15, §§15.12-31 at 71-223 (Rocky Mtn. Min. Legal Fdn. ed. 1960).

[15] H. Williams & C. Meyers, Manual of Oil and Gas Terms 134-35 (1957).

[16] *Id.* at 189.

[17] *Id.* at 134.

[18] *Id.* at 170, 281.

made under it.[19] There are many variations of these transactions applicable to individual situations or particular minerals. The following discussion covers only the primary and basic types.

A "bonus" is ordinarily a cash payment by the lessee to the lessor landowner in consideration for the execution of a mineral lease.[20] Sometimes it is not a cash payment but, in effect, constitutes an overriding royalty.

The right to a "royalty" is an interest retained by the landowner that permits the landowner to share in the return on the production of the mineral interest free of the expenses of production.[21] Ordinarily, a royalty of this nature is set as a fraction (e.g., one-eighth, one-sixth or one-fifth of the return on gross production) or as a fixed sum for, or a fixed percentage of, the "market value" of each ton or other measurement of the mineral removed. The standard depends on the mineral and the custom and usage of the area of the country involved.[22]

A "minimum royalty" is a payment in the nature of a rent paid by the lessee to the lessor.[23] It must be paid regardless of whether the mineral interest is worked or production of the mineral occurs. Its purposes, of course, are to encourage the lessee to conduct the relevant mining operations diligently, and to guarantee the lessor a definite minimum income from the lease. Such payments are common in hard mineral operation leases but are seldom found in oil and gas leases. Standard minimum royalty provisions contain exception clauses relieving the lessee from payment in case of circumstances beyond the lessee's control such as acts of God, fires, shortages of transportation equipment, strikes, etc.

From a valuation standpoint, minimum royalties should be valued like leases, subject to a discount due to the exception clauses. The value would equal the present value of the minimum royalties for the length of the lease, less an estimated discount for the possibility of reduction due to the circumstances.

An "overriding royalty" is similar to a royalty, but it is carved out of the lessee's working interest.[24] This overriding royalty may be retained by the lessor, transferred to third persons, or retained by the lessee upon assignment of the remaining working interest. Like a royalty, it is free of the expenses of production. Overriding royalty interests are more prevalent in oil and gas interests than in hard mineral interests.[25]

---

[19] *See* E. Kuntz, Oil and Gas §15.1; Helmick & Tippit, *Royalty Interests and Ore Payments,* 3 Am. L. of Min., tit 17, §17.3 at 431-82 (Rocky Mtn. Min. Legal Fdn. ed. 1967).

[20] H. Williams & C. Meyers, Manual of Oil and Gas Terms 19 (1957).

[21] *Id.* at 213-14; Helmick & Tippit, *Royalty Interests and Ore Payments,* 3 Am. L. of Min., tit 17, §17.3 at 431-82 (Rocky Mtn. Min. Legal Fdn. ed. 1967).

[22] *See* Annot., 10 A.L.R.4th 732 (1981) (cases defining the terms "market value" or "market price" as used in oil and gas leases).

[23] Helmick & Tippit, *Royalty Interests and Ore Payments,* 3 Am. L. of Min., tit 17, §17.4 at 431-82 (Rocky Mtn. Min. Legal Fdn. ed. 1967).

[24] H. Williams & C. Meyers, Manual of Oil and Gas Terms 173-74 (1957); Helmick & Tippit, *Royalty Interests and Ore Payments,* 3 Am. L. of Min., tit 17, §17.6 477-82 (Rocky Mtn. Min. Legal Fdn. ed. 1967).

[25] Helmick & Tippit, *Royalty Interests and Ore Payments,* 3 Am. L. of Min., tit 17, §17.6 431-82 (Rocky Mtn. Min. Legal Fdn. ed. 1967); Swenson, *Solid Mineral Leases,* 5 Am. L. of Min., tit 30, §30.8 at 301-84 (Rocky Mtn. Min. Legal Fdn. ed. 1967).

An overriding royalty is commonly stated as a fraction, usually one-eighth or less. It is always limited in duration to the terms of the underlying lease.

A "production payment" similarly includes a share of the mineral produced from the mineral interest and is free of the expenses of production.[26] Production payment arrangements may be used, for example, to give the lessor a bonus payable out of production rather than immediate payment, or to allow the owner of the working interest to finance the cost of production. It differs from a royalty because it terminates upon the payment of an aggregate sum. For example, a production payment may be set to equal one-eighth of production until payments received equal an aggregate value of $2,000,000. The total sum due may earn interest.[27] Production payments may be reserved by the lessor or by an assignor of the lease, or they may be carved out by the owner of the royalty or of a working interest.

The normal order of payment in the above transactions would be:

1. Bonus
2. Lessor's royalty
3. Overriding royalties
4. Production payments.

This order of payment may affect the risk of nonpayment, and thus the value, of the particular interest.

"Reserves" are the estimated quantity of the particular mineral in the mine or well that requires valuation.[28] There are basically three types of reserves: proven, probable, and prospective.[29]

Proven reserves are those reserves of the mineral that are still in the ground but that have been located and determined to be recoverable.[30] Probable reserves are reserves of the mineral that are merely estimations from geological information or prior experience. Prospective reserves are reserves of the mineral whose existence is even less certain. For most valuation purposes, only proven reserves are considered.

§7.3 The Market Approach to Mineral Interest Valuation

Determining valuation of the mineral interest from sales data of comparable properties is an important and primary technique.[31] The most difficult task in this technique—for any form of real property—is finding sufficiently comparable property for which sales

---

26 H. Williams & C. Meyers, Manual of Oil and Gas Terms 164-65 (1957).

27 *See* Estate of Frankel v. United States, 512 F.2d 1007 (5th Cir. 1975).

28 Oberbillig, *Appraisal of Mineral Property,* Encyclopedia of Real Estate Appraising 618 (3d ed., E. Friedman ed., 1978); *see also* Reg. §1.611-2(c).

29 Oberbillig, *Appraisal of Mineral Property,* Encyclopedia of Real Estate Appraising 619 (3d ed., E. Friedman ed., 1978).

30 *Id.*

31 *See* **§5.11** The Market Approach to Real Property Valuation.

information is available.[32] For mineral interests, the problem is magnified by the lack of homogeneity among different properties of the same mineral. The distinctiveness and uniqueness of each mineral interest is clear. Even within the same field, district, or area, significant differences may be present between separate interests. Much of the problem stems from the fact that mineral interests are working properties; they earn income subject to an almost unlimited range of variables.

Professional appraisers seem to have a negative attitude toward use of the market approach because mineral interests are so heterogeneous. On the other hand, the I.R.S.'s authorities indicate a general preference for its use.[33]

Despite the difficulties of identifying comparable sales of comparable properties, this technique is viable. It is employed when important valuations of mineral interests are to be made. The task is difficult but not impossible; the valuator must make an earnest and comprehensive review of sales of comparable property. In this analysis, it is necessary to identify the most important comparable features and to make adjustments if differences exist between the subject property and the property sold.[34] These adjustments should be made in the same manner as they are made whenever the market approach to valuation is employed.

A nonexclusive list of the most important comparable factors would include:[35]

1. Accessibility
2. Contemporaneousness of sale
3. Estimated life of the interest
4. Labor expenses and considerations
5. Location of the interest
6. Monthly income of the interest
7. Operating costs
8. Quality of the interest
9. Quantity or size of the interest
10. Recoverable reserves
11. Terms of leases
12. Expenses of transportation to market.

The most common technique is to find common factors. Probably the most frequently used factor is the price per appropriate unit of the mineral interest. This may be particularly useful where the only difference is one of size or quantity. When other differences exist, however, a more refined approach will be necessary.

Another common technique is to break the differences down into particular catego-

---

[32] *See* Oberbillig, *Appraisal of Mineral Property,* Encyclopedia of Real Estate Appraising 620-21 (3d ed., E. Friedman ed., 1978).

[33] *See* Reg. §1.611-2(d)(2)(i); Rev. Proc. 79-24, 1979-1 C.B. 565; I.R.S. Tax Law Course, 21-7.

[34] *See* **§5.11** The Market Approach to Real Property Valuation.

[35] *See* Reg. §1.611-2(e).

ries and to attempt to attribute some adjustment factor to each of the differences. The adjustment factors are usually stated either in the form of a lump-sum single monetary adjustment, or in monetary adjustments related specifically to the different component factors, or by index or decimal adjustments depending on the particular difference in the factors.[36]

The lump-sum adjustment method requires a thorough understanding of the market as well as other comparable factors. The index adjustment method is least desirable, because it requires an additional calculation that may change results. The component-of-adjustment method is possibly the most desirable method, because it is a compromise between the other two methods. It incorporates a degree of refinement in technique without significantly increasing the complexity of the calculations.

In making adjustments to these variables, it is very helpful to coordinate valuation determinations under the market method with the other techniques (e.g., the income, cost, and sales-of-the-asset techniques). Much of the information gathered and analyzed under these techniques is useful for the market technique, and vice versa.

Once the comparable property is identified and the appropriate adjustments are made to the sale prices for the comparable sales, it is usually necessary to compare the prices for the properties involved. Typically, the comparisons are made by identifying a common financial figure that is available for the subject property and for the comparable properties. This technique is used in the comparable sales approach for closely-held businesses.[37] Illustration VII-1 demonstrates this comparison.

Similar calculations can be made using any of the other common financial figures, or with any other comparable determinable figure known for the comparable sale property and the subject mineral interest. The most commonly used financial figures include:[38]

1. Price per economic unit, ton, barrel, etc.
2. Payout on investment (e.g., on royalties)
3. Price per separable mineral interest including well, pit or shaft
4. Production quantity of the mineral, measured on a periodical basis (e.g., day, week or year).

§7.4 The Income Method of Mineral Interest Valuation

The income method of valuation for mineral interests seems to be the most frequently used technique by professional appraisers.[39] Some courts have also expressed their acceptance of this approach.[40] When used, the income valuation technique for mineral

36 *See* **§5.11** The Market Approach to Real Property Valuation, Illustration V-7.

37 *See* **§4.17** Traded Securities Comparative Analysis.

38 *See* Fiske, *The Valuation of Oil and Gas Properties in Estates and Trusts,* 2 Rocky Mtn. Min. L. Inst. 377-79 (1956).

39 Oberbillig, *Appraisal of Mineral Property,* Encyclopedia of Real Estate Appraising 621-22 (3d ed., E. Friedman ed., 1978).

40 *See, e.g.,* Royal Mineral Assoc., 5 B.T.A. 1126 (1927).

Illustration VII-1

Assumptions	
Comparable Mineral Interest—	
Common Financial Figure	100 (Units)
Adjusted Sales Price	\$50,000
Subject Mineral Interest	
Common Financial Figure	150 (Units)
Estimated Value	V

Calculation

Comparable Interest — Subject Interest

$$\frac{\text{Common Financial Figure}}{\text{Adjusted Sales Price}} = \frac{\text{Common Financial Figure}}{\text{(Market Value)}}$$

$$\frac{100}{\$50{,}000} = \frac{150}{V}$$

$$V = \frac{150}{100 \div \$50{,}000}$$

$$V = \frac{150}{\$.002}$$

$$V = \$75{,}000$$

Estimated market value of subject mineral interest equals \$75,000.

interests is the same as it is for other assets.[41] First, it requires the determination of the future net profit or income derived from the mineral interest. Second, a determination must be made of the proper rate of capitalization or the discount rate for the purpose of attributing a present value to the future net profit or income. Because mineral interests are wasting assets with limited lives, the future net income is projected only for a specific length of time.[42] The future net income is then discounted over the life of the interest. After the current interest rate for such investments is determined, the value of the business is calculated by using either a straight-line annuity table or the Hoskold Table. The former is the preferred approach today.[43]

[41] *See* **§5.14** The Income Approach to Real Property Valuation.

[42] *See* **§2.19** Capitalization of Income.

[43] Oberbillig, *Appraisal of Mineral Property,* Encyclopedia of Real Estate Appraising 623 (3d ed., E., Friedman ed., 1978).

It is necessary to make an estimate of the total future net income that the mineral interest will produce during its life expectancy.[44] Because of the nature of the asset, this has some special requirements. For example, the following matters must be estimated:[45]

1. The total quantity of the mineral recoverable from the mineral interest measured in appropriate units (tons, pounds, ounces, barrels, thousands of cubic feet, or other measure) considering proven reserves with only slight consideration of probable and prospective reserves[46]
2. The price of the marketable units of the mineral. (Either current prices or average prices for the last five years are commonly used; a modern approach would be to use market studies to estimate the future prices throughout the life of the mineral interests)
3. The production costs including royalties, development costs, milling and other necessary refinery costs, overhead costs, marketing costs, exploration, research, development, and equipment costs, and any other related and relevant costs
4. The amount of all federal and state income and property taxes, less deductions and depreciation allowances
5. The salvage value for equipment and machinery used in the mineral development and production
6. The life expectancy of the mineral interest as a producing asset.

The income value of the asset is determined by use of the above figures. The calculations are as follows:

Worksheet VII-1

1.	Total units of mineral recoverable	______
2.	Multiply 1. by price per unit	× ______
3.	Result equals gross income per interest	______
4.	Subtract production costs	______
5.	Result	______
6.	Subtract net federal and state income and property taxes (after depletion and other allowances)	− ______
7.	Result	______
8.	Add salvage value for equipment and machinery	+ ______
9.	Gross future net income	______

[44] *Id.* at 621-22.

[45] *Id.* at 622-23; Fiske, *The Valuation of Oil and Gas Properties in Estates and Trusts,* 2 Rocky Mtn. Min. L. Inst. 382 (1956); *see also* Reg. §1.611-2(c).

[46] *See* §**7.2** The Composition of a Mineral Interest.

The gross future net income value must then be translated into market value for the whole interest, either by capitalization or by present value techniques.

The income method mandates selection of a current interest or capitalization rate.[47] Generally, the capitalization rate for mineral interests is higher due to the greater degree of risks attributable to such investments. They will run from ten to 25 percent, with most appraisals running closer to the latter category. One author stated: "In many cases a reasonable value can be obtained by taking 50 percent of the expected future net income, thus giving a return on the investment of two for one, which is the basis of trading in many actual sales."[48]

In order to find the present value of this gross amount, it is necessary to determine how the gross future net income should be distributed throughout the life of the asset.[49] One method is to assume that the income will be paid in equal annual amounts. It is frequently referred to as the "straight-line annuity" or "discount" method.

Another possible method is to allocate specific portions of the gross income among the years remaining. This requires making an estimate of the interest's productivity and profit for each year. For example, in the life of a mining interest, income usually is low in the early and later years but is high during the middle years. Consequently, it is sometimes desirable to specifically allocate the gross future net income among the various years according to what is estimated to be the production for each of those years. Such an allocation, of course, is only an estimate. When this allocation technique is used, it is necessary to determine the present value of the income allocated in each year of the life of the asset. A "present value of a future payment" table is used rather than the straight-line annuity table. The market value equals the sum of the present value of the income for each of these years.

If the allocation is a low/high/low scale, the present value determined using the "income-allocated-each-year" method is lower than that determined by using the straight-line annuity method. The same result occurs if the income is low in the early years but increases in the later years. If the high-income years are estimated to be the early years, however, and the low-income years to be the later years, the "income-allocated-each-year" method produces a market value higher than the straight-line annuity method.

The following illustration compares the two methods:

---

[47] Oberbillig, *Appraisal of Mineral Property,* Encyclopedia of Real Estate Appraising 623 (3d ed., E. Friedman ed., 1978).

[48] Fiske, *The Valuation of Oil and Gas Properties in Estates and Trusts,* 2 Rocky Mtn. Min. L. Inst. 383 (1956).

[49] Oberbillig, *Appraisal of Mineral Property,* Encyclopedia of Real Estate Appraising 623-24 (3d ed., E. Friedman ed., 1978).

Illustration VII-2

Assumptions

1. Total Future Net Income:	$2,000,000
2. Life of Asset:	10 years
3. Rate of Capitalization:	25%

Calculation

Straight Line Annuity Method

4. Divide total future net income by life expectancy to get per-year figure

$\frac{\$2{,}000{,}000}{10} = \$200{,}000$

5. Multiply per-year figure by appropriate factor on the straight-line annuity table assuming the above life expectancy and rate of capitalization

$200,000 × 3.570503 = $714,100.60

6. Estimated market value equals $714,000 (Rounded)

Income Allocated Each Year Method

7. Allocate income each year for life of asset

8. Determine present value for each year's income

9. Add present value of each year.

Year	Annual Income	Present Value
1	$100,000	$ 80,000
2	200,000	128,000
3	200,000	102,400
4	300,000	122,880
5	400,000	131,072
6	400,000	104,858
7	200,000	41,943
8	100,000	16,777
9	50,000	6,711
10	50,000	5,369
Totals	$2,000,000	$ 740,010

10. Estimated market value equals $740,000 (Rounded)

Because the earlier years had more income allocated than the later years, the market value under the "income-allocated-each-year" method is higher than it is under the straight-line annuity method.

The above illustration is applicable to royalties and production payments, too.[50] Several courts have held that the present value of one of these payments must be discounted again in order to take into account the high risk attributable to mineral interests.[51]

50 *See* §**7.2** The Composition of a Mineral Interest.

51 Estate of Frankel v. United States, 512 F.2d 1007 (5th Cir. 1975) (6% discount); E. Hightower, 41 T.C.M. (P-H) ¶72,252 (1972) (7% discount); L. Stanton, 36 T.C.M. (P-H) ¶67,039 (1967) (40% discount).

To estimate the value of mineral interests that do not appear to possess substantial present value, one could multiply production payments before depletion by a locally-developed multiplier. The primary problem is estimating the appropriate annual payments. This amount will usually be determined from actual annual production payments for the last five of ten years, if available. These payments are then averaged, or a weighted average is determined and adjusted depending on the future prospects for the payments.

This approach is very useful for many royalty and overriding royalty interests. The multiplier used will vary from mineral to mineral and from location to location. For mineral interests in Wyoming, for example, the multiplier has generally been four or five.

The following illustrates:

Illustration VII-3

Assumptions

1. 1/8th overriding royalty
2. Adjusted production payments equal $5,000 per annum before depletion
3. Multiplier equals 5.

Calculation

V = $5,000 × 5 × .125
V = $25,000 × .125
V = $3,125.

For tax purposes, it is reasonable to assume that mineral interests with an estimated value of $50,000 or more will require appraisal and thus use of the more complex technique.

§7.5 The Cost/Sale of Asset Approach to Mineral Interest Valuation

Using cost as a valuation for mineral interests has the same deficiencies as it does in other areas.[52] In fact, the problems may actually be exaggerated with mineral interests where the asset has been held for a period of time and has been consumed during that period. Mineral interests are wasting assets; the longer they are producing, the less time they have to produce in the future. Consequently, cost analysis and book value, although factors for valuation, will seldom be determinative.[53]

There is clearly at least one situation in which costs may be determinative or

[52] *See* **§2.13** Cost (Purchase Price); Tippit & Phipps, *Valuation of Mining Properties,* 4 Am. L. of Min., tit. 25, §26.6 at 577 (Rocky Mtn. Legal Fdn. ed. 1963).

[53] Tippit & Phipps, *Valuation of Mining Properties,* 4 Am. L. of Min., tit. 25, §26.9 at 580 (Rocky Mtn. Legal Fdn. ed. 1963).

particularly influential in market valuation: where costs represent the price paid for the asset very close to the valuation date.

The price at which an asset has sold may be very relevant, if not determinative, of market value.[54] Obviously, there is no better evidence of market value than the value that the asset received in the market place. This principle is as applicable to mineral interests as it is to other assets.[55] This is the rationale behind using market price data, when available, as evidence of market value.[56]

Consequently, the sale price of the subject mineral interest near the valuation date in an arm's-length transaction may constitute the best evidence of valuation.[57] Even when significant events happen between the date of sale and the valuation date requiring adjustments to the sale price, the sale price as adjusted may constitute significant evidence of valuation.[58]

It will be very helpful if other valuation techniques arrive at values that are similar to the sales price received.

§7.6 Nonproducing Mineral Interest Valuation

When mineral interests are not producing, the valuation determinations become more difficult because there is less data upon which to compare and to weigh valuation determinations. Most frequently, valuations in such situations refer to leasing arrangements for comparable property, and attempt to capitalize the appropriate rentals over the expected term.[59] The same approach to comparable leases is taken as in other valuation areas.[60] Ordinarily, the values of the most comparable leases are figured on a per-acre basis.

Another common valuation technique for nonproducing property is to refer to the opinion of those who are experienced in the field.[61] This is particularly true where these persons are in the process of buying and selling such interests and are very knowledgeable of current market conditions and transactions.

§7.7 Federal Tax Valuation Determinations For Mineral Interests

The I.R.S. sets out its position on the fair market value determination of mineral interests in its Regulations to section 611, which deals with the allowance of a deduction for depletion.[62]

---

54 *See, e.g.,* F.G. Inc. v. Commissioner, 47 F.2d 541 (7th Cir. 1931); *see also* I.R.S. App. Off., 6-4 to -8.

55 *See* §**2.11** Sales of the Asset.

56 *See* §**3.1** Introduction to Traded Securities Valuation.

57 Tippit & Phipps, *Valuation of Mining Properties,* 4 Am. L. of Min., tit. 25, §26.6 at 577 (Rocky Mtn. Legal Fdn. ed. 1963); Bourne v. Commissioner, 62 F.2d 648 (4th Cir. 1933).

58 Fiske, *The Valuation of Oil and Gas Properties in Estates and Trusts,* 2 Rocky Mtn. Min. L. Inst. 375-76 (1956).

59 Fiske, *The Valuation of Oil Properties,* 4 Oil & Gas Tax Q. 85-87 (1955).

60 *See* §**7.3** The Market Approach to Mineral Interest Valuation; §**8.3** Lease and Leasehold Valuation.

61 *See* §**7.1** Introduction to Oil and Mineral Interest Valuation.

62 I.R.C. §611; Reg. §1.611-2(d),(e).

Basically, the Regulation adopts the conventional approach of analyzing all relevant data.[63] Value must be determined as of the valuation data; subsequent events should not change that determination. The techniques mentioned include actual sales, comparable sales, costs, replacement costs, and income analysis. The Regulation states, however, that analytical appraisal methods of valuation, including present value methods using hypothetical projected income analyses, are not to be used if the value of the mineral property can be determined by cost, comparative values and replacement value of equipment, or any other method of valuation.[64]

Curiously, and almost in the same breath, the Regulation lists ten essential factors for determining a mineral interest's fair market value under the forbidden analytical appraisal method.[65] This list includes all of the usual types of information necessary to make a valuation, using a technique that attempts to determine present value from projected future income. These factors deal with quantity, quality or grade, expenses, life expectancy, profit, and rate of capitalization.

Despite the expressed limitation on analytical appraisals, in practice, the I.R.S. has considered such appraisals for what they are worth, along with other relevant evidence.[66]

Whereas under estate and gift tax provisions the I.R.S. tries to establish as high a value as possible for assets, under I.R.C. §611 the reverse is true. It is to the I.R.S.'s advantage to have a lower market value, because under this provision market value sets the basis for the property. Consequently, the lower the market value is set, the lower the taxpayer's depletion deduction allowance is, and the higher the potential capital gain on resale. This goal of the I.R.S. under I.R.C. §611 may make the Regulations less applicable to other tax issues. It is doubtful that the I.R.S. would feel restricted by these Regulations for gift and estate tax valuation issues, although it would apply them to the valuation of charitable gifts for income tax deduction purposes.

---

63 Reg. §1.611-2(d)(1).

64 Reg. §1.611-2(d)(2); *see* Green v. United States, 460 F.2d 412, 72-1 U.S.T.C. ¶9429 (5th Cir. 1972).

65 Reg. §1.611-2(e).

66 Fiske, *The Valuation of Oil and Gas Properties in Estates and Trusts*, 2 Rocky Mtn. Min. L. Inst. 381-82 (1956).

CHAPTER 8

HOW TO VALUE CONTRACTUAL PROPERTY

§8.1 Introduction to Contractual Property Valuation

This Chapter deals with the basic techniques used for valuing assets such as notes, mortgages, untraded bonds, long term leases, and leaseholds. It will also discuss the special techniques used for life insurance and annuity policies. Valuation issues concerning such properties cover all aspects of valuation determination.[1]

The valuation techniques for contractual properties are often direct and uncomplicated because the valuation factors are necessarily part of the contractual arrangement. If the contract has been properly drafted, it will set out much of the information necessary for making a valuation. Naturally, when valuation factors are not adequately covered in, or determinable from, the contractual arrangement, valuation determinations become more complex and arbitrary.

Several of the valuation terms and concepts that were explained previously should be consulted for this Chapter including:

§2.23 Actuarial Calculations

§2.8 Proof of Value

§2.15 Replacement and Reproduction Costs

[1] *See* **§1.2** When and Where Valuation Determinations are Made.

§2.3 Significance of Appraisals and Expert Testimony
§2.17 Valuation Mathematics.

§8.2 Note, Mortgage and Nontraded Bond Valuation

Promissory notes, mortgages and untraded bonds are contractual arrangements that have similar valuation attributes. It is assumed that there is no ready market for the contractual asset. If such assets are readily tradable, then market price is significant and often determinative of market value.[2] If there are similar securities or properties that are actively traded, the price received for comparable securities might also be relevant to the market value of the securities in question.[3] It is assumed in the following discussion that both of these techniques are inapplicable or unsatisfactory.

The value of notes, mortgages, and bonds, normally equals the amount of the unpaid principal plus any accrued interest up to the valuation date.[4] For tax purposes, this valuation rule is a presumption; it applies whether the contractual arrangement is secured or unsecured. The taxpayer may be able to prove, at least for gift and estate tax purposes, that value of the contractual asset should be lower. The I.R.S. will not argue, however, that the value is higher than the rule provides, notwithstanding the asset's calculable present value.[5]

In these gift and estate tax Regulations, the I.R.S. recognizes that, because of particular economic situations, notes should not always be valued at their normal face value. This rule should also be applicable to mortgages and to untraded bonds. So long as any secured property is insufficient to satisfy the note, a note may be valued at less than face value either because (1.) the note is uncollectable in whole or part due to the insolvency of the obligor or to the existence of other legal barriers to collection, or (2.) adverse or changed economic conditions have occurred (e.g., current interest rates are much higher than the interest rate on the note).[6] The same analysis is also applicable to mortgages and to untraded bonds. The burden of proving any reduction in price, of course, is clearly upon the taxpayer.

All matters that are related to the ability of the obligor to satisfy the note, mortgage or untraded bonds are relevant: for example, the value of the underlying security or collateral interest, the debtor's ability to discharge current obligations, the debtor's general solvency, other legal proceedings concerning the debtor's assets, including foreclosure proceedings, and the debtor's present and future income prospects.

The mere fact that the statute of limitations may have run against the note, mortgage, or claim is not sufficient to justify treating the obligation as valueless. The statute of limitations is an affirmative defense: the taxpayer who claims that the obligation is valueless must show that the limitation period constitutes a bar to an action against the debtor. It must be established, for example, that the debtor has not waived the

---

2 *See* **Ch. 3** How to Value Traded Securities.
3 *See* **§4.17** Traded Securities Comparative Analysis.
4 I.R.S. Tax Law Course, 25-17 to -18; Regs. §§20.2031-4, 25.2512-4; Rev. Rul. 67-276, 1967-2 C.B. 321.
5 *See* Regs. §§20.2031-4, 25.2512-4.
6 *See* I.R.S. Tax Law Course, 25-17.

defense or committed other acts that cause the limitation period to be interrupted or suspended. If the obligation is secured and the statute of limitations has run, the holder of the obligation is, then, limited to the value of the security interest.

It is also well established that interest-bearing obligations may require a valuation different from face value if its rate of return is higher or lower than prevailing market rates.[7] An interest-bearing obligation that is returning inadequate amounts of interest should be discounted. One that has a superior interest rate may be valued at a premium. All in all, the goal is to give to the interest bearing obligation the market value it deserves as if it were paying the normal rate on similar investments.

With the proper compound interest tables, calculating the discount or premium is quite simple. You need to know the following information:

1. Principal amount of the obligation
2. Interest rate of the obligation
3. Term of the obligation
4. Payback technique
5. Current interest rate.

The procedure to be used depends on whether the principal of the loan is amortized throughout the life of the loan, or whether the principal is only paid back at the termination of the obligation. The following illustrates these procedures:

Illustration VIII-1

Assumptions

1. Principal of loan equals $10,000
2. Interest rate on the loan is 9%
3. Term of the loan is 10 years
4. Payback procedure requires interest at the end of a year; the whole principal is due at the end of 10 years
5. Current rate of interest equals 12%.

Calculation

The factors used for this Illustration require a table or equivalent calculation that provides factors for determining the present value of a reversion and the present value of ordinary annuity payments, assuming an annual compound interest rate of 12 percent.[8]

---

[7] *See* E. Spiller, Financial Accounting—Basic Concepts 341-78 (1977).

[8] *See* **§2.18** The Six Principal Calculations, Table II-1.

Illustration VIII-1 (*Continued*)

Calculation (*Continued*)

Present value of $10,000 due in ten years at 12%
1. $10,000 × .321973 = $3,219.73
Present value of $900 per year for 10 years at 12%
2. $900 × 5.650223 = $5,085.20
Total present value equals the sum of 1. and 2.
3. $3,219.73 + $5,085.20 = $8,304.93

Illustration VIII-2

Assumptions

Assume the same facts as the above Illustration, except that the principal of the loan is amortized in annual payments throughout the life of the term.

Calculations

The factors used for this Illustration require a table or equivalent calculation that provides factors for determining **1.** the annual installments for the loan, assuming an annual compound interest rate of 9 percent (see Table VIII-1) and **2.** the present value of ordinary annuity payments, assuming annual compound interest rate of 12 percent.[9]
3. Installment necessary to amortize $10,000 for ten years at 9% interest.
4. $10,000 × .155820 = $1,558.20 per year
Present value of monthly payments for ten years at 12% interest.
5. $1,558.20 × 5.650223 = $8,804.18
Total present value = $8,804.18

Both calculations reveal that the face value of the loan is too high. The same approach can be used to determine the premium on an interest bearing obligation. As previously mentioned, values will not be set above face value for gift and estate tax purposes.

§8.3 Lease and Leasehold Valuation

Occasionally, it is important to determine the value of leases both to the lessor and to the lessee. From the lessor's standpoint, leases are usually part of the valuation process for the underlying asset. If the lease is for a long period of time, however, the value

9 *See* §**2.18** The Six Principal Calculations, Table II-1.

of the lease itself is the primary asset. The reversion is secondary. When this is the case, the value of the asset is determined by adding the present value of lease rentals or income flow to the present value of the reversion or what will be left of the property at expiration of the lease.[10] This valuation technique requires determination of the going rate of interest and consultation of present value tables.[11] The following illustrates:

Illustration VIII-3

Assumptions

1.	Term of lease	20 years
2.	Rent per year (Paid at beginning of year)	$12,000
3.	Value of property at end of lease	$50,000
4.	Current rate of interest	12%

Calculations

The factors used for this Illustration require a table or equivalent calculation that provides factors for determining the present value of a reversion and the present value of ordinary annuity payments, assuming an annual compound interest rate of 12 percent.[12]

Estimated Market Value = Present Value of Lease + Present Value of Reversion.

$V = (7.562003 \times \$12{,}000) + (.103667 \times \$50{,}000)$

$V = \$90{,}744.04 + \$5{,}183.35$

$V = \$95{,}927.39$

From the tenant's standpoint, the lease, sometimes called the leasehold, may also be a valuable asset. This value may be positive or negative, depending upon the fair market rentals of comparable property in comparable areas. Again valuation calculations require reference to present value tables. Ordinarily, only long-term leases will be subject to this valuation technique. Because the initial rental rate for a lease probably is at the current rate, this valuation process only arises when the valuation date falls somewhere between the beginning and the end of the lease and at a time when the going rental rate has changed.

[10] Saunders v. United States, 48 A.F.T.R.2d ¶148,481 (M.D. Ga. 1981); I.R.S. Tax Law Course, 21-23.

[11] *See* **§2.17** Valuation Mathematics.

[12] *See* **§2.18** The Six Principal Calculations, Table II-1. Using this table, you have to use an additional year for the ordinary annuity payment factor because the rent is prepaid.

Table VIII-1[a]

9% ANNUAL COMPOUND INTEREST TABLE 9%
EFFECTIVE RATE = 9% BASE = 1.09

YEARS	1 Amount Of 1 At Compound Interest $S^n = (1+i)^n$	2 Accumulation Of 1 Per Period $S_{\overline{n}\rvert} = \frac{S^n - 1}{i}$	3 Sinking Fund Factor $1/S_{\overline{n}\rvert} = \frac{i}{S - 1}$	4 Pres. Value Reversion Of 1 $V^n = \frac{1}{S^n}$	5 Present Value Ord. Annuity 1 Per Period $a_{\overline{n}\rvert} = \frac{1 - V^n}{i}$	6 Instalment To Amortize 1 $1/a_{\overline{n}\rvert} = \frac{i}{1 - V^n}$	n YEARS
1	1.090000	1.000000	1.000000	.917431	.917431	1.090000	1
2	1.188100	2.090000	.478469	.841680	1.759111	.568469	2
3	1.295029	3.278100	.305055	.772183	2.531295	.395055	3
4	1.411582	4.573129	.218669	.708425	3.239720	.308669	4
5	1.538624	5.984711	.167092	.649931	3.889651	.257092	5
6	1.667100	7.523335	.132920	.596267	4.485919	.222920	6
7	1.828039	9.200435	.108691	.547034	5.032953	.198691	7
8	1.992563	11.028474	.090674	.501866	5.534819	.180674	8
9	2.171893	13.021036	.076799	.460428	5.995247	.166799	9
10	2.367364	15.192930	.065820	.422411	6.417658	.155820	10
11	2.580426	17.560293	.056947	.387533	6.805191	.146947	11
12	2.812665	20.140720	.049651	.355535	7.160725	.139651	12
13	3.065805	22.953385	.043567	.326179	7.486904	.133567	13
14	3.341727	26.019189	.038433	.299246	7.786150	.128433	14
15	3.642482	29.360916	.034059	.274538	8.060688	.124059	15

16	3.970306	33.003399	.030300	.251870	8.312558	.120300	16
17	4.327633	36.973705	.027046	.231073	8.543631	.117046	17
18	4.717120	41.301338	.024212	.211994	8.755625	.114212	18
19	5.141661	46.018458	.021730	.194490	8.950115	.111730	19
20	5.604411	51.160120	.019546	.178431	9.128546	.109546	20
21	6.108808	56.764530	.017617	.163698	9.292244	.107617	21
22	6.658600	62.873338	.015905	.150182	9.442425	.105905	22
23	7.257874	69.531939	.014382	.137781	9.580207	.104382	23
24	7.911083	76.789813	.013023	.126405	9.706612	.103023	24
25	8.623081	84.700896	.011806	.115968	9.822580	.101806	25
26	9.399158	93.323977	.010715	.106393	9.928972	.100715	26
27	10.245082	102.723135	.009735	.097608	10.026580	.099735	27
28	11.167140	112.968217	.008852	.089548	10.116128	.098852	28
29	12.172182	124.135356	.008056	.082155	10.198283	.098056	29
30	13.267678	136.307539	.007336	.075371	10.273654	.097336	30
31	14.461770	149.575217	.006686	.069148	10.342802	.096686	31
32	15.763329	164.036987	.006096	.063438	10.406240	.096096	32
33	17.182028	179.800315	.005562	.058200	10.464441	.095562	33
34	18.728411	196.982344	.005077	.053395	10.517835	.095077	34
35	20.413968	215.710755	.004636	.048986	10.566821	.094636	35
36	22.251225	236.124723	.004235	.044941	10.611763	.094235	36
37	24.253835	258.375948	.003870	.041231	10.652993	.093870	37
38	26.436680	282.629783	.003538	.037826	10.690820	.093538	38
39	28.815982	309.066463	.003236	.034703	10.725523	.093236	39
40	31.409420	337.882445	.002960	.031838	10.757360	.092960	40

Table VIII-1 (*Continued*)

YEARS	1 Amount Of 1 At Compound Interest $S^n = (1+i)^n$	2 Accumulation Of 1 Per Period $S_{\overline{n}\vert} = \frac{S^n - 1}{i}$	3 Sinking Fund Factor $1/S_{\overline{n}\vert} = \frac{i}{S - 1}$	4 Pres. Value Reversion Of 1 $V^n = \frac{1}{S^n}$	5 Present Value Ord. Annuity 1 Per Period $a_{\overline{n}\vert} = \frac{1 - V^n}{i}$	6 Instalment To Amortize 1 $1/a_{\overline{n}\vert} = \frac{i}{1 - V^n}$	n YEARS
41	34.236268	369.291865	.002708	.029209	10.786569	.092708	41
42	37.317532	403.528133	.002478	.026797	10.813366	.092478	42
43	40.676110	440.845665	.002268	.024584	10.837951	.092268	43
44	44.336960	481.521775	.002077	.022555	10.860505	.092077	44
45	48.327286	525.858735	.001902	.020692	10.881197	.091902	45
46	52.676742	574.186021	.001742	.018984	10.900181	.091742	46
47	57.417649	626.862762	.001595	.017416	10.917597	.091595	47
48	62.585237	684.280411	.001461	.015978	10.933575	.091461	48
49	68.217908	746.865648	.001339	.014659	10.948234	.091339	49
50	74.357520	815.083556	.001227	.013449	10.961683	.091227	50
51	81.049697	889.441077	.001124	.012338	10.974021	.091124	51
52	88.344170	970.490773	.001030	.011319	10.985340	.091030	52
53	96.295145	1058.834943	.000944	.010385	10.995725	.090944	53
54	104.961708	1155.130088	.000866	.009527	11.005252	.090866	54
55	114.408262	1260.091796	.000794	.008741	11.013993	.090794	55
56	124.705005	1374.500057	.000728	.008019	11.022012	.090728	56
57	135.928456	1499.205063	.000667	.007357	11.029369	.090667	57
58	148.162017	1635.133518	.000612	.006749	11.036118	.090612	58
59	161.496598	1783.295535	.000561	.006192	11.042310	.090561	59
60	176.031292	1944.792133	.000514	.005681	11.047991	.090514	60

[a] Reproduced from Ellwood Tables for Real Estate Appraising and Financing, 4th edition, copyright 1977 by the American Institute of Real Estate Appraisers of the National Association of Realtors.

In agricultural areas where the federal government owns a significant amount of land and leases this land to farmers and ranchers, the possession of such leases may constitute a valuable asset. Although these leases are not automatically renewable, as a matter of practice, they are renewed. Consequently, farmers, ranchers and the tax collector typically rely on this renewal practice. Frequently, the value of these leases is made a part of the value of the lessor's adjacent fee lands. Occasionally, valuation of the leases is made separately.

The basic technique for valuing the leases is to determine an animal unit month for the leased land, multiply that determination by the number of acres leased, and subtract the cost of the lease and other direct expenses.[13]

§8.4 Valuation of Miscellaneous Contractual Rights

There is an indeterminable number of other contractual rights that may have value. Basically, these types of contractual rights are valued in the same way as notes, mortgages and untraded bonds.[14] The primary consideration is face value plus any accrued interest. Face value is adjusted for the same reasons, including the inability to collect due to insolvency or legal restrictions and the adverse changes in the economics of the situation. All future obligations should be discounted to their present value.[15] Furthermore, although contingencies concerning recovery do not render contractual rights valueless, they will bear on their actual value.[16]

Services are generally valued at their stipulated price, if there is one.[17] If not stipulated, the price of comparable services is determinative.

For gift tax purposes, the value of interest-free or low-interest loans is a controversial issue. The I.R.S. takes the position that the gift should be valued at the value of the use of the money.[18] For example, if a loan is to be repaid at the end of a definite period, and if we assume that a loan of this nature would ordinarily earn a specific rate of interest, the I.R.S. contends that there is a gift equal to the difference between the face value of the loan and the loan's fair market value at the date of the transaction or other applicable date.[19] The phrase "applicable date" refers to the I.R.S. contention that interest-free demand notes have a gift tax consequence for each calendar period that a return is required. The following illustrates:

---

[13] *See* **§5.8** Livestock Carrying Capacity. *See* Davis, *Appraisal of Rural Real Estate,* Encyclopedia of Real Estate Appraising, 583-602 (3d ed., E. Friedman ed., 1978).

[14] *See* **§8.2** Note, Mortgage and Nontraded Bond Valuation.

[15] Estate of G. Robinson, 69 T.C. 222 (1977).

[16] Estate of J. Curry, 74 T.C. 540 (1980).

[17] Rev. Proc. 79-24, 1979-1 C.B. 565.

[18] Rev. Rul. 73-61, 1973-1 C.B. 408.

[19] *See* E. Dickman, 49 T.C.M. (P-H) ¶80,575 (1980).

Illustration VIII-4

Assumptions	
Loan Value	$500,000
Payable	End of one year
Normal Rate of Interest	12%

Calculation[20]

Present Value of Loan = Loan Value × Factor for Present Value of Reversion
$500,000 × .892857 = $446,428.50
GV = Loan Value − Present Value of Loan
GV = $500,000 − $446,428.50
GV = $53,571.50

In effect, the I.R.S. argues that a gift of $53,571.50 has been made on the date of transfer.

The courts have ruled in favor of the I.R.S. when the interest rate on the loans is below the normal rate, particularly if the loans are unsecured and not made at arm's length.[21] However, the courts have found in favor of the taxpayers and held that interest-free demand loans are not gifts of the use of money.[22]

Obviously, if the current authority continues to prevail, interest-free loans are a method for transferring wealth without gift tax consequences. Just as obvious, the loans must be of large amounts in order to yield a meaningful tax savings, particularly given the new $10,000 gift tax exclusion.

Despite their apparent gift tax avoidance possibilities, there are limitations, hazards and counter considerations with regard to interest-free loans. Consider the following:

1. Current law protects only demand interest-free loans from gift taxation. Interest-free loans for a definite term of years may have gift tax consequences
2. The I.R.S. will scrutinize substantial interest-free loans closely, and may be willing to litigate the issue again
3. Although there may be no gift tax consequences, the unpaid portions of the loan will still be included in the lender's estate
4. Low-interest loans for a specific term are subject to gift taxation. (The lender's estate should be permitted to discount the value of these loans for estate tax purposes, however.)
5. The I.R.S. may shift its tactics and contend that the lender or borrower receives imputed interest during the term of the loan.

20 *See* **§2.18** The Six Principal Calculations, Table II-1, column 4.

21 Estate of M. Berkman, 48 T.C.M. (P-H) ¶79,046 (1949).

22 Crown v. Commissioner, 585 F.2d 234 (7th Cir. 1978); Martin v. Commissioner, 649 F.2d 1133, 48 A.F.T.R.2d ¶81-5537 (5th Cir. 1981) (persuasive dissent urging overruling of prior precedent); *but see* Hardee v. United States, 50 A.F.T.R.2d ¶82-5253 (Ct. Cl. 1982) (a trial judge's opinion held that the value of the interest-free loans were income to the borrower).

§8.5 Life Insurance Valuation

It goes without saying that life insurance is an important element in the planning of estates. Necessarily, the determination of its valuation is frequently involved, too. This Chapter discusses the valuation techniques applicable to the most common forms of life insurance.

There are a variety of techniques applicable to valuing life insurance, depending upon the purpose for which the valuation is being made: income, gift or estate tax or determination of its present value to its owner. The following four valuation techniques are used for life insurance:

1. Surrender value
2. Replacement cost
3. Adjusted interpolated terminal reserve
4. Proceeds value.

Each of the above techniques will be described and discussed below.

Because the interpolated terminal reserve is so key to an understanding of many of the valuation determinations for life insurance and annuity policies, it requires a thorough explanation. The term "terminal reserve" is defined as the reserve a life insurance company maintains on its books representing its liability on a life insurance policy or annuity policy that is issued and is still outstanding.[23] Although it can be individually calculated, the easiest method for obtaining this value is from the insurance company itself. The I.R.S. publishes Form 712 for this purpose.[24] Upon request, the insurance companies will complete this form and send it to appropriate persons.[25]

For tax valuation purposes, the terminal reserve value is both interpolated and adjusted. Interpolation is the process of adjusting the terminal reserve value between any two consecutive anniversary dates of the policy. In other words, if the valuation date does not fall on the subject policy's anniversary date, the value of the policy must be adjusted accordingly. For example, if the valuation date is four months after the last terminal reserve anniversary and eight months before the next terminal reserve anniversary, one-third of the increased value of the terminal reserve value between those dates must be added to the terminal reserve value prior to the valuation date.[26]

The value of the policy must also be adjusted to account for any unused portion of premiums paid before the valuation date and not expired by that date. This adjustment is calculated like the interpolation described above, but the increase in value equals the portion of the premiums attributable to the time after the valuation date. This amount is added to the interpolated terminal reserve value. For example, if an annual premium payment was made four months before the valuation date and had eight months of

[23] Ballentine's Law Dictionary 1266 (3d ed. 1969).

[24] *See* **§8.9** Forms and Worksheets for Life Insurance and Annuity Valuation.

[25] *Id.*

[26] *See* Reg. §25.2512-6(a)(Example 4).

unexpired coverage, two-thirds of the premium would be added to the interpolated terminal reserve value.[27]

Illustration VIII-5

ADJUSTED INTERPOLATED TERMINAL RESERVE CALCULATION

Assumptions

1.	Date of valuation	July 1, 19XX
2.	Policy anniversary date	February 1, 19XX
3.	Policy was issued on anniversary date 15 years and 5 months prior to date of valuation	
4.	Terminal reserve value at end of 15th year	$20,321
5.	Terminal reserve value at end of 16th year	$22,139
6.	Gross premium	$1,544

Calculation

1.	Terminal reserve at end of valuation year	$22,139
2.	Less terminal reserve at beginning of valuation year	–$20,321
3.	Increase in terminal reserve	$ 1,818
4.	Multiply 3. by the appropriate measure of time between prior anniversary date and valuation date (months)	× 5
5.	Result	$ 9,090
6.	Divide 5. by the appropriate measure of time for the entire year (months)	÷ 12
7.	Pro rata increase in terminal reserve	$757.50
8.	Gross premium	$ 1,544
9.	Multiply 8. by the appropriate measure of time between the valuation date and the succeeding anniversary date (months)	× 7
10.	Result	10,808
11.	Divide 10. by the appropriate measure of time for the entire year (months)	÷ 12
12.	Pro rata premium adjustment	900.67

[27] *Id.*

Illustration VIII-5 (*Continued*)

Calculation (*Continued*)		
13. Add 2., 7. and 12.		
	2.	20,321.00
	7.	757.50
	12.	900.67
14. Adjusted interpolated terminal reserve value		$21,979.17

§8.6 —Income Tax Valuation for Life Insurance

There are several income tax situations which call for valuation determinations concerning life insurance policies. The most common situations concern valuation determinations of life insurance fringe benefits to employees, and of purchases of life insurance policies by insured persons from third-person owners such as the insureds' employers. The following discussion includes only the barest information on this very technical and complex area of tax law.

Employers often provide life insurance protection for their employees as a fringe benefit. This benefit may be made as a part of a qualified pension and profit sharing plan, a split-dollar life insurance plan, or as part of a tax-sheltered annuity plan.[28] Excluding group-term life insurance for which there is a special rule, the employee recognizes income if, on the employee's death, the policy proceeds are payable either to the employee's estate or beneficiary or to the trustee of a fringe-benefit plan who then is required to pay the proceeds to the employee's estate or beneficiaries.[29] The amount of annual income attributable to the employee is only the annual cost of the pure amount at risk involved in the insurance.

Calculation of Income Taxable Amount:

1. Determine the face amount of the insurance
2. Subtract the cash value of the insurance at the end of the relevant policy year
3. Divide the result of the above calculation by 1,000
4. Multiply the result of the above calculation by the cost of the one-year premium at the insured's age.

The age of an employee-insured is set at his or her birthday closest to the beginning of the policy year.

The rate for one-year term insurance is determined from a chart recognized by the

[28] *See* E. Allen, J. Melone & J. Rosenbloom, Pension Planning 49-53 (3d ed. 1976); H. Weinstock, Planning an Estate 222-26 (1977).

[29] Reg. §1.72-16(b)(1).

I.R.S.[30] This is sometimes called the "P.S. 58 Rate." This chart is included as Appendix C. If the insurance company's rates or comparable term policies are lower, however, they may be used instead of the P.S. 58 rates.

Illustration VIII-6

INCOME TAXABLE VALUE OF LIFE INSURANCE

Assumption	
1. Face value of insurance	$100,000
2. Cash value of insurance at end of relevant policy year	$35,000
3. Age of insured nearest the beginning of the policy year	35
4. Income tax year	19XX

Calculation	
1. Face value	$100,000
2. Less cash value	−35,000
3. Pure risk	$65,000
4. Divide 3. by 1,000	÷ 1,000
5. Result	65
6. Multiply 5. by premium rate (P.S. 58 rate for 35-year-old)	$3.21
7. Taxable income for 19XX	$208.65

As indicated, there is a special income tax rule for employer paid group-term life insurance. Under I.R.C. §79, the employer-paid cost of coverage up to $50,000 is not taxable income to the employee. Employer-paid premiums for larger policies are taxable to the employee. A Regulation to I.R.C. §79 sets out the amount to be treated as income to the employee for excess employer-paid coverage.[31]

When an insured-employee purchases a life insurance policy, on which additional premiums must be paid, from his or her employer for the cash surrender value, the employee must recognize income in the amount by which the policy's adjusted interpolated terminal reserve value exceeds its cash surrender value.[32] This income must be declared in the year of the purchase.

Finally, when any insured cashes in his or her life insurance policy, income must be recognized if the cash surrender value is greater than the cost of the insurance policy.[33] In this situation, cost does not refer to replacement cost, but to the actual cost to the insured. In other words, the taxpayer-insured's tax basis equals the aggregate

30 Rev. Rul. 55-747, 1955-2 C.B. 228.

31 Reg. §1.79-3(d)(2).

32 Rev. Rul. 59-195, 1959-1 C.B. 18.

33 I.R.C. §72(e)(1)(B).

premiums. The difference in value constitutes ordinary income; this must be recognized in the year in which the surrender occurs. The same issue may arise at maturity if the insured elects to take the proceeds in a lump-sum cash payment.

§8.7 —Estate and Gift Tax Valuations for Life Insurance

It may sometimes be necessary for gift and estate tax purposes to value an insurance policy prior to the insured's death. This situation occurs when the owner of the policy transfers it inter vivos or at death to another while the insured is alive. There are two basic valuation techniques: replacement cost and adjusted interpolated terminal reserve value.

The replacement cost technique requires that you determine the replacement cost of the issuing company's comparable policies. This technique is applicable to single premium policies, to paid-up insurance policies, and to new policies on which only the first premium has been paid. The actual replacement cost equals the value of a single premium that would purchase the same policy from the same company or a comparable policy, if that policy were taken out upon the life of a person of the insured's age on the valuation date.

The adjusted interpolated terminal reserve technique is applicable to all insurance policies that have been in existence for a period of time and on which future premium payments will be made. It is also applicable to single premium policies if the transfer occurs a period of time after the purchase and comparable policies are no longer obtainable due to changes in payments and benefits.[34]

Under the circumstances described above, the interpolated terminal reserve valuation technique is applicable for both estate and gift tax purposes. For gift tax purposes, the insured may be the owner or may be someone other than the owner. For estate tax purposes, the insured and the owner must be different persons because the owner must be the decedent whose estate is being valued and the insured must still be alive at the valuation date.[35]

The interpolated terminal reserve value is also applicable where two parties have reciprocal life insurance policies. This is a common estate planning technique. The husband owns an insurance policy on his wife and the wife owns an insurance policy on her husband. Even if they die simultaneously, the I.R.S. has taken the position that each decedent's estate includes the interpolated terminal reserve value on the policy owned on the other.[36] This rule is applicable, of course, only where under state law presumes that the insured survives the beneficiary. Under the Ruling, this valuation technique is applicable even though the policy proceeds are actually paid to the decedent-beneficiary's estate under the policy's contingent beneficiary provisions.

For gift and estate tax purposes, you should deduct the amount of any loan or debt

---

[34] Regs. §§20.2031-8(a)(1)(2), 25.2512-6(a); *see* A. Edwards, 46 B.T.A. 815 (1942), *aff'd*, 135 F.2d 574 (7th Cir. 1943), *acq.* 1942-2 C.B. 6, *nonacq.* 1942-2 C.B. 24.

[35] *See* **§8.5** Life Insurance Valuation, Illustration VIII-5.

[36] Rev. Rul. 77-181, 1977-1 C.B. 272.

against the policy either from the value of the policy transferred for gift tax purposes, or as a completely separate deduction used as a claim against the gross estate.[37]

When life insurance becomes part of the insured's estate, the value of the policy is equal to the full amount receivable under the policy.[38] If the proceeds are not to be paid to the beneficiary in a lump sum, the value is the hypothetical amount that the beneficiary might have elected or that the insurance company determines is the lump-sum value of the policy proceeds. The full amount receivable includes dividends, accumulated dividends, premium refunds, and any other monetary benefit payable due to the death of the insured. This valuation technique is applicable for all forms of life insurance including ordinary life, term, group, accidental death, etc.

The test of whether insurance proceeds are part of the insured's estate is whether the insured owned or controlled any of the incidents of ownership in the policy at the time of death, whether they were exercisable alone or in conjunction with any other person.[39] In its most general sense, "incidents of ownership" is defined as "the right of the insured or his estate to the economic benefits of the policy."[40] A thorough discussion of its intricacies is left to other estate planning materials.[41]

§8.8 Annuity Valuation

Annuities can be broken into two categories: commercial and noncommercial.

The tax laws have a significant number of complex rules and limitations on the income, gift and estate taxation of annuities. No attempt here has been made to explain these rules and limitations. It is assumed for purposes of this Handbook that the annuity or portion of the annuity must be valued for estate planning purposes.

Valuation of commercial annuities for gift and estate tax purposes is comparable to valuation of life insurance under similar circumstances.[42] Presumably these annuities would also be valued in the same manner for income tax purposes.[43]

The I.R.S. has established a special valuation procedure for annuities that are issued in exchange for money or property by certain organizations. The Ruling applies to corporations, trusts, banks or foundations, but not to insurance companies.[44] After September 18, 1972, annuities from such organizations must not be valued by reference to the cost of a comparable contract purchased from an insurance company, but must be valued under tables established in the Ruling. The Ruling includes tables for single-life annuities, joint-life annuities, joint and survivor annuities, and deferred-payment

[37] Commissioner v. Procter; 142 F.2d 824 (4th Cir. 1944), *cert. denied,* 323 U.S. 756 (1944); Reg. §20.2042-1(b)(1).

[38] Reg. §20.2042-1(a)(3).

[39] Reg. §20.2042-1(c)(1).

[40] Reg. §20.2042-1(c)(2),(6).

[41] *See, e.g.,* A. Casner, Estate Planning 681-726 (4th ed. 1980).

[42] *See* **§8.5** Life Insurance Valuation; Regs. §§20.2031-10(a)(1), 25.2512-9(a)(1)(i).

[43] *See* Rev. Rul. 59-195, 1959-1 C.B. 18.

[44] Rev. Rul. 72-438 1972-2 C.B. 38.

annuities for single and joint lives. This Revenue Ruling should be consulted if an annuity of this kind must be valued.

The I.R.S. has developed a different technique for valuing noncommercial annuities, including all annuities between private parties and employees' trusts and retirement annuity contracts under I.R.C. §2039(c). It is important to note that not all annuities have to be valued for estate tax purposes. A single-life annuity with no survivorship rights or interests has an estate tax value of zero in the annuitant's estate. In addition, many kinds of annuities are exempt from federal estate taxes if certain conditions are met.[45]

The I.R.S. has developed a set of actuarial tables designed to provide a present value for these annuities.[46] The tables are calculated assuming both a three and one-half percent interest rate and a six percent interest rate on the annuity.[47] There are separate tables for males (Table A(1)) and females (Table A(2)) due to the difference in life expectancy. There are also separate tables for single-life annuities and for term-certain annuities (Table B).

The six percent tables apply to transfers and to estates of decedents dying after December 31, 1970. The three and one-half percent tables apply to the events prior to that date. Because the six percent tables apply to current events, these tables will be used for all subsequent illustrations.[48]

The Regulations also make it important to know how the payments are made. For either a single-life annuity or a term-certain annuity, an adjustment must be made depending upon whether the payments are made at the end of a semi-annual, quarterly, monthly or weekly period. If the single-life annuity is payable at the beginning of the appropriate period, the adjustment is the same as that for an annuity paid at the end with the addition of one installment payment. For a term-certain annuity, a separate adjustment is also necessary if payment is made at the beginning of the annual, semi-annual, quarterly, monthly or weekly periods. The following chart lists the adjustment factors:

Chart VIII-1

Payment Frequency	Single Life And Term Certain Payment at End	Term Certain Payment at Beginning
Annual	(No Adjustment)	1.0600
Semiannual	1.0148	1.0448
Quarterly	1.0222	1.0372
Monthly	1.0272	1.0322
Weekly	1.0291	1.0303

45 *See* I.R.C. 2039.

46 *See* **§2.23** Actuarial Calculations.

47 *See* Regs. §20.2031-7(f) (3-1/2 percent tables); §§20.2031-10(f), 25.2512-9(f) (6 percent tables).

48 These six percent tables are included at Appendix B.

To use single life annuity tables, you need to determine the following matters:

1. The beneficiary's sex
2. The beneficiary's nearest age by year
3. The frequency of annuity payments
4. The timing of payments (either at the beginning or the end of each period)
5. The amount of each annuity payment.

With this information it is easy to determine the value of the annuity for income, gift and estate tax purposes. The following illustration may aid in understanding this calculation.

Illustration VIII-7
VALUE OF SINGLE-LIFE ANNUITY

Assumptions

1. Beneficiary is female
2. Beneficiary is nearest age 58
3. Frequency of payment is monthly
4. Timing of payment is beginning of month
5. Payment is $1,000 per month for life.

Calculation

Using Reg. §20.2031-10(f) Table A(2)[49]
$1,000 × 10.9980 × 1.0272 × 12 (months) + $1,000 = $136,565.75.

The above figure would be the value of the annuity to the beneficiary. That amount would be included in a decedent's estate if the annuity was an asset of the estate and was not exempt from federal estate taxation. It also would equal the value of a taxable gift by a transferor of that annuity.[50]

49 *See* Appendix B.

50 An explanation and illustration of the process using the term certain tables is included at **§11.5** Future Interests Valuation. *See* **§8.9** Forms and Worksheets for Life Insurance and Annuity Valuation.

§8.9 Forms and Worksheets for Life Insurance and Annuity Valuation

FORM LETTER REQUESTING IRS FORM 712

In re: Estate of ____________.

Dear Sir or Madam:

This office represents the Estate of ____________. Decedent died on ________ ________, ________. Decedent's social security number is ________-________-________.

[The decedent was insured with your company under policy(ies) numbered:

____

____

Please check your records to see if other policies were issued on decedent's life].

OR

[Decedent's records indicate that decedent may have been insured by your company. Please check your records to see if any policies were issued on decedent's life.]

Please send the Internal Revenue Form 712 in [duplicate] [triplicate] for each policy issued by your company on the life of the decedent. If you have not yet paid the proceeds on any policy, please send your check therefor along with Form 712 or under separate cover.

Thank you.

Very truly yours,

Form **712**
(Rev. June 1980)
Department of the Treasury
Internal Revenue Service

Life Insurance Statement

Part I **Decedent—Insured (To be Filed with Federal Estate Tax Return, Form 706)**

1 Decedent's first name and middle initial	2 Decedent's last name	3 Decedent's social security number (if known)	4 Date of death

5 Name and address of insurance company

6 Kind of policy	7 Policy number

8 Owner's name. If decedent is not the owner, please attach copy of application.	9 Date issued	10 Assignor's name. Please attach copy of assignment.	11 Date assigned

12 Value of the policy at the time of assignment	13 Amount of premium	14 Names of beneficiaries

15 Face amount of policy . . . . . $

16 Indemnity benefits . . . . . $

17 Additional insurance . . . . . $

18 Other benefits . . . . . $

19 Principal of any indebtedness to the company deductible in determining net proceeds . . . . . $

20 Interest on indebtedness (item 19) accrued to date of death . . . . . $

21 Amount of accumulated dividends . . . . . $

22 Amount of post-mortem dividends . . . . . $

23 Amount of returned premium . . . . . $

24 Amount of proceeds if payable in one sum . . . . . $

25 Value of proceeds as of date of death (if not payable in one sum) . . . . . $

26 Policy provisions concerning deferred payments or installments.

Note: *If other than lump-sum settlement is authorized for a surviving spouse, please attach a copy of the insurance policy.*

27 Amount of installments . . . . . $

28 Date of birth, sex, and name of any person the duration of whose life may measure the number of payments.

29 Amount applied by the insurance company as a single premium representing the purchase of installment benefits . . . . . $

30 Basis (Mortality table and rate of interest) used by insurer in valuing installment benefits.

31 Was the insured the annuitant or beneficiary of any annuity contract issued by the company? . . . . . ☐ Yes ☐ No

32 Names of companies with which decedent carried other policies and amount of such policies if this information is disclosed by your records.

The undersigned officer of the above-named insurance company hereby certifies that this statement sets forth true and correct information.

Signature ▶ Title ▶ Date of Certification ▶

Instructions

Statement of Insurer.—This statement must be made, on behalf of the insurance company which issued the policy, by an officer of the company having access to the records of the company. For purposes of this statement, a facsimile signature may be used in lieu of a manual signature and, if used, shall be binding as a manual signature.

Separate Statements.—A separate statement must be filed for each policy.

Form **712** (Rev. 6–80)

Form 712 (Rev. 6–80) Page 2

Part II Living Insured
(File with Federal Gift Tax Return, Form 709. May be Filed with Federal Estate Tax Return, Form 706, where Decedent Owned Insurance on Life of Another)

SECTION A.—General Information

33 First name and middle initial of donor (or decedent)	34 Last name	35 Social security number

36 Date of gift for which valuation data submitted . . . . . ▶

37 Date of decedent's death for which valuation data submitted . . . . . ▶

SECTION B.—Policy Information

38 Name of insured		39 Sex	40 Date of birth
41 Name and address of insurance company			
42 Kind of policy	43 Policy number	44 Face amount	45 Issue date
46 Gross premium		47 Frequency of payment	
48 Assignee's name			49 Date assigned
50 If irrevocable designation of beneficiary made, name of beneficiary	51 Sex	52 Date of birth, if known	53 Date designated

54 If other than simple designation, quote in full. (Attach additional sheet if necessary.)

55 If policy is not paid-up:
- (a) Interpolated terminal reserve on date of assignment or irrevocable designation of beneficiary . . . . .
- (b) Add proportion of gross premium paid beyond date of assignment or irrevocable designation of beneficiary . . . . .
- (c) Add adjustment on account of dividends to credit of policy . . . . .
- (d) Total (add amounts on lines (a), (b), and (c)) . . . . .
- (e) Outstanding indebtedness against policy . . . . .
- (f) Net total value of the policy (for gift or estate tax purposes) (subtract amount on line (e) from amount on line (d)) . . . . .

56 If policy is either paid-up or a single premium:
- (a) Total cost, on date of assignment or irrevocable designation of beneficiary, of a single-premium policy on life of insured at attained age, for original face amount plus any additional paid-up insurance (additional face amount $..........).
  If a single-premium policy for the total face amount would not have been issued on the life of the insured as of the date specified, nevertheless, assume that such a policy could then have been purchased by the insured and state the cost thereof, using for such purpose the same formula and basis employed, on the date specified, by the company in calculating single premiums . . . . .
- (b) Adjustment on account of dividends to credit of policy . . . . .
- (c) Total (add amounts on line (a) and line (b)) . . . . .
- (d) Outstanding indebtedness against policy . . . . .
- (e) Net total value of policy (for gift or estate tax purposes) (subtract amount on line (d) from amount on line (c))

The undersigned officer of the above-named insurance company hereby certifies that this statement sets forth true and correct information.

Signature ▶ Title ▶ Date of Certification ▶

☆U.S.GPO:1980-0-313-281/5454 EI# 430814328

VALUATION OF NONCOMMERCIAL SINGLE-LIFE ANNUITIES UNDER SIX PERCENT ACTUARIAL TABLES[51]

Necessary Facts

1. Value of Annuity Installment ______

Indicate Frequency:
Weekly ____; Monthly ____; Quarterly ____; Semiannually ____;
Annually ____.

2. Nearest Actual Age of Annuitant ______

3. Sex of Annuitant M____ F____

If male, use Table A(1); if female, use Table A(2)

4. Timing For Installments

Payable at end of period ____; Payable at beginning of period ____.

Calculations

5. Installment Value ______

6. Multiply 5. by the appropriate factor that follows: × ______

Weekly	52
Monthly	12
Quarterly	4
Semiannually	2
Annually	1

7. Result from 6. × 5. ______

8. Multiply 7. by the appropriate factor from Table applicable to annuitant × ______

9. Result from 8. × 7. ______

10. Multiply 9. by the appropriate factor depending on frequency of installments: × ______

Weekly	1.0291
Monthly	1.0272
Quarterly	1.0222
Semiannually	1.0148
Annually	1.0000

11. Result from 10. × 9. ______

12. If installments are paid at the beginning of the period, add value of one installment. + ______

13. Either 11. or the result of 12. + 11. equals market value of entire annuity ______

14. If part of the annuity is excludable, multiply 13. by the nonexcludable ratio × ______

15. Result equals the market value of taxable portion ______

51 Regs. §§20.2031-10(f), 25.2512-9(f). See Appendix B.

VALUATION OF NONCOMMERCIAL TERM-CERTAIN ANNUITIES UNDER SIX PERCENT ACTUARIAL TABLES[52]

Necessary Facts

1. Value of Annuity Installment ______
Indicate Frequency:
Weekly ____; Monthly ____; Quarterly ____; Semiannually ____;
Annually ____.

2. The term certain for installments in years: Table B, Column 1 ______

3. Timing for Installments
Payable at end of period ____; Payable at beginning of period ____.

Calculations

4. Installment Value ______

5. Multiply by the appropriate factor that follows: × ______

Weekly	52
Monthly	12
Quarterly	4
Semiannually	2
Annually	1

6. Result from 5. × 4. ______

7. Multiply 6. by the appropriate factor found in 2. above × ______

8. Result for 7. × 6. ______

[Complete either 9. or 10. below, but not both].

9. If installments are paid at end of period, multiply 8. by the appropriate factor depending on frequency of installments: × ______

Weekly	1.0291
Monthly	1.0272
Quarterly	1.0222
Semiannually	1.0148
Annually	1.0000

[OR]

10. If installments are paid at the beginning of the period, multiply 8. by the appropriate factor depending on frequency of installments: × ______

Weekly	1.0303
Monthly	1.0322
Quarterly	1.0372
Semiannually	1.0448
Annually	1.0600

11. Result of either 8. × 9. or 8. × 10. equals market value of entire annuity ______

12. If part of the annuity is excludable, multiply 11. by the nonexcludable ratio ______

13. Result equals the market value of the taxable portion. ______

52 *Id.*

CHAPTER 9

HOW TO VALUE INTELLECTUAL AND OTHER UNIQUE PROPERTIES

§9.1 Introduction to Valuation of Intellectual and Unique Properties

Certain types of unique properties are found in enough estates to merit special consideration here. A unique property has some special characteristic that requires particular consideration when making valuation determinations. The properties discussed in this Chapter include patents, copyrights, trademarks and tradenames, art works, and antiques. Basically, all of these assets have a creative, intellectual or aesthetic quality calling for special valuation consideration. In addition, from an estate planning standpoint, these assets may possess substantial value.

In the process of valuing the type of assets discussed here, it is very important that adequate data be obtained and that this data be thoroughly analyzed.[1] The latter requirement means that if the asset has significant value, assistance from qualified experts is recommended and often a necessity.[2]

Several of the valuation terms and concepts that were explained previously should be consulted for this Chapter including:

§2.19 Capitalization of Income

§2.9 Fair Market Value

---

1 *See* **§1.2** When and Where Valuation Determinations Are Made.

2 *See* §**2.3** Significance of Appraisals and Expert Testimony; §**2.8** Proof of Value.

§2.10 Market
§2.8 Proof of Value
§2.11 Sales of the Asset
§2.3 Significance of Appraisals and Expert Testimony
§2.17 Valuation Mathematics.

§9.2 Patent Valuation

The task of valuing patents for estate planning purposes is an uncommon but difficult one.[3] Basically, a patent is a grant from the U. S. Patent Office to the patentee of a fixed, exclusive seventeen-year right that entitles the patentee to manufacture, use, and market the invention, process, or discovery. This exclusive right or monopoly constitutes a property interest. Because the valuation process for many patents will be extremely speculative, the employment of persons experienced with patents and their value is recommended.[4]

First, an initial determination whether a patent has any value at all must be made. Not all patents have any intrinsic or intangible value. A patent may be so obsolete or have so many alternatives so as not to possess any market power, and thus no particular special value. Consequently, it is usually suggested that you get a patent attorney's opinion on the relative value of the patent.

Generally, patents with value are those that are unique, currently useful, a part of a process or product in demand and of sufficient breadth to provide exclusive control in an adequate market. In other words, a patent, which possesses market power to set price or at least substantially affect price, has value.

Once it is determined that a patent has significant value, the second step is to ascertain its value. The most common technique is to calculate the present value of the patent's projected future income flow. In other words, what will the patent earn during its life expectancy, and what is the present value of those earnings?

The valuation calculation requires determination of the patent's earnings. If the patent is presently earning income, then its past performance plus an estimation of its future performance will be analyzed to estimate future income flow. If your patent is not producing income, then a comprehensive economic analysis of the patent is necessary in order to make this estimate.

Any estimate of earning capacity must be limited to those profits directly attributable to the patent and not to those attributable to other related tangible assets or activities. For example, earnings that are the result of personal services, marketing activities, advertising effectiveness, tangible assets or any other result of management of personal ability must be deducted from the earnings in order to arrive at a net earnings for the patent interest.

Even additional deductions from the net earnings of a patent interest may be necessary. For example, it may be required to take deductions (or what might be called

---

[3] *See* I.R.S. App. Off., 9-1 to -4.
[4] *See* §2.3 Significance of Appraisals and Expert Testimony; §2.8 Proof of Value.

discounts) such as litigation costs concerning the patent, loss of earnings due to anticipated or current patent infringement by others, starting-up costs for new patents, and the problems raised by untested markets, in order to properly treat potential or existing factors.[5]

Even under the very best circumstances, the measurement of a patent's earning capacity is a complex and speculative endeavor. For tax purposes, it has been indicated that the determination of the estimated future income flow need not be made with precision or with overwhelming proof.[6] Reasonable estimates are sufficient. For one thing, all risk factors may be considered and weighed again in determining the capitalization rate.

It is necessary, of course, for you to determine a capitalization rate in order to convert income flow into present market value. This process has been discussed several times before.[7]

As indicated above, the rate of capitalization will be affected by the speculativeness of the estimated income flow. The more speculative the income flow, the higher the rate of capitalization will be. In one case a rate of 15 percent has been permitted.[8] Significantly, the I.R.S. has indicated that the rate would be substantially greater than the rate on the safest type of investments.[9]

Because patents have a limited life, it is also necessary to estimate the remaining life of the patent. Although patents have a specific maximum life of seventeen years, it is likely that the estimated remaining life will be shorter, and in fact may be less than the time of the specific term remaining from the date of valuation. The shorter life may be appropriate because of the value of the patent in the market place. Obsolescence, noninfringing competition, market saturation, and changes in consumer desires may cause a patent to have a much shorter life than the full seventeen-year term.

Once the net future income flow and the life of the patent are determined, it is then necessary to determine present value. The two possible methods are: calculating the present value from a straight-line annuity table, or from a sinking-fund table such as the Hoskold formula.[10] The Hoskold formula has been approved for this purpose.[11] Because a patent is a wasting asset, this valuation process is similar in many ways to the valuation of mineral interests.[12]

Because patents are unique by definition, the market approach is not generally applicable to their valuation. Of course, if comparable sales data are available, this approach would be applicable. Also, if the subject patent sold in an arm's length

---

[5] *See* R.I.A., Estate Planning & Taxation Coordinator ¶82,604 at p. 82,602 (1979).

[6] I.R.S. App. Off., 9-2.

[7] *See* **§2.19** Capitalization of Income; **§4.5** Capitalization of the Business Interest's Earnings.

[8] Prophylactic Brush Co., 25 B.T.A. 676 (1932), *acq* XI-2 C.B. 8.

[9] I.R.S. App. Off., 9-4.

[10] *See* **§2.19** Capitalization of Income.

[11] B. F. Sturtevant Co. v. Commissioner, 75 F.2d 316 (1st Cir. 1935); I.R.S. Tax Law Course, 25-5 to -6.

[12] *See* **§7.4** The Income Method of Mineral Interest Valuation, Illustration VI-2, for an illustration and comparison of the two techniques for capitalizing future income flows for wasting assets.

transaction reasonably close to the valuation date, that sale price may be highly relevant and possibly determinative.[13]

Patent applications should receive the same analysis as patents. The only difference is that you must make a preliminary estimation of the application's potential for becoming a recognized patent. This adds additional risk to the patent's valuation; and that, in turn, requires either a discount from the value of the net earnings or an increase in the rate of capitalization.

§9.3 Trademark and Tradename Valuation

Occasionally, you may have to value trademarks, tradenames or other similar license arrangements. The valuation process is basically the same as it is for patents. The major difference is that there is no specified and limited length of time after which the asset's privileges expire. This means that in making the valuation of such an asset you must either select an arbitrary length of time or assume that the asset has a perpetual life like that of a closely-held business interest.[14] This decision will naturally affect the determination of the capitalization rate. The technique that is used depends upon the nature of the trademark, tradename, or other similar type of asset, and on its expected life. Some trademarks or tradenames may be expected to have an almost perpetual life. On the other hand, most trademarks or tradenames probably have a very limited, determinable life similar to patents or possibly copyrights.

If trademarks and tradenames are marketable, a market analysis approach to valuation would be relevant and appropriate.[15] Such a market analysis approach may be applicable, for example, to endorsements by well-known personalities. Endorsements may have a market value determinable from the price in the marketplace.

§9.4 Copyright Valuation

Although certainly not as common as stock and real estate, the necessity to value a copyright is not an uncommon requirement for estate planning purposes. Copyright valuation is certainly more often encountered than patent or trademark valuation.

Under existing law, copyright protection is available for any original work of authorship that is fixed in any tangible medium of expression now known or later developed and that can be perceived, reproduced, or otherwise communicated either directly or with the aid of a machine or device. The coverage is obviously very comprehensive. It includes, for example, literary and other writings, musical compositions, theatrical productions, choreographic works, pictorial, graphic, and sculptural works, motion pictures and other audio-visual materials, and sound recordings.[16]

---

[13] *See* **§2.11** Sales of the Asset.

[14] *See* **§2.19** Capitalization of Income; **§4.5** Capitalization of the Business Interest's Earnings.

[15] *See* **§2.10** Market; **§2.11** Sales of the Asset.

[16] *See* Silverman, *The Valuation of Intellectual Property in Connection with the Estates of Authors and Other Creative Persons,* 11 Miami Inst. Est. Plan ¶1101, 11-3 to -4 (1977); 17 U.S.C. §102 (1976).

With very limited exceptions, a copyright gives to the owner the exclusive rights to perform and/or authorize any of the following actions with regard to the copyrighted work:[17]

1. Reproduce it
2. Prepare derivative work from it
3. Distribute copies or phonorecords of it to the public by sale or other transfer or by rental, lease, or lending
4. Where relevant, perform it publicly
5. Where relevant, display it publicly.

In addition, these various rights may be subdivided and the exclusive right to each may be owned and enforced separately.[18]

The 1976 Copyright Act has two specific and primary durational rules. First, if the copyright was created on or after January 1, 1978, the copyright protection extends for the life of the author, or life of the last surviving author if created jointly by two or more authors, plus fifty years beyond this life or lives.[19] Second, works that were created and copyrighted prior to January 1, 1978 now have a copyright lasting up to seventy-five years. If the old copyright is in its first term, upon renewal under the old law procedure, the copyright is extended for forty-seven years. If the old copyright is into the renewal term, the renewal term is automatically extended, up to forty-seven years, to an aggregate term of seventy-five years from the date the copyright was originally secured.[20] There is also a special term of protection for works that were created before January 1, 1978 but were not published until after that date.[21] In all situations, the duration of a copyright is very generous. In fact, as will be mentioned, it probably lasts longer than the economic significance of most works.

From a valuation standpoint, it is particularly important to note that the bundle of rights created by a copyright is divisable and transferable. Each right may be sold, given, or retained as part of the owner's estate.[22] This means that valuations may be necessary for each separate right if each has economic significance.

The 1976 Copyright Act creates a "right of termination" in the owner during his or her lifetime or in a majority in interest of his spouse, children and grandchildren after his or her death.[23] This right of termination applies to any *inter vivos* transfer or license of a copyright, or any of the separate rights included in it, made by an author on or after January 1, 1978. A termination of any grant may be made at any time during a five-year period beginning at the end of thirty-five years from the date of execution

[17] 17 U.S.C. §106 (1976).

[18] Silverman, *The Valuation of Intellectual Property in Connection with the Estates of Authors and Other Creative Persons,* 11 Miami Inst. Est. Plan ¶1101.1, 11-5 (1977).

[19] 17 U.S.C. §302 (1976).

[20] 17 U.S.C. §304 (1976).

[21] 17 U.S.C. §303 (1976).

[22] Lieb & Schaaf, *Estate Planning for Creators of Intellectual Property,* 1979 Ill. L.F. 374.

[23] 17 U.S.C. §203(a)(1) (1976).

of the grant. If the grant covers the right of publication of the work, termination may take place within a five year period commencing thirty-five years from the date of publication or forty years from the date of the grant, whichever occurs first.[24] Written notice of the termination must be served on the grantee, and a copy filed in the copyright office, not less than two years nor more than ten years prior to the effective date of the termination.[25] The right of termination does not extent to works made for hire or not published as of December 31, 1977 but on which grants had been made prior to January 1, 1978.[26]

A right of termination may constitute an asset that requires valuation for estate planning purposes. This may be true even for an unexercised termination right in the owner's estate.[27]

The valuation technique for copyrights will usually be similar to that discussed for patents.[28] In most cases, the requirements are the same: determination of a future income flow and determination of the present value of that flow. It ordinarily does not make any difference whether the copyright owner receives royalties or profits in a participation agreement.

As with patents, the economic life expectancy must be determined.[29] This means that the actual life expectancy from a valuation standpoint may be significantly less than the legal life of the copyright, e.g., fifty or more years.

Unless the right to make derivative works has economic significance, the actual economic life expectancy of the copyright may be relatively short. For example, technical works may have an economic life expectancy of only one or two years. Novels may last only several years and reference works usually last no more than ten years.

On the other hand some types of copyrights have a continuing economic significance. Musical compositions, for example, may have an economic life equal to the full copyright legal life. It is clear that you must make a careful analysis of the real economics of the life expectancy of a copyright in all cases.

Copyright valuation differs in a few ways from patent valuation. Because the bundle of rights that is part of a copyright may be divided, the right to reproduce, to prepare derivative works, to distribute copies, and to perform or display publicly, separate valuations may have to be made for each of the rights which has economic significance. If the right of termination is considered a valuable asset of its own, it should be valued at the amount that a new grant of the copyright would exceed the value of the original grant of the copyright.[30]

In some situations, copyrights may be marketable. If so, the copyrights may be valued by the market approach, either by comparing the price received for comparable

---

[24] 17 U.S.C. §203(a)(3) (1976).

[25] 17 U.S.C. §203(a)(4) (1976).

[26] *See* Lieb & Schaaf, *Estate Planning for Creators of Intellectual Property,* 1979 Ill. L.F. 378.

[27] *See* Levy, *Estate Planning for Professional Songwriters After the Storm,* 8 Mem. St. U.L. Rev. 757 (1978); Lieb & Schaaf, *Estate Planning for Creators of Intellectual Propenty,* 1979 Ill. L.F. 378-79.

[28] *See* **§9.2** Patent Valuation.

[29] Silverman, *The Valuation of Intellectual Property in Connection with the Estates of Authors and Other Creative Persons,* 11 Miami Inst. Est. Plan ¶1107.3, 11-17 to -18 (1977).

[30] Lieb & Schaaf, *Estate Planning for Creators of Intellectual Property,* 1979 Ill. L.F. 397.

copyrights or by comparing earnings of comparable copyrights that have a known market value.[31]

Because of the technical nature of valuing copyrights, you will most often be wise to obtain the opinions of persons knowledgeable about copyrights and copyright law.[32]

§9.5 Artwork and Antique Valuation

In a general sense, art works and antiques are tangible personal property. Consequently, the valuation technique for these types of assets resembles the technique used for personal effects.[33] Typically, you need to identify a market and to establish a comparable market price for the asset to be valued.[34] This market and market price must be the retail-level equivalent, not the wholesale level.[35] Because of their unique status and significant value in some estate planning situations, however, they require separate consideration.

For our purposes here, artworks include drawings, prints, sculptures and antiques. It does not include literary, dramatic, musical or historical materials.[36]

The process of valuing artworks and antiques primarily involves the task of determining what the object will bring in the market place. Generally, this requires an appraisal by someone who has substantial knowledge of, and experience with, the particular market and the type of asset involved.[37] Although appraisers are recommended for all such assets, they are required for estate tax purposes for any asset valued in excess of $3,000.[38] Such asset valuations should be accompanied in the appropriate return by an appraisal signed under oath by a competent expert or experts.

The most common technique used to value such assets is to value them according to sales of comparable assets in the appropriate market, if there is one. In order to make comparisons, you must characterize works of art and antiques by type, condition, quality, and authenticity. Because almost by definition works of art and antiques are unique, comparability is a relative thing. Consequently, you will almost always have to make adjustments to the comparable sales prices in order to estimate the market value of the subject property.

Another technique that is sometimes useful is to consider the cost of the object to the owner.[39] If the owner has bought or sold the object in an arm's-length transaction

---

[31] For an explanation of the process of making valuation by way of the comparable sales approach see **§5.11** The Market Approach to Real Property Valuation. Contemporaneous, arm's length sales of the subject copyright are very significant too. *See* **§2.11** Sales of the Asset.

[32] *See* **§2.3** Significance of Appraisals and Expert Testimony; **§2.8** Proof of Value.

[33] *See* **Ch. 10** How to Value Personal Effects.

[34] Regs. §§20.2031-6(d), 25.2512-1.

[35] *See* **§2.9** Fair Market Value.

[36] *See* **§9.4** Copyright Valuation.

[37] *See* **§2.3** Significance of Appraisals and Expert Testimony.

[38] Reg. §20.2031-6(b).

[39] I.R.S. App. Off., 3-3.

reasonably close to the valuation date, the price paid may be very relevant to a determination of market value.[40]

From a tax value standpoint, the I.R.S. is often found on both sides of the issue. For gift and estate taxes, it has a desire to increase the value of such objects. For income tax charitable gift deductions, it has the desire to reduce the taxpayer's value.[41] In looking at the cases on this matter, it is very important then, to understand and to identify the I.R.S. position in the case. Consistency has not been the hobgoblin of the I.R.S.

The I.R.S. maintains an Art Advisory Panel of nationally-prominent art museum directors, art professors, and art dealers.[42] This panel is designed to systematically aid the I.R.S. in reviewing selected cases involving the valuation of major art objects.

All single works of art with a claimed value of $20,000 or more must be referred to the panel for review. If more than one such item is involved in a single case, appraisals may be submitted for a selected sample rather than all of the works. Basically, the sample must be representative as to dollar value, type of medium, period, and subject matter, and must contain examples of all appraisers and artists.[43]

The I.R.S. is very specific with regard to what a proper request to the panel must include. First, where applicable, it must include:[44]

1. An 8-inch by 10-inch or larger photograph or print of the art work
2. A complete description of the item indicating size, subject matter, medium, artist, date of creation, identification marks, and symbols or labels on the back or bottom of the work
3. Acquisition data including cost, date and manner
4. Claimed fair market value and a copy of the appraisal materials that were filed with the returns
5. Location of the art work.

In addition, if available, the request should also include the following:[45]

6. History (provenance) of the art work including authenticity
7. Exhibition record and information
8. Sales prices of other comparable works of art sold by the artists
9. Prices quoted in dealers' catalogs for the artist's work.

Ironically, the valuation set by the panel has not always been accepted by the courts. In one case, the court more than doubled the panel's valuations of a charitable gift for income tax deduction purposes.[46]

---

40 *See* **§2.11** Sales of the Asset.
41 *Compare* I.R.C. §§2031 and 2512 with I.R.C. §170.
42 I.R.M. Audit 4200, §42(16)4.1.
43 *Id.* at §42(16)4.2(b)(1)-(5).
44 *Id.* at §42(16)4.3(2)(a)-(e).
45 *Id.* at §42(16)4.3(2)(f)-(i).
46 Crocker Nat'l Bank v. United States, 39 A.F.T.R.2d ¶77-779 (C.D. Cal. 1976).

In an estate tax case dealing with the value of the artist's estate, the tax court recognized a blockage discount from the normal market value of the deceased artist's own art works because all these items were offered for sale at the same time.[47]

---

[47] Estate of D. Smith 57 T.C. 650 (1972), *aff'd on other grounds,* 510 F.2d 479 (2d Cir. 1975), *cert. denied,* 423 U.S. 827 (1975), *acq.* 1974-2 C.B. 4. *See generally* **§3.5** Blockage Discount for Traded Securities.

CHAPTER 10

HOW TO VALUE PERSONAL EFFECTS

§10.1 Introduction to Valuation of Personal Effects

The need to value personal effects usually arises in the context of inventory and appraisal of incompetents' and decedents' estates and (in larger decedents' estates) for completion of the personal effects portion of the estate tax return.[1] These items may also require valuation for gift tax purposes, including gifts to charities such as the Salvation Army and the Goodwill Industries. Some of the more frequently-traded items (such as automobiles, boats, etc.) may also require valuation for credit purposes; again, the basic techniques are the same.

The valuation standard for these assets is the same as it is for other assets.[2] The fair market value of the asset must be determined.[3] Because of the variety of type and diversity of character, it is frequently necessary to employ the services of a competent appraiser to estimate value.[4]

For estate purposes, the relevant regulation requires that, in general, all personal effects be individually itemized.[5] However, items in the same room or facility that have a value of $100 or less may be grouped. Individual items or sets of items having a total value in excess of $3,000 must have a sworn appraisal, by an expert or experts, filed

[1] *See* I.R.S, Form 706, Schedule F.

[2] *See* **§1.2** When and Where Valuation Determinations are Made.

[3] *See* **§2.9** Fair Market Value.

[4] Reg. §20.2031-6(a). *See* **§2.3** Significance of Appraisals and Expert Testimony.

[5] Reg. §20.2031-6(a).

with the return.[6] With the appraisal, the executor must also file a written, sworn statement that the list of itemized property is complete and that the appraisers were disinterested and qualified.

For estate tax purposes, the relevant I.R.S. Regulation requires that the district director must be notified of any distribution or sale of any portion of the decedent's household or personal effects prior to an investigation by an I.R.S. officer.[7] The document filed with the District Director must include both a sworn appraisal of the property and an affidavit by the personal representative that the appraisal is complete and that the appraiser is qualified. The personal representative will be notified whether or not a personal inspection will occur. The Regulation states that this procedure is designed to facilitate disposition of property and to reduce cost and inconvenience if an inspection is necessary.

Several of the valuation terms and concepts that were explained previously should be consulted for this Chapter including:

§2.9 Fair Market Value

§2.10 Market

§2.15 Replacement and Reproduction Costs

§2.11 Sales of the Asset.

§2.3 Significance of Appraisals and Expert Testimony

§10.2 Household Effects Valuation

Generally, personal items such as furniture, clothing, appliances, bedding and linens are used, worn, or obsolete, and do not carry a very substantial value. The principal technique used to value such assets is the market approach.[8] The price for which comparable goods were sold in the market is the primary criterion. Generally, casual appraisals using this technique will be accepted.[9] The price at which these items are sometimes sold reasonably close to the valuation date is also frequently accepted.[10] The valuation of household goods in a homeowner's insurance policy is not adequate documentation of market value, however.[11]

Any personal household effect of significant value must, of course, be valued in a more precise manner, perhaps by an appraisal. Special valuation techniques are required for artwork and antiques.[12] Items such as furs, jewelry and silverware also may require specific appraisals.[13]

---

6 Reg. §20.2031-6(b).

7 Reg. §20.2031-6(c).

8 *See* **§2.10** Market.

9 G. Armour, 38 T.C.M. (P-H) ¶69,245 (1969).

10 *See* **§2.9** Fair Market Value; **§2.11** Sales of the Asset.

11 V. Marlowe, 36 T.C.M. (P-H) ¶67,012 (1967).

12 *See* **§9.5** Artwork and Antique Valuation.

13 *See* **§10.3** Valuation of Precious Furs, Gems and Metals.

§10.3 Valuation of Precious Furs, Gems and Metals

Valuation issues concerning assets such as furs, gems, gold and silver arise most frequently with regard to gift, estate and income taxes. Basically, for tax purposes they must be valued at their fair market value.[14] In addition, because each particular type of asset described here has its own peculiar attributes that must be considered in the valuation, it is generally required that careful appraisals by competent and reputable appraisers be obtained.[15]

Several general characteristics are identifiable for each type of asset.

Furs: The type of animal, condition, quality, color, size of fur piece, marketability, and age are relevant factors.

Gems and Stones: Some of the important criteria include color, brilliance, size, condition, cut or setting, fashionability, and marketability.

Precious Metals: Precious metals usually are in the form of silverware and jewelry. Various factors including degree of purity, weight (usually given in troy ounces),[16] utility, desirability, condition, obsolescence, marketability and even antiquity must be assessed.

Precious Commodities: For many precious commodities, there are two identifiable markets—the investment market and the retail market. The investment market trades in diamonds (and sometimes other gems), gold, and silver bought and sold with a primary investment purpose. The retail market trades in furs, diamonds, all other gems, gold, and silver bought and sold primarily for personal adornment.

Investment gems and metals are of the highest quality and purity. The gems are flawless or near-flawless and the metals are of the highest degree of purity. Assets of this nature are clearly marketable, and a market price is usually obtainable and determinative of market value. Since market price is determined on the basis of weight, you must make or obtain a determination of the asset's weight: Carats for gems, troy ounces for metals. Quality and purity must be determined, also.

Gems and metals that are used in jewelry require a somewhat different analysis. Such assets may or may not be of the same quality or purity of the investment variety. Consequently, their value will be less than a pure weight analysis valuation.

Two distinct types of valuations of furs, gems, and metals are made in estate planning. First, the assets may have to be valued for insurance purposes—usually at replacement cost.[17] Replacement cost requires determination of the price of similar assets in the current retail market. This is clearly the highest price for the asset.

The second purpose is for gift or estate valuation. Unless the assets are new, their value will be significantly less than replacement cost. Market value for this purpose may run from one-half to one-third of replacement cost. Even precious metals, which have a determinable weight and can be reconverted to investment quality, are valued at their scrap value, usually fifty percent or less of the market price.

---

[14] *See* **§2.9** Fair Market Value.

[15] *See* **§2.3** Significance of Appraisals and Expert Testimony.

[16] *See* Reg. §20.2031-6(d).

[17] *See* **§2.15** Replacement and Reproduction Costs.

Of course, sufficiently contemporaneous arm's length sales of the asset to be valued are very significant.[18]

For gift and estate tax valuation, the federal excise tax on jewelry, furs and other similar assets must be added to their market value if the gift or bequest occurs shortly after the purchase of the asset.[19] Except as noted elsewhere, brokers' or sales commissions are not deductible from the fair market value.[20]

§10.4 Special Collections Valuation

Our society could be called collection-crazy. Almost anything can be the subject of a collection: autographs of famous persons, personal articles of clothing of famous rock stars, the more mundane stamp and coin collections. Some of these collections will have significant value; others may cost the owner a trip to the dump. As with most of the other properties discussed in this chapter, collections are usually valued using the market approach.[21] Contemporaneous arm's length sales of the collection being valued also are relevant.[22] Where collections, such as coins and stamps, have face values, the higher market values are determinative for tax purposes.[23]

Generally, all collections of economic significance require competent appraisal because each collection is so peculiar and unique that no general valuation technique can be given.[24] There is a need, however, to be particularly careful when choosing an appraiser. Many collections give rise to specialized subcollections. For example, some dealers specialize in American collections; others deal solely in foreign collections. Thus, you must match appraiser specialties with collection specialties.

For some types of collections, price list publications may give the valuator a general idea of their value. This is particularly true of the typical collections (coins, stamps and guns). However, these reference materials must be used cautiously: they do not always include current market price data. Some merely deal with estimates of market prices for the asset, estimates that often can be characterized as the "highest" price one could receive for the asset. Because the highest prices are not necessarily market prices, downward adjustments should be made to the prices, based on appraisal evidence. Not only is it unlikely that a collector could obtain such prices; even a retail dealer would find it hard to obtain them.

It is preferable that you use only price lists that report current market price information. Market price data from such lists can be extrapolated into estimates of market

---

18 *See* **§2.11** Sales of the Asset.

19 Rev. Rul. 55-71, 1955-1 C.B. 110.

20 *See* **§2.9** Fair Market Value.

21 *See* **§2.10** Market.

22 *See* **§2.11** Sales of the Asset.

23 *See* Joslin v. United States, 666 F.2d 1306 (10th Cir. 1981); Cordner v. United States, 45 A.F.T.R.2d ¶80-1677 (C.D. Cal. 1980).

24 *See* **§2.3** Significance of Appraisals and Expert Testimony.

value.[25] For small collections where valuation disagreements are not likely, the published market price data should be adequate.

The following practical suggestion may be of help:[26]

1. Unless the collection as a whole is valued at a higher value than its separate parts, collections ordinarily should be itemized and individually valued
2. Particular care must be taken to determine that items in the collection are not forgeries or counterfeits, and that they have not been improperly altered
3. The valuation of collectibles is based primarily upon age, condition, rarity and demand
4. Each type of collectible has its own vocabulary and criteria.

Collections are very much subject to market price fluctuations. Because the demand for things is based upon esthetic and emotional factors as well as need and scarcity, market prices may increase and decrease greatly and in a short period of time. These fluctuations make the marketing of collectibles very difficult, frustrating and disappointing. If you are planning to market a collection, several matters should be considered:

1. Anticipate as far in advance as possible the need to sell
2. Exercise as many avenues of sale as possible—for example, use both advertising and consignment sale
3. Be flexible with regard to the individual items to be sold—for example, offer items as a whole and individually
4. Take your time—do not necessarily take the first offer if you feel it is not sufficient.

§10.5 Vehicles Valuation

The determination of value for vehicles and other motorcraft is a very common problem, arising for gift and estate tax, loan security, and sale purposes. This discussion covers automobiles, trucks, recreational vehicles, trailers, motorcycles of all kinds, other land vehicles, boats and other watercraft, and airplanes and other aircraft. Generally, these assets are extremely marketable and have a well-defined marketplace. Consequently, the primary valuation technique is to make use of the market.[27] The market value of such assets is estimated from the market price received for comparable properties, as adjusted.

Comparability depends on such factors as make, year, model, condition, extra equipment, utility, style, mileage or time of use, size, efficiency, repair history, uniqueness, and even location. Depreciability and other issues may also be relevant. Automo-

---

[25] Use the process discussed in **§10.5** Vehicles Valuation.

[26] *See* 12 Am. Jur. Proof of Facts 2d, *Value of Coin Collection* 355 (1977).

[27] *See* **§2.10** Market.

biles, for example, depreciate very rapidly; aircraft may actually increase in market price. Currently, the fuel crisis and higher fuel costs may affect the valuation of these types of assets. Vehicles that are high fuel consumers ("gas guzzlers") tend to decrease in market price, whereas fuel efficient vehicles tend to appreciate. Ordinarily, market data will reveal these factors.

For most types of assets discussed here, publications are available to provide current market price data. These materials are available at all financial institutions and most public libraries. The following is a list of the most common publications of this nature:

Chart X-1

Automobiles	Frequency of Publication:
N.A.D.A. Official Used Car Guide (Domestic cars, imported cars and light trucks) (The Bluebook)	Monthly
CPI Cars of Particular Interest (Selected models of cars that have special marketing appeal)	Quarterly
Motorcycles and Other Two-Wheel Vehicles	
N.A.D.A. Motorcycle/Moped Appraisal Guide	Every four months
Watercraft	
N.A.D.A. Boat Appraisal Guide	Every four months
Recreational Vehicles	
N.A.D.A. Recreational Vehicle Appraisal Guide	Every four months
Aircraft	
Aircraft Price Digest	Quarterly
Special Use Vehicles	
N.A.D.A. Official Older Car, Older R.V. and Older Motorcycle Guide	Every four months

For most purposes, a reasonable extrapolation of a market price from these publications is adequate.[28] When the valuation of unusual or special use vehicles must be determined, however, it is ordinarily necessary to obtain appraisals by qualified appraisers.[29]

With the increasing popularity of mobile homes the need to make valuations of such assets increases in importance. Because mobile homes by definition are transportable, they usually fall within the category of personal effects. It is possible that a mobile home may be so fixed to the land that it would be treated as part of the land, and thus valued as an improvement on the real property. Generally, however, mobile homes are marketable apart from the land.

From a valuation determination standpoint, mobile homes are very similar to vehicles and other motorcraft. They are marketable and have a defined marketplace.

[28] *See* Brooks-Massey Dodge, Inc., 60 T.C. 884 (1973).

[29] *See* **§2.3** Significance of Appraisals and Expert Testimony.

Consequently, the market value of such assets is estimated from the adjusted market price received for comparable properties. Comparability depends on such factors as make, model, year, size, condition and other special features. Depreciability is also relevant to mobile homes as it is to motor vehicles.

For most mobile homes, publications are available to provide current market price data. For example, the N.A.D.A. Mobile Home Appraisal Guide is published every four months.

Reasonable extrapolated estimates from the market price data in such publications should be adequate. Specialized or significantly customized mobile homes ordinarily require appraisals by qualified appraisers.[30]

§10.6 Inventory Valuation

Ordinarily inventory is not valued separately from an operating business, but is merely part of the assets of the business. It happens occasionally, however, that inventory requires specific and separate valuation. The I.R.S. recognizes this in Revenue Procedure 77-12. It points out that a separate valuation for inventory must be made when a corporation purchases for a lump sum, the assets of a business containing inventory items, and when a corporation acquires assets including inventory items by liquidation of a subsidiary under I.R.C. §332 and the basis of the inventory received in liquidation must be determined. There is no reason to doubt that a separate valuation may be necessary for gift and particularly estate tax purposes where partnerships and sole proprietorships are liquidated.

The Ruling provides that the value of the inventory may be made under one or more of three techniques: market, income and cost methods. Two situations are distinguished: the inventory of a merchandising business versus of a manufacturing business.

The Ruling discusses the following three techniques and their relevant applications:[31]

1. Reproduction costs are relevant to the readily replaceable inventory of retail and wholesale merchandisers: a continuity of business premium or an obsolescence discount may require an adjustment
2. Comparable market prices are relevant to manufacturer's finished inventory: all selling costs, volume or bulk discounts, transportation charges and reasonable profits must be deducted
3. Future income flow analyses are relevant to manufacturer's finished inventory, because it best duplicates the marketing operation of a going business.

Unfinished inventory is valued the same way, but a discount for cost of completion must be deducted. The value of raw materials, however, is most reliably computed by determining replacement costs for similar quantities.

---

30 *Id.*

31 Rev. Proc. 77-12, 1977-1 C.B. 569.

CHAPTER 11

HOW TO VALUE MISCELLANEOUS PROPERTIES

§11.1 Introduction to Valuation of Miscellaneous Properties

There are a few assets that do not fit into the categories previously discussed because of their special or unusual characteristics. The assets discussed in this chapter are cash and currency, licenses and privileges, foreign assets, and future interests.[1]

Several of the valuation terms and concepts that were explained previously should be consulted for this chapter, including:

§2.23 Actuarial Calculations
§2.19 Capitalization of Income
§2.9 Fair Market Value
§2.10 Market
§2.11 Sales of the Asset
§2.3 Significance of Appraisals and Expert Testimony
§2.17 Valuation Mathematics.

[1] *See* **§1.2** When and Where Valuation Determinations are Made.

§11.2 Cash and Currency Valuation

Obviously, domestic currency is valued at its face value, whether it is in the possession of the owner, of another, or is in a bank account or other secure location.[2]

Foreign currencies are ordinarily valued at their foreign exchange rate. Closing exchange rates are usually available in the financial newspapers for each trading day. Presumably the valuation technique for foreign currencies would be that used for other securities that have their market prices listed only with closing prices.[3]

Some foreign currencies may be "blocked" by the country of origin. This means that their convertibility to U. S. dollars is restricted. For such currencies, you must identify a market in the United States and determine the exchange rates established by that market.[4] The assistance of persons who are knowledgeable and experienced in these matters is essential for these purposes.[5]

§11.3 Licenses and Privileges Valuation

Basically, a license gives its holder permission to perform certain tasks. It may or may not have economic significance, and consequently may or may not be subject to valuation. Licenses that have significant value are those that yield income and that are transferable or descendable. Whether licenses are automatically renewable, renewed in the normal order of things, or not renewable is also significant to their valuation.

There are many licenses that have significant value. In some jurisdictions, for example, liquor licenses are very valuable because they are limited in number and are transferable. The license for a radio or television broadcasting station is another high-value license.[6]

Licenses that are economically significant are valued in much the same way as other income-producing assets.[7] The primary technique is to determine the amount and duration of the future income flow, and to discount this future flow to present value.[8] If the license is considered to have a limited life, then valuation techniques used for mineral interests would be applicable.[9] The risk of nonrenewal may justify an adjustment to ordinary market value. This adjustment can be made either by reducing (discounting) the estimated future flow of income, or by increasing the rate of capitalization.

Another common method for valuing licenses is to use the market approach.[10] This approach seeks to identify sales prices for comparable properties, and adjust this price

---

2 Reg. §20.2031-5.

3 *See* **§3.11** Valuation of Bonds.

4 *See* Estate of A. Fry, 9 T.C. 503 (1947), *acq.* 1948-2 C.B. 2.

5 *See* **§2.3** Significance of Appraisals and Expert Testimony.

6 *See* Rev. Proc. 75-39, 1975-2 C.B. 569.

7 *See* **§2.19** Capitalization of Income.

8 *See* **§4.5** Capitalization of Business Interest's Earnings.

9 *See* **§7.4** The Income Method of Mineral Interest Valuation.

10 *See* **§5.11** The Market Approach to Real Property Valuation.

to set the estimated market value of the subject property. The most difficult task is to identify sufficiently comparable properties.

If the license is not transferable (e.g., a license to practice law or medicine), the license itself has no value. The underlying assets of the license, however, may have a value and require valuation. Such valuations are made according to the type of underlying assets involved: real estate, furnishings or accounts receivable, for example.

§11.4 Foreign Assets Valuation

Because the federal estate tax definition of the gross estate includes the value of the total estate of any decedent who was a citizen or resident of the United States at the time of his death no matter where such property is located, it becomes necessary to value foreign assets for estate tax purposes.[11] The valuation techniques that are used for domestic assets would also be applicable to foreign assets. Necessary proof of valuation would be similar as well. Valuations made in the foreign currency must be converted to dollars.[12] The scope of the gift tax is the same, except that the gift tax is not applicable to a nonresident noncitizen unless the property is situated within the United States.[13]

§11.5 Future Interests Valuation

Modern estate planning techniques make use of a significant number of future interests including life estates, remainders, and reversions. Although a few future legal interests are found, most of them are equitable interests that have been created in trusts.

For valuation purposes, a future interest is a present interest that is either a current possessory interest equal to less than full ownership (e.g., a life estate) or a nonpossessory interest subject to future enjoyment (e.g., a remainder). Valuation of these assets is speculative, because the actual physical possession and/or enjoyment of the asset depends upon indeterminable matters such as life expectancy and other types of volitional conduct on the part of individuals. Without the use of shortcut techniques, valuation of these assets as of a particular date would be almost impossible.

In order to systemize valuation determinations for these types of interests, it has become common usage to employ certain predetermined calculations. These calculations are commonly referred to as actuarial tables, and the I.R.S. has a full set of them for future interests.[14] Although both taxpayers and the I.R.S. have successfully argued for nonapplicability of these tables, the presumption is that they are applicable when relevant to the situation at hand.

---

[11] Reg. §20.2031-1(a).

[12] *See* **§11.2** Cash and Currency Valuation.

[13] I.R.C. §2511(a).

[14] *See* **§2.23** Actuarial Calculations.

Some of the tables set out by the I.R.S. are found in the income tax Regulations; others are found in the gift and estate tax Regulations. Where situations are interrelated, these tables are applicable interchangeably between the taxes.

The I.R.S. issues tables dealing with the following matters:

Table XI-1

Description of Table	Location
1. Term of years (income and remainder) (Table B)	
(a) Transfer before 12-31-70 (3½% interest rate)	Reg. § 20.2031-10(f)
i. Estate Tax ii. Gift Tax	Reg. §§ 20.2031-7(f), 25.2512-5(f)
(b) Transfer after 1-1-71 (6% interest rate)[15]	
i. Estate Tax ii. Gift Tax	Reg. §§ 20.2031-10(f), 25.2512-9(f)
2. Single life estates, male [Table A(1)] or female [Table A(2)][16]	(Same as above)
3. Remainder or reversion subject to single life estate, male [Table A(1)] or female [Table A(2)][17]	(Same as above)
4. Remainder interests in charitable remainder annuity trusts subject to single life estate, male [Table A(1)] or female [Table A(2)]	Reg. §§ 20.2031-10(a), (f)
5. Life interests, term of years and remainder interest in charitable unitrusts	Reg. § 1.664-4
6. Pooled Income Fund interests	Reg. § 1.642(c)-6

The I.R.S. has also published several separate pamphlets that deal with the valuation of particular future interests. Publication 723: Valuation of Last Survivor Charitable Remainders discusses:

1. Pooled income fund—valuation of a remainder interest dependent on two lives
2. Charitable remainder unitrust—valuation of a remainder interest dependent on two lives
3. Remainder interest dependent on more than two lives
4. Joint and survivor annuity values.

[15] *See* Appendix B.

[16] *Id.*

[17] *Id.*

Publication 723A: Factors at Six Percent Involving One and Two Lives is concerned with:

1. Present worth of an amount due at the death of the survivor of two persons
2. Income or annuity payable for such time as one person survives another
3. Present worth of an amount at the death of the first to die
4. Present value of income or annuity involving one life and a term of years.

Publication 723B: Valuation of Last Survivor Charitable Remainders includes two life tables for unitrust and pooled income funds.

The example portions of the above I.R.S. publications have been reproduced in Appendix E.

§11.6 —Calculations Involving Future Interests

The following will illustrate the valuation for a single life estate, a remainder interest, and a term of years using the estate tax tables assuming a six percent interest rate.[18]

Illustration XI-1

CALCULATION OF THE VALUE OF A LIFE ESTATE

Assumptions

Market value of an asset: $10,000
Life tenant's sex: Male
Life tenant's age: 65

Calculation

Using Table A(1), multiply the life estate factor (under column 3, which is to the right of the age 65 in column 1) by the market value of the asset.
.48212 × $10,000 = $4,821.20.
The life interest is worth $4,821.20.

Illustration XI-2

CALCULATION OF THE VALUE OF A REMAINDER INTEREST

Assumptions

(Same as Illustration XI-1)

[18] Reg. §20.2031-10(f).

Illustration XI-2 *(Continued)*

Calculation

Using Table A(1), multiply the remainder factor (under column 4, which is to the right of the age 65 column 1) by the market value of the asset.
.51788 × $10,000 = $5,178.80
The remainder interest is worth $5,178.80[19]

Illustration XI-3

CALCULATION OF THE VALUE OF THE INCOME INTEREST IN A TERM CERTAIN

Assumptions

Market value of asset: $10,000
Term certain: ten years

Calculation of Income Interest in Term Certain

Using Table B, multiply the term-certain factor (under column 3, which is to the right of the year 10 in column 1) by the market value of the asset.
.441605 × $10,000 = $4,416.05
The term certain income interest equals $4,416.05.

Illustration XI-4

CALCULATION OF THE VALUE OF THE REMAINDER IN A TERM CERTAIN

Assumptions

(Same as Illustration XI-3)

Calculation of the Value of the Remainder in a Term Certain

Using Table B, multiply the remainder factor (under column 4, which is to the right of the year 10 in column 1) by the market value of the asset.
.558395 × $10,000 = $5,583.95
The remainder of the term certain is worth $5,583.95.[20]

If the tables provided by the I.R.S. do not solve the problem, special factors may be requested directly from the I.R.S.[21] In addition, most I.R.S. offices will provide assistance in making calculations.

Other future interests need valuation, too. For example, defeasible remainder inter-

19 The sum of the income interest and the remainder interest equals the full market value of the asset.
20 The sum of the income interest and the remainder interest equals the full market value of the asset.
21 Reg. §20.2031-10(e); *see also* Rev. Rul. 61-88, 1961-1 C.B. 417.

ests subject to termination at the will of another are considered to be an interest in property, and must be included as part of the gross estate for estate tax purposes.[22] Consequently, the value of such an interest must be determined. No guidelines are given by the I.R.S. to make the valuation, however.

One approach to valuing interest subject to destruction is as follows: characterize the interest as an ordinary life or remainder interest and use the appropriate Tables to determine its value, and then determine a proper discount to be deducted from ordinary value because of the potential destructibility of the interest.[23] Setting the discount is, of course, the difficult task. For many situations, including the presence of a revocation power in another person, the determination may be pure speculation. The I.R.S. has stated that the mere presence of a possibility of destruction of the interest does not warrant a valuation of nominal value when there is a reasonable probability that the decedent's estate may actually obtain possession of at least some of the interest in question.[24]

If an interest's value may be determined by actuarial principles, then those principles must, of course, be used.[25]

There are other interests in the nature of future interests that may require valuation. For example, a spouse's forced share or dower right may require valuation.[26] Normally, such interests are expressed as a fraction of the estate and either as a fee or life interest. If it is a fee interest, (as a forced share usually is), then the value of the share is merely the value of the fraction of the entire estate. If it is a life interest, (as dower usually is), then the value of the right must be calculated in a manner similar to any life interest, subject to reduction due to the fraction limitation.

Similar techniques have been used to value other types of interests. For example, actuarial principles and tables have been used to determine the commuted value of support payments.[27] Any interest that either expressly or impliedly relies on lives of persons or terms of years may require the use of these principles and tables.

---

[22] Rev. Rul. 67-370, 1967-2 C.B. 324.
[23] *See* Rev. Rul. 76-472, 1976-2 C.B. 264.
[24] Rev. Rul. 67-370, 1967-2 C.B. 324.
[25] *See* Rev. Rul. 69-347, 1969-1 C.B. 227.
[26] *See* Rev. Rul. 58-13, 1958-1 C.B. 342.
[27] Rev. Rul. 71-67, 1971-1 C.B. 271.

PART III

EPILOGUE

CHAPTER 12

OVERVIEW OF ESTATE PLANNING VALUATION DECISIONS

§12.1 Generally

The previous eleven chapters may leave the reader somewhat unsatisfied. Now that you know "how" to value various assets, you may still wish to know what this means from an estate planning standpoint. Chapter 1, which dealt with the explanation of why valuations are necessary, gives a partial answer to this question. An appropriate question remains: "What control do I have over valuation?" Can the estate planner manipulate the determination? Clearly, this is not what is meant by the concept of control. Control merely refers to the exercise of legitimate action, judgment, or both, under appropriate circumstances. In this light, certainly the estate planner has control over valuation in many situations.

A basic issue that often arises is whether it is desirable to have a high or a low valuation for an asset for estate planning purposes. To solve this problem, you must identify the particular consequence of the valuation decision.

If the issue concerns the payment of gift or estate taxes, clearly, the taxpayer prefers a low valuation. These taxes are progressive: the higher the value of the assets, the higher the marginal rate of tax. But this is not the only consideration. As the estate and gift taxes apply to fewer clients (that is if inflation does not consume the new unified credits faster than they increase), estate planning valuation determinations will be directed primarily toward the issue of the asset's basis for capital gain and loss purposes. Because assets that pass as part of a person's gross estate receive a new basis, you will generally want to establish high values in order to minimize gain or maximize capital loss upon sale of the assets. Because estate tax returns are not necessary for estates below the threshold amounts,[1] you may wish to increase the value of an estate above the threshold so that the filed return serves as an indication of the stepped-up basis values for the estate's assets. This high-value philosophy is not new, but may become more prevalent because of the increased number of persons who should take advantage of it.

[1] *See* **§1.8** Estate Tax Considerations.

When you are weighing the effect of capital gains taxes versus estate taxes, it is important to compare the marginal tax rates. Whereas the effective maximum marginal rate of tax on capital gains (after the 60% deduction) is only 20 percent, the minimum marginal rate of tax, after the unified credit is deducted, is not less than 32 percent. Consequently, increasing the value of the estate will only save total taxes in estates where the estate tax does not exceed the unified credit.

There are other occasions where the taxpayer will also prefer a high valuation for assets in estate planning situations. This is very apparent when a taxpayer is making charitable contributions. In this situation, it is to the donor's advantage to substantiate high valuations for the assets because it increases the income tax deduction. In addition, if the property tax is being used as collateral for a loan, a high valuation increases the potential maximum loan amount.

It is clear, now, that an estate planner may set different values for an asset at different times. In one case, you will argue for a high value for the taxpayer; in others, a low value. The same considerations are relevant, and the same valuation techniques and procedures are used. You may, for example, want to employ an expert appraiser in either case.

Implied in the above discussion is the valuator's control over the valuation of the assets. This is more or less true. Control is not present over value if the asset's value is determined by prices set by an independent market. Without control of the market, the value of the asset is determined by outside forces that set the price for the asset in the market. Control of valuation over such assets depends upon what assets are owned by the taxpayer (e.g., shares of I.B.M. or G.M.).

For assets where market prices do not control market value, the valuator may have some leeway with regard to the valuation of the asset. This control must be carefully exercised. Proper control is either the use of specific planning techniques or the exercise of discretionary judgment over legitimately adjustable factors.

In a premortem situation, the estate planner possesses a significant degree of control over the value of a client's estate. The following is a list of the most prevalent techniques for controlling value:

1. Selecting among assets for the purpose of making *inter vivos* gifts, charitable or otherwise
2. Asset value freezing techniques with corporations and partnerships[2]
3. Buy-sell and other contractual arrangements establishing a set value.[3]

These techniques for setting or controlling the value of an estate are not available or desirable in all situations. They must be used with extreme care and consideration.

Valuation techniques inherently possess many discretionary judgment factors that can alter or affect valuations. Where market price is not determinative, a great deal of

---

2 *See* §**4.19** Weighting of Valuation Factors.

3 *See* §**4.30**—Restrictions Where Price of Resale is Set.

discretion is left to the valuator. The following are some of the most prevalent and obvious factors:

1. The capitalization rate factor for valuing income-producing assets
2. Accounting techniques for determining earnings and dividends for income-producing assets
3. The selection of, and adjustment calculations to, comparables (when using the market approach)
4. Cost data analysis under the cost approach
5. Estimation of future income flows under the income approach to valuation of assets
6. Determination of discounts and premiums for valuation of various percentages of ownership
7. The grading of quality for certain assets (under the market approach to valuation).

Despite a valuator's control either by technique or discretion, there is a practical side to the determination. The more you move away from normal techniques, factors, or adjustments, the more likely litigation may arise over the valuation issue.[4] Consequently, the cost of litigation must be considered in any valuation decision.

The Four Principles of Valuation Determinations are:

1. Be timely in making the valuation
2. Be thorough in preparation and presentation
3. Be reasonable in result
4. Be flexible.

Obedience to these four principles will, in the long run, best serve your clients and yourself.

---

[4] *See* Zorbel & Shore, *The IRS Crackdown on Valuation Abuses: How Far Does It Go: What Does It Portend,* 52 J. Tax'n 276 (1980).

APPENDIXES

A. Revenue Ruling 59–60

B. I.R.S. Actuarial Factors for Particular Annuities, Terms Certain, Income Interests and Remainder Interests

C. P.S. 58 Rates

D. Institutional Investor Study Report of the Securities and Exchange Commission, Vol. 5.

E. Actuarial Values—I.R.S. Publications 723, 723A and 723B

APPENDIX A

Rev. Rul. 59–60, as modified by Rev. Rul. 65–193.

SECTION 1. Purpose.

The purpose of this Revenue Ruling is to outline and review in general the approach, methods and factors to be considered in valuing shares of the capital stock of closely held corporations for estate tax and gift tax purposes. The methods discussed herein will apply likewise to the valuation of corporate stocks on which market quotations are either unavailable or are of such scarcity that they do not reflect the fair market value.

SEC. 2. Background and Definitions.

.01 All valuations must be made in accordance with the applicable provisions of the Internal Revenue Code of 1954 and the Federal Estate Tax and Gift Tax Regulations. Sections 2031(a), 2032 and 2512(a) of the 1954 Code (sections 811 and 1005 of the 1939 Code) require that that property to be included in the gross estate, or made the subject of a gift, shall be taxed on the basis of the value of the property at the time of death of the decedent, the alternate date if so elected, or the date of gift.

.02 Section 20.2031–1(b) of the Estate Tax Regulations (section 81.10 of the Estate Tax Regulations 105) and section 25.2512–1 of the Gift Tax Regulations (section 86.19 of Gift Tax Regulations 108) define fair market value, in effect, as the price at which the property would change hands between a willing buyer and a willing seller when the former is not under any compulsion to buy and the latter is not under any compulsion to sell, both parties having reasonable knowledge of relevant facts. Court decisions frequently state in addition that the hypothetical buyer and seller are assumed to be able, as well as willing, to trade and to be well informed about the property and concerning the market for such property.

.03 Closely held corporations are those corporations the shares of which are owned by a relatively limited number of stockholders. Often the entire stock issue is held by one family. The result of this situation is that little, if any, trading in the shares takes place. There is, therefore, no established market for the stock and such sales as occur at irregular intervals seldom reflect all of the elements of a representative transaction as defined by the term "fair market value."

SEC. 3. Approach to Valuation

.01 A determination of fair market value, being a question of fact, will depend upon the circumstances in each case. No formula can be devised that will be generally applicable to the multitude of different valuation issues arising in estate and gift tax cases. Often, an appraiser will find wide differences of opinion as to the fair market value of a particular stock. In resolving such differences, he should maintain a reasonable attitude in recognition of the fact that valuation is not an exact science. A sound valuation will be based upon all the rele vant facts, but the elements of common sense, informed judgment and reasonableness must enter into the process of weighing those facts and determining their aggregate significance.

.02 The fair market value of specific shares of stock will vary as general economic conditions change from "normal" to "boom" or "depression," that is, according to the degree of optimism or pessimism with which the investing public regards the future at the required date of appraisal. Uncertainty as to stability or continuity of the future income from a property decreases its value by increasing the risk of loss of earnings and value in the future. The value of shares of stock of a company with very uncertain future prospects is highly speculative. The appraiser must exercise his judgment as to the degree of risk attaching to the business of the corporation which issued the stock, but that judgment must be related to all of the other factors affecting value.

.03 Valuation of securities is, in essence, a prophesy as to the future and must be based on facts available at the required date of appraisal. As a generalization, the prices of stocks which are traded in volume in a free and active market by informed persons best reflect the consensus of the investing public as to what the future holds for the corporations and industries represented. When a stock is closely held, is traded infrequently, or is traded in an erratic market, some other measure of value must be used. In many instances, the next best measure may be found in the prices at which the stocks of companies engaged in the same or a similar line of business are selling in a free and open market.

SEC. 4. Factors to Consider.

.01 It is advisable to emphasize that in the valuation of the stock of closely held corporations or the stock of corporations where market quotations are either lacking or too scarce to be recognized, all available financial data, as well as all relevant factors affecting the fair market value, should be considered. The following factors, although not all-inclusive are fundamental and require careful analysis in each case:

(a) The nature of the business and the history of the enterprise from its inception.

(b) The economic outlook in general and the condition and outlook of the specific industry in particular.

(c) The book value of the stock and the financial condition of the business.

(d) The earning capacity of the company.

(e) The dividend-paying capacity.

(f) Whether or not the enterprise has goodwill or other intangible value.

(g) Sales of the stock and the size of the block of stock to be valued.

(h) The market price of stocks of corporations engaged in the same or a similar line of business having their stocks actively traded in a free and open market, either on an exchange or over-the-counter.

.02 The following is a brief discussion of each of the foregoing factors:

(a) The history of a corporate enterprise will show its past stability or instability, its growth or lack of growth, the diversity or lack of diversity of its operations, and other facts needed to form an opinion of the degree of risk involved in the business. For an enterprise which changed its form of organization but carried on the same or closely similar operations of its predecessor, the history of the former enterprise should be considered. The detail to be considered should increase with approach to the required date of appraisal, since recent events are of greatest help in predicting the future; but a study of gross and net income, and of dividends covering a long prior period, is highly desirable. The history to be studied should include, but need not be limited to, the nature of the business, its products or services, its operating and investment assets, capital structure, plant facilities, sales records and management, all of which should be considered as of the date of appraisal, with due regard for recent significant changes. Events of the past that are unlikely to recur in the future should be discounted, since value has a close relation to future expectancy.

(b) A sound appraisal of a closely held stock must consider current and prospective economic conditions as of the date of appraisal, both in the national economy and in the industry or industries with which the corporation is allied. It is important to know that the company is more or less successful than its competitors in the same industry, or that it is maintaining a stable position with respect to competitors. Equal or even greater significance may attach to the ability of the industry with which the company is allied to compete with other industries. Prospective competition which has not been a factor in prior years should be given careful attention. For example, high profits due to the novelty of its product and the lack of competition often lead to increasing competition. The public's appraisal of the future prospects of competitive industries or of competitors within an industry may be indicated by price trends in the markets for commodities and for securities. The loss of the manager of a so-called "one-man" business may have a depressing effect upon the value of the stock of such business, particularly if there is a lack of trained personnel capable of succeeding to the management of the enterprise. In valuing the stock of this type of business, therefore, the effect of the loss of the manager on the future expectancy of the business, and the absence of management-succession potentialities are pertinent factors to be taken into consideration. On the other hand, there may be factors which offset, in whole or in part, the loss of the manager's services. For instance, the nature of the business and of its assets may be such that they will not be impaired by the loss of the manager. Furthermore, the loss may be adequately covered by life insurance, or competent management might be employed on the basis of the consideration paid for the former manager's services. These, or other offsetting factors, if found to exist, should be carefully weighed against the loss of the manager's services in valuing the stock of the enterprise.

(c) Balance sheets should be obtained, preferably in the form of comparative annual statements for two or more years immediately preceding the date of appraisal, together with a balance sheet at the end of the month preceding that date, if corporate accounting will permit. Any balance sheet descriptions that are not self-explanatory, and balance sheet items comprehending diverse assets or liabilities, should be clarifed in essential detail by supporting supplemental schedules. These statements usually will disclose to the appraiser (1) liquid position (ratio of current assets to current liabilities); (2) gross and net book value of principal classes of fixed assets; (3) working capital; (4) long-term indebtedness; (5) capital structure; and (6) net worth. Consideration also should be given to any assets not essential to the operation of the business, such as investments in securities, real estate, etc. In general, such nonoperating assets will command a lower rate of return than do the operating assets, although in exceptional cases the reverse may be true. In computing the book value per share of stock, assets of the investment type should be revalued on the basis of their market price and the book value adjusted accordingly. Comparison of the company's balance sheets over several years may reveal, among other facts, such developments as the acquisition of additional production facilities or subsidiary companies, improvement in financial position, and details as to recapitalizations and other changes in the capital structure of the corporation. If the corporation has more than one class of stock outstanding, the charter or certificate of incorporation should be examined to ascertain the explicit rights and privileges of the various stock issues including: (1) voting powers, (2) preference as to dividends, and (3) preference as to assets in the event of liquidation.

(d) Detailed profit-and-loss statements should be obtained and considered for a representative period immediately prior to the required date of appraisal, preferably five or more years. Such statements should show (1) gross income by principal items; (2) principal deductions from gross income including major prior items of operating expenses, interest and other expense on each item of long-term debt, depreciation and depletion if such deductions are made, officers' salaries, in total if they appear to be reasonable or in detail if they seem to be excessive, contributions (whether or not deductible for tax purposes) that the nature of its business and its community position require the corporation to make, and taxes by principal items, including income and excess profits taxes; (3) net income available for dividends; (4) rates and amounts of dividends paid on each class of stock; (5) remaining amount carried to surplus; and (6) adjustments to, and reconciliation with, surplus as stated on the balance sheet. With profit and loss statements of this character available, the appraiser should be able to separate recurrent from nonrecurrent items of income and expense, to distinguish between operating income and investment income, and to ascertain whether or not any line of business in which the company is engaged is operated consistently at a loss and might be abandoned with benefit to the company. The percentage of earnings retained for business expansion should be noted when dividend-paying capacity is considered. Potential future income is a major factor in many valuations of closely-held stocks, and all information concerning past income which will be helpful in predicting the future should be secured. Prior earnings records usually are the most reliable guide as to the future expectancy, but resort to arbitrary five-or-ten-year averages without regard to current trends or future prospects will not produce a realistic valuation. If, for instance, a record of progressively increasing or decreasing net income is found, then greater weight may be accorded the most recent years' profits in estimating earning power. It will be helpful, in judging risk and the extent to which a business is a marginal operator, to consider deductions from income and net income in terms of percentage of sales. Major categories of cost and expense to be so analyzed include the consumption of raw materials and supplies in the case of manufacturers, processors and fabricators; the cost of purchased merchandise in the case of merchants; utility services; insurance; taxes; depletion or depreciation; and interest.

(e) Primary consideration should be given to the dividend-paying capacity of the company rather than to dividends actually paid in the past. Recognition must be given to the necessity of retaining a reasonable portion of profits in a company to meet competition. Dividend-paying capacity is a factor that must be considered in an appraisal, but dividends actually paid in the past may not have any relation to dividend-paying capacity. Specifically, the dividends paid by a closely held family company may be measured by the income needs of the stockholders or by their desire to avoid taxes on dividend receipts, instead of by the ability of the company to pay dividends. Where an actual or effective controlling interest in a corporation is to be valued, the dividend factor is not a material element, since the payment of such dividends is discretionary with the controlling stockholders. The individual or group in control can substitute salaries and bonuses for dividends, thus reducing net income and understating the dividend-paying capacity of the company. It follows, therefore, that dividends are less reliable criteria of fair market value than other applicable factors.

(f) In the final analysis, goodwill is based upon earning capacity. The presence of goodwill and its value, therefore, rests upon the excess of net earnings over and above a fair return on the net tangible assets. While the element of goodwill may be based primarily on earnings, such factors as the prestige and renown of the business, the ownership of a trade or brand name, and a record of successful operation over a prolonged period in a particular locality, also may furnish support for the inclusion of intangible value.

* * *

(g) Sales of stock of a closely held corporation should be carefully investigated to determine whether they represent transactions at arm's length. Forced or distress sales do not ordinarily reflect fair market value nor do isolated sales in small amounts necessarily control as the measure of value. This is especially true in the valuation of a controlling interest in a corporation. Since, in the case of closely held stocks, no prevailing market prices are available, there is no basis for making an adjustment for blockage. It follows, therefore, that such stocks should be valued upon a consideration of all the evidence affecting the fair market value. The size of the block of stock itself is a relevant factor to be considered. Although it is true that a minority interest in an unlisted corporation's stock is more difficult to sell than a similar block of listed stock, it is equally true that control of a corporation, either actual or in effect, representing as it does an added element of value, may justify a higher value for a specific block of stock.

(h) Section 2031(b) of the Code states, in effect, that in valuing unlisted securities the value of stock or securities of corporations engaged in the same or a similar line of business which are listed on an exchange should be taken into consideration along with all other factors. An important consideration is that the corporations to be used for comparisons have capital stocks which are actively traded by the public. In accordance with section 2031(b) of the Code, stocks listed on an exchange are to be considered first. However, if sufficient comparable companies whose stocks are listed on an exchange cannot be found, other comparable companies which have stocks actively traded in on the over-the-counter market also may be used. The essential factor is that whether the stocks are sold on an exchange or over-the-counter there is evidence of an active, free public market for the stock as of the valuation date. In selecting corporations for comparative purposes, care should be taken to use only comparable companies. Although the only restrictive requirement as to comparable corporations specified in the statute is that their lines of business be the same or similar, yet it is obvious that consideration must be given to other relevant factors in order that the most valid comparison possible will be obtained. For illustration, a corporation having one or more issues of preferred stock, bonds or debentures in addition to its common stock should not be considered to be directly comparable to one having only common stock outstanding. In like manner, a company with a declining business and decreasing markets is not comparable to one with a record of current progress and market expansion.

SEC. 5. Weight to be Accorded Various Factors.

The valuation of closely held corporate stock entails the consideration of all relevant factors as stated in section 4. Depending upon the circumstances in each case, certain factors may carry more weight than others because of the nature of the company's business. To illustrate:

(a) Earnings may be the most important criterion of value in some cases whereas asset value will receive primary consideration in others. In general, the appraiser will accord primary consideration to earnings when valuing stocks of companies which sell products or services to the public; conversely, in the investment or holding type of company, the appraiser may accord the greatest weight to the assets underlying the security to be valued.

(b) The value of the stock of a closely held investment or real estate holding company, whether or not family owned, is closely related to the value of the assets underlying the stock. For companies of this type the appraiser should determine the fair market values of the assets of the company. Operating expenses of such a company and the cost of liquidating it, if any, merit consideration when appraising the relative values of the stock and the underlying assets. The market values of the underlying assets give due weight to potential earnings and dividends of the particular items of property underlying the stock, capitalized at rates deemed proper by the investing public at the date of appraisal. A current appraisal by the investing public should be superior to the retrospective opinion of an individual. For these reasons, adjusted net worth should be accorded greater weight in valuing the stock of a closely held investment or real estate holding company, whether or not family owned, than any of the other customary yardsticks of appraisal, such as earnings and dividend paying capacity.

SEC. 6. Capitalization Rates.

In the application of certain fundamental valuation factors, such as earnings and dividends, it is necessary to capitalize the average or current results at some appropriate rate. A determination of the proper capitalization rate presents one of the most difficult problems in valuation. That there is no ready or simple solution will become apparent by a cursory check of the rates of return and dividend yields in terms of the selling prices of corporate shares listed on the major exchanges of the country. Wide variations will be found even for companies in the same industry. Moreover, the ratio will fluctuate from year to year depending upon economic conditions. Thus, no standard tables of capitalization rates applicable to closely held corporations can be formulated. Among the more important factors to be taken into consideration in deciding upon a capitalization rate in a particular case are: (1) the nature of the business; (2) the risk involved; and (3) the stability or irregularity of earnings.

SEC. 7. Average of Factors.

Because valuations cannot be made on the basis of a prescribed formula, there is no means whereby the various applicable factors in a particular case can be assigned mathematical weights in deriving the fair market value. For this reason, no useful purpose is served by taking an average of several factors (for example, book value, capitalized earnings and capitalized dividends) and basing the valuation on the result. Such a process excludes active consideration of other pertinent factors, and the end result cannot be supported by a realistic application of the significant facts in the case except by mere chance.

SEC. 8. Restrictive Agreements.

Frequently, in the valuation of closely held stock for estate and gift tax purposes, it will be found that the stock is subject to an agreement restricting its sale or transfer. Where shares of stock were acquired by a decedent subject to an option reserved by the issuing corporation to repurchase at a certain price, the option price is usually accepted as the fair market value for estate tax purposes. See Rev. Rul. 54–76, C.B. 1954–1, 194. However, in such case the option price is not determinative of fair market value for gift tax purposes. Where the option, or buy and sell agreement, is the result of voluntary action by the stockholders and is binding during the life as well as at the death of the stockholders, such agreement may or may not, depending upon the circumstances of each case, fix the value for estate tax purposes. However, such agreement is a factor to be considered, with other relevant factors, in determining fair market value. Where the stockholder is free to dispose of his shares during life and the option is to become effective only upon his death, the fair market value is not limited to the option price. It is always necessary to consider the relationship of the parties, the relative number of shares held by the decedent, and other material facts, to determine whether the agreement represents a bonafide business arrangement or is a device to pass the decedent's shares to the natural objects of his bounty for less than an adequate and full consideration in money or money's worth. In this connection see Rev. Rul. 157 C.B. 1953–2, 255, and Rev. Rul. 189, C.B. 1953–2, 294.

SEC. 9. Effect on Other Documents.

Revenue Ruling 54–77, C.B. 1954–1, 187, is hereby superseded.

APPENDIX B

I.R.S. Actuarial Factors for Particular Annuities, Terms Certain, Income Interests and Remainder Interests [Regs. 20.2031–10(f); 25.2512–9(f)]

TABLE A(1)
TABLE, SINGLE LIFE MALE, 6 PERCENT, SHOWING THE PRESENT WORTH OF AN ANNUITY, OF A LIFE INTEREST AND OF A REMAINDER INTEREST

(1) Age	(2) Annuity	(3) Life estate	(4) Remainder
0	15.6175	0.93705	0.06295
1	16.0362	.96217	.03783
2	16.0283	.96170	.03830
3	16.0089	.96053	.03947
4	15.9841	.95905	.04095
5	15.9553	.95732	.04268
6	15.9233	.95540	.04460
7	15.8885	.95331	.04669
8	15.8508	.95105	.04895
9	15.8101	.94861	.05139
10	15.7663	.94598	.05402
11	15.7194	.94316	.05684
12	15.6698	.94019	.05981
13	15.6180	.93708	.06292
14	15.5651	.93391	.06609
15	15.5115	.93069	.06931
16	15.4576	.92746	.07254
17	15.4031	.92419	.07581
18	15.3481	.92089	.07911
19	15.2918	.91751	.08249
20	15.2339	.91403	.08597
21	15.1744	.91046	.08954
22	15.1130	.90678	.09322
23	15.0487	.90292	.09708
24	14.9807	.89884	.10116
25	14.9075	.89445	.10555
26	14.8287	.88972	.11028
27	14.7442	.88465	.11535
28	14.6542	.87925	.12075
29	14.5588	.87353	.12647
30	14.4584	.86750	.13250
31	14.3528	.86117	.13883
32	14.2418	.85451	.14549
33	14.1254	.84752	.15248

TABLE A(1)—Continued

(1) Age	(2) Annuity	(3) Life estate	(4) Remainder
34	14.0034	.84020	.15980
35	13.8758	.83255	.16745
36	13.7425	.82455	.17545
37	13.6036	.81622	.18378
38	13.4591	.80755	.19245
39	13.3090	.78954	.20146
40	13.1538	.78923	.21077
41	12.9934	.77960	.22040
42	12.8279	.76967	.23033
43	12.6574	.75944	.24056
44	12.4819	.74891	.25109
45	12.3013	.73808	.26192
46	12.1158	.72695	.27305
47	11.9253	.71552	.28448
48	11.7308	.70385	.29615
49	11.5330	.69198	.30802
50	11.3329	.67997	.32003
51	11.1308	.66785	.33215
52	10.9267	.65560	.34440
53	10.7200	.64320	.35680
54	10.5100	.63060	.36940
55	10.2960	.61776	.38224
56	10.0777	.60466	.39534
57	9.8552	.59131	.40869
58	9.6297	.57778	.42222
59	9.4028	.56417	.43583
60	9.1753	.55052	.44948
61	8.9478	.53687	.46313
62	8.7202	.52321	.47679
63	8.4924	.50954	.49046
64	8.2642	.49585	.50415
65	8.0353	.48212	.51788
66	7.8060	.46836	.53164
67	7.5763	.45458	.54542
68	7.3462	.44077	.55923
69	7.1149	.42689	.57311
70	6.8823	.41294	.58706
71	6.6481	.39889	.60111
72	6.4123	.38474	.61526
73	6.1752	.37051	.62949
74	5.9373	.35624	.64376
75	5.6990	.34194	.65806
76	5.4602	.32761	.67239
77	5.2211	.31327	.68673
78	4.9825	.29895	.70105
79	4.7469	.28481	.71519

TABLE A(1)—Continued

(1) Age	(2) Annuity	(3) Life estate	(4) Remainder
80	4.5164	.27098	.72902
81	4.2955	.25773	.74227
82	4.0879	.24527	.75473
83	3.8924	.23354	.76646
84	3.7029	.22217	.77783
85	3.5117	.21070	.78930
86	3.3259	.19955	.80045
87	3.1450	.18870	.81130
88	2.9703	.17822	.82178
89	2.8052	.16831	.83169
90	2.6536	.15922	.84078
91	2.5162	.15097	.84903
92	2.3917	.14350	.85650
93	2.2801	.13681	.86319
94	2.1802	.13081	.86919
95	2.0891	.12535	.87465
96	1.9997	.11998	.88002
97	1.9145	.11487	.88513
98	1.8331	.10999	.89001
99	1.7554	.10532	.89468
100	1.6812	.10087	.89913
101	1.6101	.09661	.90339
102	1.5416	.09250	.90750
103	1.4744	.08846	.91154
104	1.4065	.08439	.91561
105	1.3334	.08000	.92000
106	1.2452	.07471	.92529
107	1.1196	.06718	.93282
108	.9043	.05426	.94574
109	.4717	.02830	.97170

TABLE A(2)
TABLE, SINGLE LIFE FEMALE, 6 PERCENT, SHOWING THE PRESENT WORTH OF A LIFE INTEREST AND OF A REMAINDER INTEREST

(1) Age	(2) Annuity	(3) Life estate	(4) Remainder
0.	15.8972	0.95383	0.04617
1.	16.2284	.97370	.02630
2.	16.2287	.97372	.02628
3.	16.2180	.97308	.02692
4.	16.2029	.97217	.02783
5.	16.1850	.97110	.02890
6.	16.1648	.96989	.03011
7.	16.1421	.96853	.03147

TABLE A(2)—Continued

(1) Age	(2) Annuity	(3) Life estate	(4) Remainder
8	16.1172	.96703	.03297
9	16.0901	.96541	.03459
10	16.0608	.96365	.03635
11	16.0293	.96176	.03824
12	15.9958	.95975	.04025
13	15.9607	.95764	.04236
14	15.9239	.95543	.04457
15	15.8856	.95314	.04686
16	15.8460	.95076	.04924
17	15.8048	.94829	.05171
18	15.7620	.94572	.05428
19	15.7172	.94303	.05697
20	15.6701	.94021	.05979
21	15.6207	.93724	.06276
22	15.5687	.93412	.06588
23	15.5141	.93085	.06915
24	15.4565	.92739	.07261
25	15.3959	.92375	.07625
26	15.3322	.91993	.08007
27	15.2652	.91591	.08409
28	15.1946	.91168	.08832
29	15.1208	.90725	.09275
30	15.0432	.90259	.09741
31	14.9622	.89773	.10227
32	14.8775	.89265	.10735
33	14.7888	.88733	.11267
34	14.6960	.88176	.11824
35	14.5989	.87593	.12407
36	14.4975	.86985	.13015
37	14.3915	.86349	.13651
38	14.2811	.85687	.14313
39	14.1663	.84998	.15002
40	14.0468	.84281	.15719
41	13.9227	.83536	.16464
42	13.7940	.82764	.17236
43	13.6604	.81962	.18038
44	13.5219	.81131	.18869
45	13.3781	.80269	.19731
46	13.2290	.79374	.20626
47	13.0746	.78448	.21552
48	12.9147	.77488	.22512
49	12.7496	.76498	.23502
50	12.5793	.75476	.24524
51	12.4039	.74423	.25577
52	12.2232	.73339	.26661
53	12.0367	.72220	.27780
54	11.8436	.71062	.28938
55	11.6432	.69859	.30141

TABLE A(2)—Continued

(1) Age	(2) Annuity	(3) Life estate	(4) Remainder
56	11.4353	.68612	.31388
57	11.2200	.67320	.32680
58	10.9980	.65988	.34012
59	10.7708	.64622	.35378
60	10.5376	.63226	.36774
61	10.3005	.61803	.38197
62	10.0587	.60352	.39648
63	9.8118	.58871	.41129
64	9.5592	.57355	.42645
65	9.3005	.55803	.44197
66	9.0352	.54211	.45789
67	8.7639	.52583	.47417
68	8.4874	.50924	.49076
69	8.2068	.49241	.50759
70	7.9234	.47540	.52460
71	7.6371	.45823	.54177
72	7.3480	.44088	.55912
73	7.0568	.42341	.57659
74	6.7645	.40587	.59413
75	6.4721	.38833	.61167
76	6.1788	.37073	.62927
77	5.8845	.35307	.64693
78	5.5910	.33546	.66454
79	5.3018	.31811	.68189
80	5.0195	.30117	.69883
81	4.7482	.28489	.71511
82	4.4892	.26935	.73065
83	4.2398	.25439	.74561
84	3.9927	.23956	.76044
85	3.7401	.22441	.77559
86	3.5016	.21010	.78990
87	3.2790	.19674	.80326
88	3.0719	.18431	.81569
89	2.8808	.17285	.82715
90	2.7068	.16241	.83759
91	2.5502	.15301	.84699
92	2.4116	.14470	.85530
93	2.2901	.13741	.86259
94	2.1839	.13103	.86897
95	2.0891	.12535	.87465
96	1.9997	.11998	.88002
97	1.9145	.11487	.88513
98	1.8331	.10999	.89001
99	1.7554	.10532	.89468
100	1.6812	.10087	.89913
101	1.6101	.09661	.90339
102	1.5416	.09250	.90750
103	1.4744	.08846	.91154

TABLE A(2)—Continued

(1) Age	(2) Annuity	(3) Life estate	(4) Remainder
104	1.4065	.08439	.91561
105	1.3334	.08000	.92000
106	1.2452	.07471	.92529
107	1.1196	.06718	.93282
108	.9043	.05426	.94574
109	.4717	.02830	.97170

TABLE B
TABLE SHOWING THE PRESENT WORTH AT 6 PERCENT OF AN ANNUITY FOR A TERM CERTAIN, OF AN INCOME INTEREST FOR A TERM CERTAIN, AND OF A REMAINDER INTEREST POSTPONED FOR A TERM CERTAIN

(1) Number of years	(2) Annuity	(3) Term certain	(4) Remainder
1........	0.9434	0.056604	0.943396
2........	1.8334	.110004	.889996
3........	2.6730	.160381	.839619
4........	3.4651	.207906	.792094
5........	4.2124	.252742	.747258
6........	4.9173	.295039	.704961
7........	5.5824	.334943	.665057
8........	6.2098	.372588	.627412
9........	6.8017	.408102	.591898
10.......	7.3601	.441605	.558395
11.......	7.8869	.473212	.526788
12.......	8.3838	.503031	.496969
13.......	8.8527	.531161	.468839
14.......	9.2950	.557699	.442301
15.......	9.7122	.582735	.417265
16.......	10.1059	.606354	.393646
17.......	10.4773	.628636	.371364
18.......	10.8276	.649656	.350344
19.......	11.1581	.669487	.330513
20.......	11.4699	.688195	.311805
21.......	11.7641	.705845	.294155
22.......	12.0416	.722495	.277505
23.......	12.3034	.738203	.261797
24.......	12.5504	.753021	.246979
25.......	12.7834	.767001	.232999
26.......	13.0032	.780190	.219810
27.......	13.2105	.792632	.207368
28.......	13.4062	.804370	.195630
29.......	13.5907	.815443	.184557
30.......	13.7648	.825890	.174110

TABLE B—Continued

(1) Number of years	(2) Annuity	(3) Term certain	(4) Remainder
31	13.9291	.835745	.164255
32	14.0840	.845043	.154957
33	14.2302	.853814	.146186
34	14.3681	.862088	.137912
35	14.4982	.869895	.130105
36	14.6210	.877259	.122741
37	14.7368	.884207	.115793
38	14.8460	.890761	.109239
39	14.9491	.896944	.103056
40	15.0463	.902778	.097222
41	15.1380	.908281	.091719
42	15.2245	.913473	.086527
43	15.3062	.918370	.081630
44	15.3832	.922991	.077009
45	15.4558	.927350	.072650
46	15.5244	.931462	.068538
47	15.5890	.935342	.064658
48	15.6500	.939002	.060998
49	15.7076	.942454	.057546
50	15.7619	.945712	.054288
51	15.8131	.948785	.051215
52	15.8614	.951684	.048316
53	15.9070	.954418	.045582
54	15.9500	.956999	.043001
55	15.9905	.959433	.040567
56	16.0288	.961729	.038271
57	16.0649	.963895	.036105
58	16.0990	.965939	.034061
59	16.1311	.967867	.032133
60	16.1614	.969686	.030314

APPENDIX C

P. S. 58 Rates
(Reproduced from Rev. Rul. 55–747)

UNIFORM ONE YEAR TERM PREMIUMS FOR $1,000 LIFE INSURANCE PROTECTION (Based on Table 38, U. S. Life Tables and Actuarial Tables (U. S. Government Printing Office, Washington, D. C.—1946), and 2½% interest.)

Age	Premium	Age	Premium	Age	Premium
15 ------	$1.27	35 ------	$3.21	55 ------	$13.74
16 ------	1.38	36 ------	3.41	56 ------	14.91
17 ------	1.48	37 ------	3.63	57 ------	16.18
18 ------	1.52	38 ------	3.87	58 ------	17.56
19 ------	1.56	39 ------	4.14	59 ------	19.08
20 ------	1.61	40 ------	4.42	60 ------	20.73
21 ------	1.67	41 ------	4.73	61 ------	22.53
22 ------	1.73	42 ------	5.07	62 ------	24.50
23 ------	1.79	43 ------	5.44	63 ------	26.63
24 ------	1.86	44 ------	5.85	64 ------	28.98
25 ------	1.93	45 ------	6.30	65 ------	31.51
26 ------	2.02	46 ------	6.78	66 ------	34.28
27 ------	2.11	47 ------	7.32	67 ------	37.31
28 ------	2.20	48 ------	7.89	68 ------	40.59
29 ------	2.31	49 ------	8.53	69 ------	44.17
30 ------	2.43	50 ------	9.22	70 ------	48.06
31 ------	2.57	51 ------	9.97	71 ------	52.29
32 ------	2.70	52 ------	10.79	72 ------	56.89
33 ------	2.86	53 ------	11.69	73 ------	61.89
34 ------	3.02	54 ------	12.67	74 ------	67.33
				75 ------	73.23

APPENDIX D

Institutional Investor Study Report of the Securities and Exchange Commission Volume 5[1]

*　　　*　　　*

8. Discounts Involved in Purchases of Common Stock

Restricted securities are usually sold at a discount from their coeval market price, if any, primarily because of the restrictions on their resale. With the information supplied by the respondents on the purchase prices of the common stock and the dates of transaction, the Study computed the implied discounts in all cases in which it was able to locate a market price for the respective security on the date of the transaction. Several factors discussed below bear consideration in connection with these computations.

a. The date on which the purchase price is agreed upon is often difficult to determine

While the Study specifically requested the respondent to report this date, in some cases the respondent indicated this date was not preserved in its records. Moreover, respondents differ in the extent to which they consider themselves committed on the so-called commitment date. Some respondents indicated that they considered the commitment binding in regard to the discount, in which case the purchase price could change between the commitment and the closing dates if the market price changed. Others considered themselves bound by the price agreed to on the commitment date. Still others did not feel bound at all until the actual closing. In some cases, where the respondent reported the date on which the transaction entered its books instead of the commitment date, the Study computed a negative discount (or a premium) by relating the purchase price to the market price on the only date available to the Study in connection with the particular transaction. The Study telephoned the respondent in most cases in which it calculated a premium and learned that the explanation often lay in a binding commitment in combination with a falling market price.[100] Therefore, the discounts computed by the Study do not always reflect the intentions of the participants in the transaction.

b. Size of purchase relative to quantity of the same security outstanding

Since the quantities of securities purchased in a private placement are often large relative to

---

[1] 92nd Congress, 1st Session, House Document No. 92–64, Part 5; reproduced in part.

[100] This effect can work either way. Part of the error is self-canceling in the average statistics reported in the tables below.

the amount available in the market, the use of the market price as the datum for evaluating the purchase price may be misleading. Large amounts of thinly traded stocks are often not available at the market price. Some respondents indicated that their purchases of restricted stock was due to their inability to acquire a large position through purchases in the open market. In some cases, respondents explained the premium they paid for the restricted stock in terms of the superior bargaining position of the issuing company. To the extent the market price is a low estimate of the true price of a large block when the buyer is the initiating party, the computed discounts may be understated. This argument, however, is symmetrical. If, as is often the case, the seller is the initiating party, the market price may overstate what that seller can in fact obtain for a large block.

c. Computation of market price

The Study used the average asked price in computing the discount for transactions in securities of issuers whose common stock is traded over-the-counter. The Study's theory was that from the point of view of the institution the datum with which to compare the purchase price is the price the institution would have had to pay on the open market. Other theories may have comparable merit. In the case of low priced stocks, the choice of market price can have a significant bearing on the computed discount.[101]

d. Computation of the discount

There is no simple way to compute the discount for the purchase of a package of securities. The Study lacked the data and the resources to separately value the components of a security package. As a result its analysis of discounts relates only to purchases of a single class of common stock in a given transaction.

Table XIV–15 shows the Study's computed discounts classified by trading market. Of the value of all transactions 7.2 percent[102] involved negative discounts (or premia) at the time of purchase; 18.2 percent involved discounts not exceeding 10 percent; 39.6 percent involved discounts not exceeding 20 percent; 62.7 percent involved discounts not exceeding 30 percent; and 88.4 percent involved discounts not exceeding 40 percent. The size of the discount varied on average among trading markets. Where 55.0 percent of purchasers of stocks listed on the NYSE sold at discounts not exceeding 20 percent, only 34.3 percent of transactions of stocks listed on the ASE and 37.0 percent of stocks traded over-the-counter were purchased at discounts not exceeding 20 percent. Where 36.1 percent of all transactions with discounts between zero and 10 percent involved OTC stocks, 93.5 percent of all transactions with discounts of 40 percent to 50 percent involved the OTC stocks of non-reporting companies. Moreover, only in the 40 to 80 percent range did non-reporting OTC companies account for a larger fraction than the reporting companies of all transactions in the range.

---

[101] The fact, shown below, that the computed discounts on OTC stocks were not higher on the average than those for ASE stocks suggest that the use of the average asked price did not bias upward the computed discounts for OTC stocks.

[102] All percentages shown in this section refer to relative value rather than numbers of transactions.

Table XIV–45

DISCOUNTS ON PURCHASE PRICE OF RESTRICTED COMMON STOCK CLASSIFIED BY TRADING MARKET

JANUARY 1, 1966 TO JUNE 30, 1969

	DISCOUNT															
	−15.0% to 0.0%		0.1 to 10.0%		10.1% to 20.0%		20.1% to 30.0%		30.1% to 40.0%		40.1% to 50.0%		50.1% to 80.0%		Total	
Trading Market	No. of Trans-actions	Value of Purchases (Dollars)	No. of Trans-actions	Value of Purchases (Dollars)	No. of Trans-actions	Value of Purchases (Dollars)	No. of Trans-actions	Value of Purchases (Dollars)	No. of Trans-actions	Value of Purchases (Dollars)	No. of Trans-actions	Value of Purchases (Dollars)	No. of Trans-actions	Value of Purchases (Dollars)	No. of Trans-actions	Value of Purchases (Dollars)
Unknown	1	1,500,000	2	2,496,583	1	205,000	0	-	2	3,332,000	0	-	1	1,259,995	7	8,793,578
New York Stock Exchange	7	3,760,663	13	15,111,798	13	24,503,988	10	17,954,085	3	11,102,501	1	1,400,000	4	5,005,068	51	78,838,103
American Stock Exchange	2	7,263,060	4	15,850,000	11	14,548,750	20	46,200,677	7	21,074,298	1	44,250	4	4,802,404	49	109,783,439
Over-the-Counter (Reporting Co.)	11	13,828,757	39	13,613,676	35	38,585,259	30	35,479,946	30	38,689,328	13	9,284,047	21	8,996,406	179	178,477,419
Over-the-Counter (Non-Reporting Co.)	5	8,329,369	9	5,265,925	18	25,122,024	17	11,229,155	25	29,423,584	20	11,377,431	18	13,505,545	112	104,253,033
TOTAL	26	34,681,849	67	52,337,982	78	102,965,021	77	110,863,863	67	123,621,711	35	22,105,728	48	33,569,418	398	480,145,572

Table XIV–46

DISCOUNTS ON PURCHASE PRICE OF RESTRICTED COMMON STOCK BY CLASS OF INSTITUTION

JANUARY 1, 1966 TO JUNE 30, 1969

	DISCOUNT															
	−15.0% to 0.0%		0.1% to 10.0%		10.1% to 20.0%		20.1% to 30.0%		30.1% to 40.0%		40.1% to 50.0%		50.1% to 80.0%		Total	
Class of Institution	No. of Trans-actions	Value of Purchases (Dollars)	No. of Trans-actions	Value of Purchases (Dollars)	No. of Trans-actions	Value of Purchases (Dollars)	No. of Trans-actions	Value of Purchases (Dollars)	No. of Trans-actions	Value of Purchases (Dollars)	No. of Trans-actions	Value of Purchases (Dollars)	No. of Trans-actions	Value of Purchases (Dollars)	No. of Trans-actions	Value of Purchases (Dollars)
Banks	6	10,803,050	17	15,021,358	31	35,624,259	26	44,586,199	18	44,581,008	9	3,838,055	12	3,047,068	119	157,500,997
Investment Advisers	7	6,012,188	13	24,429,493	27	50,390,544	26	37,654,718	32	60,149,780	16	13,630,681	16	20,695,041	137	212,962,445
Property and Liability Insurance Companies	1	1,500,000	2	1,438,375	3	2,418,279	3	7,342,061	0	-	3	1,850,000	2	1,659,995	14	16,208,710
Life Insurance Companies	5	6,909,369	2	2,029,500	8	7,735,412	13	9,720,627	8	10,174,527	2	999,993	5	3,631,414	43	41,200,842
Self-Administered Employee Benefit	4	3,109,932	29	3,733,256	2	3,653,133	3	1,748,856	0	-	0	-	2	2,000,000	40	14,245,177
Foundations	0	-	2	3,140,000	1	429,000	0	-	0	-	0	-	0	-	3	3,569,000
Educational Endowments	1	284,250	1	2,500,000	2	600,000	1	1,300,000	0	-	2	1,000,000	1	207,000	8	5,891,250
Venture Capital	2	6,063,060	1	46,000	4	2,114,394	5	8,511,402	9	8,716,396	3	786,999	10	2,328,900	34	28,567,151
TOTAL	26	34,681,849	67	52,337,982	78	102,965,021	77	110,863,863	67	123,621,711	35	22,105,728	48	33,569,418	398	480,145,572

Table XIV–46 classifies the discounts by institutional purchaser. The differences among institutional classes in regard to the discounts they obtain are largely a function of the size of the issuing companies. Investment advisers concentrated on smaller companies. These companies tend to issue stock at greater discounts. Since data on sales, earnings, and trading markets are the only relevant data available to the Study, the present analyses cannot fully evaluate the effects of portfolio risk on the size of the discount.

In addition to obtaining larger discounts, institutions can obtain compensation for bearing unusual risks by purchasing warrants at favorable prices. For example, Table XIV–31 shows that whereas there were no purchases of common stock with warrants in connection with NYSE stocks, purchases of such packages equaled 17.5 percent of the purchase of equity securities listed on the ASE or traded in the OTC market. In particular, purchases by investment advisers of equity packages were equal to 22.4 percent of all equity purchases of ASE and OTC securities. Purchases of common stock representing 39.0 percent of purchases by banks, 23.7 percent of purchases by investment advisers, and 40.5 percent by life insurance companies involved discounts not exceeding 20 percent. For discounts not exceeding 30 percent, the percentages were 67.3, 55.6, and 64.1 percent for these three classes of institutions, respectively.

Tables XIV–47 and XIV–48 show discounts classified by sales and earnings of issuer, respectively. Whereas companies with sales of under $5 million accounted for 66.4 percent of all transactions involving discounts in excess of 50.0 percent and for 68.4 percent of all transactions involving discounts of between 40.1 percent and 50.0 percent, they accounted for only 23.8 percent and 24.8 percent, respectively, of transactions involving discounts of less than 10.0 percent and of between 10.1 percent and 20.0 percent. Whereas companies with sales of $100 million or more accounted for only 6.1 percent of transactions involving discounts of more than 40.0 percent, they accounted for 21.1 percent of transactions involving discounts of not more than 20 percent.

Issuers' earnings are far more related to size of discount than are issuers' sales. For example, there were no transactions in publicly traded common stock of companies with earnings deficits in the fiscal years preceding the dates of the transactions. Whereas transactions in shares of companies with earnings of less than $1 million accounted for 93.9 percent of all transactions involving discounts of more than 40.0 percent, they accounted for only 49.4 percent of transactions involving discounts of 20.0 percent of less. The greater influence on the size of the discounts of earnings than of sales is probably due to the more proximate relationship of earnings than of sales to the riskiness of the investment.

Tables XIV–49 and XIV–50 show the average[103] discounts, in each of the years in the sample period, classified by sales and earnings of issuers, respectively. Average discounts rose over the period January 1, 1966 through June 30, 1969. They were 15.3 percent in 1966, 17.7 percent in 1967, 24.5 percent in 1968, and 27.9 percent in the first half of 1969. The averages were generally higher for the smaller companies; however, the small number of transactions in the shares of these companies makes the averages sensitive to extreme

[103] The averages are weighted by the number of transactions in each sales (or earnings) range. The averages for each range are themselves simple averages of the discounts on the individual transactions within each range.

Table XIV–47

DISCOUNTS ON PURCHASE PRICE OF RESTRICTED COMMON STOCK CLASSIFIED BY SIZE OF TRANSACTION AND SALES OF ISSUER

JANUARY 1, 1966 TO JUNE 30, 1969

(PUBLICLY HELD COMPANIES ONLY)

	DISCOUNT													
	50.1% or More		40.1% to 50.0%		30.1% to 40.0%		20.1% to 30.0%		10.1% to 20.0%		0.1% to 10.0%		Total	
Sales of Issuer (Thousands of Dollars)	No. of Trans-actions	Size of Trans-actions (Dollars)	No. of Trans-actions	Size of Trans-actions (Dollars)	No. of Trans-actions	Size of Trans-actions (Dollars)	No. of Trans-actions	Size of Trans-actions (Dollars)	No. of Trans-actions	Size of Trans-actions (Dollars)	No. of Trans-actions	Size of Trans-actions (Dollars)	No. of Trans-actions	Size of Trans-actions (Dollars)
Less than 100	11	2,894,999	7	2,554,000	17	19,642,364	16	12,197,394	6	12,267,292	9	12,566,000	66	62,122,049
100–999	7	474,040	2	1,221,000	0	-	1	500,000	1	1,018,500	2	3,877,500	13	7,091,040
1,000–4,999	8	4,605,505	13	8,170,747	12	10,675,150	15	9,865,951	10	9,351,738	3	2,295,200	61	44,964,291
5,000–19,999	6	1,620,015	4	1,147,305	13	25,986,008	25	27,238,210	24	21,441,347	47	12,750,481	119	90,183,366
20,000–99,999	3	605,689	3	4,372,676	6	11,499,250	8	11,817,954	18	22,231,737	17	36,481,954	55	87,009,260
100,000 or More	2	1,805,068	0	-	2	2,049,998	3	7,903,586	10	24,959,483	7	10,832,925	24	47,551,060
TOTAL	37	12,005,316	29	17,465,728	50	69,852,770	68	69,523,095	69	91,270,097	85	78,804,060	338	338,921,066

Table XIV–48

DISCOUNTS ON PURCHASE PRICE OF RESTRICTED COMMON STOCK CLASSIFIED BY SIZE OF TRANSACTION AND EARNINGS OF ISSUER

JANUARY 1, 1966 TO JUNE 30, 1969

(PUBLICLY HELD COMPANIES ONLY)

	DISCOUNT													
	50.1% or More		40.1% to 50.0%		30.1% to 40.0%		20.1% to 30.0%		10.1% to 20.0%		0.1% to 10.0%		Totals	
Earnings of Issuer (Thousands of Dollars)	No. of Trans-actions	Size of Trans-actions (Dollars)	No. of Trans-actions	Size of Trans-actions (Dollars)	No. of Trans-actions	Size of Trans-actions (Dollars)	No. of Trans-actions	Size of Trans-actions (Dollars)	No. of Trans-actions	Size of Trans-actions (Dollars)	No. of Trans-actions	Size of Trans-actions (Dollars)	No. of Trans-actions	Size of Trans-actions (Dollars)
Deficit	0	-	0	-	0	-	0	-	0	-	0	-	0	-
0–99	27	6,901,243	19	11,003,559	28	37,681,014	31	32,796,968	19	25,122,042	46	29,553,418	170	143,058,244
100–999	8	3,299,005	10	6,462,169	19	26,121,758	24	20,344,492	25	16,790,565	16	12,480,144	102	85,498,133
1,000–9,999	0	-	0	-	3	6,049,998	12	16,313,549	17	27,948,007	15	16,955,530	47	67,267,084
10,000 or More	2	1,805,068	0	-	0	-	1	68,086	8	21,409,483	8	19,814,968	19	43,097,605
TOTAL	37	12,005,316	29	17,465,728	50	69,852,770	68	69,523,095	69	91,270,097	85	78,804,060	338	338,921,066

Table XIV–49

AVERAGE DISCOUNTS ON PURCHASE PRICE OF RESTRICTED COMMON STOCK CLASSIFIED BY SALES OF ISSUER AND AVERAGE PERCENTAGE DISCOUNT, OVER TIME

(PUBLICLY HELD COMPANIES ONLY)

SALES OF ISSUER (THOUSANDS OF DOLLARS)

	Less Than 100		100 – 999		1,000 – 4,999		5,000 – 19,999		20,000 – 99,999		100,000 or More		Totals	
Year	No. of Trans-actions	Average Discount (Percentage)	No. of Trans-actions	Average Discount (Percentage)	No. of Trans-actions	Average Discount (Percentage)	No. of Trans-actions	Average Discount (Percentage)	No. of Trans-actions	Average Discount (Percentage)	No. of Trans-actions	Average Discount (Percentage)	No. of Trans-actions	Average Discount (Percentage)
1966	0	-	0	-	1	61.4	7	23.8	10	9.3	3	.2	21	15.3
1967	1	17.2	3	79.4	11	37.4	36	9.5	6	6.2	6	11.2	63	17.7
1968	2	25.6	5	30.0	36	32.6	47	18.7	26	23.9	11	21.1	127	24.5
1969 (First Half)	3	41.4	5	45.5	13	26.9	29	27.1	13	21.4	4	25.8	67	27.9
TOTAL	6	32.1	13	47.4	61	32.7	119	18.3	55	18.7	24	16.8	278	23.1

NOTE:
Averages of discounts are weighted by the number of transactions in each range of sales

Table XIV–50

AVERAGE DISCOUNTS ON PURCHASE PRICE OF RESTRICTED COMMON STOCK CLASSIFIED BY EARNINGS OF ISSUER AND AVERAGE PERCENTAGE DISCOUNT, OVER TIME

(PUBLICLY HELD COMPANIES ONLY)

EARNINGS OF ISSUER (THOUSANDS OF DOLLARS)

	Deficit		0 – 99		100 – 999		1,000 – 9,999		10,000 or More		Totals	
Year	No. of Trans-actions	Average Discount (Percentage)	No. of Trans-actions	Average Discount (Percentage)	No. of Trans-actions	Average Discount (Percentage)	No. of Trans-actions	Average Discount (Percentage)	No. of Trans-actions	Average Discount (Percentage)	No. of Trans-actions	Average Discount (Percentage)
1966	0	-	8	14.7	5	25.6	4	10.7	4	8.4	21	15.3
1967	0	-	35	21.8	12	19.2	12	8.1	4	4.9	63	17.7
1968	0	-	48	27.1	49	26.0	21	15.5	9	23.2	127	24.5
1969 (First Half)	0	-	19	33.3	36	26.6	10	23.8	2	19.3	67	27.9
TOTAL	0	-	110	25.6	102	25.4	47	15.0	19	15.8	278	23.1

NOTE:
Averages of discounts are weighted by the number of transactions in each range of earnings.

points. Table XIV–59 shows a monotonic decline from 25.6 percent for companies with earnings between 0 and $99,000 to 15.8 percent for companies with earnings of $10 million or more.

To capture the simultaneous influence on the size of the discount of some of the variables described above, and certain other variables, the Study regressed the discount in each transaction on dummy variables describing some of the institutional purchasers, the trading market for the publicly-held shares, the S&P index, and the size of the purchase. The estimated co-efficients attached to each of the variables and the t-values are shown in table XIV–51:

Table XIV–51
ESTIMATES OF COEFFICIENTS OF REGRESSION OF DISCOUNTS OBTAINED IN PURCHASES OF RESTRICTED COMMON STOCK ON SELECTED EXPLANATORY VARIABLES, 338 TRANSACTIONS BETWEEN JAN. 1, 1966, AND JUNE 30, 1969

Variable	Regression coefficient	t-value
Intercept	−0.512	3.22
Banks (DV)	.096	3.50
Investments advisers (DV)	.124	4.41
Life insurance companies (DV)	.107	3.07
Venture capital companies (DV)	.233	6.05
N.Y.S.E. (DV)	−.085	−2.65
A.S.E. (DV)	−.046	−1.43
O.T.C. reporting companies (DV)	−.063	−2.93
S. & P. composite index	.007	4.53
Size of purchase	−.018	−2.66

Note: The adjusted R^2 of the regression is 0.202. "DV" means dummy variable.

All variables except for the dummy variable associated with the ASE are statistically significant. The regression is read in two parts—(1) the intercept and dummy variables and (2) the last two variables. To obtain the influence on the discount of bank purchases of restricted stock of a company with securities listed on the NYSE, one sums the intercept, the coefficient for the bank dummy variable, and the coefficient for the NYSE dummy variable (−.512 +.096 −.085). To obtain the effect on discounts of purchases by venture capital companies of NYSE securities one substitutes the coefficient attached to the latter dummy variable for the coefficient attached to the bank dummy variable (−.512 +.233 −.085). Substituting the venture capital company coefficient for the bank coefficient adds 13.7 percentage points to the discount (.233 −.096). Similarly, substituting the OTC coefficient for the NYSE coefficient adds 2.2 percentage points to the discount [−0.63−(−.085)]. In effect, the dummy variables modify the intercept of the regression for each combination of independent dummy variables, in this case one institution variable and one market variable. The second part of the regression involves ordinary variables—the S&P index (coeval with the month in which the given transaction took place) and the size of the purchase. The size of the discount is positively related to the S&P index rising 0.7 percentage points for each one point change in the S&P index.[104] The discount is lower for larger purchases because larger purchases are associated with larger issuers.

Table XIV–52 summarizes the regression assuming the transaction size and the S&P index are at their mean values. The numbers in the cells were calculated in the manner described in the text above. The discounts in each cell would increase by 0.7 percentage points for each unit change in the S&P index. For example, if instead of its mean value, 98.20, the S&P index were at 100.0, the numbers in each cell would increase by 1.3 (i.e., 0.7 (100.0 − 98.2)). The average discount for the 338 transactions was 24.0 percent.

Table XIV–52
AVERAGE DISCOUNTS ON PURCHASES OF RESTRICTED COMMON STOCK CLASSIFIED BY INSTITUTIONAL PURCHASER AND TRADING MARKETS, JAN. 1, 1966-JUNE 30, 1969

	Market			
Class of institution	N.Y.S.E.	A.S.E.	OTC-R.P.G.	OTC-Non-R.P.G.
Banks	18.7	22.5	25.6	31.9
Investment advisers	21.6	25.4	28.5	34.8
Life insurance companies	19.9	23.7	26.8	33.1
Venture capital companies	32.5	36.3	39.4	45.7
Other institutions	9.2	13.0	16.1	22.4

Note: This table is based on the regression coefficients reported in Table XIV–51. The discounts are calculated on the basis of the mean value of the S. & P. index and the mean transactions size. The discounts reported in each cell would increase by 0.7 percentage points for each 1 point change in the S. & P. composite index. The discounts would decrease by 1.8 percentage points for each $1,000,000 increase in the size of transaction.

[104] This result may indicate that investors are skeptical about the permanence of rises in stock prices and, therefore, revise upward their estimate of the risk of the restricted security when stock prices are high.

APPENDIX E

Actuarial Values I
Valuation of Last Survivor Charitable Remainders
(I.R.S. Publication 723)

Explanation of Pamphlet

The tables in this pamphlet are intended primarily for use in evaluating charitable remainder interests, dependent on the death of the survivor of two or more lives, in pooled income funds and charitable remainder unitrusts. As to requests for computations to be made by the Internal Revenue Service, see section 6.

Introduction

A charitable contribution deduction may be allowable by reason of a transfer of property to (1) a pooled income fund, defined in section 642(c)(5) of the Internal Revenue Code of 1954, (2) a charitable remainder annuity trust, defined in section 664(d)(1), or (3) a charitable remainder unitrust, defined in section 664(d)(2). The definitions of the pooled income fund, charitable remainder annuity trust, and charitable remainder unitrust were added to the Code by the Tax Reform Act of 1969.

The following tables apply as indicated to the valuation of interests that are dependent on but one life:

(a) Tables G(1) and G(2), the one-life tables of section 1.642(c)–6(d) of the Income Tax Regulations, are used to determine the value of a remainder interest dependent on but one life in property transferred after July 31, 1969, to a pooled income fund for which the applicable yearly rate of return is between 2.2 and 8.0 percent, inclusive.

(b) The fair market value of the remainder interest of a charitable remainder annuity trust that is dependent on but one life is the net fair market value of the property placed in trust less the present value of the annuity computed under section 20.2031–10 of the Estate Tax Regulations by the use of the appropriate annuity factor from Table A(1) or A(2), the one-life tables set forth in such section.

(c) Tables E(1) and E(2), the one-life tables of section 1.664–4 of the Income Tax Regulations, are used to determine the value of a remainder interest dependent on but one life in property transferred to a charitable remainder unitrust having an adjusted payout rate not greater than 9 percent and meeting the limitation of section 1.664–4(b)(1) concerning the timing of amounts to be distributed during the first taxable year of the trust.

The present value of remainder interests that must await the death of the survivor of two or more measuring lives can be calculated by a method developed for Federal income, estate, and gift tax purposes by the late Charles T. Kemmerer in the National Office of the Internal Revenue Service. The method employs probabilities, herein called values of Q or values of ${}_tq_x$, that each of the given lives will have failed at the end of t years. Such probabilities are shown in Table QN of section 7. The method also employs values called K-factors that reflect a rate of interest or return or, in the case of unitrusts, a rate of payout. K-factors for various yearly rates of return are shown in Table IN and for various rates of payout in Table UN. The theory underlying the method by which the K-factors are computed and applied is based on the general theory of life contingencies and on a formula often referred to as Woolhouse's formula, with terms involving third and higher derivatives ignored. The formula may be found in Chapter IX of *Finite Differences for Actuarial Students* by Harry Freeman, Cambridge University Press (1965) and in Chapter 7 of *Life and Other Contingencies,* Volume I, by P. F. Hooker and L. H. Longley-Cook, Cambridge University Press (1953). For the resulting formulas, used in computing the Q-values and K-factors, see Appendix 1.

Following are examples of remainder interests that can be evaluated by means of the tables in sections 7 and 8.

(a) Pooled income fund: to pay income to A for life, then to B for life; remainder to charity. See section 1.

(b) Pooled income fund: to pay income to A and B in equal shares during their joint lives and all to the survivor for life; remainder to charity. See section 1.

(c) Charitable remainder unitrust created January 1, 1970: to pay at the end of the taxable year of the trust an amount equal to 5 percent of the fair market value as of the beginning of the taxable year of the trust to C and D in equal shares during their joint lives and all to the survivor for life; remainder to charity. See section 2.

(d) Same facts as (c), except that the described amount is to be paid to C for life, then to D for life; remainder to charity. See section 2.

The Kemmerer method is illustrated in sections 1 and 2. According to the method, as there illustrated, the required last survivor two-life remainder factor is the sum of 22 numbers, each of which is the product of 3 other numbers, namely, (1) a probability or value of Q from Table QN for the junior life, (2) a similar probability for Table QN for the senior life, and (3) a K-factor based on the applicable yearly rate of return in the case of a pooled income fund or on the adjusted payout rate in the case of a charitable remainder unitrust. The method is easily extended to cases involving three or more measuring lives. See section 4.

Section 1
Pooled Income Fund
Valuation of a Remainder Interest
Dependent on 2 Lives

In a case where the income from property transferred to a pooled income fund is to be paid to A for life, then to B for life, and the property itself is to be paid to charity or retained for a charitable use on the death of the survivor of A and B, charity has a remainder interest, while A and B (the "measuring lives") have successive life income interests in the property. The present value of the remainder interest equals the value of the property less the sum of the present values of the successive life income interests. Likewise, the sum of the present values of the successive life income interests equals the value of the property less the present value of the remainder interest.

Table QN and Table IN of section 7 are used together to calculate the present value of the remainder interest following two successive life income interests in a pooled income fund of $1.00. Such present value may be calculated at any rate of interest (that is, at any rate of return) that is not outside the range of rates for which K-factors are provided in Table IN, namely, from 2.2 percent to 8.0 percent, inclusive. It is assumed that at least one of the measuring lives is younger than age 70 nearest birthday. In a case where the ages nearest birthday of the junior measuring life is greater than 69 but less than 90, the method of section 3 should be used.

For purposes of computing the present value of a remainder interest in a pooled income fund, the rate of return to be assumed in the computation is the applicable "yearly rate of return" of the pooled income fund, determined in accordance with section 1.642(c)–6 of the Income Tax Regulations. In the example below, the applicable yearly rate of return (6.2 percent) is a rate for which factors are provided in Table IN.

Example 1.

G transfers $100,000 of property to a pooled income fund on January 1, 1970, and provides that the income from the property is to be paid to A (a woman aged 68) for life and then to B (a man aged 74) for life, with remainder to charity. The highest yearly rate of return earned by the fund for its 3 preceding taxable years is 6.2 percent. At that rate of return, the present value of charity's remainder interest is $42,549, determined as follows:

The computation of present value in this case employs three columns of multipliers:

(a) Two columns of Q-values from Table QN that reflect the mortality of the two measuring lives involved. Each of the columns in Table QN shows the probabilities that a life of given age and sex will not be living at the end of the number of years indicated under "*t* " in the margin, namely, at the end of 5, 10, 15, . . ., 110 years. There are thus 22 entries in each column. (In actuarial notation, ${}_tq_x$ represents the probability that a life now aged *x* will not be living *t* years hence. The 22 Q-values are merely values of ${}_tq_x$.) The two columns from Table QN to be used in the present example are those labeled "68F" and "74M", namely, those reflecting the mortality of a woman aged 68 and a man aged 74, respectively.

(b) A column of K-factors from Table IN that reflects a yearly rate of return ("YRR") of 6.2 percent. There appear in the margin of Table IN the same 22 values of *t* (5, 10, 15, . . ., 110) that appear in Table QN. Similarly, as in Table QN, each column in Table IN contains 22 entries. The column in Table IN to be used in the present example is the one labeled "YYR = 6.2%".

It is convenient to use a columnar work sheet for the computation. The details are shown in Exhibit 1. In the margin to the left of Column (1) are entered line numbers (1 through 22) and the values of *t* (5 through 110, advancing by steps of 5) that appear in the left margin of Table QN. In Columns (1) and (2) are copied the Q-values from Table QN for the junior and senior life, respectively. On each of the 22 lines, the entry in Column (1) is to be multiplied by the entry in Column (2), and the result (rounded to 6 decimal places) entered in Column (3). In Column (4) are copied the 22 K-factors from Table IN for a yearly rate of return of 6.2 percent. To help insure that the entries were correctly copied into Column (4), add them and compare the total with the total shown in Table IN for those entries. Next, on each of the

22 lines, the entry in Column (3) is multiplied by the entry in Column (4), and the result, rounded to 6 decimal places, entered in Column (5). Finally, the entries in Column (5) are summed. The sum, rounded to 5 decimal places, of the 22 entries in Column (5) is the required remainder factor: 0.425493 rounded to 5 decimal places is 0.42549. Thus, at a rate of interest (rate of return) of 6.2 percent, the present value of $1.00 due at the death of the last to die of a woman aged 68 and a man aged 74 is $0.42549. Therefore, the required present value of the remainder interest is $100,000 × 0.42549 or $42,549.

In Example 1, a number of entries in Column (4) are carried forward without change into Column (5). Such duplication occurs whenever the entry in Column (3) equals 1.0. The columns could have been shortened if those entries in Column (4) that were carried forward without change to Column (5) had been consolidated in Column (4), and only their total carried forward to Column (5). The method is illustrated in Example 2. Little or no shortening is possible, however, if the junior life is aged 30 or younger.

Example 2.

The results obtained in Example 1 can be more quickly obtained by consolidating (lumping together) those K-factors that in Exhibit 1 appeared opposite an entry of 1.0 in Column (3).

Thus, in Exhibit 1, the first entry of 1.0 in Column (3) appears on line 9 opposite $t = 45$. This means that the computation can be shortened to 9 lines. The details are shown in Exhibit 2. The K-factors that would normally appear on lines 9 through 22 of Column (4) should be summed and the sum (.077329) entered on line 9 of both Column (4) and Column (5). Except for these two entries, the first 9 lines of the computation are the same as in Example 1. In Columns (1) and (2) are copied the first 9 Q-values from Table QN for the junior and senior life, respectively. On each of the 9 lines, the entry in Column (1) is to be multiplied by the entry in Column (2), and the result (rounded to 6 decimal places) entered in Column (3). In Column (4) are copied the first 8 K-factors from Table IN for a yearly rate of return of 6.2 percent, and on the first 8 lines of Column (5) are entered the results (rounded to 6 decimal places) obtained by multiplying the entry in Column (3) by the entry on the same line in Column (4). The 9 lines of Column (4) and Column (5) are then summed.

The sum of the entries in Column (4) is a check value. It should agree with the sum shown for the column of K-factors in Table IN: 0.857659.

The sum of the entries in Column (5), rounded to 5 decimal places, is the required remainder factor: 0.42549.

If the facts are the same as those of Example 1 except that the income is payable to A and B in equal shares during their joint lives and all to the survivor for life, the present value at 6.2 percent of the remainder is the same ($42.549) as in Example 1. The value of the remainder is not affected by how the income is apportioned between A and B during their joint lives.

If the facts are unlike those of Example 1 because the applicable yearly rate of return of the pooled income fund is between two neighboring rates of return for which columns are provided in Table IN, the factor for the present value of the remainder interest should be determined by linear interpolation between two factors computed at the closest neighboring rates of return. The method is illustrated by the following example.

Exhibit 1.

Line No.	Values of t	Values of Q 68F (1)	Values of Q 74M (2)	Col. (1) *times* Col. (2) (3)	K-factors. YRR = 6.2% (4)	Col. (3) *times* Col. (4) (5)
1	5	.139259	.328007	.045678	.222778	.010176
2	10	.327421	.639001	.209222	.164911	.034503
3	15	.562454	.859012	.483155	.122075	.058981
4	20	.790103	.966727	.763814	.090366	.069023
5	25	.940973	.995509	.936747	.066893	.062662
6	30	.991038	.999678	.990719	.049518	.049058
7	35	.999262	.999989	.999251	.036655	.036628
8	40	.999971	1.	.999971	.027134	.027133
9	45	1.	1.	1.	.020086	.020086
10	50	1.	1.	1.	.014869	.014869
11	55	1.	1.	1.	.011006	.011006
12	60	1.	1.	1.	.008148	.008148
13	65	1.	1.	1.	.006031	.006031
14	70	1.	1.	1.	.004465	.004465
15	75	1.	1.	1.	.003305	.003305
16	80	1.	1.	1.	.002446	.002446
17	85	1.	1.	1.	.001811	.001811
18	90	1.	1.	1.	.001341	.001341
19	95	1.	1.	1.	.000992	.000992
20	100	1.	1.	1.	.000735	.000735
21	105	1.	1.	1.	.000544	.000544
22	110	1.	1.	1.	.001550	.001550
					.857659	.425493

Exhibit 2

Line No.	Values of t	Values of Q 68F (1)	Values of Q 74M (2)	Col. (1) *times* Col. (2) (3)	K-factors. YRR = 6.2% (4)	Col. (3) *times* Col. (4) (5)
1	5	.139259	.328007	.045678	.222778	.010176
2	10	.327421	.639001	.209222	.164911	.034503
3	15	.562454	.859012	.483155	.122075	.058981
4	20	.790103	.966727	.763814	.090366	.069023
5	25	.940973	.995509	.936747	.066893	.062662
6	30	.991038	.999678	.990719	.049518	.049058
7	35	.999262	.999989	.999251	.036655	.036628
8	40	.999971	1.000000	.999971	.027134	.027133
9	45–110	1.000000	1.000000	1.000000	.077329*	.077329
					.857659	.425493

*sum of lines 9 through 22

Example 3.

The facts are the same as in Example 1 except that the highest yearly rate of return earned by the fund for its 3 preceding taxable years is 6.344 percent. At that rate of return, the present value of charity's remainder interest is $41,806, determined as follows:

The rate of return next above and below 6.344 percent for which K-factors are provided in Table IN are 6.4 and 6.2 percent. Use the method of Example 1 or Example 2 to find (to 6 decimal places) at each of those two rates of return the factors for the present value of the remainder interest. The factor for the present value of the remainder interest at a 6.344 percent rate of return is then determined by linear interpolation as follows:

(1)	Present value at 6.2 percent (See Example 2.)	0.425493
(2)	Present value at 6.4 percent (Details omitted)	0.415171
(3)	Decrease: line (1) less line (2)	0.010322
(4)	Proportion of decrease to be taken into account: $(6.344-6.2) \div (6.400-6.2) = 144 \div 200$	0.72
(5)	Amount of decrease to be taken into account: 0.72×0.010322	0.007432
(6)	Present value at 6.344 percent Line (1) less line (5)	0.418061
(7)	Same, rounded to 5 decimal places .	0.41806

Based on the foregoing, the required present value is $100,000 × 0.41806 or $41,806.

Section 2
Charitable Remainder Unitrust
Valuation of a Remainder Interest
Dependent on 2 Lives

Table QN and Table UN of section 7 are used together to calculate the present value of a remainder interest dependent on two lives in a charitable remainder unitrust provided that the limitation of section 1.664–4(b)(1) of the regulations is met concerning the timing of amounts to be distributed during the first taxable year of the trust. (For example, such limitation is not met if the aggregate amount distributed as of any date during the first taxable year of the trust, X percent of the taxable year having elapsed, exceeds X percent of the entire amount distributable during that taxable year.)

It is assumed that at least one of the measuring lives is younger than age 70 nearest birthday. In a case where the age nearest birthday of the junior measuring life is greater than 69 but less than 90, see section 3.

For purposes of computing the present value of a remainder interest in a charitable remainder unitrust, the "adjusted payout rate" to be used in the computation is the adjusted payout rate determined in accordance with section 1.644–4 of the regulations.

The method of computation is the same for a unitrust as for a pooled income fund except that in the case of a unitrust the K-factors are taken from Table UN, while in the case of a pooled income fund the factors are taken from Table IN. For an example of a computation that employs K-factors from Table IN, see Example 1.

Example 4.

H, a man aged 74, transfers $100,000 to a charitable remainder unitrust on January 1, 1970. The trust instrument requires that the trust pay at the end of the taxable year of the trust 5 percent of the fair market value as of the beginning of the taxable year of the trust to H during his lifetime and then to W, a woman aged 68, during her lifetime. The adjusted payout rate, determined in accordance with section 1.644–4 of the regulations is 4.717 percent. The present value of the remainder interest is $49,807, determined as follows:

The adjusted payout rates next below and above 4.717 percent for which K-factors are provided in Table UN are 4.6 and 4.8 percent. The required remainder factor must be determined by linear interpolation between one remainder factor based on an adjusted payout rate of 4.6 percent and another based on an adjusted payout rate of 4.8 percent.

Exhibit 3

Line No.	Values of t	Values of Q: Junior Life: 68F (1)	Values of Q: Senior Life: 74M (2)	Col. (1) *times* Col. (2) (3)	K-factors. APR = 4.8% (4)	Col. (3) *times* Col. (4) (5)
1	5	.139259	.328007	.045678	.192402	.008789
2	10	.327421	.639001	.209222	.150450	.031477
3	15	.562454	.859012	.483155	.117646	.056841
4	20	.790103	.966727	.763814	.091995	.070267
5	25	.940973	.995509	.936747	.071936	.067386
6	30	.991038	.999678	.990719	.056251	.055729
7	35	.999262	.999989	.999251	.043986	.043953
8	40	.999971	1.000000	.999971	.034396	.034395
9	45–110	1.000000	1.000000	1.000000	.123354*	.123354
					.882416	.492191

*sum of lines 9 through 22

Details of the computation based on the 4.8 percent rate are shown in Exhibit 3. From Table QN, values of Q for the junior life (aged 68, female) are to be copied into Column (1), and those for the senior life (aged 74, male) into Column (2). From Table UN, K-factors for an adjusted payout rate of 4.8 percent ("APR = 4.8%") are to be copied into Column (4). Each entry in Column (3) is the product, rounded to 6 decimal figures, of the corresponding entries in Columns (1) and (2). Similarly, each entry in Column (5) is the product of the entries in Columns (3) and (4). However, as in Example 2, the columns have been shortened by the procedure for consolidating K-factors that is explained in section 1. Accordingly, Column (4) contains only the first 8 K-factors from Table UN and on line 9 the total (0.123354) of the 14 remaining K-factors.

To help insure that the entries were correctly copied into Column (4), add them and compare the total with the total shown in Table UN for those entries.

The sum (0.492191) of the entries in Column (5) is the factor (unrounded) for the present value of the remainder interest at the 4.8 percent rate.

When the computation is repeated after substituting new K-factors from Table UN at a 4.6 percent rate, it will be found that the sum of the entries in the new Column (5) is 0.506358.

The factors for the present value of the remainder interest at an adjusted payout rate of 4.717 percent is then determined by linear interpolation as follows:

(1)	Present value at 4.6% rate	0.506358
(2)	Present value at 4.8% rate	0.492191
(3)	Decrease: line (1) less line (2)	0.014167
(4)	Proportion of decrease to be taken into account: $(4.717-4.6)\div(4.8-4.6)=117\div200$	.0.585
(5)	Amount of decrease to be taken into account: 0.585×0.014167	0.008288
(6)	Present value at 4.717% rate: line (1) less line (5)	0.498070
(7)	Same, rounded to 5 decimal places ..	0.49807

Based on the foregoing, the required present value is $100,000 × 0.49807 or $49,807.

If the facts are the same as those of Example 4 except that the designated annual payment is payable to H and W in equal shares during their joint lives and all to the survivor for life, the present value of the remainder is the same as in Example 4: $49,807. The value of the remainder is not affected by how the annual payment is apportioned between H and W during their joint lives. What matters is that the rate of payment from the trust does not change during the joint lives and the life of the survivor of the measuring lives.

If the rate of payment from the trust can change during the joint lives and the life of the survivor of the measuring lives, a special computation is required, and the tables of sections 7 and 8 do not apply. Example: In the case of a charitable remainder unitrust that calls for a 5 percent payment to each of H and W for their respective lives, the rate of payment from the trust can change (from 10 percent to 5 percent) during the term that ends with the death of the last survivor of H and W. As to actuarial computations by the Internal Revenue Service, see section 6.

Section 3
Age of Junior Life 70 but Less Than 90

Where the age nearest birthday of the junior measuring life is 70 or more, Tables QN, IN, and UN should not be used. Where such age is 70 but less than 90, Tables QN2, IN2, and UN2 of section 8 should be used instead.

For example, if the ages of the measuring lives are 69 and 95, Table QN should be used with Table IN in the case of a pooled income fund, and with Table UN in the case of a charitable remainder unitrust. If the ages are 70 and 72, Table QN2 should be used with Table IN2 in the case of a pooled income fund, and with Table UN2 in the case of a charitable remainder unitrust.

The columns of Tables QN, IN, and UN show 22 entries for values of *t* at 5-year intervals, whereas the columns of Tables QN2, IN2, and UN2 show 20 entries for values of *t* at 2-year intervals. Table QN should not be used with Table IN2 or Table UN2; nor should Table QN2 be used with Table IN or Table UN.

The methods of applying the tables computed at 2-year intervals are the same as the methods shown in Examples 1 to 4 of applying the tables computed at 5-year intervals. The method in a case involving a pooled income fund is illustrated in Example 5. No example is given of a similar computation involving a charitable remainder unitrust; all that would be changed is that the column of K-factors would be taken from Table UN2 rather than Table IN2.

Example 5.

G transfers $100,000 of property to a pooled income fund on January 1, 1970, and provides that the income from the property is to be paid to A (a man aged 70) for life and then to B (a woman aged 86) for life. The highest yearly rate of return earned by the fund for its 3 preceding taxable years is 6.2 percent. At that rate of return, the present value of charity's remainder interest is $54,577, determined as follows:

The details of the computation are shown in Exhibit 4. In the margin to the left of Column (1) are entered line numbers (1 through 20) and the values of *t* that appear in the left margin of Table QN2 (2 through 40). From Table QN2, the values of Q for the junior life (aged 70, male) are copied into Column (1), and those for the senior life (aged 86, female) into Column (2). From Table IN2, K-factors for a yearly rate of return 6.2 percent ("YYR = 6.2%) are copied into Column (4).

Each entry in Column (3) is the product, rounded to 6 decimal places, of the corresponding entries in Columns (1) and (2). Similarly, each entry in Column (5) is the product of the entries in Columns (3) and (4).

The sum of the entries in Column (4) is a check value. It should agree with the sum shown for the column of K-factors in Table IN2: 0.941618.

The sum .(0.545765) of the entries in Column (5), rounded to 5 decimal places, is the applicable remainder factor: 0.54577. Accordingly, the required present value of the charitable remainder interest is $100,000 × 0.54577 or $54,577.

Section 4
Remainder Interests Dependent on More Than 2 Lives

The method described in the preceding sections, whereby the factor for the value of a last survivor remainder interest is obtained by summing the line-by-line products of columns of

Exhibit 4

Line No.	Values of t	Values of Q 70M (1)	86F (2)	Col. (1) *times* Col. (2) (3)	K-factors. YRR = 6.2% (4)	Col. (3) *times* Col. (4) (5)
1	2	.099610	.291950	.029081	.106735	.003104
2	4	.202282	.540339	.109301	.094636	.010344
3	6	.306906	.729821	.223986	.083909	.018794
4	8	.411760	.856996	.352877	.074398	.026253
5	10	.515734	.931250	.480277	.065965	.031681
6	12	.617506	.969768	.598838	.058487	.035024
7	14	.712024	.987933	.703432	.051858	.036479
8	16	.792914	.995666	.789478	.045979	.036299
9	18	.859645	.998612	.858452	.040768	.034997
10	20	.911785	.999607	.911427	.036146	.032944
11	22	.949305	.999903	.949213	.032049	.030421
12	24	.973457	1.000000	.973457	.028416	.027662
13	26	.987267	1.000000	.987267	.025195	.024874
14	28	.994401	1.000000	.994401	.022339	.022214
15	30	.997765	1.000000	.997765	.019807	.019763
16	32	.999197	1.000000	.999197	.017562	.017548
17	34	.999743	1.000000	.999743	.015571	.015567
18	36	.999927	1.000000	.999927	.013806	.013805
19	38	.999982	1.000000	.999982	.012241	.012241
20	40	1.000000	1.000000	1.000000	.095751	.095751
					.941618	.545765

Q-values and a column of K-factors, is easily extended to cases involving three or more measuring lives. The ages of the measuring lives should be arranged in ascending order, and columns of Q-values for those measuring lives copied in the same order onto a columnar work sheet. For example, if it is required to determine a 6 percent rate of interest or return, the present value of a remainder interest in a pooled income fund that falls in at the death of the survivor of three women aged 20, 30, and 40, the columnar headings and the entries on the first line in each column would be as follows:

Column (1): Values of Q from Table QN
(age 20F) 003493

Column (2): Values of Q from Table QN
(age 30F) 006115

Column (3): Product: Column (1) *times*
Column (2) 000021

Column (4): Value of Q from Table QN
(age 40F) 013695

Column (5): Product: Column (3) *times*
Column (4) . . . . - 0 -

Column (6): K-factors from Table IN
(YRR = 6.0%) 217833
Column (7): Product: Column (5) *times*
Column (6) . . . . - 0 -

The sum of the entries in Column (7) is 0.035615 (details omitted). Thus, the required remainder factor is 0.03562.

If the most junior of the measuring lives is aged 70 nearest birthday or older, the method of computation would be similar, but the values of Q for all the lives would be taken from Table QN2 rather than Table QN, and the K-factors from Table IN2 or UN2 rather than Table IN or UN.

The method outlined in the preceding sections is not applicable unless there are at least two measuring lives.

Section 5
Joint and Survivor Annuity Values

The formula shown below can be used to determine the present values of joint and survivor annuities. It can be used, for example, to determine the present value, at 6 percent interest, of a joint and survivor annuity payable by a charitable remainder annuity trust.

Suppose that A and R, present values computed at the rate of interest i per annum, are further defined as follows:

A = The present value of a complete annuity of \$1 per annum, payable at the end of each year during the joint lives and the life of the survivor of two or more designated persons.

R = The present value of a payment of \$1 due at the (moment of) death of the survivor of such designated persons.

Then the relationship between A and R is given by the following formula:

$$A = (1 - R)/i.$$

R is the factor for the present value of the remainder interest in a pooled income fund having i as the applicable yearly rate of return. If the value of R is known, then A can be determined by the formula. The value of R computed to 5 decimal places should be used in the formula.

Example 6.

The formula of this section and the value of R obtained in section 4 may be used to compute the present value at 6 percent interest of an annuity of \$1 per annum payable during the joint lives and the life of the survivor of 3 women aged 20, 30, and 40.

The value of R to 5 decimal places, determined in section 4, is 0.03562. In the formula for A, the numerator is $1 - R$ or 0.96438; hence

$$A = \frac{1 - R}{i}$$

$$= \frac{.96438}{.06}$$

$$= 16.0730.$$

That is, the present value at 6 percent interest of a complete annuity of $1 per annum payable at the end of each year during the joint lives and the life of the survivor of 3 women aged 20, 30, and 40 is $16.0730. Thus, if the amount of the annuity were $100 per annum, its present value at the 6 percent interest rate would be $100 × 16.0730 or $1,607.30.

Section 6. Actuarial Computations by the Internal Revenue Service

Section 1.642(c)-6(a)(2) of the Income Tax Regulations provides that if the computation of the value of the remainder interest of a pooled income fund requires the use of a factor which is not provided in section 1.642(c)-6(d), the Commissioner of Internal Revenue may, if conditions permit, supply the factor upon request. The request must be accompanied by a statement of the pooled income fund's yearly rate of return and of the date of birth and sex of each measuring life and by copies of the relevant instruments. Section 1.642(c)-6(d) provides tables to be used in determining factors for the present value of remainder interests, dependent on but one life, in pooled income funds for which the yearly rate of return is within the range 2.2 to 8.0 percent.

Section 1.664–4(a)(3) of the regulations provides that if the computation of the value of the remainder interest in a charitable remainder unitrust requires the use of a factor which is not provided in section 1.664–4(b), the Commissioner may, if conditions permit, supply the factor upon request. The request must be accompanied by a statement of the date of birth and sex of each measuring life and by copies of the relevant instruments. Section 1.664–4(b) provides tables to be used in determining factors for the present value of remainder interests, dependent on but one life, in charitable remainder unitrusts for which the adjusted payout rate is within the range 4.717 to 9.0 percent.

Section 1.664–2(c) of the regulations provides that the fair market value of the remainder interest of a charitable remainder annuity trust is the net fair market value of the property placed in trust less the present value of the annuity, computed under section 20.2031–10 of the Estate Tax Regulations. Section 20.2031–10 provides tables for the valuation of annuities (and of life estates and remainder interests) that are dependent on but one life. A special factor must be used if the interest to be valued is dependent on the continuation or the termination of more than one life or upon a term certain concurrent with one or more lives. The factor is to be computed on the basis of interest at the rate of 6 percent a year, compounded annually, and life contingencies determined, as to each male and female life involved, from the values of l_x that are set forth in columns (2) and (3), respectively, on Table LN of section 20.2031–10(f) of the regulations. (Such values of l_x are, except for differences in rounding, the same as shown for total males and total females in Tables 2 and 3, respectively, of United States Life Tables and Actuarial Tables: 1959–61, published by the U.S. Department of Health, Education, and Welfare.)

Section 20.2055–2(a) of the Estate Tax Regulations, relating to the estate tax charitable deduction, provides that if a special factor is required under that section in the case of an actual decedent, the Commissioner may, if conditions permit, furnish the factor to the executor upon request. The request must be accompanied by a statement of the sex and date of birth of each measuring life and by copies of the relevant instruments.

Similarly, section 25.2522(a)-2(a) of the Gift Tax Regulations, relating to the gift tax charitable deduction, provides that if a special factor is required under that section in the case of an actual gift, the Commissioner may, if conditions permit, furnish the factor to the donor upon request. The request must be accompanied by a statement of the sex and date of birth of each measuring life and by copies of the relevant instruments.

Actuarial Values II
Factors at 6 Percent Involving One and Two Lives
(I.R.S. Publication 723A)

First Part
Text and Examples
Explanation of Pamphlet

The tables and examples of this publication supplement Tables A(1) and A(2) and Table B of the estate and gift tax regulations. See section 20.2031–10 of the estate tax regulations and section 25.2512–9 of the gift tax regulations.

1. LAST-TO-DIE FACTORS BASED ON TABLE LT6

Table LT6 sets forth factors for the present worth of $1.00 due at the death of the survivor of two persons. The factors have been computed on the basis of interest at the rate of 6 percent a year, compounded annually, and life contingencies determined, as to each male and female life involved, from the values of l_x that are set forth in Table LN of section 20.2031–10(f) of the Estate Tax Regulations. Table LN contains values of l_x taken from the life table for total males and the life table for total females appearing as Tables 2 and 3, respectively, in *United States Life Tables: 1959–61,* published by the Department of Health, Education, and Welfare, Public Health Service, except that for technical reasons Table LN employs graduated data, furnished by that Department, to increase the number of significant figures shown at ages greater than 86 (male) and 90 (female).

The factors in Table LT6 are arranged according to difference in age. Determine the ages nearest birthday of the two lives involved and the number of years' difference between those ages. Enter column (1) of Table LT6 with the age difference. Opposite the age difference in column (1), find the age of the senior life in column (2) and the age of the junior life in column (3). Opposite the latter age, find the appropriate remainder factor in column (4), (5), (6), or (7), according to whether the senior and junior lives are respectively (4) male-female, (5) male-male, (6) female-female, or (7) female-male.

Example 1.

The factor for the present worth of $1.00 due at the death of the survivor of two women aged 54 and 51 is $0.17748. Here the age difference is 3 and the senior age is 54. The factor 0.17748 is found in column (6) of Table LT6 opposite the figure 3 in column (1) and the figure 54 in column (2).

Table LT6 contains remainder factors only. Tables A(1) and A(2) contain annuity and income (life estate) factors as well as remainder factors, but the factors are related by definite formulas. For example, in Table A(1) the three factors opposite age 45 are:

Annuity factor, age 45M	$12.3013
Income (life estate) factor, age 45M	0.73808
Remainder factor, age 45M	0.26192

The formulas giving the relationships among any triplet of factors from Tables A(1) and A(2) are:

Formula (1): Income factor = $1.00 *less* Remainder factor.
Formula (2): Income factor = Annuity factor *times* 0.06.
Formula (3): Annuity factor = Income factor *divided by* 0.06.

For example, using the above factors for age 45 male:

(1) $1.00 less Remainder factor = $1.00 − 0.26192
= $0.73808
= Income factor.
(2) Annuity factor times 0.06 = $12.3013 × 0.06
= $0.73808
= Income factor.
(3) Income factor ÷ 0.06 = $0.73808 ÷ 0.06
= $12.3013
= Annuity factor.

The above formulas hold because in Tables A(1) and A(2) the remainder factors are factors for remainders payable immediately on death, and the annuity factors are factors for the present worth of "complete" life annuities, that is, annuities that provide a final fractional payment proportionate to the time elapsed between the date of the last full payment and the date of the death that terminates the annuity.

The remainder factors of Table LT6 are factors for remainders payable immediately on death, and the above formulas can be used to determine the income and annuity factors that correspond to the remainder factors given in Table LT6. Thus, Formula (1), above, and the appropriate remainder factor from Table LT6 can be used to determine the factor for the present worth of the right to receive the income from $1.00 until the death of the survivor of two persons.

Example 2.

The factor for the present worth of the right to receive the income from $1.00 until the death of the survivor of two women aged 52 and 50 is 0.83542, determined as follows:

Senior age	52F
Junior age	50F
Difference in age	2

Remainder factor, Table LT6, column (6) $0.16458

From Formula (1):

$$\begin{aligned}\text{Income factor} &= \$1.00 \textit{ less } \text{Remainder factor}\\ &= \$1.00 - \$0.16458 = \$0.83542.\end{aligned}$$

Similarly, Formula (3) can be used to determine the factor for the present worth of an annuity of $1.00 per annum payable annually until the death of the survivor of the two measuring lives.

Example 3.

The factor for the present worth of an annuity of $1.00 per annum payable annually until the death of the survivor of a man aged 59 and a woman aged 58 is $12.2300, determined as follows:

Senior age	59M
Junior age	58F
Difference in age	1

Remainder factor, Table LT6, column (4)	$0.26620
Income factor ($1.00 *less* $0.26620)	0.73380

From Formula (3):

$$\begin{aligned}\text{Annuity factor} &= \text{Income factor} \div 0.06\\ &= \$0.73380 \div 0.06 = \$12.2300.\end{aligned}$$

2. INCOME OR ANNUITY PAYABLE FOR SUCH TIME AS ONE PERSON SURVIVES ANOTHER

If the income from $1.00 is payable to X for life, then to Y for life, the factor for the present worth of the combined interests of X and Y can be determined by the method of Example 2. A factor for the life interest of X can be obtained from Table A(1) or A(2). The factor for Y's secondary life estate can then be determined by subtraction.

Example 4.

The factor for the present worth of the right to receive the income from $1.00 for such time as Y, a woman aged 52, shall survive X, a woman aged 50, is $0.08066, determined as follows:

Assume that the income from $1.00 is payable to X for life, then to Y for life:

Factor for combined rights of X and Y. See Example 2	$0.83542
Less: Factor, Table A(2), for life estate of X, aged 50F	0.75476
Factor for secondary life estate of Y, aged 52F	$0.08066

Similarly, if an annuity of $1.00 per annum is payable to X for life, then to Y for life, the factor for the present worth of the combined annuities of X and Y can be determined by the method of Example 3. A factor for the life annuity of X can be obtained from Table A(1) or A(2). The factor for Y's secondary (survivorship) life annuity can then be determined by subtraction.

Example 5.

The factor for the present worth of an annuity of $1.00 per annum payable annually for such time as Y, a man aged 59, shall survive X, a woman aged 58, is $1.2320, determined as follows:
Assume that an annuity of $1.00 per annum in annual payments is payable to X for life then to Y for life:

Factor for combined rights of X and Y. See Example 3	$12.2300
Less: Factor, Table A(2), for life annuity of X, aged 58F	10.9980
Factor for secondary life annuity of Y, aged 59M	$1.2320

3. FIRST-TO-DIE FACTORS

Let F, L, A, and B be defined as follows:

F = the present worth of $1.00 due at the death of the first to die of X and Y,
L = the present worth of $1.00 due at the death of the last to die of X and Y,
A = the present worth of $1.00 due at the death of X, and
B = the present worth of $1.00 due at the death of Y.

A fundamental relationship between F, L, A, and B is:

$$F + L = A + B.$$

This can be rewritten as a useful formula for obtaining the value of F, since the value of L can be obtained from Table LT6 and the values of A and B from Table A(1) and/or Table A(2):

Formula (4): $F = A + B - L.$

The following example illustrates the use of the formula:

Example 6.

The factor for the present worth of $1.00 due at the death of the first to die of a man aged 59 and a woman aged 58 is $0.50975, determined as follows:

(1) Remainder factor, Table A(1), for $1.00 due at death of man aged 59	$0.43583
(2) Remainder factor, Table A(2), for $1.00 due at death of woman aged 58	$0.34012
(3) Remainder factor, Table LT6, for $1.00 due at death of survivor of them	0.26620
(4) Required remainder factor: Item (1) + Item (2) − Item (3)	0.50975

The factor for the present worth of the right to receive the income from $1.00 until the death of the first to die of two persons can be determined by subtracting from $1.00 the present worth, computed as in Example 6, of $1.00 due at such death. Finally, the present worth of an annuity of $1.00 per annum payable annually until the death of the first to die of such two persons can be obtained by dividing the income factor of the preceding sentence by 0.06.

Example 7.

The factor for the present worth of an annuity of $1.00 per annum payable annually until the death of the first to die of a man aged 59 and a woman aged 58 is $8.1708, obtained as follows:

(1) Remainder factor: Present worth of $1.00 due at the death of the first to die of the two persons (See Example 6)	$0.50975
(2) Income factor: $1.00 less Item (1)	$0.49025
(3) Annuity factor: Item (2) ÷ 0.06	$8.1708

4. FACTORS INVOLVING ONE LIFE AND A TERM OF YEARS

The columns of Tables H(1) and H(2) are called "commutation columns." The use of these columns is illustrated in Examples 8 through 11. Example 12 illustrates the use of Table LN.

Example 8.

The factor for the present worth of a temporary annuity of $1.00 per annum payable annually for 10 years or until the prior death of a woman aged 42 is $7.2449, determined as follows:

Initial age	42F
Term of years	10
Terminal age	52F

(1) N-factor, Table H(2), age 42F 112,320.829
(2) N-factor, Table H(2), age 52F 53,327.602
(3) Difference: Item (1) less Item (2) 58,993.227
(4) D-factor, Table H(2), age 42F 8,142.748
(5) Required factor: Item (3) ÷ Item (4) 7.2449

Example 9.

The factor for the present worth of $1.00 due at the death of a man aged 45 provided such death occurs within 15 years is $0.10707, determined as follows:

Initial age	45M
Term of years	15
Terminal age	60M

(1) M-factor, Table H(1), age 45M 1,702.89614
(2) M-factor, Table H(1), age 60M 1,006.76431
(3) Difference: Item (1) less Item (2) 696.13183
(4) D-factor, Table H(1), age 45M 6,501.600
(5) Required factor: Item (3) ÷ Item (4) 0.10707

Example 10.

The factor for the present worth of the right to receive the income from $1.00 for 10 years or until the prior death of a woman aged 42 is $0.43469, determined as follows:

The required factor is 6 percent of the corresponding temporary annuity factor, which, from Example 8, is $7.2449. Therefore the required factor is $7.2449 × 0.06 or $0.43469.

Example 11.

The factor for the present worth of the right of a woman aged 21 to receive $1.00 upon attaining age 30 is $0.58763, determined as follows:

Initial age	21F
Terminal age	30F

(1) D-factor, Table H(2), age 30F 16,713.88
(2) D-factor, Table H(2), age 21F 28,443.06
(3) Required factor: Item (1) ÷ Item (2) 0.58763

Example 12.

The probability that a woman aged 21 will be alive at age 30 is 0.992781, determined as follows:

Initial age	21F
Terminal age	30F

(1) *l*-value, Table LN, age 30F	95,996
(2) *l*-value, Table LN, age 21F	96,694
(3) Required probability: Item (1) ÷ Item (2) .	0.992781

Table MN contains values of the *force of mortalilty* (u_x) derived from the *l*-values shown in Table LN.

* * *

Actuarial Values I
Valuation of Last Survivor Charitable Remainders
Part B
Two-Life Tables for Unitrusts and Pooled Income Funds
(I.R.S. Publication 723B)

Explanation of Publication

These two-life tables and the accompanying text and examples are designated Part B of "Actuarial Values I: Valuation of Last Survivor Charitable Remainders."

At its next printing, Publication 723 (12–70), which sets forth the so-called Kemmerer method of valuation of last survivor remainders, will be designated Part A of "Actuarial Values I: Valuation of Last Survivor Charitable Remainders." The Kemmerer method should continue to be used in cases not covered by the present tables, for example, in cases involving three or more lives.

Use of Tables

A charitable contribution deduction may be allowable by reason of a transfer of property to (1) a pooled income fund, defined in section 642(c)(5) of the Internal Revenue Code of 1954, (2) a charitable remainder annuity trust, defined in section 664(d)(1), or (3) a charitable remainder unitrust, defined in section 664(d)(2) and (d)(3). The definitions of the pooled income fund, charitable remainder annuity trust, and charitable remainder unitrust were added to the Code by the Tax Reform Act of 1969.

The present tables, Tables E(3) and G(3), set forth factors representing the present worth of remainder interests, dependent on the death of the survivor of two persons, in charitable remainder unitrusts and pooled income funds. Factors are not provided in the tables for ages below 30 or above 90. (If a factor is required that involves an age below 30 or above 90,

Publication 723 should be used. Publication 723 continues to apply, as appropriate, in cases involving three or more lives.)

In the case of a charitable remainder annuity trust from which an annuity is to be paid during the joint lives and the life of the survivor of two measuring lives, the present value of the annuity should be determined by the use of Publication 723A. If there are three or more measuring lives, the present value of the annuity should be determined by the use of Publication 723.

Table E(3)

Table E(3) sets forth remainder factors to be used in the case of a trust that qualifies as a charitable remainder unitrust under section 664 of the Internal Revenue Code of 1954 and that provides a payout at a fixed percentage rate during the joint lives and the life of the survivor of two persons. Table E(3) does not apply where the payout during the joint lives is not at the same rate as the payout during the life of the survivor, nor does it apply where a portion of the corpus is to be removed from the trust at the death of the first to die of the two persons. However, it does apply in the case of a payout to A and B in equal shares during their joint lives and all to the survivor for life.

The factors in Table E(3) are arranged in five parts, reflecting the following "adjusted payout rates," as determined under section 1.664–4 of the Income Tax Regulations:

Part 1	4.6 to 6.0%
Part 2	6.2 to 7.6%
Part 3	7.8 to 9.2%
Part 4	9.4 to 10.8%
Part 5	11.0 to 12.4%

Within each part, the factors are arranged according to the difference in the ages nearest birthday of the two measuring lives, starting with difference in age zero. This difference in age appears in the margin of the table, in the column labeled with the letter "D." Following this difference in age are the two ages involved. Beneath each pair of ages is an array of letters:

M f	denoting	male and junior female
M m	"	male and junior male
F f	"	female and junior female
F m	"	female and junior male

Thus, if the measuring lives were a female aged 34 nearest birthday and a male aged 31 nearest birthday, the required factor would be found on the 4th line following those ages, opposite the letters "F m," in the appropriate part of Table E(3):

D	Ages
3	34:31

M f	1st line
M m	2nd "
F f	3rd "
F m	4th "

If the measuring lives were two women, the required factor would be found on the 3rd line, opposite the letters "F f."

If the adjusted payout rate is an amount that is between adjusted payout rates for which factors are provided in Table E(3), a linear interpolation must be made.

Example 1.

On January 1, 1970, C, a man aged 34 nearest birthday, transfers $100,000 to a charitable remainder unitrust. The trust instrument requires that the trustee pay at the end of each taxable year of the trust 5 percent of the fair market value of the trust assets as of the beginning of the taxable year of the trust to C for life and then to his wife A, aged 31, for life. The adjusted payout rate is 4.717 percent (5% × 0.943396, factor from Table F, section 1.664–4(b)(5) of the Income Tax Regulations). The present value of the remainder interest is $10,503, computed as follows:

Table E(3), Part 1
Ages 34M : 31f

Factor at 4.600%	0.11075
Factor at 4.800%	0.10097
Difference	0.00978

$$\frac{4.717\% - 4.600\%}{4.800\% - 4.600\%} = \frac{X}{0.00978}$$

$X = 0.00572$

Factor at 4.600%	0.11075
Less: X	0.00572
Interpolated factor	0.10503
Present value of remainder interest ($100,000 × 0.10503)	$10,503

Table G(3)

Table G(3) is applicable in the case of a trust that qualifies as a pooled income fund under section 642(c)(5) of the Internal Revenue Code of 1954, where an income interest is retained for the joint lives and the life of the survivor of two persons. Thus, within the 30 to 90 year age limits referred to above, Table G(3) would apply in the case of a qualified trust that is to pay its net income to A for life, then to B for life, or to A and B in equal shares during their joint lives and all to the survivor for life.

The factors in Table G(3) are arranged in five parts, reflecting the following "yearly rates of return," as determined under section 1.642(c)-6 of the Income Tax Regulations:

Part 1	2.2 to 3.6%
Part 2	3.8 to 5.2%
Part 3	5.4 to 6.8%
Part 4	7.0 to 8.4%
Part 5	8.6 to 10.0%

Within each part, the factors, like those of Table E(3), are arranged according to the difference in the ages nearest birthday of the two measuring lives, starting with difference in age zero. This difference in age appears in the margin of the table, in the column labeled with the letter "D." Following this difference in age are the two ages involved. Beneath each pair of ages is an array of letters:

M f	denoting	male and junior female
M m	"	male and junior female
F f	"	female and junior female
F m	"	female and junior male

Thus, if the measuring lives were a male aged 36 nearest birthday and a female aged 32 nearest birthday, the required factor would be found on the 1st line following their ages, opposite the letters "M f," in the appropriate part of Table G(3):

D	Ages	
4	36:32	
	M f	1st line
	M m	2nd "
	F f	3rd "
	F m	4th "

If the measuring lives were both male, the required factor would be found on the 2nd line, opposite the letters "M m."

If the applicable yearly rate of return is a percentage that is between yearly rates of return for which factors are provided in Table G(3), a linear interpolation must be made.

Example 2.

On January 1, 1970, M, a man aged 36 nearest birthday, transfers $100,000 to a pooled income fund, reserving an income interest in such property to himself for life and then to his wife B, aged 32, for life. The highest yearly rate of return earned by the fund for its 3 preceding taxable years is 5.692 percent. The present value of the remainder interest is $8,299, computed as follows:

Table G(3), Part 3
Ages 36M : 32f

Factor at 5.600%	0.08600
Factor at 5.800%	0.07945
Difference	0.00655

$$\frac{5.692\% - 5.600\%}{5.800\% - 5.600\%} = \frac{X}{0.00655}$$

$X = 0.00301$

Factor at 5.000%	0.08600
Less: X	0.00301
Interpolated factor	0.08299
Present value of remainder interest ($100,000 × 0.08299)	$8,299

* * *

TABLE OF STATUTES (I.R.C.)

I.R.C. §	*Book §*	*I.R.C. §*	*Book §*
61(a)(3)	§1.13	2032A(b)(3)	§5.22
72(e)(1)(B)	§8.6	2032A(c)	§5.23
165(c)(3)	§1.13	2032A(c)(2)(E)	§5.20
165(e)	§1.13	2032A(e)	§5.21
166(b)	§1.13	2032A(e)(4)	§5.20
167(a)	§1.13	2032A(e)(7)	§§5.20, 5.24
170	§9.5	2032A(e)(8)	§§5.20, 5.25
301(b)(1)	§1.13	2032A(e)(13)	§5.20
303	§1.9	2033	§4.21
303(b)(2)	§1.9	2035	§4.21
307(a)	§1.13	2035(b)	§1.12
331(a)	§1.13	2035(d)(2)	§1.12
341(c)(1)(A)	§1.13	2036	§4.21
341(e)(1)(C)	§1.13	2037	§§1.2, 4.21
341(e)(8)	§1.13	2037(b)	§2.24
356(a)(1)	§1.13	2038	§4.21
356(b)	§1.13	2039(c)	§8.8
361(b)	§1.13	2040	§4.21
368(a)(2)(B)(iii)	§1.13	2041	§4.21
404(a)(3)	§1.12	2042(2)	§2.24
542(a)(2)	§1.13	2053(a)(4)	§5.22
543(a)(6)(A)	§1.13	2503	§1.12
611	§§6.3, 7.7	2503(b)	§§1.12, 2.24
851(b)(4)	§1.13	2504(c)	§1.12
851(c)(1)	§1.13	2505	§1.12
1011	§1.13	2511(a)	§11.4
1014	§1.13	2512	§§1.2, 9.5
1015	§1.13	2611-2614	§1.2
2011	§1.11	2613(a)	§1.2
2031	§§1.2, 1.8, 9.5	2613(b)	§1.2
		6018	§1.8
2032	§1.8	6166	§1.9
2032A	§§1.1, 1.9, 2.16, 5.20, 5.21 5.22, 5.23, 5.24, 5.25	6166A	§1.9
		6324B	§5.23
		6601(j)	§1.9
		7517	§2.28
		7517(a)	§2.28
2032A(a)(2)	§5.22	7517(b)	§2.28
2032A(b)(1)	§5.22	7517(c)	§2.28
2032A(b)(2)	§5.20		

TABLE OF TREASURY REGULATIONS

Reg. §	*Book §*	*Reg. §*	*Book §*
25.2512-2(b)(3)(Example 1)	§3.3	25.2512-5(f)	§§2.23, 8.8
25.2512-2(b)(3)(Example 5)	§3.11	25.2512-6(a)	§8.7
25.2512-2(c)	§§3.3, 3.11	25.2512-6(a)(Example 4)	§8.5
25.2512-2(d)	§§3.3, 3.11	25.2512-9(a)(1)(i)	§8.8
25.2512-2(e)	§§3.1, 3.6, 4.11	25.2512-9(f)	§§2.23, 8.8, 8.9
25.2512-3	§4.9	301.7517-1	§2.28
25.2512-4	§8.2		

TABLE OF REVENUE RULINGS, REVENUE PROCEDURES AND LETTER RULINGS

Revenue Ruling	*Book §*
189, 1953-2 C.B. 284	§4.30
53-156, 1953-2 C.B. 253	§3.12
54-76, 1954-1 C.B. 194	§4.30
54-97, 1954-1 C.B. 113	§1.13
54-399, 1954-2 C.B. 279	§3.3
55-71, 1955-1 C.B. 110	§10.3
55-278, 1955-1 C.B. 471	§3.11, 3.12
55-747, 1955-2 C.B. 228	§§2.23, 8.6
58-13, 1958-1 C.B. 342	§11.6
58-402, 1958-2 C.B. 15	§1.1
59-60, 1959-1 C.B. 237	§§1.14, 4.1, 4.3, 4.4, 4.5, 4.6, 4.7, 4.9, 4.18, 4.21, 4.25, 4.27, 4.29, 4.30
59-195, 1959-1 C.B. 18	§§8.6, 8.8
60-124, 1960-1 C.B. 368	§3.3
61-88, 1961-1 C.B. 417	§§2.24, 11.6
65-192, 1965-2 C.B. 259	§4.9
66-110, 1966-1 C.B. 12	§2.23
66-307, 1966-2 C.B. 429	§2.24
67-276, 1967-2 C.B. 321	§8.2
67-370, 1967-2 C.B. 324	§11.6
68-269, 1968-1 C.B. 399	§3.12
68-272, 1968-1 C.B. 394	§3.2
68-609, 1968-2 C.B. 327	§§4.3, 4.5, 4.7
68-610, 1968-2 C.B. 405	§3.3
69-347, 1969-1 C.B. 227	§11.6
69-489, 1969-2 C.B. 172	§§3.11, 3.12
71-67, 1971-1 C.B. 271	§§2.24, 11.6

Revenue Ruling	*Book §*
72-438, 1972-2 C.B. 38	§8.8
73-61, 1973-1 C.B. 408	§8.4
76-472, 1976-2 C.B. 264	§11.6
77-181, 1977-1 C.B. 272	§8.7
77-195, 1977-1 C.B. 295	§2.24
77-287, 1977-2 C.B. 319	§§3.8, 3.9, 3.10, 4.26
77-358, 1977-2 C.B. 342	§2.24
78-367, 1978-2 C.B. 249	§4.3
79-7, 1979-1 C.B. 294	§4.21
79-189, 1979-1 C.B. 293	§4.24
80-179, 1980-2 C.B. 253	§4.24
81-170, 1981-25 I.R.B. 18	§4.24
81-253, 1981-43 I.R.B. 10	§4.22
82-104, 1982-21 I.R.B. 7	§5.24

Revenue Procedure	*Book §*
65-19, 1965-2 C.B. 1002	§2.9
66-49, 1966-2 C.B. 1257	§§2.6, 2.29
69-18, 1969-2 C.B. 300	§3.12
75-39, 1975-2 C.B. 569	§§4.5, 11.3
77-12, 1977-1 C.B. 569	§10.6
79-24, 1979-1 C.B. 565	§§5.10, 5.11, 5.12, 5.17, 7.3, 8.4

Letter Ruling	*Book §*
8010017	§4.22
8034005	§5.6
8046012	§5.20
8114058	§5.12
8132011	§1.12

TABLE OF CASES

Supreme Court	***Book §***
Cartwright; United States v., 411 U.S. 546 (1973)	§3.4
Consolidated Rock Prods. Co. v. Du Bois, 312 U.S. 510 (1941)	§3.14
Elmhurst Cemetery Co. v. Commissioner, 300 U.S. 37 (1937)	§§2.3, 2.8
Miller; United States v., 317 U.S. 369 (1943)	§1.5
Protective Committee v. Anderson, 390 U.S. 414 (1968)	§3.14
Salvage; Helvering v., 297 U.S. 106 (1936)	§4.30
Estate of Sternberger; Commissioner v., 348 U.S. 187 (1955)	§2.24
Tex-Penn Co.; Helvering v., 300 U.S. 481 (1937)	§4.31
Welch v. Helvering, 290 U.S. 111 (1933)	§§1.5, 2.8

Federal Circuit Court of Appeals	***Book §***
Andrews v. Commissioner, 135 F.2d 314 (2d Cir. 1943), *cert. denied,* 320 U.S. 748 (1943)	§2.8
Armstrong's Estate v. Commissioner, 146 F.2d 457 (7th Cir. 1944)	§4.30
Bourne v. Commissioner, 62 F.2d 648 (4th Cir. 1933)	§7.5
Estate of Bright v. United States, 658 F.2d 999 (5th Cir. 1981)	§§4.21, 4.22
Bull v. Smith, 119 F.2d 490 (2d Cir. 1941)	§3.5
Colonial Fabrics v. Commissioner, 202 F.2d 105 (2d Cir. 1953), *cert. denied,* 346 U.S. 814 (1953)	§1.5
Crown v. Commissioner, 585 F.2d 234 (7th Cir. 1978)	§8.4
Cullers v. Commissioner, 237 F.2d 611 (8th Cir. 1956)	§2.7
F.G. Inc. v. Commissioner, 47 F.2d 541 (7th Cir. 1931)	§7.5
Estate of Frankel v. United States, 512 F.2d 1007 (5th Cir. 1975)	§§7.1, 7.2, 7.4
Goldman v. Commissioner, 388 F.2d 476 (6th Cir. 1967)	§§1.5, 2.10
Groff v. Munford, 150 F.2d 825 (2d Cir. 1945)	§3.5
Green v. United States, 460 F.2d 412, 72-1 U.S.T.C. ¶9429 (5th Cir. 1972)	§7.7
In re Hill's Estate, 193 F.2d 724 (2d Cir. 1952)	§2.24
Joslin v. United States, 666 F.2d 1306 (10th Cir. 1981)	§10.4
Estate of Lion v. Commissioner, 438 F.2d 56 (4th Cir. 1971), *cert. denied,* 404 U.S. 870 (1971)	§2.24
Loesch & Green Const. Co. v. Commissioner, 211 F.2d 210 (6th Cir. 1954)	§2.3
Louis v. United States, 369 F.2d 263 (7th Cir. 1966)	§4.6
Estate of Manny; United States v., 645 F.2d 163 (2d Cir. 1981)	§3.12
Maresi; Commissioner v., 156 F.2d 929 (2d Cir. 1946)	§2.24
Martin v. Commissioner, 649 F.2d 1133, 48 A.F.T.R.2d ¶81-5537 (5th Cir. 1981)	§8.4
Maryland Nat'l Bank v. United States, 609 F.2d 1078 (4th Cir. 1979)	§2.24
May v. McGowan, 194 F.2d 396 (2d Cir. 1952)	§1.1
Montrose Cemetery Co. v. Commissioner, 105 F.2d 238 (7th Cir. 1939), *aff'd,* 309 U.S. 622 (1940)	§5.14

Federal Circuit Court of Appeals (continued)	*Book §*
Mott v. Commissioner, 139 F.2d 317 (6th Cir. 1943)	§3.6
Newell v. Commissioner, 66 F.2d 102 (7th Cir. 1933)	§4.27
O'Bryan Brothers v. Commissioner, 127 F.2d 645 (6th Cir. 1942), *cert. denied,* 317 U.S. 647 (1942)	§4.6
Phipps v. Commissioner, 127 F.2d 214 (10th Cir. 1942), *aff'g* 43 B.T.A. 1010 (1941), *cert. denied,* 317 U.S. 645 (1942)	§§3.6, 4.21
Procter; Commissioner v., 142 F.2d 824 (4th Cir. 1944), *cert. denied,* 323 U.S. 756 (1944)	§8.7
Richardson v. Commissioner, 151 F.2d 102 (2d Cir. 1945), *cert. denied,* 326 U.S. 796 (1946)	§3.5
Robinson v. United States, 632 F.2d 822 (9th Cir. 1980)	§2.24
Rushton v. Commissioner, 498 F.2d 88 (5th Cir. 1974)	§3.5
Spitzer v. Commissioner, 153 F.2d 967 (8th Cir. 1946)	§4.30
B. F. Sturtevant Co. v. Commissioner, 75 F.2d 316 (1st Cir. 1935)	§9.2
Tracy v. Commissioner, 53 F.2d 575 (6th Cir. 1931), *cert. denied,* 287 U.S. 632 (1932)	§2.8
Weber v. Rasquin, 101 F.2d 62 (2d Cir. 1939)	§4.24
Worcester County Trust Co. v Commissioner, 134 F.2d 578 (1st Cir. 1943)	§4.31
Zanuck v. Commissioner, 149 F.2d 714 (9th Cir. 1945)	§3.14

Federal District Court	*Book §*
Bader v. United States, 172 F. Supp. 833 (S.D. Ill. 1959)	§§4.19, 4.24
Baltimore Nat'l Bank v. United States, 136 F. Supp. 642 (D. Md. 1955)	§§4.26, 4.30
Bartram v. Graham, 157 F. Supp. 757 (D. Conn. 1957)	§4.24
Belser v. Edwards, 54-1 U.S.T.C. (CCH) ¶10,942 (M.D.Ga. 1954)	§4.30
Bishop Trust Co., Ltd., Adm'r. v. United States, 50-1 U.S.T.C. (CCH) ¶10,764 (D. Hawaii 1950)	§4.24
Blackard v. Jones, 62 F. Supp. 234 (W.D. Okla. 1944)	§4.24
Blackburn v. United States, 60-2 U.S.T.C. (CCH) ¶11,964 (D. Ind. 1960)	§4.24
Blanchard v. United States, 291 F. Supp. 348 (S.D. Iowa 1968)	§4.22
Brown v. Commissioner, 35-2 U.S.T.C. (CCH) ¶9557 (D. Kan. 1935)	§4.24
Clark v. United States, 36 A.F.T.R.2d ¶75-6417 (E.D.N.C. 1975)	§4.21
Cordner v. United States, 45 A.F.T.R.2d ¶80-1677 (C.D. Cal. 1980)	§10.4
Cravens v. Welch, 10 F. Supp. 94 (S.D. Cal. 1935)	§4.24
Crocker Nat'l Bank v. United States, 39 A.F.T.R.2d ¶77-779 (C.D. Cal. 1976)	§9.5
Driver v. United States, 38 A.F.T.R.2d ¶76-6315 (W.D. Wis. 1976)	§4.22
Drybrough v. United States, 208 F. Supp. 279 (W.D. Ky., 1962)	§4.24
Forbes v. Hassett, 38 F. Supp. 62 (D. Mass. 1941)	§4.24
Goss v. Fitzpatrick, 97 F. Supp. 765 (D. Conn. 1951)	§4.24
Hicks v. United States, 335 F. Supp. 474 (D. Colo. 1971)	§4.24
Lewis v. United States, 27 A.F.T.R.2d ¶71-1650 (D. Wyo. 1970)	§2.9
Mathews v. United States, 226 F. Supp. 1003 (E.D. N.Y. 1964)	§4.31
Estate of McGinn v. Granquist, 55-2 U.S.T.C. (CCH) ¶11,566 (D. Ore. 1954)	§4.24
Obermer v. United States, 238 F. Supp. 29 (D. Hawaii 1964)	§§4.4, 4.21, 4.24
Roth v. United States, 48 A.F.T.R.2d ¶148,468, (E.D.Mo. 1981)	§4.30
St. Joseph Bank & Trust Co. v. United States, 48 A.F.T.R. 1561 (N.D. Ind. 1953)	§3.5
Saunders v. United States, 48 A.F.T.R.2d ¶148,481 (M.D. Ga. 1981)	§§2.14, 5.6, 5.14, 8.2
Schnorbach v. Kavanagh, 102 F. Supp. 828 (W.D. Mich. 1951)	§§1.4, 3.5
Slimp's Estate, 48 A.F.T.R. 1572 (W.D. Tex. 1954)	§4.22
Tishman v. United States, 207 F. Supp. 830 (E.D. Va. 1959)	§4.24
Whittemore v. Fitzpatrick, 127 F. Supp. 710 (D. Conn. 1954)	§§4.21, 4.23, 4.24

Federal District Court (continued)	***Book §***
Worthen v. United States, 192 F. Supp. 727 (D. Mass. 1961)	§4.24

Federal Court of Claims	***Books §***
Campbell v. United States, 48 A.F.T.R.2d ¶81-5068 (Ct. Cl. 1981)	§3.9
Central Trust Co. v. United States, 305 F.2d 393 (Ct. Cl. 1962)	§§4.19, 4.24, 4.26
Estate of Ridgely v. United States, 180 Ct. Cl. 1220 (1967)	§3.5
Righter v. United States, 439 F.2d 1204 (Ct. Cl. 1971)	§4.19
Estate of Tully v. United States, 78-1 U.S.T.C. (CCH) ¶13,228 (Ct. Cl. 1978)	§§4.24, 4.28

Board of Tax Appeal	***Book §***
Estate of E. Andrews, 13 B.T.A. 651 (1928)	§4.24
Estate of M. Baer, 3 B.T.A. 881 (1926)	§4.24
Estate of J. Barclay, 2 B.T.A. 696 (1925)	§4.24
Estate of H. Brittingham, 46 B.T.A. 1278 (1942)	§4.24
C. Cook, 2 B.T.A. 126 (1925)	§4.24
J. Couzens, 11 B.T.A. 1040 (1928)	§4.24
A. Edwards, 46 B.T.A. 815 (1942), *aff'd,* 135 F.2d 574 (7th Cir. 1943), *acq.* 1942-2 C.B. 6, *nonacq.* 1942-2 C.B. 24	§8.7
A. Evans, Trustee, 29 B.T.A. 710 (1934)	§1.13
George D. Harter Bank, Ex'r, 38 B.T.A. 387 (1938)	§4.24
Estate of J. Gregory, 41 B.T.A. 1340 (1940)	§4.24
M. Hooper, 41 B.T.A. 114 (1940)	§4.24
Estate of L. Kaffie, 44 B.T.A. 843 (1941)	§4.24
M. Kopple, 35 B.T.A. 1056 (1937), *acq.* 1937-1 C.B. 14	§4.31
W. Laird, 29 B.T.A. 196; 38 B.T.A. 926 (1933)	§4.24
Estate of D. McColgan, 10 B.T.A. 958 (1930)	§4.24
Estate of L. McKitterick, 42 B.T.A. 130 (1940)	§3.1
L. Phipps, 43 B.T.A. 1010 (1941), *aff'd,* 127 F.2d 214 (10th Cir. 1941), *cert. denied,* 317 U.S. 645 (1942)	§4.21
Estate of J. Pitts, 19 B.T.A. 288 (1930)	§4.24
Prophylactic Brush Co., 25 B.T.A. 676 (1932), *acq.* XI-2 C.B. 8	§9.2
Royal Mineral Assoc., 5 B.T.A. 1126 (1927)	§7.4
Estate of L. Sanderson, 16 B.T.A. 1022 (1929)	§4.24
Second Nat'l Bank & Trust Co., 39 B.T.A. 1242 (1939)	§4.24
Estate of F. Staunton, 29 B.T.A. 376 (1933)	§4.24
Estate of W. Stewart, 31 B.T.A. 201 (1934)	§4.24
H.Testard, 6 B.T.A.M. (P-H) ¶37,272 (1937)	§2.3
Estate of M. Vail, 42 B.T.A. 1478 (1940)	§4.24
C. Wilson, 5 B.T.A. 615 (1926), *acq.* VI-1 C.B. 6	§5.12

Tax Court	***Book §***
Estate of B. Bischoff, 69 T.C. 32 (1977)	§§4.23, 4.24
Brooks-Massey Dodge, Inc., 60 T.C. 884 (1973)	§10.5
Buffalo Tool & Die Mfg. Co., 74 T.C. 441 (1980)	§1.4
N. Campanari, 5 T.C. 488 (1945)	§4.24
Estate of F. Cruikshank, 9 T.C. 162 (1947)	§§4.4, 4.24
Estate of J. Curry, 74 T.C. 540 (1980)	§8.4
H. Dupont, 2 T.C. 246 (1943), *nonacq.* 1943 C.B. 30	§3.5
Duncan Industries, Inc, 75 T.C. 266 (1979)	§2.11
H. Epstein, 53 T.C. 459 (1969), *acq.* 1970-2 C.B. xix	§1.5
Estate of A. Fry, 9 T.C. 503 (1947), *acq.* 1948-2 C.B. 2	§11.2
Estate of E. Gooel, 68 T.C. 504 (1977)	§2.24
Estate of M. Heckscher, 63 T.C. 485 (1975)	§2.24
Estate of S. Henry, 4 T.C. 423 (1944), *aff'd,* 161 F.2d 574 (3d Cir. 1947), *acq.* 1945 C.B. 4	§§2.24, 5.6

Tax Court (continued)	*Book §*
Estate of J. Huntsman, 66 T.C. 861 (1976), *acq.* 1977-1 C.B. 1	§4.27
G. Johnson, 74 T.C. 89 (1980)	§3.1
Estate of H. Johnson, 77 T.C. 120 (1981)	§4.28
P. Kalech, 23 T.C. 672 (1955), *acq.* 1955-2 C.B. 7	§4.30
W. King, 18 T.C. 414 (1952), *acq.* 1953-1 C.B. 5	§3.12
Estate of W. Lee, 33 T.C. 1064 (1960)	§4.21
Estate of H. Leyman, 40 T.C. 100 (1963)	§4.24
Estate of O. Littick, 31 T.C. 181 (1958), *acq.* 1959-2 C.B. 5	§4.30
M. Messing, 48 T.C. 502 (1967)	§4.24
Estate of W. Piper, 72 T.C. 1062 (1979)	§3.9
Estate of C. Prell, 48 T.C. 67 (1967)	§3.5
Estate of G. Robinson, 69 T.C. 222 (1977)	§8.4
Estate of A. Salt, 17 T.C. 92 (1951), *acq.* 1952-1 C.B. 4	§4.30
Estate of L. Schroeder, 13 T.C. 259 (1949)	§4.24
Estate of E. Simmie, 69 T.C. 890 (1978), *aff'd,* 632 F.2d 93 (9th Cir. 1980)	§3.12
Estate of D. Smith 57 T.C. 650 (1972), *aff'd on other grounds* 510 F.2d 479 (2d Cir. 1975), *cert. denied,* 423 U.S. 827 (1975), *acq.* 1974-2 C.B. 4	§§1.5, 9.5
Estate of G. Trammell, 18 T.C. 662 (1952), *acq.* 1953-1 C.B. 6	§4.30
Estate of L. Weil, 22 T.C. 1267 (1954), *acq.* 1955-2 C.B. 10	§4.30
Wolfsen Land & Cattle Co., 72 T.C. 1 (1979)	§5.11

Tax Court Memorandum	*Book §*
G. Armour, 38 T.C.M. (P-H) ¶69,245 (1969)	§10.2
Estate of M. Berkman, 48 T.C.M. (P-H) ¶79,046 (1979)	§8.4
W. Bollenbach, 43 T.C.M. (P-H) ¶74,270 (1974)	§4.24
Estate of G. Brown, 46 T.C.M. (P-H) ¶77,085 (1977)	§4.24
Estate of M. Brush, 32 T.C.M. (P-H) ¶63,186 (1963)	§3.6
Buffalo Tool & Die Mfg. Co., 50 T.C.M. (P-H) ¶81,457 (1981)	§1.4
C. Chamberlin, 12 T.C.M. (P-H) ¶43,347 (1943)	§§4.30, 4.31
Estate of L. Cotchett, 43 T.C.M. ¶74,031 (1974)	§4.24
W. Cullman, 50 T.C.M. (P-H) ¶81,666 (1981)	§5.6
P. Dean, 29 T.C.M. (P-H) ¶60,054 (1960)	§4.24
E. Dickman, 49 T.C.M. (P-H) ¶80,575 (1980)	§8.4
Estate of E. Dooly, 41 T.C.M. (P-H) ¶72,164 (1972)	§4.24
Estate of T. Folks, 51 T.C.M. (P-H) ¶82,043 (1982)	§§2.3, 3.5, 4.24, 4.28, 5.6
E. Gallun, 43 T.C.M. (P-H) ¶74,284 (1974)	§4.24
Estate of J. Garrett, 22 T.C.M. (P-H) ¶53,329 (1953)	§4.24
Estate of E. Goodrich, 47 T.C.M. (P-H) ¶78,248 (1978)	§4.12
Estate of C. Grootemaat, 48 T.C.M. (P-H) ¶79,049 (1979)	§4.24
Estate of D. Hayes, 42 T.C.M. (P-H) ¶73,236 (1973)	§4.24
Estate of G. Helmers, 19 T.C.M. (P-H) ¶50,154 (1950)	§4.24
Estate of C. Heppenstall, 18 T.C.M. (P-H) ¶49,034 (1949)	§4.21
Estate of C. Herter, 23 T.C.M. (P-H) ¶54,105 (1954)	§4.24
E. Hightower, 41 T.C.M. (P-H) ¶72,252 (1972)	§7.4
Estate of M. Iacono, 49 T.C.M. (P-H) ¶80,520 (1980)	§5.6
Estate of O. Johnson, 12 T.C.M. (P-H) ¶43,264 (1943)	§4.24
Estate of S. Katz, 37 T.C.M. (P-H) ¶68,171 (1968)	§4.24
Estate of E. Kirkpatrick, 44 T.C.M. (P-H) ¶75,344 (1975)	§§4.23, 4.24
S. Koffler, 47 T.C.M. (P-H) ¶78,159 (1978)	§4.12
J. Lagrew, 45 T.C.M. (P-H) ¶76,310 (1976)	§4.24
Estate of A. Larson, 13 T.C.M. (P-H) ¶44,168 (1944)	§3.5
Estate of A. Little, 51 T.C.M. (P-H) ¶82,026 (1982)	§§1.4, 3.6, 3.9, 3.10

TABLE OF TEXTS AND TREATISES

Text or Treatise	*Book §*
E. Allen, J. Melone & J. Rosenbloom, Pension Planning (3d ed. 1976)	§8.6
American Institute of Real Estate Appraisers (AIREA), The Appraisal of Real Estate (7th ed. 1978)	§§5.1, 5.9
American Law of Property (A.J. Casner ed. 1952)	§7.2
American Society of Farm Managers and Rural Appraisers, Inc., Rural Appraisal Manual (5th ed. 1979)	§§5.1, 5.8
Ballentine's Law Dictionary (3d ed. 1969)	§8.5
W. Behrenfeld, Estate Planning Desk Book (4th ed. 1978)	§1.11
L. Bernstein, The Analysis of Financial Statements (1978)	§§4.1, 4.5, 4.6, 4.14
H. Bloomenthal, Securities and Federal Corporate Law (1980)	§3.8
J. Bonbright, Valuation of Property (1937)	§§1.1, 1.4, 1.15, 2.13, 4.4
C. Breeding, F. Burke & G. Burton, Income Taxation of Natural Resources (1977)	§6.3
F. Burke, Valuation and Valuation Planning for Closely Held Business (1981)	§4.28
A. Casner, Estate Planning (4th ed. 1980)	§8.7
G. Christy & J. Clendenin, Introduction to Investments (7th ed. 1978)	§§3.2, 3.4, 3.5
Collier on Bankruptcy (15th ed. 1980)	§3.14
S. Davidson, C. Stickney & R. Weil, Accounting; The Language of Business (4th ed. 1979)	§§2.12, 2.13, 4.5
Doane, Rural Appraisal Handbook (1947)	§§6.2, 6.4, 6.5
Ellwood Tables for Real Estate Appraising and Financing, Part I-II (Compiled for the AIREA by L. W. Ellwood) (3d. ed. 1970)	§§2.18, 8.2
Encyclopedia of Real Estate Appraising (3d ed., E. Friedman ed., 1978)	§§2.5, 2.17, 2.21, 2.25, 5.1, 5.7, 5.9, 5.10, 5.11, 5.12, 5.14, 5.15, 5.17, 5.19, 6.3, 7.1, 7.2, 7.3, 7.4, 8.3
W. Fletcher, Cyclopedia of Corporations (1971)	§4.6
S. Goldberg, Private Placements and Restricted Securities (1979)	§3.8
N. Harl, Agricultural Law (1982)	§6.3
I.B.P. Lawyer's Desk Book (6th ed. 1980)	§1.11
Internal Revenue Manual-Audit (CCH 1977)	§9.5
Internal Revenue Service, Appeals Officer Valuation Training Program (1980)	§§1.5, 2.3, 2.11, 3.5, 4.1, 4.7, 4.9, 4.13, 4.17, 4.18, 4.23, 7.5, 9.2, 9.5

Text or Treatise	*Book §*
Internal Revenue Service, Estate, Gift and Generation Skipping Tax Law Course for Attorneys (1979)	§§1.5, 2.3, 2.12, 2.15, 2.19, 2.21, 3.2, 3.3, 3.4, 3.6, 3.9, 4.7, 4.8, 4.23, 5.5, 5.6, 5.14, 5.15, 7.3, 8.2, 8.3, 9.2
I. Johnson, Selling Real Estate by Mortgage-Equity Analysis (1976)	§§5.15, 5.16
L. Kazmier, Basic Statistics for Business and Economics (1979)	§2.25
D. Kelly & D. Ludtke, Estate Planning for Farmers and Ranchers (1980)	§§5.20, 5.21, 6.1, 6.2
S. Kess, B. Westlin & R. Whitman, Financial and Estate Planning (CCH)	§4.29
J. Kolb, Section 2032A: Special Valuation of Farm and Business Property (1981)	§§5.20, 5.21, 5.24
E. Kuntz, Oil and Gas (1962)	§7.2
H. O'Neal, Close Corporations Law and Practice (2d ed. 1971)	§§4.10, 4.23, 4.29
R. Parks, Examination and Valuation of Mineral Property (4th ed. 1957)	§7.1
S. Pratt, Valuing a Business–The Analysis and Appraisal of Closely-Held Companies (1981)	§4.17
R.I.A., Estate Planning & Taxation Coordinator (1979)	§§1.1, 9.2
A. Ring, The Valuation of Real Estate (2d ed. 1970)	§§1.1, 2.21, 5.1, 5.11, 5.19
S.E.C., Institutional Investor Study Rep. (1971)	§3.9
W. Sharpe, Investments (1978)	§3.2
E. Spiller, Financial Accounting–Basic Concepts (1977)	§§2.23, 4.7, 8.2
J. Van Horne, Financial Management and Policy (5th ed. 1980)	§§4.14, 4.15
Webster's New Collegiate Dictionary (1977)	§2.10
H. Weinstock, Planning an Estate (1977)	§8.6
H. Williams & C. Meyers, Manual of Oil and Gas Terms (1957)	§7.2

TABLE OF ARTICLES

Article	Book §
Gelman, *An Economist-Financial Analyst's Approach to Valuing Stock of a Closely-Held Company,* 36 J. Tax'n 353 (1972)	§4.23
Gettel, *"Good Grief," ANOTHER Method of Selecting Capitalization Rates,* 46 Appraisal J. 90 (1978)	§5.15
Haneberg, *The Actuarial Process,* 36-S N.Y.U. Inst. Fed. Tax'n 225 (1978)	§2.23
Harnack, *Techniques in Preparing a Valuation Case,* 30 N.Y.U. Inst. Fed. Tax'n 163 (1972)	§2.29
Helmick & Tippit, *Royalty Interests and Ore Payments,* 3 Am. L. of Min., tit 17, at pp. 431-82 (Rocky Mtn. Min. Legal Fdn. ed. 1967)	§7.2
Hocky, *Blockage,* 248 T.M. (1979)	§3.5
Jensen, *Stock Valuation Formulas for Estate and Gift Taxes,* 117 Tr. & Est. 238 (1978)	§§2.19, 4.5
Kascle, *Valuation of Closely Held Corporations,* 43 Taxes–The Tax Magazine 454 (1965)	§4.5
Korner, *Issues and Problems in Valuing Closely Held Business Interests for Estate Tax Purposes, Especially Partnership Interests,* 30 N.Y.U. Inst. Fed. Tax'n 185 (1972)	§4.9
Krahmer & Henderer, *Valuation of Shares of Closely Held Corporation,* 221 T.M. A-57 (1978)	§§3.1, 4.4, 4.5, 4.6, 4.7, 4.8, 4.21, 4.25, 4.29, 4.30, 4.31
Lamson, *Factors That Will Substantiate the Valuation of a Closely Held Corporation,* 34 J. Tax'n 226 (1971)	§4.5
Levy, *Estate Planning for Professional Songwriters After the Storm,* 8 Mem. St. U.L. Rev. 751 (1978)	§9.4
Lieb & Schaaf, *Estate Planning for Creators of Intellectual Property,* 1979 Ill. L.F. 373	§9.4
Lyons & Whitman, *Valuing Closely Held Corporations and Publicly Traded Securities with Limited Marketability: Approaches to Allowable Discounts From Gross Values,* 33 Bus. Law 2213 (1978)	§§4.23, 4.26, 4.27
Maher, *An Objective Measure for a Discount for a Minority Interest and a Premium for a Controlling Interest,* 57 Taxes–The Tax Magazine 449 (1979)	§4.25
Maher, *Application of Key Man Discount in the Valuation of Closely Held Businesses,* 55 Taxes–The Tax Magazine 377 (1977)	§4.27
Maher, *Discounts for Lack of Marketability for Closely Held Business Interests,* 54 Taxes–The Tax Magazine 562 (1976)	§4.26
Martin & Sandford, *Applying Fair Market Value Appraisal Techniques to Closely Held Preferred Stock,* 56 Taxes–The Tax Magazine 108 (1978)	§4.12
Martz, Carrell & Kirgis, *Conveyancing and Status of Mineral Interests,* 3 Am. L. of Min., tit. 15, at pp. 71-223 (Rocky Mtn. Min. Legal Fdn. ed. 1960)	§7.2
Moroney, *Most Courts Overvalue Closely Held Stocks,* 51 Taxes–The Tax Magazine 144 (1973)	§4.23
Parks, *Valuation of Mineral Property,* Real Estate Appraiser 37-46 (May-June 1972)	§7.1
Rams, *Judicial Valuation of Dissenting Shareholder Interest,* 8 Lincoln L. Rev. 74 (1973)	§3.14
Real Estate Review, *Financial Analysis of Real Estate Investment,* Portfolio No. 7 (1975)	§2.22
Schreier & Joy, *Judicial Valuation of "Close" Corporation Stock: Alice in Wonderland Revisited,* 31 Okla. L. Rev. 853 (1978)	§§4.4, 4.5, 4.17, 4.19, 4.23

Article	*Book §*
Silverman, *The Valuation of Intellectual Property in Connection with the Estates of Authors and Other Creative Persons,* 11 Miami Inst. Est. Plan ¶1100, at p. 11-1 (1977)	§9.4
Smith, *Court Decisions Now Recognize Valuation Discounts for Community Property Interest,* 53 J. Tax'n 28 (1980)	§4.21
Smith, *Issues and Problems in the Valuation of Real Estate,* 30 N.Y.U. Inst. Fed. Tax'n 209 (1972)	§5.12
Solberg, *Valuing Restricted Securities: What Factors Do the Courts and the Service Look For?,* 51 J. Tax'n 150 (1979)	§3.8
Starkey, *Valuation of Closely-Held Corporation Stock: Book Value v. Capitalization of Earnings,* 2 Est. Plan. 37 (1974)	§4.4
Stechel, *Restrictive Buy-Sell Agreements Can Limit Estate Tax Value of A Business Interest,* 44 J. Tax'n 360 (1976)	§4.29
Swenson, *Solid Mineral Leases,* 5 Am. L. of Min., tit 30, at pp. 301-84 (Rocky Mtn. Min. Legal Fdn. ed. 1967)	§7.2
Tippit & Phipps, *Valuation of Mining Properties,* 4 Am. L. of Min., tit. 25, at p. 567 (1963)	§§7.1, 7.5
Treanor & Johnson, *Valuation of Community Property Minority Interests Reflect Judicial Inconsistencies,* 52 J. Tax'n 356 (1980)	§4.21
Webster, *Ascertainable Value,* 19 N.Y.U. Inst. Fed. Tax'n 509 (1961)	§1.1
Wiley, *Valuing Large Holdings of Publicly Traded Stock: The "Blockage" Problem,* 8 U. Miami Inst. Est. Plan. ¶74.800, at p. 8-1 (1974)	§3.5
Zorbel & Shore, *The IRS Crackdown on Valuation Abuses: How Far Does It Go: What Does It Portend,* 52 J. Tax'n 276 (1980)	§12.1
Comment, *Depreciability of Going Concern Value,* 122 U. Pa. L. Rev. 484 (1973)	§4.7
Comment, *Estate and Gift Tax Valuation: Discounts of Partnership Interests,* 59 Neb. L. Rev. 737 (1980)	§4.9
Comment, *Restricted Securities Need Not Be Restricted When Valuing for Federal Estate and Gift Tax Purposes,* 31 Tax. Law. 482 (1978)	§3.10
Comment, *The Dissenting Shareholders Appraisal Remedy,* 30 Okla. L. Rev. 629 (1977)	§3.14
Note, *Valuation of Dissenters' Stock Under Appraisal Statutes,* 79 Harv. L. Rev. 1453 (1966)	§3.14

TABLE OF MISCELLANEOUS REFERENCES

United States Code	*Book §*
15 U.S.C. §77(b)(1) (1976)	§3.8
17 U.S.C. §102 (1976)	§9.4
17 U.S.C. §106 (1976)	§9.4
17 U.S.C. §203(a)(1) (1976)	§9.4
17 U.S.C. §203(a)(3) (1976)	§9.4
17 U.S.C. §203(a)(4) (1976)	§9.4
17 U.S.C. §302 (1976)	§9.4
17 U.S.C. §303 (1976)	§9.4
17 U.S.C. §304 (1976)	§9.4

Economic Recovery Tax Act of 1981 Sections	*Book §*
401	§1.8
421	§§5.21, 5.24
421(a)	§5.22
421(f)	§5.24
422	§1.9
422(b)	§1.9
441	§1.12
442	§1.9
442(b)(1)	§1.9

Code of Federal Regulations	*Book §*
Tit. 7 §53.120	§6.4
Tit. 7 §53.121	§6.4
Tit. 7 §53.122	§6.4
Tit. 7 §53.122(f)	§6.4
Tit. 7 §53.130	§6.4
Tit. 7 §53.132(c)	§6.4
Tit. 7 §53.150	§6.4
Tit. 7 §53.151	§6.4
Tit. 7 §53.152(d)	§6.4
Tit. 7 §53.152(j)	§6.4
Tit. 7 §53.158	§6.4
Tit. 7 §53.203 (b)(1)	§6.4
Tit. 7 §53.203 (c)	§6.4
Tit. 7 §53.204	§6.4

Code of Federal Regulations (continued)	*Book §*
Tit. 7 §53.205	§6.4
Tit. 7 §2853.102-.107	§6.5
Tit. 7 §2853.112-.117	§6.5
Tit. 7 §2853.122-.127	§6.5
Tit. 7 §2853.132-.137	§6.5
Tit. 7 §2856.200-.234	§6.5
Tit. 7 §2870.200-.271	§6.5
Tit. 7 §2870.200-.332	§6.4
Tit. 7 §2870.300-.332	§6.5
Tit. 8 §57.1-.13	§6.2
Tit. 8 §57.50-.52	§6.2
Tit. 8 §61.101-.104	§6.2
Tit. 8 §68.101-.122	§6.2
Tit. 8 §68.201-.213	§6.2
Tit. 8 §68.251-.264	§6.2
Tit. 8 §68.301-.316	§6.2
Tit. 8 §68.401-.410	§6.2
Tit. 8 §68.501-.510	§6.2
Tit. 8 §68.601-.611	§6.2
Tit. 17 §230.144	§3.8
Tit. 17 §230.405	§3.8
Tit. 31 §306.28	§3.12
Tit. 31 §351.1-.12	§3.12

Miscellaneous References	*Book §*
Annot., Valuation of Closely Held Stock for Federal Estate Tax Purposes Under § 2031(b) of the Internal Revenue Code of 1954 (26 U.S.C.S. § 2031(b)), and Supplementing Regulations, 22 A.L.R. Fed 31 (1975)	§4.10
Annot., Admissibility On Issue of Value of Real Property of Evidence of Sale Price of Other Real Property, 174 A.L.R. 386 (1948)	§5.12
Annot., Unaccepted Offer for Purchase or Sale of Real Property as Evidence of Value, 7 A.L.R.2d 781 (1949)	§5.12
Annot., Valuation of Stock of Dissenting Stockholders in Case of Consolidation or Merger of Corporation, Sale of Its Assets, or the Like, 48 A.L.R.3d 430 (1973)	§3.14
Annot., Meaning of, and Proper Method for Determining, Market Value or Market Price in Oil and Gas Lease Requiring Royalty to be Paid on Standard Measured by such Terms, 10 A.L.R.4th 732 (1981)	§7.2
H.R. Rep. No. 1380, 94th Cong., 2d Sess. 61, *reprinted in* 1976 U.S. Code Cong. & Ad. News 3415	§2.28
I.R.S. Instructions for Form 706 (Rev. 6-82)	§§2.29, 10.1
I.R.S. Instructions for Form 709 (Rev. 7-82)	§2.29
I.R.S. Publication 723, Valuation of Last Survivor Charitable Remainders (12-70)	§11.5
I.R.S. Publication 723A, Factors at 6 Percent Involving One and Two Lives (12-70)	§11.5
I.R.S. Publication 723B, Valuation of Last Surviving Charitable Remainders (11-71)	§11.5
2 P.O.F., Appraisals 1 (1959)	§§2.3, 2.15, 5.14
2 P.O.F. 2d, Valuation of Stock of Closely Held Corporations 1 (1974)	§4.10
3 P.O.F 2d, Rental Value of Realty 457 (1974)	§5.14
5 P.O.F. 2d, Market Value of Single-Family Residence–Market Comparison Appraisal 411 (1975)	§5.11
12 P.O.F. 2d, Value of Coin Collection 355 (1977)	§10.4

INDEX